Roll of Honour

To Private Horace Groom

13th Battalion Durham Light Infantry
Enlisted 10 November 1914
Killed in action attacking the Beaurevoir Line
Saturday, 5 October 1918

And some there be, which have no memorial; who are perished, as though they had never been; and are become as though they had never been born; and their children after them.

Ecclesiasticus 44:9

Roll of Honour

Schooling and the
Great War 1914–1919

Barry Blades

Pen & Sword
MILITARY

First published in Great Britain in 2015 by
Pen & Sword Military
an imprint of
Pen & Sword Books Ltd
47 Church Street
Barnsley
South Yorkshire
S70 2AS

ISBN 978 1 47382 105 7

Typeset in Ehrhardt by
Mac Style Ltd, Bridlington, East Yorkshire
Printed and bound in the UK by CPI Group (UK) Ltd,
Croydon, CRO 4YY

Pen & Sword Books Ltd incorporates the imprints of Pen & Sword
Archaeology, Atlas, Aviation, Battleground, Discovery, Family History,
History, Maritime, Military, Naval, Politics, Railways, Select, Transport,
True Crime, and Fiction, Frontline Books, Leo Cooper, Praetorian Press,
Seaforth Publishing and Wharncliffe.

For a complete list of Pen & Sword titles please contact
PEN & SWORD BOOKS LIMITED
47 Church Street, Barnsley, South Yorkshire, S70 2AS, England
E-mail: enquiries@pen-and-sword.co.uk
Website: www.pen-and-sword.co.uk

Contents

Acknowledgements   vi
Abbreviations   viii
A Note on Sources   x
Foreword   xii
Prologue   xiv
Introduction   xvi

Part I: Call-to-Arms!   1

Chapter 1   Ante-bellum   3

Chapter 2   Roll of Honour   26

Part II: Schools at War   49

Chapter 3   On Campaign   51

Chapter 4   Lessons in War   68

Chapter 5   On the Front Line   86

Chapter 6   Alma Mater   113

Part III: Teachers at War   121

Chapter 7   Patriots   123

Chapter 8   Temporary Gentlemen   149

Part IV: Aftermath   169

Chapter 9   Peace   171

Chapter 10   The Fallen   183

Chapter 11   The Forgotten   203

Epilogue   216
Notes   217
Bibliography   243
Index   256

Acknowledgements

The production of this book owes an enormous debt of gratitude to many individuals and institutions. The original research stemmed from my earlier work on the history of Deacon's School in Peterborough, a project stimulated by former colleagues, friends and Old Deaconians Brian Anthony and the late Wilf Saul. I was equally fortunate to have other wise mentors at the University College London (UCL) Institute of Education (IOE), where the late Professor Richard Aldrich and Dr David Crook guided me through the broader contexts of the History of Education and the intricacies and demands of academic research. My thanks for such support and encouragement also extend to Professor Gary McCulloch at the IOE and to Dr Peter Cunningham at the University of Cambridge. The archivists and librarians at the IOE also deserve a special mention. Sarah Aitchison, Rebecca Webster, Jessica Womack, Alix Kingston and Kathryn Hannan have helped enormously by introducing me to their collections related to the London Day Training College, the National Union of Women Teachers and the Girls' Public Day School Trust. The impressive collection of School Histories in the IOE Library has been a major source of research material. I thank the hundreds of authors of such works for providing so much rich detail about their schools and hope that in some small way *Roll of Honour* serves to tell some of their stories to a wider audience.

Additional material has been made available by archivists in other institutions. I would like to thank Richard Hillier and Elisabeth Kingston at Peterborough Library and Archives for allowing me to use images of Edward Adams and extracts from the Peterborough Practising School Logbook, and for retrieving material from the Deacon's School Archive which is now safely deposited there. Thanks also to Paul Richards and the volunteers at True's Yard Museum in King's Lynn for material relating to Joseph Dines and St Nicholas Boys' School, and to Janet Friedlander at the National Union of Teachers Headquarters in London for granting access to an original copy of the NUT *War Record* (1920). My thanks to all those school archivists throughout the land who do such an important job in preserving the essential links to the past for their individual institutions. Rachel Hassell at Sherborne School, Dr Christine Joy at Manchester High School for Girls and Peter Harrod at Christ's Hospital School in Lincoln have all been especially helpful. I owe a particular debt to the archivists and historians of Harrow County High School for Boys who first told the story of the school and of its pupils and teachers, such as Bob Hart and Russell Wheeler, namely Alex Bateman, Jeffrey Maynard and Trevor May. My gratitude also to Adam Cree for permission to use his research material relating to Susannah Knight in Chorley, and to Keith Haines for his work on Corrie Chase at Campbell College. I am particularly indebted to Sir Anthony Seldon for writing the Foreword to this book and for giving me the opportunity to share my research with conference audiences. His recent *Public Schools and the Great War – A Generation Lost* (Pen & Sword Books, 2013, co-authored with David Walsh), contained invaluable information and data provided by many individual public schools, which I have used to augment my own research and conclusions.

In addition to the aforementioned, the following have also helped in different ways by granting permission to use images and information in their collections or by providing links to other relevant material: Bruce Anderson (Rusholme Archive), Dr Charles Barber (Geoffrey Barber letters), Mark Dodd (Genealogy Forum), John Duncan (Newbattle At War), Brian Elsey (Wigan World), Jane King (Peterborough War Memorials), Maurice Palmer (The Wellingborough Album), Lianne Smith (King's College, London) and Emma Wootton (World War I School Archives). To all the above, and to all those local historians whose websites have added to my knowledge of individual people, institutions and localities in the Great War, I extend my sincere thanks and appreciation.

The majority of photographic and other images contained in *Roll of Honour* come from my own collection of original postcards, newspapers, magazines and other ephemera from the Great War period. These are referred to in the photographic plate sections as (Blades Collection), and will eventually be donated to the IOE in London. Other images were kindly provided by individuals and organisations mentioned above. The Imperial War Museum in London granted permission to include the image of Lieutenant Commander Archibald Buckle. I have endeavored, without success, to contact representatives of Aberdeen University Press for permission to use the image of Ishobel Ross.

My thanks to current and former members of staff at Pen & Sword Books Ltd, including Eloise Hansen, Lisa Hooson and Jen Newby, for commissioning *Roll of Honour* and for agreeing to publish two future related volumes on Schooling and the Great War.

Finally, my thanks to family past; it was they who first stimulated my love of history with their early gifts of medals in toffee boxes and recollections of ordinary men and women doing extraordinary things in extraordinary times. Family present – my wife Heather, sons Richard and Stephen, father Keith and grandaughter Daisy – continue to be the most important sources of inspiration, encouragement and support today.

Abbreviations

ANZAC	Australian and New Zealand Army Corps
BEF	British Expeditionary Force
CO	Conscientious Objector
CWGC	Commonwealth War Graves Commission
DSO	Distinguished Service Order
GPDST	Girls' Public Day School Trust
HCSB	Harrow County School for Boys
HMC	Head Masters' Conference
HMI	His (Her) Majesty's Inspector
HMS	His (Her) Majesty's Ship
ILP	Independent Labour Party
IOE	Institute of Education
JTS	Junior Technical School
LCC	London County Council
LDTC	London Day Training College
LEA	Local Education Authority
MC	Military Cross
MHSG	Manchester High School for Girls
MM	Military Medal
NCO	Non-Commissioned Officer
NFWT	National Federation of Women Teachers
NTS	Naval Training School
NUT	National Union of Teachers
NUWT	National Union of Women Teachers
OCB	Officer Cadet Battalion
OTC	Officer Training Corps
POW	Prisoner of War
PT	Physical Training
RAF	Royal Air Force
RAMC	Royal Army Medical Corps
RFA	Royal Field Artillery
RFC	Royal Flying Corps
RGA	Royal Garrison Artillery
RND	Royal Naval Division

RNVR	Royal Naval Volunteer Reserve
SWH	Scottish Women's Hospital
TS	Training Ship
UCL	University College London
VAD	Voluntary Aid Detachment
VC	Victoria Cross
WAAC	Women's Army Auxiliary Corps
WHWTA	West Ham Women Teachers' Association
WSPU	Women's Social and Political Union
YMCA	Young Men's Christian Association

A Note on Sources

The School Histories Collection in the Library and Archives at the University College London Institute of Education (IOE) was a major resource when conducting the research for this book. The IOE collection consists of hundreds of monographs of individual British schools, covering a range of institutions which span the educational spectrum. The voluminous histories of elite public schools stand next to brief studies of charity schools for waifs and strays. Publications marking the centenaries of ancient and modern secondary grammar schools are shelved next to accounts of elementary schools which no longer exist or have been absorbed into other institutions. Many of these histories of schools – the vast majority relating to English, Welsh and Scottish institutions – were written by alumni, former pupils or teachers determined to place on record the distinctive development and particular achievements of their Alma Mater. It is all too easy for the outsider to criticise the esoteric, celebratory and partisan nature of these rarely-analytical publications, the great majority of which were intended primarily for the individual school community itself. Yet, in many ways, what may at first appear to be their greatest weakness is, for the historian investigating the history of education more generally, their greatest strength. The rich detail, the human stories and the 'relatively obscure anecdotage' contained in such histories says so much about the ethos, culture and formative traditions of individual institutions.[1] These 'secondary' sources thus become a form of 'primary' material when the researcher asks questions relating to continuity and change in, for example, hierarchies of schooling. Many of the histories were, of course, constructed using primary sources, their authors making full use of the archive material still retained by many institutions: school logbooks, magazines, headteachers' annual reports, governors' minutes, the records of alumni organisations, and ephemera including school photographs and fixture lists.[2] *Roll of Honour* has extracted relevant material from over one hundred such histories, using direct evidence from the original archive material wherever possible, and being sensitive to issues related to the accuracy and reliability of the original authors.

School histories vary considerably in their coverage of educational activities during the Great War. Few focus exclusively on their experience of the years 1914–19.[3] In some, there is little or no reference at all to the impact of the war on the daily life of the school,[4] or to the conflict in general.[5] In others, the wartime experiences of alumni take centre stage.[6] Some of the most informative histories chart the war service and experience of the new secondary schools established in the wake of Balfour's 1902 Education Act for whom the war was an opportunity to establish their status and credentials.[7]

Using these histories alone would create no more than a patchwork account of the way in which British schools experienced the deluge of war.[8] Many other sources have therefore been used to construct this history of *Schooling and the Great War*. Material from original archive collections for individual schools, teacher training colleges, and teachers' associations has been included. This has been drawn from institutional archives and deposited collections in libraries, record offices and museums. The Great War Centenary Commemorations have resulted in a wealth of similar primary accounts being presented on internet websites and other forms of media. Some of this material has also found its way into this book, albeit with the usual caveats regarding authenticity and reliability. By synthesising school-produced primary and secondary sources with official directives such as Board of Education Circulars, *Roll of Honour* links central national imperatives with the everyday actions and experiences of ordinary people.[9] Contemporary fiction and autobiographies have been used to add period 'texture', 'feeling' and 'insight'. Local and national periodicals and newspapers also bring together the histories of war and histories of schooling. Oral testimony is used sparingly.[10] Secondary publications relating to the history of education generally have been used to provide a broader context of the function and provision of schooling; published texts on the military and wider social aspects of the Great War fulfil a similar function.

Finally, this is a book about Britain, and schooling, and wartime. I have endeavoured to include educational institutions of all kinds and from all parts of these islands;[11] to present a view of the war from a different standpoint to that normally taken; to examine the impact of events overseas on individuals and institutions on the home front; and to recall the experience of those who have often been forgotten but are worthy of our consideration. The extent to which I have been successful in my attempts will be judged by the reader.

Foreword by Sir Anthony Seldon

Master of Wellington College

I first met Barry Blades at a conference about schools and the Great War, held at Wellington College in 2012. I had become fascinated by the topic because Wellington, where I am head, lost 707 pupils in the war, the third highest number of any school in Britain. I knew very little about the topic and wanted to know more. Barry gave a wonderful talk and opened up a completely new world to me. He had conducted extensive research into the impact of the schools on the war, and vice-versa, and delegates were fascinated. I thought at the time that he must write a book on the subject. Now he has.

The focus of the conference was on the public schools, but it became obvious that Barry's research, conducted over more than a decade, was not confined to the wartime experience of the elite schools, nor to the battlefield experiences of school alumni. Much has been written about public schools and the war, not the least by the schools themselves, but few published works have dealt with the impact of the first 'total war' on the schools which were attended by the majority of British schoolchildren at the time. That impact, as this book reveals, was profound for many educational institutions and their local communities. In 1914 the demands of war led to the involvement of many schools in recruitment drives, whilst the buildings of others were requisitioned for military or medical purposes. Rolls of Honour recorded the names of teachers, older students and 'Old Boys' – and 'Old Girls' – who had departed for military service. In the classroom, pupils charted the advances, promotions and fates of their new set of heroes. Pupils and teachers fought their own wartime campaigns, providing comforts for 'their boys' on the battle fronts, collecting ingredients for munitions, making the *matériel* of war, donating their 'War Savings', and 'Digging for Victory' in response to major food shortages. They suffered the horrors of war on the home front, especially those under the flightpaths of Zeppelin and Gotha bomber aircraft. In 1918 they welcomed peace, remembered the dead, and tried to return to some semblance of normality.

Roll of Honour describes the wartime experience of 'schools' of all designations: Public, Preparatory, Grammar, High, County, Secondary, Technical, Elementary, Reformatory, Military. It looks at the education of boys and girls, and at forms of schooling beyond the classroom and formal educational institutions. By doing so, we are able to see the experience with a much greater sense of perspective. The book discusses how all schools operated within a fragmentary national and local system, which was based upon widely held contemporary notions of social and educational status.

The place of one's school in the hierarchy of schooling was often a key determinant of an individual's wartime status and experience. In *Roll of Honour*, the crucial role of the great public schools in producing leaders of men – and the great sacrifices made by them in wartime – is tempered by the assertion that the 'Lost Generation' was but part of a greater, but at times forgotten, 'Lost Citizenry'. Schools of all kinds, and in all parts of this country, paid the price for sending their alumni off to fight in foreign fields.

Roll of Honour is an important contribution to our understanding of the Great War. This book places individual schools at the centre of the action, but they are inextricably linked to the military campaigns on the Western Front and other theatres of war. Schools looked out from Blighty across the English Channel to where the fighting was taking place, whilst their alumni looked back to their Alma Mater from the trenches, air fields or naval patrols. Myriad faces of war challenge familiar stereotypes. Dr Blades has opened up a major and neglected part of the history of 1914–19 and has performed a great service in enriching our understanding of events a hundred years ago.

Sir Anthony Seldon

Prologue

For Bob Hart and his companions from Harrow County School for Boys, the halcyon days of summer 1914 came to dramatic and abrupt end. Whilst pupils from more prestigious schools were back at home for the vacation or attending the Public Schools Officer Training Corps annual camps at Aldershot and elsewhere, this particular school contingent was already entrained for the continent of Europe. Their destination was the city of Freiburg in southern Germany.

Most observers at the time would probably have urged caution when the notion of a school excursion to Germany was first mooted. Relations between Britain and its continental rival had become steadily worse in the first years of the twentieth century as these two European great powers competed for colonies and raced to produce armaments. The British government sought security in a Triple Entente involving its allies France and Russia, the popular press published 'Made in Germany' scare stories, and public opinion called for the building of ever-more *Dreadnought* battleships to counter the naval threat from the new continental superpower. Bob and his generation of British schoolboys, avid readers of the novels of G.A. Henty and popular action adventure comics such as *The Captain* and *The Boys' Own*, would have been well versed in stories of espionage and military action involving the Germanic enemy, the Hun.

In 1911 Bob Hart was one of the first boys to attend the newly opened Harrow County School for Boys, a small secondary school situated just two miles away from its more famous and historic namesake, Harrow School. Three years later he was School Captain, the most senior pupil in the school. When Bob and the small group of fellow pupils and teachers – Mr King and Mr Pettersson – set out on their great adventure on Thursday, 30 July 1914, few of their contemporaries had yet recognised the significance of an event which had taken place one month earlier, at Sarajevo in the distant Balkans.

The Harrow County party crossed the English Channel, travelled through Belgium and then entered Germany without incident. On reaching the great German fortress city of Metz, however, schoolboy enthusiasm for travel in foreign parts was tempered somewhat by an awareness that the German army was on the move. Bob and his friends noticed great numbers of troops moving westwards. At Strasbourg their train was held up for lengthy periods to allow troop trains to pass. On the following day, Friday, 31 July, and after a long and arduous journey, they eventually arrived at their destination. They were clearly unexpected guests.

Their German hosts, who were far more aware of the beginnings of the war fever that would soon engulf most of Europe, explained that whilst food was scarce they were nevertheless welcome to stay. The following day the Harrow County party debated the merits of either remaining in Freiburg and making the most of the situation, or returning home to England as soon as possible and before the diplomatic, and increasingly military, situation got any worse. The decision was finally made for them. Later that same day, Saturday, August 1 1914, Germany declared war on Russia and began its mobilisation in earnest.

Having experienced difficulties on the outward part of their journey, Bob and the others decided upon an alternative route back to England. Their return journey took them through the Rhine Valley via Cologne and on to Coblenz. Once more they witnessed the confusion created by the mass movement of troops. This time, however, the situation was much more fraught with danger and speed was of the essence. Following the requisitioning of supplies for the Schlieffen Plan armies bound for France, food shortages had led to localised civilian panic. From Coblenz they travelled to Herbesthal. From there they caught a train to the Belgian border. Their luck held as they crossed the frontier without being delayed and then made their way to the port of Ostend. On Sunday, August 2 they re-crossed the Channel and arrived in London, tired and very hungry, at around midnight. One of Bob's school friends wrote at the time:

We had been away for about four days, had slept properly twice, had had only two official meals, and had considerable luck in getting over our course of about 2,000 miles. Last but not least we had only twice washed, and at Charing Cross we discovered that the frontier at Herbesthal had been closed two hours after we had crossed.[1]

Back in England, Bob and his schoolfellows must have reflected upon how fortunate they had been to return home unscathed after such an eventful journey at such a momentous time. On August 4 1914, Britain finally declared war when Germany failed to respect Belgian neutrality. Millions of British troops, many of them straight from schools such as Harrow County, served in what would become known by contemporaries as the Great War. Of those in the school party who made the journey to Freiburg on the eve of war in July 1914, seven later saw active service. Lance Corporal Robert David Hart of the Honourable Artillery Company was one of them. In 1915 he crossed the Channel once more, this time as part of the British Expeditionary Force on the Western Front.

Introduction

Lance Corporal Robert Hart (Plate 1) was just nineteen when he was killed in action on 15 November 1916 during the British assault on the French village of Beaumont Hamel. Unlike many of his contemporaries who are still remembered and celebrated today, Bob Hart did not attend an elite school or ancient university. He did not become a commissioned officer, and won no awards for gallantry. Today, Bob is still honoured by his school community as one of the schoolboy heroes worthy of annual remembrance.[1] Few beyond the walls of that particular institution, however, know that he too belongs to the ranks of the 'Lost Generation', the 'doomed youth' of 1914 who have been both praised and pitied since the Great War ended nearly a century ago. Bob's story tells of great promise, but of even greater tragedy. As a narrative of a young life cut short by war it is of intrinsic interest but, given the huge number of casualties sustained by British, allied and enemy forces during the conflict of 1914–19, it is hardly exceptional. Nonetheless, it is important, for it reveals one of the myriad faces of a war which encompassed far more than its customary representations and traditional histories. It is a story which says so much more about who and what we choose to value and to remember.

We are all familiar with the Great War. Perhaps we are too familiar, readily accepting and then reinforcing what we already 'know' about this cataclysmic event in our history. In Britain, our collective knowledge of this particular war – perhaps above all others – is well rehearsed and all pervasive. In many of our schools, teachers and students have rarely deviated from a script which has become formulaic and seldom interrogated: the Great War as a consequence of European nationalism and militarism, the all-embracing war fever of 1914 which blinded so many to the realities of armed conflict, and the incompetence of generals who condemned millions to the horrors of trench warfare and experiences which were both pitiful and ultimately futile. Beyond school, many people have fought the war by proxy as they research the service history of family members who responded to the call-to-arms in 1914.[2] Battlefield tourism has allowed thousands to see something of the legacy of mass-industrialised warfare in the fields of Flanders, or to confirm the impossibility of offensive action from the beaches of Gallipoli. A culture of remembrance, created in the aftermath of the Great War and re-invigorated in the twenty-first century by Centenary Commemorations, continues to emphasise the horrors of war and the seemingly senseless sacrifice of the nation's citizens.

Thousands of books about the Great War have been published by British and Commonwealth historians. Some are brilliantly informative,[3] or contain moving portrayals of personal tragedy.[4] Others reinforce the perversely comforting horror stories we have been led to expect; stories which we take at face value and from which we make generalisations.[5] The vast majority of these books focus primarily on the military conflict. Collectively, this 'Tommy in the trenches' tradition has established a powerful lexicon which is used as shorthand to describe a seemingly universal wartime experience: stalemate, trenches, mud, slaughter, sacrifice. Many of these works deploy powerful visual imagery from the battle fronts,[6] and present the authentic voices of combatants in their oral testimony and letters home to loved ones, former colleagues and schoolfriends.[7] The canonical literature of the war poets, such as Wilfred Owen and Siegfried Sassoon,[8] and the autobiographies of disillusionment written by Edmund Blunden, Robert Graves and Vera Brittain,[9] for example, all contribute to and validate the vocabulary of suffering and waste. The final utterances of Harry Patch and other war veterans and survivors have been captured for posterity so that we may never forget just how truly awful the war was.[10]

What so many of the narrative accounts of the Great War fail to address, however, are the more complex issues. Alternative understandings, variations and inconsistencies have all but disappeared from non-academic publications. Similarly, celebrated London West End theatre productions,[11] recent historical fiction,[12] and even television comedy programmes,[13] whatever their real merits as social commentary, political critique or pure entertainment, have contributed to an iterative process which confirms what is now taken as read. Lasting truths may well be revealed when issues of great importance and magnitude are reduced to their very essence,[14] but *Blackadder Goes Forth* is but a snapshot of a far more nuanced story.

This is not to deny the evident horrors of the Great War, nor to diminish the real suffering experienced by millions of individuals and their communities. British deaths resulting from military action and its after-effects amounted to over 720,000.[15] The economic cost of the war was enormous. The psychological impact of the war on the millions of individuals who experienced unforeseen, unfamiliar and often unwelcome activities is immeasurable. Over-simplistic stereotypes and generalisations may well be the inevitable consequence of genuine attempts to make sense of a war which truly was 'great', a war which surpassed all previous conflicts in its scale and intensity. The familiar caricatures, however, are mere representations of what we now *believe* the Great War to have been; they do not represent the entirety of the war as it was experienced.[16] For many of the men and women of 1914 to 1919 the Great War was not meaningless or futile; it was a war that had to be fought and had to be won, whatever the cost.[17]

This book shifts our gaze. Our collective fixation with the trenches is put to one side. 'Tommy' appears, but is no longer centre stage or the only actor. Instead, the conflict is viewed by many different people – soldiers and civilians, adults and children – with multiple perspectives, and from different standpoints and particular localities. This book widens our gaze. So much has been written about the undoubtedly important wartime experience of front-line military personnel. Far less attention has been paid to the experiences of other groups who also contributed to the war effort, the civilians living 'largely in the shadows',[18] although the changing role and status of some groups of women has been well documented.[19] If we look beyond the much-studied combatants and war-workers – the soldiers in the mud of Flanders and the munitionettes in their factories – then the war experience of British citizens between 1914 and 1919 becomes increasingly diverse and multi-faceted. Myriad faces of war begin to appear on stage. Some are familiar, but not in the context of a nation at war. Others, who might have previously led 'indistinct lives',[20] illustrate both the enormous demands made *upon* individuals by a nation state mobilised for total war, and the huge and varied contributions made *by* them. In a British population of some 40 million people in 1914, the war produced wildly differing reactions, experiences and meanings.[21]

Roll of Honour is based upon the premise that in the total war of 1914–19, wartime service extended beyond combatants in the front line. Indeed, the very concept of the 'front' itself is redefined. Since the 1980s the British home front has attracted more attention from historians. Much of this work, however, has investigated the impact of war *on* Britain, rather than constructing a view of the war *from* Britain. What might be gained from a study of one type of institution in wartime, looking out as well as looking in; seeing the Great War from Blighty, from the streets of the home front, and in particular from the perspective of communities connected inextricably to those serving on other battle fronts?

Roll of Honour places the nation's schools at the centre of the action. A similar approach to studying the myriad faces of the conflict, and thus finding new ways of reading the past and refining the more generalised grand narratives,[22] might be taken for other institutions. Unlike business corporations, factories, government agencies, or even hospitals, schools are institutions with which we are all familiar. The experience of schooling is universal, albeit gained in different times, forms and geographical locations, and observed through different cultural lenses. The relationship between education and war, however, is complex. Schooling, in all its various guises, conditions personal values, attitudes and expectations. It shapes individual and collective identities, but its outcomes are diverse. Schools might prepare the nation's children for war – or peace. Conversely, war has the potential for major disruption and transformation of educational provision and outcomes – or, alternatively, for validation of the status quo. The Great War did have an enormous, but not necessarily a widespread or lasting, impact on British schools.

Roll of Honour is not the first book to shine 'a light that has not been cast before'.[23] Peter Parker's *The Old Lie: the Great War and the Public-School Ethos*

(1987) provided a detailed analysis of the way in which the culture of elite schools prepared boys from privileged backgrounds to play their part as leaders of men in future conflicts.[24] More recently, Sir Anthony Seldon and David Walsh have vividly portrayed the enormous and costly contribution made by pupils and teachers from the country's leading private fee-paying schools.[25] In *Public Schools and the Great War: the Generation Lost* they have argued that the Centenary Commemorations of the Great War provide an ideal opportunity for individual schools 'to research and celebrate their past pupils who fought, and examine why they fought'.[26] The wartime experiences of some institutions have already appeared in such titles as *Kitchener's Lost Boys*, *The Boys of Shakespeare's School* and *Tig's Boys*.[27] Most of these books, frequently constructed from surviving correspondence to and from school alumni, contain poignant accounts of combatants and casualties, but references to the impact of the war on the daily ebb and flow of school life are often no more than incidental.

Most British children, of course, did not attend such schools. The provision of schooling was framed within a hierarchy of education based firmly upon social class, family origins and the ability to pay. The children of the masses attended elementary schools. Relatively few children from the working classes progressed to some form of secondary education and even fewer went on to higher education and the universities. The wartime experience of the majority of children, unlike their counterparts in the Second World War,[28] has yet to be illuminated. To some extent this book is an attempt to redress the balance, and to respond to the appeal of Seldon and Walsh to research the Great War experience of schools of all types.[29] *Roll of Honour* is not simply confined to the wartime history of non-elite schools, however. Instead, it examines the experience and impact of war across the hierarchy of schooling. It explores the response to war of privately-funded preparatory schools as well as some of the great public schools. It considers the ways in which reformed and newly-created secondary schools emulated institutions of superior social standing and used opportunities created by the war to forge new identities and traditions. The massive contribution to the war effort of public-financed elementary schools is highlighted, as is the role of different forms of technical, reformatory and military education before and during the Great War. Boys' schools *and* girls' schools provide personal and institutional cameos of wartime experiences. The war of 1914–19 was a war in which all the nation's schoolchildren were called upon to serve King and Country.

The *dramatis personae* who appear on stage in *Roll of Honour* constitute a varied cast. Those who inhabited our schools during the Great War included the headteachers and governors who were charged by the British Government with mobilising their school communities; the school masters, whose enlistment, conscription or conscientious objection to military service changed lives and career paths; the school mistresses, appointed 'for the duration of the war only', who sought to demonstrate their interchangeability in male-dominated institutions; the school alumni who thought of school whilst knee deep in mud; and finally, of course, the schoolchildren themselves, whose collection campaigns added vital resources to the war economy.

Each of these groups contained individuals with myriad faces of their own. The lives in wartime of men, women and children may often appear to conform to our familiar groupings and characterisations, but it is important to understand 'the complexity of human behaviour, particularly in times of great turmoil or catastrophe'.[30] Each individual was a multi-faceted actor capable of wearing different hats at different times and in different contexts. Each had multiple affiliations. They were more than simply 'Tommy', or 'Schoolmaster', or an 'Old Boy' of the school. In many cases they were all of these things and more. Contemporaries often referred to the existential gap which existed between those who fought in the trenches and those who stayed at home, but the dynamics of a nation at war created an intimate relationship between battle front and home front.[31] During the Great War schools did much to cultivate this crucial symbiotic relationship. Just as there was no typical 'Tommy', similarly, in the early twentieth century there was no typical school, or teacher or pupil.

The voices from the diverse school communities of the period, for so long part of a hidden history of our social past, are now emerging from the archives and bear witness to the huge range and complexity of wartime experience. The Great War Centenary has prompted many schools to explore their own archives and to re-tell the stories which are uniquely theirs. School logbooks, admissions registers, magazines, prize day reports and governors' minutes have been re-discovered, dusted off and, increasingly, digitised and offered to a wider audience by way of the internet.[32] School Rolls of Honour, in particular, take the researcher back to a time when the number of alumni joining the colours was a matter of enormous institutional pride. School memorials containing the 'saddening list' of names of 'The Fallen' reflect the real cost in human terms of that particular community's contribution to a national war effort.[33] Such records, with their references to regiments joined, commissions gained and decorations awarded, reveal so much about an individual school's place in the social and educational hierarchy of the period.

Contemporary records such as these challenge many of the generalised and pre-conceived notions of the war by allowing us to re-focus our gaze periodically. They make possible a close-up view of the war as it unfolded for those present at the time. Day-by-day school logbook entries and termly magazines, in particular, provide a sense of immediacy which contrasts sharply with how later observers, often with insufficient awareness of timescales, visualise and understand the war. The archives reflect individual and group response to national and local events. They chronicle features of local and institutional context, the immediacy of decisions to be taken, and the personal concerns and attitudes which changed as the war dragged on over four long years. The impact of the call-to-arms in August 1914, at a point when most observers believed that the war would be over by Christmas, is an obvious example of an event which elicited different responses from the nation's schools. Similarly, the published lists of Old Boy casualties in the wake of the great military offensives on the Somme in 1916 and at Passchendaele in 1917 had an inevitable sobering effect upon many, but not all, school communities. Some institutions responded to shortages of food caused by the German U-boat campaign by introducing rationing, whilst others dug up their formerly sacrosanct playing fields and grew more vegetables. More male teachers were called up for military service in the wake of the German Spring Offensive of 1918, leading some secondary boys' schools to employ women 'masters' for the first time. In November of that same year, news that the war had ended, and indeed had been won in the final March to Victory and German surrender, was greeted with mixed feelings.

The Great War made huge demands on British schools. Almost immediately following the outbreak of war in August 1914 schools were galvanised into action. They quickly became part of a national effort to wage total war. Some educational institutions lost some or all of their buildings and playing fields, requisitioned by the authorities for use by the military or medical services. Many senior pupils in the secondary schools heeded the call to join Kitchener's New Armies, as did thousands of teachers whose prolonged absences from the classroom created enormous staffing problems. Headteachers throughout the country produced Rolls of Honour, listing the names, ranks and regiments of their Old Boys, and sometimes Old Girls. Pupils knitted balaclavas to keep the boys in khaki warm, raised money for the wounded and prisoners of war, and made and supplied war *matériel* as part of a revised wartime curriculum. Other children, especially those in the elementary schools, started their working lives prematurely, replacing elders who had gone off to fight and bringing in the harvest. Former pupils entrenched in foreign fields thought of their schools as well as their homes. Their Alma Mater had given them a code of behaviour and a set of beliefs which helped them to endure and to make some sense of the war. When the war finally ended, and the Armistice of 1918 and Peace of 1919 had been celebrated, the nation's schools became an important focus for a culture of communal remembrance. Hundreds of thousands of British citizens who, like Bob Hart, had made the ultimate sacrifice on the battlefields of Europe and beyond did not return home to Blighty. School war memorials of all shapes, sizes and degrees of elaboration were unveiled for The Fallen, but many of those who returned from the war were simply forgotten.

Part I

Call-to-Arms!

Who'll earn the Empire's thanks –
Will you, my laddie?
Who'll swell the victor's ranks –
Will you my laddie?
When that procession comes,
Banners and rolling drums –
Who'll stand and bite his thumbs –
Will you, my laddie?

Jesse Pope (1915)
The Call

Chapter 1

Ante-bellum

The river of death has brimmed his banks,
And England's far, and Honour a name,
But the voice of a schoolboy rallies the ranks:
"Play up! Play up! And play the game!"
This is the word that year by year,
While in her place the school is set,
Every one of her sons must hear,
And none that hears it dare forget.

Sir Henry Newbolt (1892)
Vitaï Lampada (The Torch of Life)

B ob Hart was one of the first boys through the impressive front entrance doors to Harrow County School for Boys. He and his fellow new boys numbered just 73, but by the eve of war in 1914, when Bob and the school party embarked upon their eventful trip to Germany, Harrow County had reached its full complement of 300 pupils. The school had opened officially on Saturday, 21 January 1911 after almost a decade of heated and often acrimonious local debate. County Alderman A.K. Carlyon JP was the new school's first Chairman of Governors. He had been a leading campaigner for the creation of additional secondary school places in the growing Urban District of Harrow. The Governors of the prestigious Harrow School – *the* Harrow School – had entered into negotiations with Middlesex County Council with a view to either expanding part of their own public school or jointly supporting the establishment of a new school. Protracted discussions ended with a compromise that few had anticipated; a new, separate and fully rate-supported secondary school situated just two miles away from its historic neighbour. With more than a hint of exasperation and black humour Alderman Carlyon gave Harrow County its motto: *Virtus Non Stemma*, literally 'Worth Not Birth'. A popular local translation was 'Pluck not Pedigree'. Mr Ernest Young BSc, latterly headmaster of the Lower School of John Lyon at Harrow School, became the first headmaster of Harrow County. He quickly established a local, regional and national reputation for his upstart school.[1] Bob Hart joined one of the new types of secondary school; one which offered wider opportunities and combined progressive and enlightened ideals with popular and traditional forms of schooling.

The opening of Harrow County School for Boys took place in a different world. It was a world which was identified by those who endured the greatest conflict their country had ever seen as the 'ante-bellum' – the time before the war. The Great War, as it was called at the time, became the great dividing line in history. Before the war everything was different. The war changed everything. After the war nothing would be the same, or so it was believed and often stated. The halcyon days which preceded the outbreak of hostilities in August 1914 were depicted in stark contrast to the storm, or deluge, which engulfed all those who lived through it. The late Victorian and Edwardian period is thus usually portrayed as a period of calm and relative stability. As far as the provision of education was concerned, however, this was a time of contested principles and controversy. Since 1833 the state had become increasingly involved in the provision of education in England. Demand for education from a growing middle class, combined with a belated and often begrudging recognition of the need to educate the masses, resulted in the creation of a compromised patchwork of schooling characterised by local and social diversity. There was an education system of sorts; a series of arrangements directed centrally by the Board of Education in London but controlled locally by many different interest groups: the Church of England and its Nonconformist counterparts, numerous charities and private institutions. Forster's 1870 Education Act and Balfour's 1902 Education Act filled in some of the gaps in the provision of elementary and secondary education respectively and established protocols for funding. Before the Great War British society was class based and hierarchical, and so was the provision of schooling.

Balfour's Act and the Regulations which followed re-defined and re-structured the framework of secondary schooling in England and Wales. In his speech introducing the Education Bill in the House of Commons in March 1902, Prime Minister Arthur Balfour referred explicitly to the 'imperfect condition' and 'insufficiency of the supply of secondary education'.[2] The 1902 Act was intended to remedy deficiencies in both the quantity and quality of secondary education available, and to make clear the differences and limited connections between the elementary and secondary sectors. Financial support was given to schools officially recognised by the Board of Education. In return, such schools were subject to regulation by the Board and inspection by His Majesty's Inspectors of Schools (HMI).

Many existing schools, such as former charity schools and endowed grammar schools, took advantage of the funding on offer. These schools varied in size and clientele, but collectively they offered diverse forms of 'middle-class education', as secondary education was often referred to at the time. Balfour's Act gave many educational institutions formal status and recognition, as well as a timely infusion of much-needed financial support after years of precarious existence relying upon incomes derived from original endowments and the pursuit of fee-paying pupils.

Deacon's School in Peterborough, for example, founded by Thomas Deacon in 1722 as a charity school for 'twenty poor boys', accepted much-needed financial support in 1902 and became a 'Secondary School (Division B)'. Its neighbour, The King's School, one of the many traditional cathedral grammar schools founded during the Tudor period, decided that regulation by the Board of Education was too high a price to pay for the additional funding.[3]

The 1902 Act also created Local Education Authorities. Under the new legislation county councils and boroughs were directed to provide not only elementary school places, as had the School Boards which they replaced, but also to take 'such steps as seem to them desirable, to supply or aid the supply of education other than elementary education'.[4] Hence, Middlesex County Council was able to counter the arguments of those who opposed the expansion, and public funding, of secondary education and open five new secondary schools in 1911, including Harrow County School for Boys.[5]

The new secondary schools attracted ambitious parents from the 'intermediate' classes: the amorphous and constantly shifting social groupings referred to by sociologists as the lower-middle and upper-working classes. School success and survival depended upon the extent to which individual institutions, operating within very particular local frameworks of schooling, were able to attract parents supportive of the curriculum on offer and, more importantly, able and willing to pay the required school fees.[6] At Harrow County the majority of pupils were fee-payers. Others were 'free-placers': bright boys, drawn mostly from the neighbouring elementary schools, who had won funded scholarships through competitive examination in line with the Board of Education's *Free Place Regulations* of 1907.

But what, exactly, would the new or reformed secondary schools such as Harrow County and Deacon's School actually teach? What sort of ethos and culture would they espouse and cultivate? Sir Robert Morant at the Board of Education provided an answer to the first question. The 1904 *Regulations for Secondary Schools* established an academic curriculum in the newly recognised secondary schools similar to that provided in the great public schools. It was a curriculum, or list of subjects, not too dissimilar from the National Curriculum operating in English and Welsh secondary schools today: English language and literature, geography, history, mathematics, science, drawing, manual work, physical exercises and at least one foreign language. This was the basis of a 'general' rather than 'classical' education. It is clear from the curriculum designed by Ernest Young at Harrow County that, subject to periodic HMI visitations and recommendations, the new secondary schools were given sufficient flexibility to be able to respond to local conditions. Some schools even introduced vocational subjects such as bookkeeping and shorthand in order to satisfy parental demand for 'useful' subjects and to enhance their pupils' prospects of employment in local economies which were dependent upon huge armies of male clerks and apprentices.[7]

In answer to the second question, many of the post–1902 secondary schools consciously copied the public schools. They adopted important and highly visible cultural symbols, such as school uniforms, houses systems, magazines, debating societies, prefects and team sports. Many of the genteel patterns and traditions of the elite schools were fixed one level lower in the new schools by schoolmasters who themselves were products of, or had taught at, the public schools.[8] This 'diffusion' model enabled 'intermediate' schools to emulate their superiors in the great public schools and distance themselves from their perceived inferiors in the elementary schools surrounding them.[9] History, tradition and reputation still differentiated the great schools from the new foundations. The Great War, however, and despite the disruption it created and the loss in human life it incurred, provided an early opportunity for schools like Harrow County School for Boys to create their own traditions, heroes and history and, ultimately, to establish their credentials. Bob Hart's schooling set him aside from the masses and gave him the opportunity to become one day, possibly, a gentleman.

Not all the post–1902 schools were boys' schools. In Cheltenham, for example, Pate's Grammar School for Girls was opened in 1905 for the daughters of tradesmen, clerical workers and those employed in the lower ranks of the professions. The daughters of 'gentlefolk' were already taught elsewhere, in Cheltenham Ladies' College.[10] Many County High Schools (Plate 2), including the Harrow County School for Girls which opened in 1914, were created to cater for girls from the 'middling' classes. As a trade advertisement for the Wellingborough County High School for Girls demonstrated, however, the curriculum on offer was often distinctly gender based and included subjects such as Cookery and Laundry.[11] Most girls who attended secondary schools were fee-payers. Increasingly, however, scholarships funded by Local Education Authorities were made available to bright girls as well as boys from the elementary schools. In theory at least, this 'scholarship ladder' allowed able girls from lower-middle and working-class homes to progress into higher education and employment. Wellingborough County High provided training for careers in 'Medicine, Dispensing, Teaching, Art, Civil Service, Nursing, etc.'. In practice, however, few young women generally entered the higher professions. Instead, many became teachers and nurses. Nevertheless, with the expansion of secondary school places, increasing numbers of girls were able to experience an education which emulated that provided by the best girls' boarding schools. Manchester High School for Girls, for example, was founded in 1874. In her School Report of 1914, Head Mistress Sara Burstall, who had herself attended the independent North London Collegiate School, stated with evident pride that the school contained 600 girls aged 9 to 19 taught by 41 Mistresses.[12]

The reformed secondary schools did not sit in splendid isolation. Whatever their official Board of Education designation, the real status of each school was determined by their relationship to other schools. More prestigious institutions, their popularity and success built upon years of service to the local and, in some cases, national community, were a constant reminder of the school's place in society. The ancient grammar schools already provided a traditional secondary education in many British towns and cities. Some, like King's School Canterbury (founded 597 AD), had existed in one form or another since the early Middle Ages. Originally linked to monasteries or other religious establishments, they prepared able boys for careers in the Church or royal and noble households. They had taught almost exclusively Latin and Greek grammar in an age when vernacular English was rarely used for official purposes. The English Reformation of the sixteenth century and the consequent dissolution of the monasteries saw the growth of new grammar schools founded by royal patronage, for example the King Edward VI Grammar Schools in Retford and Totnes, or by private endowment. Some, like Manchester Grammar School, eventually joined the ranks of the elite fee-paying public schools. By the 1870s, however, many grammar schools had few pupils and low standards of teaching and learning. From 1879 the Endowed Schools Commission breathed new life into them, broadening their curricula and their appeal. By 1914 these schools, usually catering for fee-paying day boys and displaying many of the academic and cultural features of the public schools, were once again attracting discerning middle-class parents and competing with the likes of Harrow County School for Boys.

At the apex of the hierarchy of schooling were the great public schools. These were the institutions which had traditionally educated the nation's elite: the sons of the landowning aristocracy and the wealthy upper-middle classes. They were often ancient foundations, steeped in tradition and held in high esteem. In England, public schools such as Westminster (founded 1371), Winchester (1382), Eton (1440), Shrewsbury (1552), Rugby (1567), Harrow (1572), Uppingham (1584) and Charterhouse (1611) could boast pedigrees which stretched back centuries. They were joined in the nineteenth century by others such as Marlborough College (1843), Wellington College (1859) and Malvern (1862), independent schools established primarily 'to instil into the new middle classes the values of the old gentry'.[13] Membership of the Head Masters' Conference (HMC) and, from 1889, a listing in the *Public Schools Yearbook*, signified status as a leading 'Public School'.[14] Links with the universities of Cambridge and Oxford ensured a virtual monopoly in the preparation of future leaders for politics, the armed forces and the major professions.

There were nearly 200 British public schools in 1914,[15] and they varied enormously in size and reputation. The most prestigious schools with boarding facilities, such as Harrow School (Plate 3), attracted fee-paying clientele from a broad regional and sometimes national base. In London and others cities, day pupils were also admitted by institutions such as Dulwich College, St Paul's and Latymer Upper. Smaller public schools were found throughout Britain. In Wales,

Bangor Grammar School and Christ College, Brecon had 76 and 120 pupils on roll respectively in 1914. Irish public schools were differentiated by religion. Campbell College in Belfast admitted boys from the Protestant community; St Columba's in Dublin was a Catholic foundation. In Scotland, the city of Edinburgh alone boasted five major public schools, including George Heriot's, the largest institution of its kind with 1,400 pupils. Merchiston Castle School was far smaller, with 196 pupils on roll when the Great War began. As befitted one of the key providers of imperial personnel, the public school model of education was also exported to the Dominions, and assumed familiar forms at Sydney Grammar School, Upper Canada College, King's Auckland and St John's Johannesburg.

The public schools taught the 'Classics'. Their curriculum was dominated by the study of Latin and Greek, but most also found time to teach English, mathematics, modern foreign languages, history and geography. The teaching of science (Plate 4) in the public schools was not universal. Rugby and Oundle pioneered the teaching of the subject at a time when the study of science and engineering were deemed appropriate for the skilled working classes, but not for gentlemen. The great majority of public school headmasters were classicists.[16] The ability to 'conjure up classical illusions' and quote verbatim from the works of the ancients was deemed by these influential educators to be far more important than the ability to innovate, design or make.[17] The pecking order of subjects was evident to the public schoolboys themselves. In the latter stages of the Great War, a conflict terrifyingly transformed by science and technology, Evelyn Waugh and his fellow pupils at Lancing College still regarded those boys taking science at school as 'a socially inferior race'.[18]

The process of schooling at these elite institutions was far more than traditional learning from a list of subjects. For generations of schoolboys before 1914, attendance at a public school was an all-embracing, immersive and conditioning experience. Moreover, it was the crucial preparation for the key role the boys would play during the Great War. Throughout the Victorian era the public schools had served the nation well, providing colonial administrators for the growing British Empire and young subalterns for its imperial wars in Africa and the Far East. The 'Public School Ethos' stressed the importance of 'character'. This was not simply an innate God-given quality, although 'good breeding' was often regarded as a pre-requisite, but was, instead, an attribute which could be formed by careful nurturing in a cloistered environment. The formation of character became the central purpose of many public schools during the nineteenth century. Duty, loyalty, patriotism and self-sacrifice. These were the essential concepts upon which character would be moulded; the ideals which were 'inextricably bound up with the concept of a ruling class'.[19] Duty and loyalty were owed to monarch, regiment, school and house. Patriotism was 'virtually exalted into a religion (and to die for one's country was the supreme sacrifice'.[20] Chivalric images abounded in school magazines, in the stained glass windows in the chapel, and in the trophies awarded to schoolboy heroes on the playing field.[21] Boys were made into men in an overtly masculine and strictly hierarchical, regimented and disciplined society of headmasters, housemasters, prefects and boys. Scholarly achievement, sporting prowess, social poise and the acceptance of responsibility were the desired indicators of the character-building process. Boarding schools, with their potential to manage a boy's leisure time as well as his academic programme, were particularly effective vehicles for cultivating 'gentlemanly' ethics and attitudes.[22]

Sport was a fundamental part of the public school curriculum. The late nineteenth and early twentieth centuries witnessed the development of many team sports. Public schools were often instrumental in the process of game codification, governance and expansion. Fixtures between schools and local clubs were commonplace. Fixtures against other schools, first recorded in the 1805 cricket match between Eton and Harrow at Lord's Cricket Ground in London, reflected a school's place, or ambitions, in the educational hierarchy. Football, cricket and rowing (Plate 5) were the sporting activities of choice for elite schools and their imitators. Not all the great public schools played 'rugger'. Many, such as Charterhouse, played the round ball version of football. For most socially ambitious schools, however, it was Rugby Union, a game for gentlemen that was the preferred code, even if its players, as Kipling noted, appeared at times to be 'muddied oafs'.[23] Teachers, too, were expected to be sporting role models, combining the attributes of scholar and athlete,[24] and many school teams comprised boys and masters. The acquisition and development of school playing fields became an important signifier of a school's educational and social status. These expensive assets were important locations of indoctrination.

Playing the game on the playing fields of Eton and elsewhere was about more than just the game itself. The development of team games in the public schools and beyond was based on 'the subscription to the belief that important expressive and instrumental qualities can be promoted, in particular loyalty, self-control, perseverance, fairness and courage, both moral and physical'.[25] Team games, advocates argued, developed manliness, character, leadership skills and *esprit de corps*. Charles Hodges, Headmaster of Shore, the Sydney Church of England Grammar School in Australia, claimed in his Speech Day Report of 1901 that 'Opportunities for the practice of those virtues which stamp the real man – courage, vigour, chivalry, straightforwardness – are found perhaps more frequently in the playing field than upon the school benches'.[26] Many schools instigated and encouraged a 'games cult' – or 'mania' – which gloried athleticism and deified success.[27] Most pupils subscribed to the cult. Norman Musgrave Dillon attended Haileybury where 'Sport was very important ... the main aspiration above work and classical knowledge was to become a member of the rugby fifteen'.[28] The Captain of the XI or XV epitomised the hero of the age. School magazines, honours boards and Speech Day reports regularly praised their contribution to the good name of 'The School'. Gentlemanly behaviour and 'good form' on the playing field were regarded as highly as skill, determination and bravery – just the attributes required of an imperial elite and, after 1914, of subaltern officers on the Western Front.

Playing for one's school and fighting for the Empire were, for public school masters and boys, part of the same continuum.[29] The cry of 'Play up! Play up! And play the game!' applied equally to the battlefield as to the cricket field. Linking the two experiences were the Cadet Corps established in many public schools before the Great War. During the nineteenth century many schools established paramilitary units as part of the wider Volunteer Movement which attracted many British citizens into part-time soldiering. The corps at Harrow School (Plate 6), one of the first to be established in 1859, was attached to the 5th (West) Middlesex Volunteer Rifle Corps. Divided into three companies and with a Band, Cyclist and Signalling sections, the Harrow School Cadet Corps held parades, drills and field days and attended summer camps with cadets from other schools. Some public schools developed an even more overt military tradition during the Victorian era. Blundell's School in Tiverton, for example, established a Cadet Corps in 1898 as part of the Devon Militia. The school also had a Special Army Class, which enabled Blundell's to compete with Eton and Wellington College in preparing entrants for the military academies at Sandhurst and Woolwich. Over one hundred former pupils fought in the Boer War of 1899–1902. Before the outbreak of war in 1914 there were nearly 240 Old Blundellians serving with the colours, many of them in India.[30] Other schools had belatedly introduced the corps. Founded in 1904 as part of the 4th Battalion South Wales Borderers, Monmouth School Cadet Corps was by 1906 'in full swing. It promises to be exceedingly smart and efficient, and from being rough and indisciplined it has learnt to serve and obey'.[31]

Public school cadets were given early instruction in military discipline and the use of weaponry. Senior pupils and masters served as non-commissioned officers (NCOs) and officers of the corps. After the Haldane Reforms of 1908 the Cadet Corps became an integral part of Britain's military establishment. Haldane created an Expeditionary Force supported by a restructured and expanded reserve force, which included Cadet Corps – now renamed Officer Training Corps (OTC). Army Order 160 of 1908 established Senior Division OTC in universities and Junior Division OTC in public schools. By 1912 there were 55 university and 155 public school OTC contingents. Haldane had thus linked schooling to preparation for war. The nation's elite educational institutions would henceforth develop military skills to a common and exacting standard. In times of war they would supply officers to the army. Whatever else they might have been, the public schools had become 'schools for subalterns'.[32]

A multitude of smaller private schools, charging fees sufficient to ensure a degree of relative social exclusivity, emulated their more prestigious counterparts and transmitted the same values. Many were preparatory schools, catering for younger pupils intending to join the public schools in their early teens. The core purpose of these 'incubation pens' was to 'mould their charges for the public school experience'.[33] The games cult was a crucial part of the preparation, as were modified forms of militarisation. At Belmont School, a small proprietary private school in Brighton founded by its headmaster Mr G.L. Evans and suitably assisted by Mrs Evans, the Head Boy was 'Captain' MacTier. Upland House School, a small preparatory institution founded in Epsom in 1884, contained only nineteen boys aged nine to thirteen in 1911. The school was too small and the boys too young for the school to meet the requirements for establishing a Cadet Corps but, nevertheless, activities at Upland House included drill and shooting. In 1908, and in the wake of the Haldane reforms, Headmaster George Burgess proudly reported in the school magazine that:

> I am glad to say that nearly all my Old Boys join their Cadet Corps when they go to the Public Schools, and I have had proof of the advantage derived from the drill and shooting learnt here. At a time when recruits are wanted for the Territorial Army, I hope Upland House Boys will come to the front in showing an example of unselfish patriotism.[34]

Grammar schools and the new secondary schools also introduced opportunities for schoolboy soldiering. Aubrey Baggley, a pupil at Burton Grammar School during the Boer War, recalled the introduction of 'Military Drill' with Sergeant Major Maher and short-range rifle-shooting at targets under the covered shed in the playground.[35] Hackney Downs School in London, formerly a Grocers' Company foundation but from 1907 maintained by London County Council, operated a School Battalion. The six companies were based on the existing house structure, with House Captains as company commanders and House Prefects making up the other officers. Despite several previous disbandments, from 1905 the battalion was put on an almost permanent footing by the headmaster, William Jenkyn Thomas.[36] In 1909 a Cadet Corps was founded at Northampton Grammar School despite the rejection by the governors of a previous proposal due to the potential expense. The Northampton boys did a great deal of marching, drilling and shooting, and sent teams to compete with public school cadets at the Boys' Bisley shooting competition. In 1914 the school's 180 cadets were affiliated to the 4th Battalion Northamptonshire Regiment and, for the first time, wore cadet uniforms.[37] The War Office turned down the request for a school OTC made by the governors of Hutcheson's Grammar School in Glasgow. Undeterred, the School Trust financed their own Cadet Corps, which was 'in drilling order' by January 1914. When one governor protested at a proposal to form a pipe band, on the grounds that it would encourage a 'spirit of militarism', headmaster King Gillies replied that the corps 'would help to develop the esprit and voluntary submission to authority that would ultimately dispense with all forcible methods in the classroom'. By December 1915 over 100 boys at Hutcheson's had joined the corps, paying a subscription fee of 2s.6d. for the privilege of membership. They too had close links to the regular army, having affiliated to the 7th Battalion (Cameronians) Scottish Rifles.[38]

There were, of course, many who did not subscribe to the 'corps' or its ideals. Even compulsory membership of the OTC, introduced by the majority of public schools by 1914, did not prevent individual cadets undermining the military regime through deliberate acts of sloppiness, as Cadet Waugh at Lancing recorded later.[39] Some schools introduced other forms of 'military' service in addition, or as alternatives, to the OTC. In 1907 Robert Baden-Powell, who had served as a military scout during the Boer War, held an experimental camp for boys on Brownsea Island near Poole in Dorset. The twenty-two 'Scouts' who attended that first gathering became the pioneers for a youth movement that caught the public imagination and grew rapidly into an international organisation. Some boys were clearly attracted to the less-militaristic activities which being a scout, rather than a cadet, offered. John Wilkinson, an early recruit, later recalled that 'There was no Army about it – never military – it was quite the reverse. It was the outdoor life, camping and cooking, birds and animals, and singing'.[40] Forms of military drill were, however, practiced by other scout troops.[41] *Scouting for Boys* proclaimed a message which was responded to by many community groups. Manchester Grammar School, having founded an OTC in 1910, introduced a scout troop two years later after a visit to the school by the evangelistic Baden-Powell.[42] In November 1911 'B–P' visited Harrow County School for Boys following an invitation from Ernest Young. After the Chief Scout's address to a large audience of parents the school scout troop the 4th Harrow was founded and the headmaster, now Scoutmaster Young, became one of its most dedicated propagandists. Within a month, 114 of the 185 boys, including Bob Hart, had been enrolled. In this particular school, the Boy Scout movement provided the opportunities for character building, not the cadet corps.

For many decades before the Great War the public schools and their imitators had educated the nation's boys, albeit that minority of boys from the 'respectable' classes of society who could afford the fees. The development of schooling for their sisters, however, had taken place relatively recently. Girls from genteel families were traditionally educated at home, usually by private tutors. Their 'education' was essentially a preparation for eligibility for marriage. Before the development of girls' boarding schools in the second half of the nineteenth century, the few girls from the upper classes who did have some form of formal education were prepared for the drawing room rather than for public life. Private tuition or small private establishments gave them a social rather than intellectual education, often comprising a narrow curriculum of foreign language recitation, music and dancing, and the practice of graces and other 'accomplishments'. The pioneering work of Miss Buss at North London Collegiate School (1850) and Miss Beale at Cheltenham Ladies College (1853) led the way for more fee-paying schools for girls, with broader curriculum offerings which included subjects such as English language and literature, mathematics, history and geography, and participation in team sports such as hockey (Plate 7). At Nottingham High School for Girls, an institutional member of the Girls' Public Day School Trust (GPDST), Miss Clark, the Head Mistress, introduced several features, including classical, debating and Shakespeare societies, which would have been familiar to those in the boys' public schools. An Old Girls Association was established. The school built a boarding house. In 1903 a Form Drill Competition was introduced in lieu of a cadet corps.[43]

Before the Great War the public schools educated an elite minority. New publicly-maintained schools catered for an increasing number of other children from the middling and intermediate classes of society. The vast majority of British children, however, did not and could not attend secondary school. It was not until after the Second World War that all children in England and Wales were able to progress automatically from primary to secondary education. The 1944 Education Act provided a 'Secondary Education for All' irrespective of parental means or a child's scholarly potential. Until that point, however, elementary and secondary schooling were two barely connected educational experiences, separate pathways intended for the 'Two Nations' identified many years before by Prime Minister Benjamin Disraeli, their disjuncture regularised by the reform of schooling during the Edwardian period. The 1902 Education Act was driven by 'the need for directing elite groups to keep things under control'.[44] Successive Board of Education Regulations clearly defined the differences between elementary and secondary education to ensure the existence of two parallel systems, each with a distinct social function. The class divide was 'buttressed by the educational system'.[45] Secondary schools were not intended for the working classes. With the exception of a privileged few – the extremely able scholarship winners whose parents could afford the additional incidental costs of secondary schooling – working-class children were consigned to the elementary schools. The system thus fostered social stability, or so it was argued by its proponents, whilst facilitating very limited social mobility. Boys from the 'upper strata' of society were ten times more likely than those from 'skilled manual' or 'routine clerical' homes to receive a secondary education – and seventeen times more likely than those from the 'less-skilled working class'.[46]

It is important, however, to remember the social context of the years before the Great War. Victorian and Edwardian Britain 'contained not one, but several worlds within it'.[47] British society was incredibly diverse, but given a degree of order by class-based hierarchical structures. Schooling had traditionally reflected social divisions and still does.[48] The middle classes viewed secondary education as their preserve, a buyable commodity.[49] Private fee-paying schools deliberately pitched their charges at the desired clientele's ability to pay. Government officials and respectable ratepayers were equally concerned about the confusion and financial implications created by the flood of children who had been staying on in the elementary schools or even going on to 'higher grade' schools provided by some of the post-1870 School Boards.[50] In an age when few advocated equal opportunities in education,[51] the 1902 Education Act was consistent with popular opinion. The social reality of education was given a statutory basis.

The first concerted attempts to educate the British masses took place in the nineteenth century. The Industrial Revolution, enormous population growth and rapid urbanisation changed the demography of the country. W.E. Forster, the architect of the 1870 Education Act, recognised the social and political implications, and potential dangers, of such massive and wide-scale change and stated that 'we should educate our future masters'. The Act increased the provision of basic – or elementary – education for the masses, not by building 'state' schools but by encouraging existing organisations and new local initiatives. The Church of England and the British and Foreign School Society had founded National Schools and British Schools respectively since the early nineteenth century. These supplemented the existing provision for children in parochial schools and other often small and poorly resourced private schools. The 1870 Act attempted to 'fill in the gaps', enabling local School Boards, funded by the rates rather than central government, to establish Board Schools providing elementary education only. The Board of Education's *Revised Code* ensured that such schools taught a rudimentary curriculum based upon the 'three Rs' – 'Reading, Riting and Reckoning' – and HMI ensured conformity by regular visitation and inspection of schools.

It may well be true to say that the poor are always with us, but, despite the Victorian 'age of progress', in Edwardian England the poor were both numerous and highly visible. Many working-class families were large, but they were regulated by high infant mortality. There was no welfare state, doctors' fees were often prohibitive and charity was scorned by many. Leonard Thompson, a farm labourer in the village of Akenfield which was described so lyrically and movingly by Ronald Blythe, recalled just how harsh life could be for rural families with many children and little food or fresh water.[52] Conditions in the towns and cities were rarely any better. Edith Turner recalled attending a London County Council (LCC) school despite having no shoes on her feet.[53] Amidst widespread fears and concerns about the physical and moral health of the poorest children, elementary schools became part of a civilising mission, especially in the poorest districts of the new industrial towns and cities.[54] The function of schooling was rarely to enlighten the recipients; at best it was intended to help ameliorate the dire symptoms of poverty, and at worst to provide a labouring class comprised of individuals who accepted their lot in life and their place in the social and economic hierarchy. In order to rescue the poor from corruption and bad influences, elementary schooling involved a strong emphasis on religious teaching, especially in church schools, combined with deference to authority.[55] One of the oft-interviewed veterans of the Great War, Albert 'Smiler' Marshall, remembered the importance placed on manners and the raising of caps to the gentry.[56] At Hornby School in Lancashire the school logbook entry for 6 February 1905 records the judgement made by the Diocesan Inspectors: 'The whole tone of the school is decidedly good. And the children are reverent and good mannered'. For those who could afford no better form of schooling for their children, the elementary schools provided a little learning, combined it with a great deal of godliness and discipline, and instilled in their charges respect for authority.

The emphasis on the development of basic literacy and numeracy, epitomised in the routine teaching of the 'three Rs', left time nonetheless for other subjects in the elementary school curriculum. Practical subjects invariably conformed to gender stereotypes: boys worked with wood and metal in preparation for their employment as artisans and labourers (Plate 8), and girls developed the domestic skills (Plate 9) deemed necessary for their future lives as wives and mothers. At Peterborough Practising School, a school attached to St Peter's Training College for intending teachers, pupils were taught about 'Citizenship', a theme which was to reappear as a compulsory National Curriculum cross-curricular element in all English and Welsh state schools some eight decades later.[57] This involved fostering 'attitudes and values which would be conducive to the furtherance of Empire', a form of 'education for imperialism', which was particularly prevalent in the period 1900–1905.[58] Loyalty and obedience became paramount virtues, and were clearly expected, as in schools for the social classes above them, to extend beyond the confines of the immediate community.

In so many of the pre-war photographs of elementary schools we see drab, gas-lit, monotone images of regimented pupils. The children of that Edwardian generation often appear tired and dull. In some cases they pose for the camera whilst sitting on their hands to discourage fidgeting. They are rarely engaged in learning as we would know it today. Standing by the sides or at the back of the bleak utilitarian classrooms are the schoolteachers: stiff and upright, model disciplinarians. These images may well convey the reality of schooling for many children in many schools at the time, but the real world of the child was lived in colour, not sepia tones. Despite the prevalence of rote learning and classroom order maintained by harsh discipline, schooling could be colourful and exciting. The Victorian and Edwardian notion of 'Empire', whatever we may feel about imperialism and its consequences a century later, carried with it tales of great historic and momentous deeds. 'Drum and trumpet' textbooks may have reinforced social stereotypes, propagated often inaccurate and poisonous myths, and romanticised war,[59] but it was this very romance and national myth-building process which captivated so many teachers and schoolchildren at the time. Lessons in school promoted salutary examples of such valued 'British' attributes as endurance, persistence and, as in so much of the iconography in the elite schools, self-sacrifice. Geography lessons demonstrated the greatness of our empire, and history lessons remembered great military and naval victories and the achievements of explorers.[60] At the Peterborough Practising School, poetry reading lessons took place weekly, and in 1907 included a class reading of Tennyson's epic poem *Charge of the Light Brigade*.[61] In many schools, the school hall was decked out with a large Union Jack, or with the captions such as 'For God, King and Country'. Classroom walls, displaying maps, scenes from history, and the portraits of British military and naval commanders and intrepid voyagers, conveyed similar colourful – and powerful – messages. Here were the constant reminders of the 'tangible expressions of patriotism ... men to be admired, respected and emulated'.[62]

The Boer War, despite its administrative blunders and military disasters, provided real opportunities for schools to spread the message of imperialism and to militarise their pupils. At Fleet Road School in Hampstead, one of the most ambitious and successful of the LCC elementary schools, Head of the Infants Department, Louise Walker, encouraged children to dress up in military uniforms, especially if, like pupil John Jones who attended school in his miniature Royal Artillery uniform, their fathers were serving in the armed forces. During the Boer War Miss Walker also produced action songs such as *Off to the War*, in which two infants played mother and son bidding a tearful farewell, the son 'at duty's call' to 'protect Old England from a foe'.[63] At Dronfield Junior School near Sheffield, pupils were encouraged to make collections for the Transvaal War Fund, and holidays were awarded for the relief of the besieged garrison towns of Ladysmith and Mafeking.[64] The Boer War generated its own crop of anniversaries and heroes. It added to a growing, almost religious, fervour of patriotism that existed in society at large, and was both reflected and further developed in schools. Akenfield resident Leonard Thompson recalled: 'It was all "my country" – country, country, country. You heard nothing else'. Local boys would march through the village singing about the latest heroes: 'Lords Roberts and Kitchener, Generals Buller and White, all dressed in khaki, going out to fight'.[65]

In the wake of the Boer War, Empire Day (Plate 10) became the major opportunity for schools to develop national solidarity and imperialist attitudes, and to fly the flag for King, Country and Empire. First observed in Canada in the 1890s, Empire Day was promoted in Britain in 1902 by Reginald Brabazon, the Earl of Meath, as part of his campaign for patriotism in the elementary school curriculum. Intended to be held each year on 24 May, the anniversary of Queen Victoria's birthday, Empire Day was an early example of how schools have been 'key devices for the development and transmission of a sense of nationhood'.[66]

George Baden (sic) White remembered the boys in his school dressing up on Empire Day and representing the colonies, with Britannia as the centrepiece of the display. Young George, along with fellow pupils wearing a red, white or blue cap, loved every minute of it.[67] LEA-maintained elementary schools often observed the day in accordance with a common format, with lessons on the British Empire in the morning followed by a holiday in the afternoon.[68] In 1906 the pupils of Dronfield Junior School spent their Empire Day learning about the duties and responsibilities of citizenship, singing national songs and giving three cheers for King and Empire. The girls also wrote essays entitled 'What qualities were needed to make good colonists?'[69] The Akenfield school logbook records that on 30 May 1907 the children were taught how to salute the national flag and were given lessons on the 'Growth and Extent of the British Empire'.[70]

In some cities, children from all the elementary schools would congregate in promenades, parks or sports grounds to parade or form human flags. In 1907 a Union Jack formation consisting of over 3,000 local schoolchildren was created at Bramhall Lane, home of Sheffield United FC. At such gatherings brass bands played and local dignitaries made rousing speeches.[71] Empire Day rituals continued to be observed during the Great War. The logbook entry for 24 May 1916 at Stibbington School, Peterborough, describes the activities:

> At 11 a.m. the children assembled in the playground where after Hymn and Prayer the Union Jack was unfurled. The National Anthem and Patriotic songs were sung and after a 'March past' and saluting the flag the children were regaled with cake and lemonade and sweets.[72]

Empire Day was observed enthusiastically in many schools, but the rituals were not universally adopted. The London School Board, which administered the majority of the capital's elementary – or 'Board' – schools until 1902, was not originally supportive of the 'patriotic movement' of the 1890s. Empire Day was not officially sanctioned nationally until 1916, by which time Britain was using every available device to promote patriotism at home and solidarity with the imperial Dominions.

The centrally directed but locally administered education system still left room for institutional initiative by teachers who were themselves imbued with the patriotic and imperialist spirit. Many headteachers routinely recorded in their school logbooks the anniversaries of spectacular military triumphs such as Waterloo and Trafalgar, and then described the commemorative lessons taught by their staff. More recent events and their associated heroes were also eulogised. Alfred Whitehouse, headteacher of St Nicholas Boys' School in King's Lynn since it first opened in 1884, taught the whole school a 'Lesson on Endurance, Captain Scott and the South Pole' in February 1914, just months after news that the expedition had ended in tragedy.[73] 'Endurance' for schoolchildren was exemplified by habitual good conduct and, especially, by punctual and regular attendance. The latter was rewarded in many schools and local authorities by the award of medals and bars identical in style to military campaign medals. According to the logbook entry for 4 April 1901 at Hornby School in Lancashire, for example, 'Margaret Kelsall, Alice Ripley, Sarah Ellen Hodgson and Fred Ripley have never missed' and were therefore eligible for 'Colonel W.H. Foster's Attendance Medals'.[74]

The physical health of the nation also became a national priority in the decade before the Great War. Widely accepted notions of the 'physical deterioration of the race', influenced by the ideas of Social Darwinists and eugenicists, led to calls in Britain for 'National Efficiency'. This meant different things to different social and economic interest groups, but it had quite clear and specific implications for the function of schooling, particularly for the education of girls. The relationship between motherhood and nationhood was considered crucial.[75] Contemporary opinion was divided as to whether it was women's employment outside the home or maternal ignorance of effective child care that was to blame for the high infant mortality rate and poor physical condition of many children.[76] In response to the 1904 *Report of the Inter-departmental Committee on Physical Deterioration*, commissioned after complaints from the army about the poor physical specimens enlisting in the Boer War, the Board of Education decided that better schooling for the masses might at least overcome some of the ignorance. The Board issued more regulations which dealt with the preparation of girls for motherhood. The teaching of domestic subjects – or 'housework' – became a key part of the curriculum for girls in the maintained elementary and secondary schools. The new Liberal government elected in 1906 also empowered LEAs to provide school meals and introduced school-based medical examinations for children.

As in Britain's elite schools and their secondary school imitators, sport became an important feature of school life in the elementary sector. At Fleet Road School, headteacher W.B. Adams deliberately imported features of public-school culture into what soon became known as the 'Eton of the Board Schools'. The school's prize-givings were often glittering social occasions. Fleet Road pupils excelled in music competitions. They also developed their sporting prowess and gained a reputation for success.[77] Elsewhere, elementary schools arranged fixtures between their teams: usually football for the boys and rounders for the girls.

Organised school sport was not the only opportunity available to develop healthy bodies. Education for imperialism demanded the improvement of physical attributes in all children.[78] Once again, schools were expected to be key locations for the transformation of the nation's human stock. Lessons in 'Drill' became a feature of many schools during the Victorian era, spurred on originally in the 1860s by public reaction to both the deficiencies of the British armed forces in the Crimean War and the growth of Prussia as a major continental power.[79] The Volunteer Movement of the 1860s and 1870s attracted teachers to its ranks, such as

John Martin of St Augustine's School in Peterborough, who introduced elements of military drill into their school activities.[80] Drill, it was argued, was a powerful instrument of socialisation, inculcating habits of obedience and acceptance of discipline.[81] It contributed to good order in schools, institutions which were relatively recent social innovations containing elements of society with the potential for disorder. Drill had evident health benefits. For boys from the elementary schools it developed a better physique and a degree of soldierly fitness. Finally, it served the military needs of the nation, providing the massed 'other ranks', the drilled followers destined to be led by the products of the public-school Cadet Corps and OTC. Despite the increasing importation of militarist elements into the school curriculum, however, there was by the late nineteenth century, and even during the Boer War, a debate about the nature of physical education.[82] For girls, especially, there was a move away from military style drill towards the adoption of forms of exercise, such as Swedish gymnastics, which were more consistent with the notion of health for motherhood. Nevertheless, when in 1909 the Board of Education issued *The Syllabus of Physical Exercises for Public Elementary Schools*, lesson outlines (Plate 11) still contained phrases such as 'Form ranks', 'Attention', 'Stand easy', 'Class, fall in', 'Eyes right, lines straight'.[83]

There were some children whose later education was based entirely upon preparation for a life in the army or navy. Military and naval schools, often established by charitable institutions, catered predominantly for boys from the poorer classes. The Marine Society, founded in 1756 by Joseph Hanway, provided naval training for boys, many of whom had been rescued from the Poor Law workhouses of London. By 1911 the society, with its training ship *Warspite*, had sent 65,667 boys and young men to sea, of whom 28,538 had gone into the Royal Navy.[84] From the 1860s similar training was provided on the River Thames at Greenhithe by the National Refuges for Homeless and Destitute Children on the *Chichester* and *Arethusa*. The latter, on which boys were known by their numbers and not their names, was built in 1849, saw action in the Crimea, and claims the distinction of being the last British ship to go into battle under sail.[85] Some training establishments were ashore – a ship on land. The Watts Naval Training School (NTS) in Norfolk had previously been a school for orphans and destitute boys set up by Dr Thomas Barnado. In April 1906 the school was officially opened as a Training School but was often referred to as a Training Ship. Commander H.C. Martin was the first captain of the school, assisted by fifteen other staff who were responsible for the training and welfare of the 300 pupils. Discipline was harsh and conditions spartan for the selected Barnado's Boys being prepared for a life at sea. Dr Barnardo himself recognised

> the immense importance of the Training Ship as a means of discipline and
> training for the unwanted youth of our great towns, and also as the very best

method of furnishing the requirements of our Mercantile Marine and of our Royal Navy.[86]

Watts NTS was officially classified as a Secondary Technical School, and suitable boys were admitted from the age of eleven. They followed a two-year general education course before commencing, usually at fourteen, nautical technical training. Musical training was also available for boys intending to join the Royal Marines or other military bands.[87] There was no compulsion to join the navy, but the vast majority of Watts pupils ultimately did so. Many of the boys who trained at Watts and other training ships served in the Royal Navy during the Great War. Claude Choles, the last of the 1914–18 veterans to serve in both world wars, and the last surviving Australian combat veteran of the Great War, joined TS *Mercury* in 1915 at the age of fourteen. Two years later he was serving aboard HMS *Revenge*, part of the British Grand Fleet, and later witnessed the scuppering of the German High Seas Fleet at Scapa Flow.[88]

The majority of boys selected for the training ships were poor 'but of good character'. Some, like Claude Choles, deliberately chose a career at sea and their parents paid the required training fees. For others, a life at sea was chosen for them. Some juvenile delinquents were sentenced to this form of rigorous 'schooling', serving time on reformatory ships, notably the *Cornwall* on the Thames at Purfleet and the *Akbar* on Merseyside.[89] The education of children who had broken the law, or were in need of care and protection away from the bad influence of criminal homes and neighbourhoods, was a major concern, especially in the rapidly expanding factory towns. The Industrial Schools Act of 1857 made provision through the courts for vagrant, destitute and disorderly children to attend schools, often miles away from home, where they would be reformed by teaching them a trade. Once again, charitable provision was available. In Scotland, Mrs Kibble's Reformatory School was founded in 1859 and received boys who were lawbreakers. The majority were illiterate. Not surprisingly the educational regime at Kibble focused on the 'three Rs', plus a large dose of religious instruction, plenty of physical exercise and, with the intention of making the boys useful members of society, vocational training. Many of the boys were later sent 'on release' to work in the colonies as child migrant labour. In the nine months before the outbreak of war in 1914, seventeen Kibble boys went as 'farmers' to South Australia alone.[90] In London, pupils at the East Lewisham Industrial School stayed on until they were sixteen, but could be granted permission to leave at the age of fourteen if joining the army or working in the mines.

'National Efficiency', taken to its logical conclusions, might well have meant moving away from traditional modes of schooling and curriculum provision. Despite the Industrial Revolution, however, and Britain's early industrial and technological supremacy, the provision for technical education was far from clear.

A series of international exhibitions in London – the Great Exhibition of 1851 – and Paris in 1867 and 1878 'showed the British what their continental neighbours were achieving through the methods of the classroom rather than the workshop'.[91] The establishment of the Samuelson Commission in 1881 reflected growing British concern with foreign economic competition, but evidence presented to the commission indicated little serious provision for secondary technical education. The educational reforms of the Victorian and Edwardian era did not remedy this situation; instead they systematised and replicated the 'classical' education so valued by elite social groups. Board of Education Regulations stipulated an 'elementary' education for the masses and a 'general', or 'liberal', education for those fortunate enough to attend secondary schools. A good 'liberal' education, without undue or early specialisation, was the making of a man; 'vocational' education was the making of a tradesman.[92] Unlike in Germany, one of Britain's major economic competitors and perceived threats, as illustrated in the 'Made in Germany' scare of 1896,[93] there were few opportunities in the majority of British secondary schools to 'worship the modern, the useful, the technocratic, the scientific'.[94] Industrialisation had led to complex methods of production. New techniques demanded new types of workers: skilled mechanics and engineers, together with the clerks for the growing number of incidental administrative and commercial functions associated with production on a huge scale.[95] Secondary schools could provide the latter, but which forms of schooling would provide the former, the skilled technicians?

There was widespread public interest in science and technology generally in the late nineteenth century,[96] but this was not translated into systematic or national provision for technical education. Instead, local initiative led to the establishment of diverse forms of institutions which attempted to meet specific economic needs. Of the 898 officially recognised and grant-funded secondary schools operating in 1912, 74 had a distinct vocational bias in their curriculum.[97] Some were clearly 'intermediate' schools, sitting uneasily between the secondary and elementary schools. They were often located near to traditional grammar schools and provided just enough secondary education for the children of tradesmen and artisans. A detailed case study of education in Peterborough in the nineteenth and early twentieth centuries, for example, demonstrates how hierarchies of schooling operated even within the secondary sector. A school's position was not fixed, but altered over time as new schools opened and older schools responded to demographic change. The King's School, founded in 1541, continued to provide the officially approved classical curriculum for the sons of the professional classes, albeit in competition with some nearby public schools such as Oundle and Kimbolton. Deacon's School prepared boys for occupations similar to those of their fathers: shopkeepers, small farmers, teachers, clerks and, increasingly, engineers.[98] Institutional imperatives for survival led to schools such as Deacon's introducing more flexible curriculum offerings, which included 'useful' subjects designed to meet local employment needs. Technical education, as distinct from workplace training, often took place out of school. Peterborough School of Science, Art and Technology and its successor institution, the County Technical School, for example, provided education and training for employed young adults in part-time evening classes, a model popular with wage-earning school leavers, their parents and employers. In the decade before the Great War some overt technical education did take place in a number of newly-established Junior Technical Schools (JTS). The JTS imitated elements of the German *Fortbildungschulen* and French *Ecoles Primaire Superieure*.[99] By 1914 the Board of Education had recognised twenty-seven JTS for boys and ten for girls. LEAs received funding to establish JTS. Their pupils, mostly 13-year-old elementary school leavers, were prepared for the lower rungs of the vocational ladder: boys for semi-skilled artisan and industrial trades, girls for domestic work. Fees averaged £3 per year. Courses, usually of short duration, were taught mostly in the local technical colleges.[100] The JTS were never intended to provide secondary education; the 1913 Regulations expressly stated that such schools would not offer 'secondary school features', such as the teaching of foreign languages or preparation for external examinations.[101] The JTS were yet another example of the official British predilection for 'filling in the gaps' in educational provision. JTS were separate, inferior and ultimately unsuccessful forms of schooling.[102] The Admission Register for Peterborough JTS lists only thirty-one male students, all aged thirteen to fourteen and admitted to engineering courses for the year 1913–14.[103] By 1915, only nine students were enrolled, and in 1917 the school was closed. Some JTS did succeed in placing pupils in skilled and responsible employment.[104] Nationally, however, many JTS were short-lived or achieved relatively little. In Leeds, for example, pupils at the 3 JTS had a poor completion rate: of 144 leavers, 50 per cent had left within a year and only 18 pupils completed the full course.[105]

Despite two world wars and the rapid advance of technological innovation and application in the twentieth century, technical education has remained the poor relation of schooling. The Tripartite System of secondary schooling introduced by the 1944 Education Act, with its formal hierarchy of Grammar, Technical and Modern schools, reinforced notions of educational worth, despite initial assertions that the three types of schooling were different in kind rather than status. In our current century, despite repeated and familiar calls for parity of esteem in schools and wider society for vocational and technical subjects, the 'gold standard' traditional subjects of the Edwardian Board of Education Regulations continue to dominate the school curriculum.

For most families before the Great War, the provision of formal schooling was a relatively recent phenomenon, reaching back one or two generations at most. Before the advent of free and compulsory schooling, education had been a commodity that few could afford and was in a form that was not necessarily valued, especially if it came at the cost of rendering children unavailable for early employment. Learning had traditionally taken place elsewhere: in the home, on the land, in small workshops, at church or chapel or Sunday school, within local community clubs and organisations, and from daily social interaction with other children and adults. As Mark Twain famously exclaimed, he had never let his schooling get in the way of a good education. For those who had gained 'a little learning' in school, newspapers, magazines and popular literature expanded childhood and adolescent horizons. New forms of media introduced them to unfamiliar and changing worlds beyond their village or urban terraces. The children of the twenty-first century often take fast-paced technological change for granted, but for Bob Hart, Edith Turner, Claude Choles and the other children of the pre-war generation the impact of change was enormous. Great War veteran Harry Patch saw his first car and aeroplane at the age of fourteen in 1912.[106] How exciting the world must have seemed in the years before the Great War, at least for those not ground down by poverty and neglect.

Schoolboy magazines proliferated before and during the war. Their vivid and often graphic accounts of daring deeds on the battlefields or adventures in the far-flung outposts of the Empire conditioned impressionable young minds and established cultural norms. *The Magnet, Chums, The Captain, The Boy's Own Paper* (Plate 12) and many others extolled the virtues of team spirit and personal sacrifice. Schoolboy heroes abounded. Most magazines were aimed at a wide market, but *The Captain* catered mainly for a more select readership, namely the boys from the public schools. There were publications for girls too. The 1906 *Girl's Realm Annual* contained articles on diverse topics – violet farming, hockey and photography - along with 'good literature' with titles such as *The Mysterious Vases* and *A Little Gypsy Lass*.[107] An enduring feature in many magazines for boys was the depiction of life in the boarding school – a microcosm of life on the games field and preparation for the officers' mess or remote colonial hill stations. *Tom Brown's School Days*, published in 1857 by Thomas Hughes, 'an Old Boy of Rugby', modelled the 'public-school story'; a genre which is still alive over a century later in the *Harry Potter* novels of J.K. Rowling.[108] Such stories exemplified codes of behaviour which reached a far wider audience beyond the cloistered walls of the public schools.[109] Stories for schoolgirls by Angela Brazil, such as *The Nicest Girl in the School* (1909), served much the same purpose.

War was an ever-present and popular theme in many of the publications for boys. War was expected, and expected sooner rather than later. War with Germany – albeit a literary war in a fictional serialisation – was already being fought in the pages of *Chums* from December 1913.[110] The philosopher Bertrand Russell referred to the 'whole foul literature of 'glory' ... with which the minds of children are polluted'.[111] War was glorified and romanticised, empires mythologised, and concepts of honour, duty and manliness positioned centre stage in dramatic reconstructions of a civilisation superior to all others, or so it was claimed. A chivalric brotherhood fought their wars against alien 'Kultur' and inferior colonial subjects as keenly as they played their sport in school.[112] Artists, poets and popular writers added to the inner personal narrative of millions of British adolescents.[113] Illustrations of battle scenes, like Newbolt's poems, were more heroic than realistic. Rudyard Kipling wrote of colonial masters and servants in *The Man Who Would Be King* and numerous other stories and poems. His evocative depictions of the Indian Raj, for example, thrilled and fascinated British children and adults alike. George Alfred Henty, the historian A.J.P. Taylor's favourite author as a schoolboy,[114] contributed articles to *The Boy's Own Paper* and was editor of *Union Jack*, another popular paper. Henty became the acknowledged master of historical fiction in which young adventurers served with Clive in India and Wolfe in Canada, fought under the flags of Drake and Nelson in their naval wars against the Spanish and French, and made pioneering journeys through alien terrain which established British dominions abroad.

The adult addiction to playing at soldiers, so clearly demonstrated by the enthusiasm for the Volunteer, Militia and Yeomanry movements in the late Victorian period, especially amongst the middle classes, extended to their children. In addition to popular literature, there were many other ways in which childhood and adolescence were militarised. Dressing up in gendered uniforms – boys as soldiers, girls as nurses – was a common feature in many countries before the Great War. The British royal family and its network of royal cousins throughout Europe made this fashionable. In 1846, engravings of the young Prince of Wales, wearing a replica naval uniform worn by ratings on the Royal Yacht, started a fashion trend which lasted decades and extended well beyond the British Isles. Many school photographs from the pre-war period attest to the popularity of 'sailor suits'. Cultural ephemera such as postcards, board games, cigarette cards and jigsaws, with their stirring and colourful images of brave warriors and heroes through the ages, were powerful agents of militarisation. Toy soldiers, inexpensive and produced in their millions before the Great War, may well have added to the notion that war was a game to be played rather than a curse to be endured.[115]

Youth organisations also served as agents of schooling in an age of militarism and imperialism. The OTC, directly affiliated to the elite schools, were not available to the great majority of British children. After 1907 the Boy Scout movement, and then the Girl Guides from 1910, attracted a wider cross-section of society. Some youth movements, however, were targeted directly at the working classes. The Boys' Brigade was founded in Glasgow in 1883 by William Alexander Smith. His background as both a Sunday School teacher at North Woodside Mission Sabbath School and as an enthusiastic lieutenant in the Volunteers explains the quasi-religious and quasi-military nature of the new organisation. The Brigade's stated objective was:

The advancement of Christ's Kingdom among Boys and the promotion of habits of Reverence, Discipline, Self-Respect, and all that tends towards a true Christian Manliness.

The word 'Obedience' was added later to the list of 'habits' which, it was believed, would rescue disadvantaged and potentially deviant working-class boys from temptation and indolence. Smith's boys took part in gymnastics classes, played team games, paraded with dummy rifles,[116] and wore uniforms. They too would develop the personal fitness, esprit-de-corps and group regimentation that was a feature of schooling for boys from higher social groups. Similar organisations included the openly militaristic Church Lads' Brigade, the Jewish Lads' Brigade and the non-denominational Lads' Drill Association. Military-style bands were also popular. By 1914, a distinctive British youth culture had developed.[117] The movements were highly organised and, collectively, they managed to enroll some 40 per cent of the nation's adolescent boys.[118]

By 1914 the children of Britain had been subjected to a nexus of formal and informal modes of schooling, each according to their social class. The traditional curriculum had been augmented by cultural, sporting and military activities, both in and out of school, which were intended to create a nation ready and willing to meet the demands of Britain and its empire. British schools had produced leaders and followers, officers and other ranks, and at least a few who might understand the science and technology behind new forms of warfare. Britain stood ready to face the challenge from Germany or any other erstwhile enemy which, many felt, would surely come. As Nial Ferguson has noted, 'it would be easy to argue that the First World War happened at least partly because people expected it to happen'.[119] In fact, when war finally came in August 1914, it took many by surprise.

Chapter 2

Roll of Honour

Hoarse, booming drums of the regiment,
Little souls who thirst for fight,
These men were born to drill and die.
The unexplained glory flies above them,
Great is the battle-god, great, and his kingdom –
A field where a thousand corpses lie.

Stephen Crane (1899)
Do Not Weep, Maiden, For War is Kind

B ob Hart and the party from Harrow County School for Boys were not the only ones rushing back home as the storm clouds of war began to break over Europe. Whilst Bob and his fellow pupils had been travelling to and from Germany, another party of sixty Boy Scouts from Harrow County were back in Britain, enjoying their 'Great Trek' through the Mendips – and accompanied by a dozen German scouts from Dresden. They too decided to return home prematurely. On 4 August 1914, the day Britain declared war on Germany, Harrow County headteacher Ernest Young wrote:

Our German friends went home yesterday. With heads erect they stepped from the ranks, saluted, and passed away from sight. For the sake of pleasant memories (I hope) that, if they were in the ranks of the soldiers, they were fighting on the Eastern rather than the Western Front.[1]

Boy Scouts from Bristol Grammar School were also heading home. They had recently set up camp in Boulogne and had witnessed the French call-to-arms when mobilisation orders were posted on 1 August 1914. Two days later, during their return crossing to England, they saw in the waters of the Channel their first signs of what would become a new form of warfare – the periscope of a submarine.[2]

Returning to Britain in some haste were several schoolteachers. Some, like Susannah Knight (Plate 13) of St Gregory's School in Chorley, had been enjoying their summer vacations abroad when the commencement of hostilities was formally announced. Susannah had spent the summer in Switzerland and was in France when war was declared. She was absent from school when St Gregory's began the new autumn term. A school logbook entry noted:

1914

10 August: Miss Knight, Assistant Teacher, unable to return to school, detained in France on account of the war.

Miss Knight finally reached England and resumed her teaching duties nearly two weeks later.[3] Other teachers had been employed in what were now enemy countries. Beatrice Kelsey, an English governess in Vienna started her journey home on a train full of Austrian army reservists. In the febrile atmosphere in the days and weeks following the declarations of war, any foreigner was regarded with suspicion. Beatrice was arrested in Cologne on Friday, 7 August, but was soon released from custody and eventually reached Harwich six days later.[4]

Some British pupils and teachers failed to make it home before the continental frontiers finally slammed shut their gates for the duration of the war. Hector Munro, a senior pupil at Hutcheson's Grammar School in Glasgow, had been travelling in Germany in order to develop his foreign language skills. He was detained and then interned in a German prisoner of war (POW) camp for the duration of the war.[5] A similar fate awaited Mr Latham, the Latin Master at Aberystwyth County School in Wales. His honeymoon in Germany also ended abruptly and was followed by imprisonment.[6] By far the greatest tragedy, however, befell a teacher returning to Britain after teaching abroad. In *Meeting the Enemy*, Richard van Emden describes how Henry Hadley became the first British fatality of the Great War. Educated at Cheltenham College, and a former commissioned officer in the West India Regiment, Henry Hadley had taught in Germany for nearly four years. On his way home on 3 August, accompanied by his housekeeper on a crowded train full of German troops, the 51-year-old schoolteacher was involved in a heated and very public exchange with a waiter in the restaurant car. He then returned to his carriage. Some time later, and just short of the Belgian border, he stepped into the train's corridor and was shot in the stomach by Lieutenant Nicolay, a German officer. Henry cried out "They've shot me, Mrs Pratley, I am a done man". He was taken to hospital and died at 03.15 German Time on 5 August. Lieutenant Nicolay reported that Henry Hadley had been vague about his travel plans, was acting suspiciously, and had raised his stick at the officer when confronted.[7]

Back in Britain, the European crisis started to have repercussions for other groups and individuals. In late July and early August 1914 hundreds of schoolboys and their schoolmasters were attending the annual Public Schools OTC Camps (Plate 14), unwittingly preparing for 'the real thing'. The OTC from Wellington and Marlborough were in Wiltshire, Shrewsbury and Repton were at Hasley Park in Rugeley,[8] the Oakham contingent were encamped on Cannock Chase,[9] and the King's College Taunton cadets combined with several other school corps in the OTC camp at Aldershot.[10] Other schools had made their own local arrangements. The OTC at Merchant Taylors' School in Liverpool, for example, were on manoeuvres with the King's Liverpool Rifles. Throughout the country, young men and boys were preparing for war. Some, like 14-year-old Kenneth Cummins, later recalled how limited their military training had seemed that summer, consisting mainly of marching behind the regimental band.[11] War had not yet been declared, but since the assassination of the Archduke Franz Ferdinand at Sarajevo there had been intense diplomatic activity in the capital cities of Europe. Tom Kirk, a Cadet Sergeant in the Giggleswick School OTC, was aware of the developing crisis and later recalled the tense atmosphere in which his particular camp took place:

> With war looming we began to take ourselves very seriously under the command of the chaplain. At the end of the summer term, we took a train to Rugeley, Staffordshire. We were housed in tents – but war was now inevitable, so our tents were handed over to the army. We spent the last two nights in the open, which was no hardship.[12]

Following the German declaration of war on France on Monday, 3 August the various OTC contingents received orders to strike camp, accompanied by news that the military authorities would be requisitioning much of their equipment. The following day Britain declared war on Germany and the boy soldiers were escorted back to their schools.[13] One young member of the Shrewsbury School OTC complained in a letter home, without any sense of irony, that his cadet camp had been ruined by 'this beastly war'.[14]

Within days of the British declaration, many of the same boys' schoolmasters were recalled to their Territorial units. The BEF was mobilising, and the pre-war part-time soldiers, with commissions in the corps or reserve, now became full-time combatants. Many senior boys, experienced cadets, were granted commissions and began their journeys to battalion headquarters. This was not 'war fever'. It was a deliberate and essential element of British war planning as embodied in the Haldane Reforms, namely the systematic call up of public school and university men whose OTC experience had qualified and prepared them for this moment. For the public schools, August 1914 was thus 'a moment of high drama … but one that rapidly turned to tragedy'.[15]

It had all happened so quickly. The author Dennis Wheatley recalled in his memoirs how, as a 17-year-old schoolboy at Dulwich College during the seemingly endless summer of 1914, he had observed the diplomatic and then military crises unfolding. At first, there was little reason to believe that events in the distant Balkans would have any repercussions for British schoolboys such as Dennis; they were far too busy enjoying their cricket matches in the final weeks of term. When the Archduke Franz Ferdinand, heir to the Austro-Hungarian throne, was assassinated by Bosnian separatists on 28 June, 'no one thought much about it'.[16] Likewise, the British government, led by Liberal Prime Minister Herbert Henry Asquith, was far too preoccupied with domestic issues and growing tensions in Ulster to be overly concerned with the consequent diplomatic rift between the Hapsburg Empire and Serbia.[17] The governments of Europe, however, many combining a catastrophic combination of absolute rule wielded by incompetent monarchs and administrations led by obsequious royal officials, were sleepwalking towards war.[18] Economic rivalry, arms races, alliance systems and a proliferation of nationalist movements in the old empires had created the pre-conditions for war, but the capitals of Europe had seen out previous diplomatic crises without resorting to armed conflict. Despite the Austrian ultimatum to Serbia, diplomatic machinations in Berlin and St Petersburg, and then the epic blunders of mobilisation, Britain still prevaricated and resisted any temptation or demand to take sides or intervene in this particular crisis. The Triple Alliance between Russia, France and Great Britain did not automatically commit the latter to military action. Nevertheless, uncertainty about London's foreign policy may well have made a continental war more rather than less likely.[19] The German ultimatum to Belgium and, especially, the defiant but dignified response of the Belgian government to a naked threat of aggression, changed everything.[20] Britain's 'good name', as signatory to the 1839 Treaty of London which had guaranteed Belgian independence, was at stake. Unlike their co-signatories Germany, the sanctity of Belgian territory was a matter of honour, integrity and reputation. Even members of the Cabinet who had argued against military intervention – men like David Lloyd George, a staunch opponent of the Boer War – now conceded that Britain would have to fight.

The declaration of war against Germany on 4 August 1914 by Prime Minister Asquith, an 'Old Citizen' of City of London School, was the signal for the mobilisation of British armed forces. The BEF preparations were quickly underway. This relatively small army, composed of regular professional soldiers and the trained part-timers of the Territorial battalions, was primed, as its name suggested, to launch an expedition onto the continent of Europe. Three days after the declaration, with a prescience shared by few contemporaries, Field Marshal Lord Kitchener asked the British Parliament to sanction an increase in army numbers. This war would be fought by mass conscript armies and last years rather than months. Kitchener demanded a 'New Army' of 500,000 men and began with an urgent, and now legendary, personal appeal for what later became known as 'The First Hundred Thousand'. Recruiting Offices appeared in every city and town throughout the land. The response was staggering. Between 4 August and 12 September 478,893 volunteers came forward, all ready to serve their King and Country.[21] By the end of the year, when early predictions that the war would be 'over by Christmas' had been tragically confounded, Kitchener's appeal had delivered a total of 1,186,337 new recruits to the army.[22] This was a new type of British army: a 'people's army' – or 'citizen army' – drawn from those previously employed in the fields, factories, workshops, mines, offices, great country houses, hotels and retail stores throughout the land.

The phenomenon of mass enlistment in Britain has become part of the Great War legend and mythology, but its causes are complex and nuanced.[23] The notion of a people carried away to war by a form of mass hysteria – 'war fever' – is an insufficient explanation as to why so many young men, in all of the belligerent nations, rushed to join the colours in 1914. After weeks of tense diplomatic activity, the actual declaration of war and commencement of hostilities may well have released pent-up emotions and generated excitement. To say, however, that the citizens of 1914 were duped or misguided into war is far too simplistic and denies them the personal agency and respect that we today have come to expect for ourselves. Undoubtedly there were some who got carried away, succumbed to peer and other pressures, made rash and impulsive decisions and entered military service precipitately. For other individuals, however, the decision to enlist was considered, evaluated against potential personal losses and gains, and born of an idealism based on established values. Whilst many of these ideals and values had been conditioned by exposure to new forms of media – and the process of schooling future citizens described in the previous chapter – they were, nevertheless, real and tangible, and often held with deep conviction. We overrate the power of the state, schools and newspapers if we truly believe that a whole nation could be so easily nationalised and manipulated against its will.[24]

However unfashionable the concept of patriotism may or may not be today, it was, nevertheless, a key motivational factor for many in August 1914. The obligation of duty to King and Country was widely accepted. War was regarded as an extension, rather than failure, of diplomacy. This patriotism was not simply an embodiment of jingoism. In Britain, it was defensive rather than offensive patriotism.[25] Mass enlistment was fuelled by a widespread and genuine fear of German militarism and 'Prussian' domination of Europe,[26] a fear that was only exacerbated as the Schlieffen Plan directed wave upon wave of German troops over the border and into Belgium. There was heartfelt sympathy for the plight of Belgian refugees which, admittedly, was strengthened by lurid press coverage of imagined atrocities committed by 'the Hun'. Some 'outrages' were real, however. The deliberate destruction by fire of the renowned library at the University of Louvain convinced many of the well educated in society that German 'Kultur' was a threat to civilisation. Early military reversals and a BEF retreat after the first major encounter at Mons, described in exaggerated fashion as a 'terrible defeat' in the 'Amiens Dispatch' printed in *The Times* on 30 August,[27] shattered confidences and convinced many that the homeland itself was under threat. Men flocked to the colours in even greater numbers. Erstwhile opponents of the war, including many in the Labour movement, gradually accepted its reality,[28] or at least, as the war dragged on, the requirement for total commitment to a total war.

Some young men may well have had less altruistic reasons for leaving their homes and jobs. War had provided an opportunity for travel overseas and the real possibility of an adventure with their 'pals' alongside them. They were part of something vital and not to be missed. They could escape from the drudgery of academic routines or mundane employment, for a while at least. These recruits knew *why* they were fighting – or at least they were aware of the individual decisions which had brought them before the recruiting sergeant – but not necessarily *what* they were fighting for.[29] Others saw the war as an intrusion. Harry Patch, aged sixteen when war began, claimed he 'wasn't at all patriotic'. He simply wanted to continue his apprenticeship as a plumber.[30] Conversely, lay offs in many non-vital industries at the start of the war prompted some unemployed men to enlist.[31] There were geographic and occupational disparities, too. In comparison with Scotland, Welsh reactions generally to the war were lukewarm,[32] and there was a relative reluctance to enlist in Ireland,[33] a member of the United Kingdom in which different communities had begun preparing for a possible civil war before August 1914. Most enlisted men came from urban rather than rural areas, and clerks outnumbered miners and railwaymen.[34] Some individuals were indifferent. Others watched the unfolding events of autumn 1914 and chose the moment of their enlistment carefully. German conduct of the war, especially the naval bombardment of Scarborough, the Hartlepools and Whitby on 16 December 1914, followed in January and May 1915 by Zeppelin raids and the sinking of RMS *Lusitania*, prompted thousands of new enlistments.[35] Nevertheless, the two and a half million men who had responded to Lord Kitchener's appeal by the end of 1915, impressive though this feat undoubtedly was, represented only some 25 per cent of those eligible for military service.[36]

The impact of enlistment was felt by virtually all British institutions. Few of the nation's schools were able to escape from the complex social, economic and increasingly military web which was being mobilised for war, even if they had wanted to. Published school histories, their authors having the advantage of knowing what carnage was to follow, often sentimentalise the response by individual institutions to the call-to-arms of 1914. The wartime history of a Methodist public school in Canterbury, for example, describes how:

> The outside world of war hammered on the heavy doors of Kent College and shouted up at its dormitory windows. The inmates made no attempt to deny its demands, and one by one slipped away.[37]

Many British schools did respond with evident enthusiasm. Headteachers reminded Old Boys who had been members of their school's OTC that God had indeed matched them with this hour and that duty called.[38] They also encouraged members of their wider school communities to do their duty to King and Country – and at the same time honour the school and its name – by enlisting. At Colfe's Grammar School in Lewisham, London, the school magazine *Colfensia* was quick off the mark to galvanise all those with affiliations to the school. Its 1914 edition stated, unequivocally, the reason for, and urgency of, joining the fight:

> Since going to press a deadly struggle has arisen, full of danger to civilisation. The cruel military despotism of Prussia must be crushed at all costs. The place of every single man is at the front. In great numbers Old Colfeians have gone quietly to the posts of duty.[39]

The call of duty echoed throughout the British Empire. In distant Australia, John Refshauge, Principal of Ballarat Agricultural High School in Victoria, used the *School Magazine* of December 1914 to alert pupils old and new to the 'voice of duty' calling 'the sport-loving Australian'.[40]

Some recent school leavers about to go up to university, or school alumni who were already undergraduates, elected to join the increasing number of New Army battalions rather than resume their studies at the beginning of the new academic year. At Oundle School, some of the senior boys who had been expected to return to the school after the long vacation had already taken commissions or were on battalion waiting lists.[41] Eager prospective recruits, especially those from the public schools looking for commissions, 'milked old boy and other social connections for all they were worth'.[42]

Some schools attempted to form their own military units similar to the 'Pals Battalions' that had emerged as men from similar occupations, or even sporting interests, chose to go to war together. City of London School tried to form an Old Citizen Company of the 3rd Battalion Middlesex Regiment. At the time, however, OCs were eagerly joining every possible type of unit and the attempt was ultimately unsuccessful.[43] In Scotland, Glasgow Academy men did form their own company in the 17th Highland Light Infantry.[44] One of the legendary 'pals' battalions was based originally upon old school ties. Many of the recruits to the 10th Battalion Lincolnshire Regiment – the 'Grimsby Chums' – were former pupils of Wintringham School. They were joined by a large contingent of Worksop College Old Boys. Wintringham School was not one of the ancient public schools. Founded originally as a Technical College, its early involvement as an agent for recruitment demonstrates how different types of school rushed to establish their patriotic, military and institutional credentials. Many Old Edwardians from King Edward VII School in Sheffield, a secondary school founded only nine years before the war, joined the 12th (City of Sheffield) Battalion York and Lancaster Regiment, known more famously as the 'Sheffield Pals'.[45] They had responded to recruitment placards directing them 'TO BERLIN – VIA THE CORN EXCHANGE'. Within days of enlisting they were taking part in military drill sessions at Bramhall Lane, home of Sheffield United FC and site of former Empire Day celebrations.[46]

Some of the new battalions aimed to recruit men from similar educational backgrounds, rather than from a specific school. In London, the 16th Middlesex

(Public Schools) Battalion was open only to public school and university men. The Universities and Public Schools Brigade, comprising four battalions of the Royal Fusiliers, was similarly founded for men who had attended university or famous fee-paying private schools. One of the most active recruiters for the brigade was John Paton, Head Master of Manchester Grammar School.[47] In Bristol, the *Magazine* published by Kingswood School, a Methodist foundation with no prior military tradition, displayed in heavy type a notice inviting old boys willing to enlist to write at once to the 'Public Schools and University Men's Brigade'.[48] Many former pupils of the elite schools clearly preferred to serve in the ranks alongside fellows from similar educational and, most importantly, social backgrounds rather than take commissions to lead the common 'Tommy Atkins' in the far less prestigious Service battalions in county regiments.

Schoolteachers and other staff were also joining the forces as the new academic year was about to begin or in the first days of the new autumn term. At Wellington College, ten masters and twenty college servants left to re-join Territorial battalions or to enlist in new ones.[49] George Arthur Tryon, housemaster at Oundle and captain of the school's OTC, volunteered for service immediately. He was commissioned into the 6th Battalion King's Royal Rifle Corps and within two months was posted to France to join the BEF. Teachers from less-prestigious schools were also reporting for duty. Many had prior military experience. Captain Dugald Blue, a graduate of the University of Glasgow, was a classics teacher at Hutcheson's Grammar School in the same city. As a part-time Volunteer who had previously served in Rhodesia, he too had a pressing commitment to re-join the colours immediately upon the outbreak of war.[50] John Paulson had been a Cadet Sergeant in the University of London OTC. In 1911, whilst teaching at Orme Boys' School in Newcastle–under–Lyme, he was awarded a commission in the part-time Special Reserve and was thus duty bound to make the swift transition to full-time warrior when the call-to-arms was sounded. Newly qualified teacher Arthur Schofield, fresh from Borough Road College in London, was appointed at the end of the 1913–14 academic year to teach mathematics at Deacon's School, Peterborough. The events of August changed everything. Arthur failed to join his new colleagues in the staff room at the beginning of term as expected. Private Schofield had joined the Northamptonshire Regiment.[51]

Teachers from the elementary schools throughout Britain also responded to Lord Kitchener's appeal for men. In the Isle of Ely, for example, an area of ancient fens and rich farmland on the western borders of East Anglia, three elementary school headteachers and thirteen assistant teachers enlisted in the first weeks of the war.[52] They included Old Deaconian Edgar Felix Law, Assistant Master at Broad Street Boys School, Whittlesey, who departed by train from Peterborough on Wednesday, 7 August with other local recruits to the 6th Battalion Northamptonshire Regiment. Also leaving Peterborough for military training on the same day was Albert Herbert, a fellow Old Boy of Deacon's School and latterly teacher at St Mark's School in the city. Albert enlisted in Whitsed's Light infantry (2nd Battalion Northamptonshire Regiment), one of the many units raised by patriotic elected councillors and local worthies.[53] Councillor Isaac Whitsed and Major Shipley Ellis, who also happened to be Governors of Deacon's School, were key figures in recruitment activity in their particular locality.[54]

The excitement of mass enlistment and mobilisation was tangible. Patriotic meetings, emotionally charged speeches, bands playing martial music, flags flying, newly enlisted men marching and parading – these were days of jubilation, tinged, nevertheless, with some trepidation and thoughts of what this new war might bring.[55] Many children experienced first hand the decisions to enlist made by fathers, brothers, uncles, cousins and older schoolfellows. They shared with them the cheap exhilaration of taking the 'King's Shilling' at the nearby recruiting office. They attended LEA-organised recruitment marches in their hundreds (Plate 16), calling upon adult males to enlist. They lined the roads and gathered *en masse* at train stations to cheer the new heroes as they started their journeys to the training camps. Many of the children were in school groups, released from the classroom for the occasion by headteachers who were themselves caught up in the whirlwind of patriotic enthusiasm. In the Essex village of Birdbrook, children from the local junior school lined the road 'to give the eleven recruits a hearty send off'.[56] When Edwin G. Jones, the Geography Master at Aberystwyth County School, left to join the London Welsh Battalion of the Royal Welch Fusiliers in December, a group of his students were there at the railway station to cheer him on his way.[57] In these heady days, and for a generation of schoolchildren and their elders raised on notions of military adventure and glory abroad, the reality of war was yet to make its presence felt. Cheering soon gave way to mourning as the casualties mounted and the obituaries were listed in the local and national newspapers. The death of the same Mr Jones eighteen months later plunged the whole of his former school into sorrow.[58]

Within weeks of Lord Kitchener's appeal, schools throughout the country began to produce 'Rolls of Honour'. These lists of names became tangible evidence of an individual community's commitment to the war effort. They were not unique to schools or to Britain. They were produced by factories, offices, churches, chapels, masonic lodges and youth organisations; in fact, by any community grouping which felt the need to celebrate the contribution being made by its members or constituents. They were produced both in the British Dominions and in enemy states such as Germany, where they were known as Rolls of Service. Schools, ancient and newly-founded institutions alike, were particularly keen to record their new heroes. Rolls of Honour became symbols of institutional pride. Some listed names only. Those containing name, rank and military unit, sometimes in order of military seniority, provide clues as to the position of that particular school in the hierarchy of schooling. The regional nature of recruitment is often very evident, with many Old Boys joining their local county regiments or city battalions. Rolls of Honour varied greatly in their design and format. Some were very large, ornately decorated and framed wall hangings intended for public display. Others were simply typed lists in school magazines. Some schools purchased commercially produced templates and filled in the details in ink by hand, as was the case with the Roll of Honour for Oldbury Tabernacle Schools in the West Midlands (Plate 15). Less formal rolls were kept by many elementary school headteachers who recorded names and details in school logbooks or, as at Monikie School near Dundee in Scotland, published unsophisticated school-made booklets.[59]

Rolls of Honour were clearly intended to be motivational devices. They were produced to remind others that they too should be making a military contribution to the war effort; an exhortation not simply to former pupils, but to those still at school. As *The War Pictorial* reminded the children of Britain as late as August 1918, the Roll of Honour:

Serves as an inspiration to boys and girls, and a permanent reminder that they, too, are called upon to play what part they can in the great struggle.[60]

Compiling the Roll of Honour was not an easy task. The speed of mobilisation in 1914, the number of new units looking to attract recruits, and the continuation of enlistment throughout 1915 created enormous difficulties for those in schools with responsibility for writing up the lists of alumni who had joined the armed forces. Many former pupils had moved away from the locality of the school, some to the outposts of empire, in search of employment or further education and training. Tracking down Old Boys – and Old Girls who had joined nursing and other ancillary units – and accurately recording details of their newly joined battalion and rank awarded on enlistment was time consuming and haphazard. Updating individual service records to include promotions and transfers to other regiments or theatres of war was no less difficult. That so many schools did so is testimony to the importance they placed on their Roll of Honour. This was their war, their story.

The headmaster and staff at Preston Grammar School in Lancashire, for example, began collecting information about Old Boys in the services almost as soon as war was declared. In October 1914 the school sought further information from outside sources by making an appeal for information in a letter to the editor of the *Lancashire Daily Post*:

Sir, – May I ask the hospitality of your columns in order to beg of your readers who are acquainted with old Preston Grammar School Boys who have enlisted to send me their names that they may be recorded by me. – Yours &c, Norman Trewby, Headmaster, Grammar School, Preston. October 9th.

Each edition of *Hoghtonian*, the school magazine, contained a Roll of Honour and appealed for further information. It was far more efficient to have regular updates in the magazine than to amend the grand and elaborate honours boards. On Prize Days, Mr Trewby made the same appeal. Further details were gleaned from parents, Old Boys in the same units and, later, from scanning the casualty lists published in the newspapers.[61]

Early lists of serving Old Boys and staff were also published by schools in the local press, not simply as public declarations of institutional pride, but as deliberate attempts to glean further information. In Ireland, the Headmaster of Larne Grammar School in County Antrim, James MacQuillan, wrote to the *Larne Times*:

> Sir, I enclose a list of Larne Grammar School boys who are at present serving with the colours. We are preparing a roll of honour ... There are many of your readers who know much more about the old boys of the school than I can claim to know, and if they kindly inform me of any names omitted I shall be very grateful.

Mr MacQuillan's prototype Roll of Honour contained forty-four names. In all, over sixty members of the Larne Grammar School community were to serve in the Great War.[62] At Aberystwyth County School, Assistant Mistress S.E. Thomas published a Roll of Honour in the *Ystwythian* magazine and wrote an accompanying 'Khaki Column' which gave details of the named men's exploits in foreign fields – 'censor permitting'.[63] Each successive issue of a school magazine contained a longer roll-call of heroes. The October 1914 copy of the *Gaytonian*, edited by Bob Hart at Harrow County, listed the first eight members of the school to join the forces, adding by way of explanation for the relatively small number of Old Boys on active service: 'We are a very young school as yet and not many of our children are yet quite old enough to serve the Motherland'. In all, some 160 Old Gaytonians fought for their King and Country.[64] Newport High School for Boys, another relatively new secondary school founded in 1896, published the names of 400 Old Boys in the December 1915 edition of *The Magazine*, an increase from 150 in December 1914.[65]

The proportion of commissioned to non-commissioned men in any particular school Roll of Honour says so much about the status of the institution and the social origins of pupils who attended it. For boys in the elite schools, the outbreak of war in August 1914 put an end to playing at war, although membership of the OTC involved far more than that, and forced them to confront the realities of armed combat. Their patriotic fervour is patently obvious from the numbers volunteering for service throughout 1914.[66] Their leadership skills and personal bravery were about to be tested. Most public schools had cultivated the qualities needed by this generation of young men not only to fight, but to assume command of other warriors. The public schoolboy was the traditional source of supply for officers, and, with his OTC preparation was, according to the historian John Lewis-Stempel, 'ready and waiting in the wings of history'.[67]

The contribution to the British war effort of the great public schools is particularly well documented in individual school histories and other publications.[68] Many of their stories – and obituaries – are now available on school internet websites. Over five and a half thousand (5,656) Old Etonians are known to have served in the Great War. Old Boys from Manchester Grammar School (3,566), Cheltenham (3,540), Charterhouse (3,500), Wellington (3,500), Marlborough (3,418), Rugby (3,244), Clifton (3,063) and Dulwich (3,036) also joined the forces. More than thirty other famous English public schools, including Harrow (2,917), each recorded the wartime service of more than a thousand Old Boys or, in the case of Cheltenham Ladies College, Old Girls (2,000). In Scotland, 3,102 former pupils of George Watson's School in Edinburgh served, as did thousands from Glasgow High School (2,700) and George Heriot's in Edinburgh (2,637). Irish public schools, both Catholic and Protestant foundations, also sent sizeable contingents, such as those from Clongowes Wood near Dublin (604) and the Royal Belfast Academic Institution (703). The vast majority of former pupils from the schools listed above, some of the largest and most prestigious schools in Britain, became commissioned officers at the point of joining the armed forces.

Less widely known is the military contribution of some of the smaller public schools. In Wales, the wartime history of Christ College Brecon has been particularly well documented by researchers with strong ties to the school, both at the time and more recently.[69] Founded by King Henry VIII in 1541, this small boarding and day school, with only 120 pupils on roll in 1914, eventually listed a total of 447 alumni and masters on the various incarnations of its Roll of Honour. The process of tracking down Old Boy volunteers began in the early weeks of the war and the results were published in the school magazine, *The Breconian*. It was the remarkable persistence of Canon A.E. Donaldson, however, which resulted in the publication of a separate booklet in 1916 entitled *Roll of Honour & War List*. Canon Donaldson taught at Christ College Brecon from 1902 to 1955 and undertook numerous roles as Master, Housemaster and Chaplain. His 1916 *War List* contained 324 names and other details; the names of men and boys known personally to the Canon and his colleagues. The vast majority of these former pupils, over 90 per cent, joined the army, with far fewer involved in naval or air force duties. Not surprisingly, many on the list – some one in three – joined Welsh units, such as the Royal Welsh Fusiliers, the Welch Regiment and the South Wales Borderers. As befitted the products of a school for gentlemen, many Old Breconians were commissioned on entering the armed forces in the first two years of the conflict. Canon Donaldson recorded the details of 218 men (68 per cent) who were officers, a list which included front-line company and battalion commanders and well as military Chaplains, Surgeons, Engineers and Officer Cadets in training. For a public school, the figure of ninety-nine (33 per cent) for 'other ranks' might appear to be somewhat high, especially as those listed as NCOs amounted to only seventeen men. The figure for 'privates', however, disguises the fact that some in this grouping had elected to join one of the more prestigious units such as the Public Schools Brigade, the Artists Rifles and the Honourable Artillery Company. Other former pupils were returning to fight for Britain having previously emigrated to the Dominions. The advantages bestowed on those with a British public-school education did not automatically transfer to the award of commissions in units raised in Canada and Australia.

British preparatory schools, attended by younger age pupils prior to their schooling in the public schools, also produced their lists of alumni responding to the nation's call. Winchester House School in Deal, for example, recorded the names of over fifty Old Boys in the July 1915 edition of the *WHS Magazine*. By that date the school could boast thirty commissioned officers and two NCOs. The remainder had no record of rank or, in five cases, regiment. Such were the difficulties of compiling accurate lists in the first months of the war. Seven Old Boys, however, had joined the Honourable Artillery Company, presumably as privates.[70]

It would be wrong to assume that all public schoolboys were officers, or that all officers were public schoolboys. Some products of the public school system had neither the inclination nor, indeed, the ability to secure a commission in His Majesty's armed forces in time of war. Charles Glass Playfair Laidlaw, for example, had all the credentials necessary for obtaining a commission, but appears to have put unit before rank. At the Perse School in Cambridge he was a member of the Cricket XI, Captain of Football, Head of School and a sergeant in the Cadet Corps. In 1909 he went up to St John's College, Cambridge to read Natural Science and gained further research scholarships at Gonville and Caius College and at Imperial College of Science and Technology, London. When war came, however, he enlisted as a private in the 14th Battalion (The London Scottish) The London Regiment.[71]

The notion that British officers came solely from the public schools is a fallacy. By March 1915, 22 of the 143 former pupils of Dartford Grammar School who had enlisted were commissioned officers. The figure for Maidstone Grammar School was 17 out of 120.[72] Grammar school Old Boys may not have been considered automatic candidates for commissions, especially at the beginning of the war, but many did subsequently attain the rank of second lieutenant and above. The celebrated case of R.C. Sherriff, however, exemplifies the difficulties of those from the 'wrong type' of school in 1914. A former scholar and sportsman at Kingston Grammar School (Plate 5), and for a year before the war employed as an insurance clerk, his initial attempt to gain a commission was unsuccessful. He was informed by the recruiting officer at his interview in August for a commission in the army that 'all applicants for commissions must be selected from the recognised public schools, and yours is not among them'.[73] Despite its ancient foundation and displaying many of the trappings of the elite institutions, including representation in the Public School Cup rowing races at Molesey Regatta,[74] Kingston Grammar School's status was ambiguous. Robert Sherriff subsequently became a captain in the 9th Battalion East Surrey Regiment, fought at Passchendaele and won a Military Cross. After the war he wrote the much-acclaimed *Journey's End*.[75]

For the products of schools positioned even further down the educational and social hierarchy, the award of a commission was even more difficult to attain. Boys from the lower classes and non-professional occupational backgrounds were, by general public consensus, not 'gentlemen'. As an officer was a gentleman, and a gentleman had, by definition, the pre-requisite qualities and background to be an officer, the great majority of men educated in the intermediate and, especially, elementary schools became 'other ranks' on entering the armed forces. The Roll of Honour for Deacon's School in Peterborough first appeared in the Easter 1915 edition of *The Deaconian*. It contained a list of 128 Old Deaconians who were known to have enlisted in the first six months of the war. Nearly half had joined locally based units, such as the Northamptonshire Regiment, the Peterborough Battalion of the Royal Field Artillery (RFA) and the Huntingdonshire Cyclist Battalion. Seven former pupils had joined the Royal Navy.[76] Of those listed, sixty-one had additional details of military rank. Ten of the 61 (16 per cent) were commissioned officers (including one Officer Cadet at Sandhurst Military College), 28 (46 per cent) were NCOs, and 23 (38 per cent) were privates or of equivalent rank. The rank recorded was not necessarily the rank allocated at the time of enlistment but the rank attained by the time the list was compiled. Some men had enlisted as army privates but had been awarded a commission subsequently. Private Edgar Felix Law of the Northamptonshire Regiment had become Second Lieutenant Law by the time the Deacon's School Roll of Honour had been published.

Most of the men who had been educated in British elementary schools became privates on enlistment. The Roll of Honour of 'Ducie Avenue Old Boys serving in His Majesty's Forces During the Great War, 1914' is typical of many produced by schools educating predominantly working-class children. Of the 246 former pupils listed, only 7 (3 per cent) were commissioned officers, 38 (15 per cent) were NCOs and 201 (82 per cent) were privates. Over 100 of them joined the Manchester Regiment. The statistics for Armadale Public School in the mining district of West Lothian in Scotland, where the term 'public school', a school genuinely for the wider public, denoted a school similar in status and provision to an English elementary school for the working classes, reflect the school's ranking and demographic base. The proportion of officers to other ranks on the Armadale

Roll of Honour is identical to that of Ducie Avenue School. With its ornate format and meticulous hand-written entries, the Armadale roll lists 10 officers (3 per cent of the total), 60 NCOs (15 per cent) and 319 privates (82 per cent) or equivalent. The figures for former pupils of Monikie Public School who enlisted before the end of 1915 are very similar: 2 commissioned officers (4 per cent), 4 NCOs (8 per cent) and 45 privates (88 per cent).

The structure of the British armed forces in the early months of the Great War thus reflected British society more generally; a world where birth, class, wealth and the right kind of schooling counted for more than innate talent or aptitude for the task in hand. It was not an alien structure, but one which rested on widely accepted notions of hierarchy. A small elite maintained and vigorously promoted their perceived entitlement to lead; the majority of the populace acquiesced with varying degrees of deference. The Great War, a war fought on a scale not previously witnessed, expected or experienced, severely tested such notions. Changes did take place, albeit 'for the duration of the war only'.

As the Great War dragged on, and more and more men were drawn into the conflict, Rolls of Honour 'acted as living documents, recording the fate of those from the community who were in the forces'.[77] Most, given the undoubted difficulties in collecting information, were reasonably accurate.[78] The growing requirement for 'war economy', however, led to an end to the publication of many school magazines for the duration of the war. The growing number of war-related casualties had an enormous psychological as well as physical impact, and led incidentally to a transformation in the recording process for many schools. The Roll of Honour began to assume a new title and contained additional details. What had started as a statement of institutional celebration and pride became a sorrowful and mournful record of lost friends and school fellows: the names of The Fallen.

One of the highlights of the school year at King Edward VII School in Sheffield School was the school lecture. In November 1914 the lecture was given by the then Vice-Chancellor of Sheffield University, H.A.L. Fisher. More famous later as the chief architect of the 1918 Education Act, Fisher addressed the assembled boys and masters on the 'Causes and Issues of the War', referring to Germany's perfidiousness and Britain's necessary and traditional response to protect her interests.[79] Britain had responded to the German invasion of Belgium and the consequent threat to the French and British Channel ports. Schools throughout the country, said Fisher, had encouraged their communities to rally around the flag and to be part of the nation's military response.

For some schools, however, this was an especially difficult time. The Quaker witness against war might have resulted in wholesale conscientious objection by members of their school communities. The realities of war and, especially, the appeal for national support, created an ethical dilemma for individuals and institutions. Quaker communities were patently aware that 'here was a decision of life importance, and yet one on which equally sincere and alive men and women might have opposed convictions'. The war record of Old Scholars of The Friends School, Saffron Walden, for example, demonstrated clearly the fault lines created by the Great War: 'those who gave their lives in battle keep company with those who tried to help heal the ravages of war by ambulance or relief work'.[80]

Schools without overt religious foundations also faced a stern test of the fundamental principles upon which they had been formed. King Alfred School, an independent school established by the Fabians in North London in 1898, was a very different institution to the majority of conventional elementary and secondary schools. It had been founded as part of the Progressive Movement in education; a 'rationalist' school which emphasised practical education and was based on secular, not religious, tenets and principles. John Russell, its headteacher, blamed the outbreak of war upon 'the intense competitive spirit which dominated nations and their education systems'. He condemned the way in which this was disguised by 'an increased flood of cheap emotion, of patriotic insincerities, of organised passion, and of reckless injustice'. Russell hoped, however, that some good would emerge, nevertheless, from the turmoil of war: 'the triumph of those values for which King Alfred School stood'.[81] Truth may be the first casualty of war, but idealism runs a close second. The war in Belgium rapidly became the European War, then the Great War or First World War as it was later designated. It was difficult to stand aside, remain aloof or be indifferent to a war which gradually encompassed not simply the boys at the battle fronts, but all the nation's citizens: men and women, young and old, combatants and non-combatants. Bedales, a radical, non-authoritarian and early co-educational private school was a member of the internationalist New School Movement. Its pupils, drawn from many different countries by its distinctive philosophy, were confronted by the reality of an all-consuming European war. They were forced to make difficult decisions. Bedalians fought on both sides in the Great War. By end of 1914 'seventy percent of those who had been to the school were serving the war effort in some capacity or other'.[82] As Trotsky later remarked, 'You may not be interested in war, but war is interested in you'.[83]

Despite all the diplomatic and military excitement which had taken place over the summer months, the majority of headteachers, school governors and LEAs had hoped to re-open their schools at the start of the new autumn term and carry on with 'business as usual'.[84] To paraphrase Trotsky, however, the war wanted the schools – or at least some of their buildings and playing fields. In the final months of 1914 the British army was on the move, not yet in the fields of Flanders, but on the roads and railways of the mother country. The inhabitants of towns and cities throughout the land were witness to the dislocation this deployment inevitably created. Their senses were assaulted by the sights and sounds of the infantry marching, cavalry horses being harnessed and the transportation of the *matériel* of war. The mobilisation of the BEF and the initial recruitment and organisation of Kitchener's New Army was a massive undertaking which necessitated billets and training facilities. The demands of war took priority over the demands of the new academic year.

Many schools were requisitioned, often at incredibly short notice. Schools had been used for other non-educational purposes in the past. Hornby School, for example, was one of many which had been used as a polling station in Parliamentary Elections, in this particular case 'for electing [the] Member for Lancaster Division'.[85] More recently, schools had opened their doors as recruiting centres, but this had commenced during the summer holiday when schools were not in session. In London, George Green's School in Poplar was used as a recruitment centre for a month from 11 August, processing some 2,000 volunteers.[86] The Huntingdonshire Cyclists Battalion, which used the premises of the Old Fletton Council School in Peterborough for some of its recruiting meetings, travelled on 6 August to Grimsby and marched straight into its new quarters: Littlecote Council School.[87] Newly-raised battalions throughout the land were likewise engaged in establishing their bases and awaiting further orders. The speed and scale of requisitioning schools and other public buildings for billeting troops and other war-related purposes was unprecedented.

Elementary schools under LEA control were particularly vulnerable to the myriad needs and demands of the military authorities. The Board of Education stipulated that permission from 'the responsible education authority' was required before a school could be used by the military.[88] In Bedfordshire, ten schools in St Albans were requisitioned, despite parental complaints to the LEA about the consequent dislocation to their children's education. Some local authorities, such as that in Hemel Hempstead, also made protests on the basis of the logistical difficulties of finding alternative provision for schoolchildren.[89] Many children and their teachers were hosted by nearby schools, experiencing a double shift system of part-time schooling. Others were simply relocated to other available buildings such as church halls. For some the disruption was temporary, for others their closure or displacement was for the duration of the war. In the first three months of the war 705 elementary schools in England and Wales were requisitioned by the military authorities for use as billets, stores and offices. By April of the following year, this figure had dropped to 178 schools,[90] a reflection of how many battalions had moved on after their initial training.

Many school buildings and facilities bore the strain of hosting hundreds of men whose minds were elsewhere. Whilst the troops were preoccupied with thoughts of war and the necessary preparation for it, headteachers counted the material cost to their schools. William Clark at East Boldon School, an elementary school in South Tyneside, noted that the 300 troops billeted there had caused numerous breakages of school property and used over 27,000 gallons of water.[91] The Board of Education issued *Circular 892* in March 1915, giving details of 'Compensation for Military Occupation of School Buildings'. It also referred to the Army Council's confidence 'that all persons concerned will welcome this opportunity of contributing to the welfare of the troops during this period of emergency'.

Secondary institutions were not immune from the pressures of military deployment. By 1 November 1914, thirty-three maintained secondary schools and fifteen Technical Schools had been requisitioned, although these numbers decreased to eighteen and fourteen respectively by April 1915.[92] The Duke of York's Royal Military School was fully evacuated to Hutton near Brentwood for the duration of the war. Originally established in Chelsea to provide an education for the orphans of British servicemen killed in the Napoleonic Wars, it had relocated to Dover only five years before the Great War. Its site on the south east coast was of strategic importance and was used as a transit point for troops going to and from the Western Front throughout the war. Most secondary schools remained *in situ*, but many suffered military 'invasions' of one kind or another nevertheless. When George Clifford Diamond resumed his studies after the holidays he found that half of Cardiff High School had been occupied by the Royal Army Medical Corps (RAMC). What struck him most was 'the bad language and worse temper of sergeants'.[93] At King Edward VI School, Retford, corrugated iron huts were provided for the displaced High School girls. Most of the buildings at Morpeth Grammar School were requisitioned in 1914. The school retained use of the Library and one other small room, but much of its teaching took place in the rented Presbyterian Hall. This, and the nearby Congregational Hall, continued to be used even after the departure of the troops as numbers in the school grew.[94] Even where schools were not needed for billeting, their premises were used when vacant. During the 1914 Christmas holiday period the Royal Welch Fusiliers used Aberystwyth County School to give lectures to their men on military tactics.[95] When the Local Defence Corps asked Harrow County School for Boys for permission to use their lecture room for evening drill sessions, however, the school agreed but stipulated the use of rubber-soled shoes so as not to damage the recently polished floor.[96] Some schools chose not to cooperate with the authorities. In Wales, Caernarvon County School stated their unwillingness to place school buildings at the disposal of the War Office.[97] On Merseyside, Merchant Taylors' School for Girls in Crosby had proudly become the first and only secondary school in the area to accommodate troops in the early weeks of the war. When the army asked for an extension of the arrangement through the winter months of 1914–15 the governors nevertheless decided that education came first and refused the request. When the occupying troops moved on soon afterwards, the school was disinfected and redecorated before opening its doors to the pupils again on 14 September.[98] Relations between the school and the troops appear not to have been severed irreparably; the Head Mistress of the school, Miss Shackleton, subsequently invited the Commanding Officer of the South Lancashire Regiment to distribute the school prizes at the end of that autumn term.

The once-sacrosanct playing fields of some schools, including public schools, were obvious targets for the military in its preparations for war. On 1 August 1914, before war had even been declared, units of the Lancashire Fusiliers arrived at Hymers College in Hull. They set up camp around the running track, established their headquarters in the sports pavilion, and placed a soldier on duty by the telephone in the school office.[99] Detachments of the Highland Mountain Brigade occupied Huntingdon Grammar School, 'their horses ... tethered in rows across the sports field'.[100] Damage caused to these hard-won and expensive symbols of school status and sporting prowess was inevitable. In these patriotic times, however, complaints from headteachers and school governors tended to be confined to the minutes of their meetings rather than aired openly. Such was the case at Deacon's School following reports on the state of the field after the departure the Royal Engineers.[101] In 1915, with no signs of an early victory, school sports facilities continued to be appropriated. In London, the Queen's Westminster Rifles used the playground and gym of Hackney Downs School to improve the fitness of new recruits.[102]

The Great War produced casualties on an enormous and unprecedented scale. A constant stream of badly wounded men flowed from the initial engagements in Belgium and then from each new theatre of war. The number of critical cases soon began to overwhelm the medical facilities in the field and necessitated a huge logistical operation to return men to Blighty for further treatment, convalescence and rehabilitation. Many civilian hospitals were rapidly converted to receive the casualties. Other contingency plans involved supplementing existing medical provision by converting suitable buildings into military hospitals as soon as hostilities commenced. Once again, urgent military and, in this case medical, priorities superseded existing educational needs. Schools were amongst a range of public and private buildings that were requisitioned for use as military hospitals. In November 1914, thirty-three elementary and ten secondary schools were occupied for medical purposes. Demand for such facilities did not decrease. Within six months sixty elementary and seventeen secondary schools had been converted to care for the casualties of war.[103] In the hectic days which followed the British declaration of war, not everything went according to plan. Winifred Sturge at The Mount School, a Quaker boarding school for girls in York, was one of many who had not even suspected 'the coming tragedy'. On 5 August, however, she received a telegram informing her that the school buildings had been requisitioned. Red Cross nurses arrived shortly afterwards, and rows of hospital beds were set up in classrooms, the dining room and the gymnasium. And then – nothing happened. By the end of August The Mount School was vacated. The authorities had decided to use the Friends Meeting House in York instead.[104]

Lincoln Grammar School was one of the first schools to be commandeered, converted and used for the treatment of wounded soldiers (Plate 17).[105] In August 1914 it became a Territorial Force General Hospital and eventually formed part of Northern Command as the 4th Northern General Hospital. The original school buildings in Wragby Road were converted into operating theatres and wards, and twenty new huts on the school field provided additional accommodation for hospital patients. The professional services in the General Hospitals were provided by the RAMC and Queen Alexandra's Imperial Military Nursing Service. They were supported by volunteers from the Red Cross, St John's Ambulance, Young Men's Christian Association and Voluntary Aid Detachments (VAD). The 4th Northern provided beds for 41 officers and 1,126 other ranks and treated 45,000 casualties during the war. The needs of the country in time of war were clearly met by this particular conversion of school to hospital. The October 1914 edition of *The Lincolnian* contained an editorial which reminded the school community of its duty to help British servicemen 'in our country's peril', and to do so with pride and at 'whatever personal inconvenience'. The school itself had been massively inconvenienced, but it had not closed, and it had been able to open its doors to pupils at the beginning of the school year in new buildings on a new site. As reported in *The Lincolnian*, those in authority had used the six weeks of holidays after the outbreak of war to build a temporary school on Lindum Terrace which was 'excellent in every way'. Even the boarders had been found accommodation in 'very comfortable quarters' in the nearby, and possibly appropriately named, Coldbath House. The all-important school games and sports fixtures took place on Lindum Cricket Ground for the duration.[106]

In Manchester, the re-organisation of schooling to serve the needs of the military was even more extensive and involved several schools. The Central High School for Boys in Whitworth Street provided 520 hospital beds in 1914. It became the headquarters of the 2nd Western General Hospital, later commanding 25,000 beds in the Manchester area. Ducie Avenue School in Whitworth Park gave up its buildings as well as many former pupils to the war effort. Moseley Road School in Fallowfield was also requisitioned, and the newly constructed Heald Place School in Rusholme became a hospital before any teachers or pupils could start their teaching and learning there.[107] Alternative provision was made for the children's education in other schools in the city. Manchester High School for Girls (MHSG), in particular, played a key role in alleviating the effects of the 'national crisis' by accommodating pupils from Central High School and Ducie Avenue School. Hundreds of other students, including a thousand from the Municipal School of Domestic Economy, attended evening classes in the MHSG buildings.[108] Private schools in the area were also used as hospitals. Founded in 1854, originally as the Manchester Warehousemen and Clerks Orphan School, the co-educational Cheadle Hulme School was partly refurbished by the Red Cross and provided twenty-four beds in the main school building by March 1915. At the height of the Battle of the Somme in September 1916 a further forty-one beds were found by displacing some of the girl boarders from their dormitory. As the war dragged on and the casualties mounted, a marquee and two asbestos buildings were constructed on the girls' playground in 1917, giving a total capacity of 100 beds. By the end of the war the hospital at Cheadle Hume School had treated 1,402 casualties.

Throughout Britain there were similar experiences of conversion and displacement. The Board of Education reported in 1915 that 'In the great majority of cases the loss of the school premises has not been allowed to stop the work of the school'.[109] These were difficult times for everyone, but schools generally responded positively and adjusted accordingly. Nevertheless, the frustration of some headteachers is evident in their logbook entries. The Meeching Boys' School in Newhaven, Sussex, became a military hospital on 12 October 1914. The school was relocated to the church room and the congregational room, but these buildings were also subject to wartime demands other than those of the school. Just four days later the school had to close for two days so that a concert raising funds for the families of servicemen could be held in the new premises. On 14 December the school logbook records that the 'Children assembled as normal this morning but at 9.15 they were dismissed as the buildings were required by the military authorities'. The following month the children had to vacate the school by 4 p.m. 'owing to new lighting restrictions'.[110]

During the four years of war, and with casualties counted in their millions, further requisitions of schools took place. In Scotland, the Beach Road Council Schools in Litherland were taken over by the Medical Department of the War Office in 1917. The newly-named Seaforth Hospital accommodated up to 210 patients, whilst the Junior Boys and the Junior Girls had their lessons in the Wesleyan Sunday School building and St Philip's Church Hall respectively.[111] Thousands of additional hospital beds were provided for British and allied soldiers, sailors and airmen in buildings formerly occupied by the nation's schoolchildren. For a few individuals, both their schooling and their wartime hospital were in the very same buildings. Corporal Ralph Pearson of the 19th Battalion Durham Light Infantry, a former Head Boy of the Trent Bridge Elementary School in Nottingham, was later treated in the military hospital established there for wounds received in Flanders, just weeks before the war ended. He also died there, aged twenty, in April 1919.[112]

For the majority of schools which managed to escape the immediate demands of the military for their premises, the outbreak of war, nevertheless, created new problems to be addressed and disruptions to be managed. Some were caused by factors external to the school: staffing difficulties caused by recruitment campaigns; closures to accommodate military medical examinations; transport problems for pupils – and subsequent school closures – when the railways were used to move troops.[113] The task confronting new schools which were scheduled to open at the start of the new school year in 1914 must have seemed particularly daunting. In London, Cardinal Vaughan Memorial School, a Catholic public school in Kensington which opened on 21 September, had little opportunity to celebrate its foundation. Britain was at war; a formal opening ceremony would, it was decided, be inappropriate in the circumstances.[114] In schools where development projects were already underway, or were planned for implementation in the academic year 1914–15, important decisions also had to be made. In Derbyshire, the building programme which had started earlier in the year at the Herbert Strutt School in Belper continued despite the war. The school had been opened in 1909 and was recognised by the Board of Education as a provider of secondary education. Herbert Strutt, its founder and benefactor, ordered the building contractor, in quasi-military terms, to go 'full steam ahead'. Despite the inevitable disruption caused by the building works, by February 1916 the school had built and furnished new classrooms, laboratories and dining facilities.[115] Building projects scheduled for schools elsewhere were put on hold.

The country had been at war for a month when Alfred Whitehouse, headteacher of St Nicholas Boys' School in King's Lynn recorded in his logbook: '31 August. Re-opened after the Midsummer holiday'.[116] His counterpart at Silver Street Senior Boys' School in Edmonton, Middlesex, also made a formal note of events of importance to the school: 'August 31. Re-opened after holiday. During the holiday the whole exterior of the school has been redecorated'.[117] There was similarly no mention of the war in the logbook for Peterborough Practising School until 1 September 1914, when Mr L.C. Pullan noted the departure of one of his teaching staff: 'Mr J. Gooding has enlisted in the Northamptonshire Regiment'.[118] For the people of Britain, war had traditionally been fought on the continent of Europe, in distant colonies or on the high seas. The demands of war came sooner than expected, even to those schools and communities which still believed themselves to be sufficiently distant from the fighting. This new war quickly began to re-define the arena of warfare, and both the practice of war and those who might be its practitioners – or victims. Schools began to prepare for a conflict which might not be 'over by Christmas' and might even involve those left behind in school, rather than the Old Boys who had made their way to the battle fronts across the English Channel. For some, the prospect of military action was very real indeed. In Deal on the Kent coast, boys at Winchester House School were early eye-witnesses to hostilities; an event which created enormous excitement amongst the boys, but which was far too close for comfort for the school authorities. Pupil Stuart Meikle later recalled the naval action on 11 November 1914:

Our first introduction to the activities of war was an enormous explosion which disturbed our Geometry lesson. We all hastened to the Deal front to witness the sinking of HMS *Niger*, the first British ship, so we were told, to be sunk in home waters; the *Niger* had been torpedoed by a German submarine.

Submarine U-12 of the German Imperial Navy was subsequently destroyed by ships of the Royal Navy in 1915, by which time Winchester House School had decided to relocate inland to the relatively safer surroundings of Canterbury. Unfortunately, its new premises, Kenfield Hall, were under the flight path to London of a new menace to the home front – the German Zeppelin airship. In 1918 the school moved once more, to its present site in Brackley in Northamptonshire, in the very centre of England.[119] Other schools similarly prepared for the worst. The committee which governed Ayton School, a Quaker institution in the North of England, had a contingency plan. Should the Germans invade Yorkshire, Ayton School was primed for a swift evacuation. The headmaster, Mr Herbert Dennis, was instructed to keep £100 in gold in the safe; various farms in Fryup Dale had agreed to accommodate the girls; the boys would look after themselves.[120]

Part II

Schools at War

The home front is always underrated by the Generals in the Field. And yet that is where the Great War was won and lost.

David Lloyd George (1938)
War Memoirs

Chapter 3

On Campaign

The war made it clear, in its demand for efficient man-power and woman-power, that the children of a nation are its real reserve capital, and that physical neglect and imperfect education were waste of capital on a prodigious scale.

The Times History of the War (1918)

In the first weeks and months of the Great War, Britain's Boy Scouts were kept busy. With so many men making their way to their battalions, either as Territorials or Kitchener's New Army recruits about to start their basic training, the members of Baden-Powell's new quasi-military youth organisation became an early incarnation of the Home Guard. The first into action were the St Albans Scouts.[1] Having organised a 24-hour rota, they were ready to answer the call of duty. Throughout August 1914 they moved furniture to the nearby military hospital. They made bandages and looked after officers' horses. Others quickly followed their example. In Woodford in Essex, the Bancroft's School Scout Troop carried messages for local war organisations which, in these days of frenetic activity, were springing up everywhere.[2] Throughout the country, Scouts patrolled vulnerable coastlines and safeguarded points of strategic importance such as railways, bridges and telegraph lines. During their 12-hour shifts, boys from the Peterborough and District Scout troops guarded the Great North Road and recorded car numbers.[3] Elsewhere, older Boys Scouts who had already left school were expected to go to work in uniform and be available for deployment at a moment's notice. Younger Scouts were released from school and formed anti-sabotage patrols.[4] The Scout Troop at Bristol Cathedral School, a unit founded just months before the start of hostilities, conducted night time road patrols but recorded, much to their obvious disappointment, 'no encounters with German spies'.[5]

Schools, youth organisations and the people of Britain more generally were clearly anticipating the possibility of a foreign invasion in the autumn of 1914. When it came, however, it was not a landing of German forces to be resisted, but the far more benign arrival of families from an allied country. Belgian refugees began to arrive in Britain after fleeing from the advancing Schlieffen Plan armies and the subsequent German occupation of their country. Between August 1914 and May 1915 a quarter of a million of them crossed the English Channel. There was an immediate, widespread and enthusiastic commitment to aid the 'gallant little Belgians'. Local Belgian Refugee Committees were quickly established throughout Britain in addition to national organisations, such as the Belgian Relief Fund which was set up to help victims of the war still in their mother country.[6] Many Belgian refugee families included children of school age. In the first year of the war, some 30,000 refugee children were provided with school places arranged by genuinely well-meaning but somewhat paternalistic local committees. Here was an early opportunity for middle and upper-class philanthropists on the home front to make a real contribution to the war effort. Schools, and their governors, teachers and pupils, similarly recognised that welcoming the needy refugee children, whatever the consequent logistical difficulties and additional dislocation, was a way of 'doing one's bit'.[7] LEAs had a statutory obligation to educate all children of elementary school age in their area, hence many refugee children were initially absorbed into existing local authority schools.

The initial concentration of refugees in London and other large urban areas, and the religious and linguistic differences within the Belgian community itself, called for additional measures. The LCC-maintained Old Poland Street School in Westminster accommodated over 200 Belgian children of Jewish origin and faith by the end of December 1914. The school building was originally a workhouse, but in the first year of war it contained four mixed age and gender classes. Furniture was provided by the LCC which also funded the four classroom teachers, three of whom were Flemish and possessed only rudimentary English language skills. History was taught in English, whilst arithmetic was taught in Flemish; geography was taught in both Flemish and French. The Jewish Free School in the city also arranged two additional classes for Belgian boys. Their initial instruction was in Yiddish, but as their grasp of English improved they were moved into mainstream classes.[8] Such were the complexities of schooling in wartime for some children, but at least – many pupils, parents, teachers and school authorities believed – these arrangements were only temporary.

Further afield, as refugee families were dispersed beyond the main cities, their children were found places in other local authority schools. In January 1915, for example, headteacher Frank Amos at Badsey Council School in Evesham admitted his first Belgian refugee, 6-year-old Maria van de Wyngaert.[9] Small rural schools also felt the impact of war. Headmaster Charles Bailey Allerton noted in the logbook for Barnack School in Northamptonshire the admission of two Belgian children from Ostend on 14 December 1914.[10] As in London, religious denominations provided education for refugee children in faith-based schools. In Peterborough, the Roman Catholic All Souls School established special classes for Belgian children. They were taught by the Sisters of Charity and, after 1915, by a Belgian schoolmaster. Appointed on a salary of £40 per annum, he taught seven pupils in the upper school and twelve infants.[11]

Some refugee children attended secondary schools. At Hackney Downs School in London, for example, thirty Belgian boys were admitted.[12] For new arrivals who had recently fled their homeland and begun new and very insecure lives in a foreign land, the fees charged by many post-elementary institutions would have been prohibitive. Many schools showed compassion in this matter, however, generously awarding free places to Belgian children. This was the case in Wales at Gowerton Intermediate School in Glamorgan,[13] and at Aberystwyth County School, where free places were given to Belgian children as early as 7 October 1914 by special resolution of the governors.[14] In England, the Herbert Strutt School in Belper was similarly welcoming but continued, nevertheless, to maintain high expectations and standards from all who attended, whatever their backgrounds. One 16-year-old Belgian boy was subsequently withdrawn from the school for failing to make sufficient effort and progress.[15] Places for refugees were also made available by headteachers and governors at some of the elite public schools. Eton admitted twenty Belgian boys, and refugees from Belgium, France and Serbia were taken in by Sherborne and St Edwards, Oxford.[16] Some schools, however, whilst offering to take in the newcomers, maintained their established admissions criteria. Lionel Ford, Head Master of Harrow School, stated on 9 November 1914 that, unlike the unfortunate Belgian pupil presenting himself to the school on that very day, prospective pupils had 'to be of the right sort' and be able to speak English and Latin.[17]

Despite their different backgrounds and experiences, there were few incidents of poor behaviour between British and Belgian children in schools. Minor tensions occurred, generally related to the importance of particular cultural activities. At the newly opened Cardinal Vaughan Memorial School in London, for example, an appreciation of the iconic place of sport in British education was an important rite of passage for the thirteen new boys from Belgium. An English pupil at the school noted:

> There were some Belgian boys amongst us, not too popular until we taught them to play cricket and football, and not to do things that were 'not done' in an English Public school.[18]

From 1915 there was a gradual withdrawal of Belgian children from British schools. Many refugee parents had recognised the limited educational value of learning in existing schools when children so evidently struggled with language difficulties. Their children, too, commented unfavourably on other differences, particularly in relation to the perceived harshness of discipline and the use of prefects in their new schools.[19] As the war dragged on, temporary arrangements no longer sufficed for many Belgian parents and the refugee communities in which they lived. An increasing number, intent on returning to their home country at some point in the future, requested that their children be given tuition in their own language and follow a Belgian curriculum. The generous hospitality of their hosts in their evident time of need was most welcome; full assimilation of their children into British culture via the media of British schooling was not. A distinctive 'Belgian' education is what many requested; taught in Belgian schools by Belgian teachers – in Britain – 'for the duration of the war only'.

By the end of the war 100 Belgian primary and 15 secondary schools, catering for some 10,000 pupils, had been opened. They were funded jointly by local Refugee Committees, wealthy members of the Belgian ex-patriot community and the Belgian government. Some were small-scale additions to existing provision, as in Peterborough where the Roman Catholic authorities augmented the provision for refugee children at All Souls School with a further sixteen places at the Belgian School in Cowgate.[20] The Belgian National School of Manchester was on a much larger scale, with 265 pupils and 6 teachers.[21] On 3 April 1916, The King Albert School opened in Kensal Rise, London, named after the King of the Belgians who steadfastly maintained throughout the war a small but symbolic sector of the Western Front in Flanders. Funds for its establishment and maintenance were provided by the Belgian Government, the English Board of Education and the LEA, Willesden Urban District Council. The school accommodated sixty Belgian pupils in the rooms of The Sunday School at Brondesbury Congregational Church. The boys were taught by M. Pieters, and the girls by Mlle Rosalie Jansen.[22] Provision for the schooling of Belgian children was even more specific in the town of Elisabethville in Tyne and Wear. Named after the Queen of the Belgians, Elisabethville was a Belgian enclave; a purpose-built town and a sovereign state in its own right. Its 6,000 inhabitants included refugees and wounded Belgian servicemen employed in a huge munitions factory. Families lived in cottages and single men were housed in hostels. The gated complex, guarded by Belgian *Gendarmes*, was self-contained, with shops, church, cemetery – and a school with Belgian teachers and a Belgian curriculum.[23]

Hospitality for the Belgian refugees extended beyond the provision of formal schooling. British schoolchildren also supported Belgian families in different ways. Some schools, such as St Nicholas Boys' School in King's Lynn, made regular donations to the Belgian Refugee Fund (Plate 18).[24] In the Peterborough area the children of Fletton County Council School sacrificed their 'sweet money' and pledged a collective ten shillings each week to help the refugees recently arrived in the city. Girls at the County Secondary School worked collaboratively with the Peterborough Refugee Committee to provide a hostel close by in Cromwell Road. The same pupils made weekly contributions, which were sufficient to meet the needs of the Belgian family who lived there. They visited the family and played with the children. Occasionally, girls took the children back to their own homes for tea.[25] Girls at the Mount School in York also helped to prepare accommodation for Belgian refugees in nearby Acomb.[26] Once housed, Belgian refugees were often then provided with some of the other necessitates of life. Appeals for clothes and food for the refugees appeared in *The Magpie*, the magazine produced by the secondary girls at George Dixon Schools in Birmingham.[27] In such simple, but generous and heartwarming ways, British schoolchildren contributed to the relief of a humanitarian crisis created by the Great War. It was just one of many ways in which they became involved in the war effort.

The Belgian refugees who fled to Britain were essentially temporary visitors from abroad. Four years of exile from their own land forced them to make do, to make compromises and to ensure that their cultural and national identities were not eroded by exposure to British schooling. They were foreigners and, therefore, aliens,[28] albeit 'friendly aliens'. They were wartime allies who had heroically resisted Britain's enemies, were worthy of British compassion and material assistance, and were consequently welcomed as honoured guests. This was not the case, however, for others designated as 'aliens' in wartime Britain. Anti-German hysteria in the early weeks of the war took a particularly insidious form when it was applied to those, including schoolchildren, with 'alien' origins or even foreign sounding names. They were particularly vulnerable to the possibility of discrimination or hostility, even from some of the authorities responsible for their welfare. In February 1915, for example, the Minutes of the Managers of the LCC-controlled Lambeth Central and Special Schools stated that children who had been identified as 'aliens' were not to be admitted to the borough's Central schools 'if other children properly qualified are available'.[29] In some cases families felt compelled to change their surnames – often the only signifier of these otherwise British citizens of long standing. This was the case even in some of the elite fee-paying schools. On returning to Lancing College for the start of the new term in September 1914, Evelyn Waugh noted that some German names had been anglicised: fellow pupil Kaiser had, perhaps understandably given the new climate of war, changed his name to Kingsley.[30]

For the majority of children in British schools, however, the Great War brought a heady mixture of emotions – excitement, trepidation and uncertainty among them – but at least they were to be 'part of it'. Their involvement was necessary and their contribution valued. Their 'King and Country' needed them too, just as it had made explicit the need for more and yet more men for the armed forces. The war of 1914–19 was the first 'Total War'; a war in which all the nation's citizens were expected to serve in some capacity, and schoolchildren were no exception. The children of Britain were, indeed, a reserve force, and there were millions of them ready, and mostly willing, to be deployed. In August 1914, children in the 193 elite public schools numbered just over 50,000.[31] There were a further 200,000 pupils in over 1,000 voluntary aided and state funded secondary schools, and over 7,000,000 on roll in the 20,000 or so elementary schools.[32] The call-to-arms of 1914 extended far beyond those who were members of the OTC and the Scout movement, or those who had come into early contact with refugees from the continental battle zones. Millions of children in thousands of schools throughout Britain volunteered – or were 'volunteered' by their teachers, families and community groups – in myriad ways. Their production of comforts and their many collection campaigns helped maintain the morale of troops at the front and provided much needed funds for charities, additional food supplies and war *matériel*. Some children ended their school careers prematurely to join the forces or to provide cheap labour in the fields and factories in place of the men now fighting on the battle fronts. A few were subjected to the horrors of new forms of warfare which targeted the civilian population. At times the schoolchildren of Britain even dressed like military personnel or auxiliary forces. The Great War was their war; a war fought on the home front.

This commitment to the war took many forms and lasted throughout the four years of conflict. In the autumn term 1914 schoolchildren were encouraged by their teachers to make or provide items for the troops who were stationed on the battle fields of the Western Front and beyond. These comforts took many forms. Items of clothing, especially gloves and balaclavas, were particularly well-received and often much needed by British troops as the especially harsh winter of 1914–15 set in. Also popular were contributions of cigarettes, pots of jam and other small luxuries for men living, by then, in the cold and mud of the trenches or still in the training camps. Schoolchildren made, provided or raised money to fund such items. Some initiatives came from the children themselves; other 'campaigns' were encouraged by enterprising teachers. Pupils at College Road Council School in Moseley, for example, knitted socks and collected candles for the troops.[33] Some of 'the more nimble boys' at Bancrofts's School, a public school in Essex, were taught how to knit large socks and balaclava helmets.[34]

Other activities were prompted by a multitude of local and national patriotic or humanitarian organisations which were keen to mobilise schoolchildren to assist in their particular contributions to the war effort. The logbook for Sychdyn School in Flintshire, Wales, records the way in which one local organisation encouraged schoolchildren to take part in the 'knitting frenzy' (Plate 19) which was sweeping the country at the time. Headteacher Mr J. R. Macfarlane noted:

1914
25 November: This morning I received from Mrs Ivor Davies, 4lbs of wool and twelve sets of needles from the Soughton Committee in order that the upper – standard girls should knit scarves for the troops.

22 December: This morning I forwarded fifteen scarves and seven pairs of mittens to Mrs Ivor Davies, Bryn Siriol.[35]

Appeals by members of the British royal family for the production of comforts were particularly popular and successful. Queen Mary called for 300,000 pairs of socks for the men at the Front. The girls of Aberystwyth County School, determined to do their bit, responded by setting up a School Wool Fund.[36] Their counterparts at Caernarvon County School in the principality responded likewise to the appeal from 17-year-old Princess Mary, daughter of King George V and Queen Mary and Patron of the Girls' Patriotic Union of Secondary Schools,[37] for girls to knit articles for the troops.[38] In return for their donation of fourteen shillings to the Soldiers and Sailors Christmas Fund, the Infants of Market Street Schools in Ely received a letter of thanks from the princess. They also had the satisfaction of knowing that a serviceman somewhere was enjoying the contents of a Princess Mary's Christmas Gift – an embossed tin containing tobacco, confectionary, a Christmas card and other small but useful or comforting items.

Very often comforts were sent directly to units that had been raised locally. Throughout September 1914 girls in the senior classes at Badsey Council School in Evesham used their needlework lessons to produce shirts and socks for men of the Worcestershire Regiment.[39] In October 1914, the pupils and teachers at Barnack School 'sent cigarettes to all Barnack men on service – about forty-five in number', followed by 'fourteen pairs of knitted mittens for men of the Northamptonshire Regiment' in December.[40] Elementary school pupils at East Boldon in South Tyneside knitted sixty-two pairs of socks and thirty-three mufflers for the Boldon Soldiers Comforts Fund. Prizes were awarded by the school to pupils making the best products, on the condition that the producer washed the knitted item thoroughly before presenting it for judging.[41] Frederick Longbottom, appointed headteacher of Hornby School in Lancashire just weeks after the war began, made several references to knitting in his logbook. Children at his school began subscriptions in late-November for the purchase of wool 'for knitting socks for the soldiers'. By early December they had raised over twenty-one shillings for the project, and by February 1915 the socks were ready to be distributed:

3rd February: Five local young men, who are serving in the army, called in school to receive the socks and scarfs which have been knitted by the scholars. They are going to the Front in a few weeks time.

Some months later, on 24 June, Mr Irving Alderson, one of the local soldiers who was serving with the Territorials, 'called in school during the afternoon to thank the children for the socks they supplied'. The humble pair of socks, new and dry and recently arrived from kindly supporters back home, was 'symptomatic of a wider yearning for home comforts, for a sense of well-being and security'.[42] Socks, especially, were always appreciated by the men in the trenches. Such close connection with the men at the Front, however, could sometimes be a mixed blessing. Regular contact between the school and local men fighting abroad made the war seem nearer and more personal, but that relative closeness and familiarity could equally expose young children to the grim reality of war. Irving Alderson was killed in action shortly after his visit to Hornby School. On 25 September 1915 the school flag was hoisted at half-mast in his memory.[43] The real meaning of war – a war very different from that portrayed in the stories of heroism and glory in *The Boys' Own* and other schoolboy magazines – was experienced by increasing numbers of schoolchildren in the first year of the conflict.

Where former pupils of the school had joined local battalions there was even more incentive to send comforts to the trenches. On 27 June 1916 Inverness Royal Academy held a fete to raise money for the 'Camerons Comforts and Academy War Fund'. In a magazine article entitled 'Pupils' Work for Sailors and Soldiers', the writer referred with pride to the 782 items which the pupils had been able to provide for Old Academy Boys, the Cameron Highlanders and other good causes. The comforts included 'socks, seamen's stockings, scarves, cuffs, cardigans, face cloths, handkerchiefs, cigarettes etc. etc.'.[44] Former pupil teachers were not forgotten by their schools. Oswald Ash, serving in France, had his army rations supplemented by food parcels sent from East Boldon School, until he was killed by a shell in 1916.[45]

Schools continued to support men in the armed forces throughout the war, both directly and indirectly, via the many civic and charitable organisations, which provided comforts and equipment for them. In addition to the production of home-made comforts, many schools contributed financially, forwarding sums of money raised by pupil subscription, periodic collections or by a multitude of fund-raising activities. When the locally recruited 1st/5th Battalion of the Norfolk Regiment were sent to the Dardanelles as part of the British, French and ANZAC forces taking part in the Gallipoli Campaign in 1915, pupils at St Nicholas Boys' School contributed £1. 6s. to the Mayor of King's Lynn Fund.[46] Pupils at George Green's School in London made a similar contribution to the Mayor of Poplar's 'Plum-Pudding Fund'.[47] Barnack School was particularly enterprising. Headteacher Charles Allerton noted in his logbook in April 1915 that the children had gathered primroses, which were then sent by train to the nearby town of Stamford to be sold at one penny a bunch. All proceeds went to the Red Cross and St John's Ambulance.[48] Other organisations which benefitted from financial contributions from British schools included the Star and Garter Home for severely wounded servicemen,[49] the Welsh Soldiers Fund,[50] the Soldiers and Sailors Employment Society,[51] the Blinded Soldiers Children Fund,[52] and the YMCA,[53] to name but a few. Ensuring that the boys at the front were able to celebrate Christmas with at least a modicum of cheer was a major priority. The Overseas Club in London provided a valuable service in sending Christmas Day Gifts to servicemen at the Front, and rewarded individual pupil contributors with a personalised certificate (Plate 20).

Some of the recipients of comforts managed to send back messages of both thanks and encouragement. Private A. Pickles, his military unit and wartime location deliberately excluded from the official 'thanking the donor' postcard, wrote:

> Dear Children and Teacher,
> I have received the tobacco and find it excellent. Wishing the children and you the best of health and success to your school. As I reside in Grimsby when in civil life I am nearly a neighbour. Thanking the children for their pennies as it is the pennies that will win the war and give cheer to Tommy Atkins.

Schools occasionally sent the men comforts of a somewhat unusual nature, such as sporting goods. After all, the men were not engaged in fighting all of the time, and leisure pursuits and team games, usually behind the front lines, were considered good for morale. Following the receipt of one such gift, a letter of thanks appeared in the Spring 1915 edition of *The Magpie*,[54] the magazine of George Dixon School in Birmingham:

> 16 February 1915.
> Dear Girls,
>   I am writing on behalf of my chums and myself to thank you for the football you so kindly sent us and which we appreciate very much.
>   Driver A. Chervas, A.S.C.
>   C/O Queen Victoria's Rifles
>   British Expeditionary Force

The morale of soldiers throughout the centuries and across the globe has often depended upon ordinary comforts and discomforts.[55] The receipt of a letter or, even better, a parcel from people back home, whether from family or new friends and supporters, was generally well-received, much-appreciated and invariably encouraged. Letters and gifts made a world of difference to 'Tommy Atkins'. Someone cared, was concerned about their welfare, and was thinking of them. Tangible demonstrations of compassion and support did not, however, preclude individual letter writers from making far less altruistic comments about the war and the common enemy. The children of West Town Infants School in Peterborough, for example, wrote letters to soldiers, one of which read:

> I shall be glad when the Kaiser is dead.
> I hope you are killing a lot of Germans.
> I wish I could come to the front and be a drummer boy.[56]

The generosity of school communities extended beyond Britain to her allies. Nationally organised Flag Days for the French Red Cross and its Serbian equivalent were particularly well-supported. Collectively, school concerts, raffles, bazaars, waste paper collections and numerous other activities raised significant amounts of money – a contribution to humanitarian good causes, which did much to mitigate the worst effects of the war.

One group of British soldiers and civilians on the continent of Europe became a particular focus of support: prisoners of war (POW). National organisations such as the Prisoner of War National Relief Fund acted as a channel for monetary contributions from schools. St Nicholas Boys' School in King's Lynn sent £1. 1s. 0d. to the fund as early as April 1915.[57] Pupils at Bacup and Rawtenstall Grammar School in Lancashire sent food parcels and money to an individual POW via the Red Cross.[58] He was one of many POW who were 'adopted' by schools. Each Form Group at Hampton School near Richmond adopted their own POW in Germany 'and kept him in his comforts and sometimes necessaries'.[59] Letters of thanks reached the donor schools, as at North London Collegiate School, where Head Mistress Mrs Bryant read out the letters from the POW to the girls in their assemblies.[60] Lance Corporal Barnes, a POW adopted by Norwich High School, visited the school after his repatriation in 1918, much to the girls' pleasure.[61] One school had a particular reason for supporting a POW. Hector Munro of Hutcheson's Grammar School, the young Scot who had found it impossible to get back home when the war began, received a Christmas parcel from his old school containing the 'necessaries' that might make life in his prison camp more bearable.[62]

The newly established military hospitals, and the wounded men they treated, provided ample opportunity for schools to 'do their bit' for the war effort. The never-ending stream of casualties made enormous and expensive demands upon medical supplies and staffing at all levels of expertise. Some schools, for example North London Collegiate School and Haberdashers' Aske's Hatcham Girls' School, raised funds to sponsor hospital beds at home and abroad; the former contributed thirty shillings each week for two beds at the Great Northern Hospital;[63] the latter raised £100 for two 'Hatcham' beds in the Scottish Women's Hospitals in France and Serbia.[64] New hospitals needed new equipment, and the boys from Barrow Grammar School in Cumbria provided some of the non-specialist items such as bed rests and bed tables, which they had made as part of their 'Special Efforts' in their 'Handicraft School'.[65] Girls from private and secondary schools, in particular, were drawn to voluntary work for – and in some cases, in – military hospitals situated near to their schools. At Merchant Taylor's School for Girls in Crosby the pupils spent their Friday afternoon sessions making swabs and bandages for the hospitals, as well as shirts and primitive gas masks for the troops.[66] The Hatcham girls made shirts, bed jackets and surgical stockings.[67] Girls from Manchester High School (Plate 21) made similar items for their local hospital.[68] Some pupils and their teachers acted as much-needed ancillary staff. Members of the Godolphin School community in Salisbury worked in the kitchen of their local hospital at weekends.[69] The previously sheltered girls of Norwich High School found that the war provided them with very different challenges. In addition to their sewing parties, canteen work and agricultural efforts, which had 'succeeded in ousting more light-hearted school activities', some of the senior girls were set to work on the mangles in the laundry at the Norfolk and Norwich Hospital.[70]

The morale of hospitalised servicemen was also considered by British school-children. Once again, the collection and production of simple comforts for the wounded became a priority for many schools. The seventy-five jars of jam sent by the children of Alconbury School near Huntingdon to hospitals in London must presumably have involved teachers and parents as well.[71] The one hundredweight of jam produced by the boys of Bramshaw School in Hampshire – as early as October 1914 for the wounded soldiers being treated in Netley Hospital – would also have been a major logistical operation for a small village school.[72] The children of Ysgol Sychdyn in Wales had a particularly close relationship with the wounded men in the nearby Leeswood Hall Hospital. In October 1915, every child at the school brought in a single potato from home, collectively 'to be sent as a gift' to the hospital. Three months later, one of the recipients, Quartermaster B. Lloyd Parry, sent a letter of thanks on behalf of those convalescing at Leeswood Hall, for another welcome gift from the school: six chairs 'kindly sent for the use of the soldiers'.[73]

These creature comforts undoubtedly brought some cheer to men recovering from the physical wounds inflicted upon them in the trenches of the Western Front and other theatres of war. For many of these young servicemen, however, the trauma of experience on the battlefield, followed by weeks and months in hospital, brought additional psychological problems. Often far from home and devoid of non-military activities and associations, soldiers in recovery were prone to feelings of isolation, boredom and depression. In extreme cases, nothing but professional counselling and lengthy spells of treatment would suffice. For many men recovering in hospital, however, simple forms of personal contact and entertainment, especially those provided by young people full of cheer and enthusiasm, helped to alleviate some aspects of a prolonged convalescence. Visitors to the hospital wards were particularly welcomed by the wounded men, especially when the schoolchildren brought gifts which would occupy the patient for some time afterwards. Girls from Merchant Taylors' School, for example, regularly visited the wounded and donated books and magazines which had been collected in school.[74] Visits to schools by the walking wounded were also much appreciated by host and guests alike. Servicemen were often invited to join in a school's celebration of Empire Day.[75] Even more exciting and cheering were the school concerts and dramatic productions which were put on especially for hospital inmates. The School Choir at Colfe's Grammar School in London sang to wounded soldiers,[76] as did the pupils of Holy Trinity Girls' School in Trowbridge.[77] An entertainment and tea for the wounded was organised once or twice a term by the girls at Godolphin School in Salisbury which, the Headmistress explained, was part of their way of demonstrating that 'the war came first'. After all, they too had fathers and brothers away fighting.[78] An article in the Autumn 1915 edition of *School Magazine* produced by Norwich High School describes the scene at one such school event:

> The cheery blue-clad Tommies arrived early and were received by the Head Mistress, Miss Wise, who spoke a few words of welcome to each man. Those Tommies deserved (a) VC for their courage in facing something even worse than the Huns – a room full of schoolgirls, who for the most part hung together in a crowd at the back of the room. After the soldiers had had time to settle down, the entertainment began.

The girls sang and danced for the invited audience of men, dressed in their hospital 'blues', from the Norfolk and Norwich Hospital. The musical offering included a rendition by girls with blacked faces of *Ten Little Nigger Boys* (sic), much to the amusement, apparently, of all there. The proceedings concluded with the communal singing of the National Anthem.[79]

Support of various kinds was also extended to the families of wounded men, and to those of soldiers, sailors and airmen still away from home on active service. Boys from Hackney Downs School in London raised funds and delivered parcels of clothes to servicemen's wives and families in their borough.[80] North London Collegiate School supported The Sunshine League, an organisation which collected old clothes for the far-less privileged children of the city's East End whose families had been hit badly by the demands of the wartime economy.[81]

In ways such as these, in which schools deliberately contributed to the welfare of combatants and their wider communities, and joined with other local and national relief groups in doing so, the inter-connectivity of those involved in Britain's Great War was clearly demonstrated. 'Tommy' was undoubtedly at the sharp end – on the Western Front, in Gallipoli or Mesopotamia, to name but a few of the new killing fields – and his wartime experience was significantly different in scale and impact to that of the majority of his compatriots back in Blighty. The oft-quoted chasm of experience and understanding between those at the Front and those at home was nonetheless lessened and rendered less inflexible by the charitable activities of the nation's schoolchildren and their teachers.

The war, as we now know, would not be 'over by Christmas'. The war of 1914–19 was a different form of conflict, one which could no longer be fought, as previously, solely by the dispatch of an expeditionary force to foreign fields. This war, the unprecedented 'Great War', took new forms and created enormous challenges at home as well as abroad. It began to make demands which profoundly disturbed the rhythms and patterns of everyday life. A form of 'war collectivism' developed, in which 'patriotic, organised labour' was mobilised,[82] using existing institutions and, as became increasingly necessary, centralised directives and control. Civilians, as well as soldiers, now had 'campaigns' to be fought and objectives to be achieved. Individual institutions continued to make their own contributions, based upon local initiative and institutional imperatives but, increasingly, they were prompted into war-related action by external authorities.

For schools, a series of collection campaigns absorbed their patriotic energies. Some campaigns continued the practice of supporting the troops by providing them with foodstuffs of various kinds. The Children's Egg Week, a national campaign in February 1916, was taken up by many schools. There was a similar response to the National Egg Collection for sick and wounded soldiers which lasted for three years. In some schools, children wrote their names and details of their school on the eggs before sending them off to the collection centres. When Captain M.J.H. Drummond received a gift of eggs whilst convalescing in hospital, on each one was written the message 'Wishing you good luck from Violet Palmer, Girls Council School, Thetford'.[83] Charlie White, a pupil at Busbridge School in Godalming, received a letter of thanks in May 1917 from the recipient of his donated egg. Petty Officer Cox, writing from the Royal Naval Hospital in Hull, took the opportunity to tell Charlie of 'the part our ship has played in this great war which I hope will soon be brought to a glorious end'.[84]

Schoolchildren throughout Britain collected blackberries and other plant material from the hedgerows and fields. In September 1917, and again the following year, County Education Committees, under direction from the Food Controller at the Ministry of Food in London, issued instructions to the headteachers of schools under their control to organise the collection of blackberries growing wild in their locality. Schools were to close for one afternoon session so that the collection could be made by the pupils (Plate 22). The logbook of Stibbington School near Peterborough makes it clear that the blackberry campaign was instigated by central government:

1917
19 October: In accordance with the request of the Food Production Dept. the School closed for the afternoon for the children to gather blackberries for the army and navy jam... 50lbs. of blackberries have been forwarded to the Government Jam Factory.[85]

In many schools the foraging expeditions lasted over several weeks until early October. The result of all this extra-curricular activity, albeit in school time, could at times be very impressive. The pupils of Meeching Boys School in Newhaven may well have welcomed the opportunity to escape their formal lessons in the classroom; by the time their 1918 campaign ended on 3 October they had collected one ton of blackberries.[86] Whortleberries – or Bilberry, Vaccinium Myrtillus – were also collected for use in jams, pies and some herbal remedies. Other collection campaigns targeted acorns and chestnuts, used at first for animal fodder. Dandelion roots were collected – over 500lbs of them by the children of Evesham's Badsey Council School alone – for use in the manufacture of medicinal drugs.[87]

Collecting the fruits of the fields was a useful and relatively innocuous activity. Such seasonal campaigns were generally popular and very productive, and gave children and their teachers yet another opportunity for patriotic involvement and a break from lessons indoors. Most schools genuinely wanted to help the war effort, but there was also an expectation that they would do so. Local dignitaries and school managers were often 'quick to judge the patriotism of teachers and pupils through their war-related activities'. In Hertfordshire, for example, members of education committees such as H.F. Herbert pressed successfully for the local authority to make collections for approved war-related charities mandatory for all maintained elementary schools in the county.[88] National Efficiency in wartime demanded an organised, compliant and, above all, cheap labour force. School collection campaigns provided just that. Local patriotic groups and individual worthies galvanised the populations of schools in much the same way as they had promoted recruitment to the New Army battalions.

The line between indirect and direct involvement in the war effort, however, is a fine one. The original collection campaigns, with their clear emphasis on charitable works and the welfare of the wounded or men posted far from home, supported the military enterprise indirectly. Collecting horse chestnuts and acorns for use in the manufacture of deadly munitions and the development of chemical warfare, however, involved the schoolchildren of Britain far more directly in the industrialised processes which helped men to kill each other on the battlefield. During the Great War the British Army and the Royal Navy used 248 million high-explosive shells. On the Western Front, the heavy guns of the Royal Artillery were one of several key weapons which determined the nature of trench warfare and the great offensives which attempted to break the stalemate. In the wake of the German U-boat campaign, however, cordite – the key product used as a propellant for shells – was in short supply. The importation of raw materials such as maize from the United States of America (USA), which were necessary ingredients for the production of acetone (used as a solvent in cordite production), was severely jeopardised by enemy submarine action. In response to this crisis, David Lloyd George MP, Minister of Munitions and successor to H.H. Asquith as Prime Minister in December 1916, commissioned a series of experiments to find alternative sources of acetone. Dr Chaim Weizman of Manchester University (and later President of Israel, 1948–1950) discovered that horse chestnuts – the humble 'conker' of children's games in their backyards and school playgrounds – could be used to make acetone. A notice in *The Times* published on 26 July 1917 stated that:

Chestnut seeds, not the green husks, are required by the Ministry of Munitions. The nuts will replace cereals which have been necessary for the production of an article of great importance in the prosecution of the war.

At the request of the Minister of Munitions, the Board of Education issued *Circular 1009* on 15 August 1917, making very clear its expectation that:

School children could give most valuable assistance in collecting the chestnuts, and by so doing make a definite contribution to national efficiency. It is suggested, therefore, that the Governing Bodies, Managers and Teachers of Schools should organise the efforts of the children for the purpose.

Thousands of tons of horse chestnuts were collected by schoolchildren throughout the country in the last months of 1917. Schools in the Wiltshire town of Chippenham alone collected six tons of horse chestnuts, with the pupils of Ivy Lane School contributing a quarter of the total amount.[89] The conkers were then bagged up and sent to a top-secret processing plant in King's Lynn in Norfolk. For security reasons the general public, and the schools, were not told the exact reason for this huge national collection campaign, nor the precise location of the production facility. Headteachers, however, must have had some idea about the use that their horse chestnut harvest would be put to. Several, including Charles Allerton at Barnack School in Northamptonshire, noted in their logbooks that the collection was to be 'stored to await despatch to the Ministry of Propellant Supplies'.[90] In total, 3,000 tons of horse chestnuts reached the Synthetic Products Company premises, renamed 'His Majesty's Factory', in Alexandra Dock in King's Lynn. The factory had been producing small quantities of acetone distilled from potatoes since 1915. Production of acetone using horse chestnuts finally began April 1918, but ceased three months later. The experiment ultimately failed. Logistical problems had left many bags of horse chestnuts rotting at railway stations. The raw material was found to be a poor quality source of acetone. The U-boat menace had been countered by the convoy system, and trans-Atlantic trade was safer for the import of supplies of maize.

Pupils and teachers in British schools also became war financiers. The sheer scale and longevity of the Great War made enormous demands on the national economy. The new technologies of warfare were far more expensive to produce than the relatively small amounts of equipment demanded by previous campaigns. Collection campaigns had successfully raised funds for a multitude of good causes, but many of these activities had been of a local and sporadic nature. This war demanded new and far more systematic methods of tapping into patriotic enthusiasm and commitment in order to extract money from the people's pockets. Britain was not alone in establishing so-called 'War Savings' schemes; similar models designed to add to the country's war chest were introduced in France and the USA. Buying savings 'bonds', certificates or weekly stamps encouraged thrift and a sense of individual and communal contribution. Such war financing schemes were often aimed squarely at the school system; existing organisational frameworks, from central policy makers through to individual institutions, facilitated the processes needed for the collection and auditing of funds. Prompted by the National War Savings Committee, the Board of Education issued *Circular 949* in May 1916 encouraging LEAs to promote the campaign. It contained a pamphlet entitled *War Savings – How Everybody Can Help to Win the War*, which was distributed to maintained schools and taken home by pupils to discuss with their parents.[91] War Savings Clubs and Associations were quickly established in many schools, whilst others contributed to local associations. A War Savings Committee was formed at St Nicholas Boys' School in King's Lynn in July 1916, and on 7 September the school's 'War Savings Association No 1451/29' came into existence.[92] Throughout Britain individual schools raised thousands of pounds and issued hundreds of War Certificates. Wartime newspapers contained features and photographs of schoolchildren handing over their pennies to their teachers. The January 1918 edition of *The War Pictorial*, for example, reported on the 460 'child investors' at Gibbons School in Willesden who collectively contributed a weekly sum of £9–10. In Wales, the Cardiganshire War Savings Committee calculated in September 1917 that of the £233,000 collected in the county, £219,000 had been forwarded by School Associations. Elementary schools had made an average contribution of £2,100, and each child in such schools an average of £4.[93] By the end of the war over 14,000 British schools had taken part in the savings campaign.[94] In what became a competitive endeavour, one of the most successful War Savings Associations was that formed at Newbattle School in Midlothian (Plate 23). Many of the school's pupils came from mining families. Only one other school in the whole country – Eton College – collected more War Savings during the Great War.[95]

As the war dragged on into 1917 and 1918, new national fund-raising initiatives added impetus to the War Savings programme. Schoolchildren could now allocate their pennies to schemes which supported the funding of dedicated weapons of war. The Spring 1918 edition of Caldicott School's magazine illustrates the way in which some preparatory school pupils in Buckinghamshire, with the help of their teachers, helped to finance the war:

The school has responded splendidly to the call for War Bonds, and more especially for 'Aeroplane Week'. Many thanks are due to Miss Ingram for spending so much of her time in looking after the accounts. At the beginning of this term it dawned upon us that we had been getting very slack in the matter of War Savings and in letter-writing. On January 20th, we made up our minds that something should be done to raise us again to our old standard, when we saved £12 in one term. There is nothing like striking while the iron is hot, so we decided there and then to open a Tank Bank.

One of the boys made a small, but apparently very realistic, wooden tank, which was christened 'Charlie' in memory of the first Caldicott boy on the school Roll of Honour. The money box was designed to swallow sixpences, and within a few weeks contained over £27. The magazine article continued with an appeal to former pupils:

> When 'Charlie' is asked what he did in the Great War, we think that he will be able to say that he did his 'bit'! Any old boys who would like to save their sixpences by joining our Association are asked to communicate with the Secretary, who will receive their money gladly.[96]

In July 1918, in the Welsh valley town of Tredegar, the children of the Georgetown Schools marched in procession to deposit their War Savings Association collection of £178.19.06. A real tank, which the infants had christened 'Egbert', was there to greet them.[97]

Chapter 4

Lessons in War

Education is simply the soul of a society as it passes from one generation to another.

G.K. Chesterton

The girls of Christ's Hospital School in Hertford were particularly busy during the Great War. They knitted comforts, supported Queen Mary's Needlework Guild, assisted their local VAD hospital, joined the Girl Guides and collected horse chestnuts. Worthwhile activities such as these all required time and additional resources, but schools throughout the country engaged in similar wartime campaigns. In the elementary schools the collection campaigns similarly absorbed the efforts of pupils and teachers alike, and strictly 'educational' work suffered in some institutions as a result.[1] In the secondary and especially the public schools, the important but increasing demands of the OTC meant that there was less time available for the formal subject-based curriculum. It appeared to many observers at the time that the Great War had made a huge impact on each and every one of the nation's schools.[2]

Despite the fact that the British system of schooling was centrally directed and, in the case of maintained schools, locally administered, individual institutions and their leaders ultimately determined a school's response to any given initiative – even in wartime. Consequently, the range of direct involvement by schools in war-related activities was extremely wide. At one end of the spectrum, the war effort was, or at least perceived to be by those involved, all-consuming. The Great War 'completely dominated' the life of Bolton School,[3] for example. The magazines of many secondary schools referred frequently to the varied and unstinting contributions of their pupils and alumni. Elementary school logbooks generally make numerous references to key dates and events which impinged directly upon the institution itself. At the other extreme, however, there were schools, such as the Calton Road Schools in Gloucester, where there was not a single mention of the war in the logbook entries made between 1914 and 1919.[4]

Many schools modified their curriculum activities to suit wartime conditions and demands. The pre-war curriculum, determined primarily by tradition in the fee-paying sector and by Board of Education Regulations in publically-maintained schools, was adapted rather than supplanted. The wartime curriculum was remarkably similar to that operating in schools before 1914. In most schools the traditional subjects remained. There were, however, some early casualties of war. Every effort was made to keep the curriculum intact at Bedford Girls' Modern School but the study of German was considered to be unpatriotic and consequently discontinued.[5] City of London School also dropped German from the Classical Sixth's curriculum and, in common with Manchester High School for Girls and Northampton Grammar School amongst others,[6] began teaching Russian classes in 1916. This gesture of support for one of Britain's key allies was clearly provisional; the subject was discontinued in 1918 'probably as a gesture of disapproval at the Russian Revolution'.[7] The teaching of science in some schools also suffered, not through curriculum decisions but because of difficulties with supplies of materials and equipment necessary for laboratory experiments. In response to demands for medical supplies, of which there was an acute shortage as battlefield casualties mounted, the Herbert Strutt School in Belper donated large stocks of costly chemicals to the detriment of the teaching of science. Mr Tunnicliffe, headmaster and chemistry teacher, extolled the virtues of the British-made laboratory glassware purchased as a substitute for the German equipment manufactured in Jena which was no longer available. Unfortunately, however, he and the Senior Science Class soon managed to break all the patently substandard retorts.[8] Colfe's Grammar School also abandoned Practical Chemistry because of difficulty in obtaining chemicals in wartime.[9]

In other subjects, discussion of the latest war news, initiated by both pupils and teachers, inevitably impinged upon 'normal' lessons. This war, a war which involved every member of the community, their families, friends and neighbours, normalised such discourse in ways which would have been deemed inappropriate in most schools in the pre-war period. The events of 1914, and the personal trauma and dislocation which followed, were far too important to be put on one side for consideration later. Educationists in the twenty-first century extoll the virtues of making learning relevant to the lives of learners. For the children, and teachers, of 1914 to 1919 the war mattered; it affected them all in one way or another; it pervaded school classrooms, corridors, boarding houses, playing fields and the staff common room.

In some subjects, of course, discussion of war-related events was more likely to be considered a legitimate and even valuable use of teaching and learning time. History and geography lessons, in particular, became even more overt vehicles for the promotion of patriotic values and discussion of current events. Subject content and classroom activities frequently contained topical exemplar material and reflected the new realities of war. Miss Daley's history lessons at Aberystwyth County School, for example, often began with the latest news from the Front as reported by, or about, Old Boys of the school. When former pupil Ned Harries was awarded the Military Cross, Miss Daley reported the news to her class with 'pride in her eyes'.[10] St Mary's Boys' School in Hitchin revised its geography syllabus. Countries and regions previously ignored, but where British and allied forces were fighting during the war – Egypt, the Persian Gulf, the Balkan States and German West Africa – were now officially, and with the sanction of the local HMI, studied in schools.[11]

Formal lessons were supplemented by other activities which did much to enhance the wartime atmosphere. Music lessons and concerts – and group singing in classrooms or social time generally – reflected the nation's patriotic and jingoistic spirit. Many songs, including this example for children in elementary schools, contained the tried and tested formula of references to God, King and Country:

> There's a land, a dear land,
> Where the rights of the free
> Are as firm as the earth
> And as wide as the sea.
> Where the primroses bloom
> And the nightingales sing
> And an honest man
> Is as good as the King.
> Home of brave men and the girls they adore,
> Westland, bestland, my land, thy land,
> England wave-guarded and green to the shore,
> God bless our Empire and King evermore.[12]

Songs sung by pupils in the secondary schools included parodies of well-known rhymes, brought right up to date by topical references to new features of the war. At the 1917 Christmas Concert at King Edward VII Grammar School, Melton Mowbray, held in aid of King George's Fund for Sailors, Form 2b recited *Ten Little Zeppelins*. The Choir Master on this occasion was none other than Malcolm Sargent, at that time a teacher at the school.[13] The Sixth Form of George Green's School in Poplar borrowed a classic from the British soldiers' repertoire – *Tipperary* – for their social event.[14] On occasions, however, the mood could be far more sombre. The war, after all, was a serious business. Marjorie Llewellyn, a schoolgirl in wartime Sheffield, later recalled:

We had evening assembly every night and special prayers were said for the soldiers. We always sang the last verse of 'Eternal Father' and then the hymn 'Holy Father in Thy Mercy', and then said the prayer 'Lighten our Darkness'. This went on every night all through the war.[15]

In the pre-war period many classroom walls were adorned with maps and biblical images. In wartime more maps and charts appeared. Many were produced by newspapers such as *The Daily Telegraph*. These new visual aids were used explicitly by teachers to further their pupils' understanding of the conflict as it unfolded. Marjorie Llewellyn remembered that in her school:

> Schooldays were very different once the war had started. We had great maps in each of the classrooms and every day we used flags to mark the progress of the war on both fronts – in Gallipoli and then on the Somme when that started. There was a keen interest taken in this because we could see how it was progressing.[16]

Charting the great advances by 'our boys', in reality recorded on maps rather than on the ground and followed inevitably by reports of limited gains and mounting numbers of casualties, was not unique to British classrooms. Pupils in Germany similarly followed newspaper reports of their 'victorious' armies – and sang patriotic songs and observed famous victories – with intense interest.[17] Later in the war, the History Room at Colfe's Grammar School exhibited a far more realistic approach to the cost of the war by displaying a chart showing the allied tonnage sunk by enemy submarines.[18]

At key points in the school calendar, whole school sessions might be given over to similar patriotic themes and activities. Empire Day, Trafalgar Day, St George's Day and, in Wales, St David's Day were not new; indeed, they had been key elements in the wider curriculum and education of children in the years before 1914. In wartime, however, these anniversarial events assumed new meaning and significance. In some schools the format of Empire Day remained essentially unchanged. At Badsey Council School in Evesham, for example, the May 1916 celebrations retained the usual formula: the classes marched, saluted the Union Jack, and sang patriotic songs including the National Anthem.[19] The children at Highgate Primary School, however, added to the occasion by wearing the badges of their fathers' regiments. One of the children, whose father was a post-master and hence in a non-military reserved occupation, decided that 'I must have a badge as well as the others and, not to be left out, got one from a chemist's shop on Grand Parade'.[20] In Wales, the 1916 Empire Day celebrations at Northop National School also included an address and subsequent essay writing assignment on the theme of 'Empire', followed by a collection for the Overseas Club.

St David's Day was observed in many Welsh schools. On 1 March 1915 Northop School celebrated the occasion in what a local newspaper report – a copy of which was inserted in the school logbook – described as a very patriotic spirit. The vicar Rev. T.H. Vaughan gave an address, there were special lessons on patriotism given by Headmaster J.R. Richardson and, most importantly, the names on the Roll of Honour were read out to the assembled children. The newspaper went on to report that:

Patriotic songs were heartily sung and cheers for king and country were vociferously given. A half holiday was granted to mark the day. Before dispersing each child was presented with an orange by Miss Vaughan. A collection of photographs of all the old boys who are with the colours is being made for display on school walls.[21]

Secondary schools in the principality also celebrated the day. Headmaster E.P. Evans at Caernarvon County School paid tribute to past and present national heroes: Owain Glyndwr, and the Welsh regiments serving in France.[22]

The Great War provided additional opportunities for nationalistic celebration. Victories by British and Dominion forces, especially during a war that often brought long lists of casualties but little cheer, were always worthy of note and were occasions marked by many schools. The logbook entry of 11 December 1917 for Amberley Parochial School in Gloucestershire, for example, states: 'Upon the capture of Jerusalem the Union Jack was hoisted and saluted by the children at 9.30 a.m.'.[23] Now that Britain was at war, new Allies were added to the list of countries studied in schools. 'Flag Days' for each allied nation often included lessons on that particularly country's geography, history and culture. In numerous school concerts, dramatic productions and Prize Distributions, the national anthems of the Allies were sung. On 11 December 1915, those assembled in the hall at Caernarvon County School were treated to a rendition of the Belgian national anthem by M. Borrey, a Belgian refugee invited especially to the school's 'social evening'. His 'very touching performance' was followed by a response from a school group, which involved singing *La Marseillaise* and the Russian Tsarist national anthem, *God the All-Terrible*.[24]

Other opportunities for encouraging patriotic sentiments, values and actions included assemblies and lectures given by invited speakers. Many of these talks were no more than blatant attempts to spread official propaganda and to secure further recruits to the armed services in the future.[25] The lectures usually concentrated upon distinctly military themes and were generally aimed at male audiences. In February 1916 a logbook entry for Pound Lane School in Epsom noted that Lieutenant Commander H. Chamberlain gave a lecture on 'The War', but 'to the boys only'.[26] The importance of the Royal Navy was another regular theme for visiting speakers and, for some school communities, an unquestionably important one. The boys of St Nicholas School in King's Lynn came from the town's traditional fishing and seafaring community known as the North End. Many of the boys' fathers had joined the Royal Naval Volunteer Reserve (RNVR) and saw wartime action at sea. Indeed, several fathers – and former pupils of the school – had been killed in action on 22 September 1914 when HMS *Hogue*, HMS *Cressy* and HMS *Aboukir* were torpedoed and sunk by German submarine U-9 in the North Sea. Deeply saddened by this tragedy but evidently undaunted, Alfred

Whitehouse, the school's headteacher, continued to promote a career at sea for his boys, as these two school logbook entries clearly indicate:

1915
14 January: Short lecture by permission of LEA on Watts Naval School by Mr Berry.

1917
30 October: Suitable lesson on 'Our Navy' given on Monday.

Schools with no obvious naval connections or tradition also received copies of *Our Sure Shield the Navy* in 1916, 'to be used in connection with the teaching of the use of sea power and Britain'.[27] In the wake of the Battle of Jutland in 1916 the County Council in Hertfordshire recommended to the managers of maintained elementary schools that naval history, and especially 'the use of British Sea Power', be regarded as 'an essential branch' of education. The topic was duly included in new editions of class readers used in the authority's schools.[28]

The machinery of government gave direction and guidance to local initiative. In January 1915 the children of the Georgetown Schools in Tredegar each received a book entitled *What Shall We Do For Britain?*[29] To mark St David's Day in 1916 the Welsh Department of the Board of Education published a booklet for schools, which contained suggestions for the teaching of patriotism.[30] The British government promoted works of propaganda to children of school age from the earliest months of the war. The War Propaganda Bureau under Charles Masterman MP commissioned popular authors including John Buchan – author of *The Thirty-Nine Steps* and *Greenmantle*, and appointed Director of the Department of Information in January 1917 – to convey overtly nationalistic messages to a young, impressionable and captive audience in the nation's schools. In *Why Britain Went to War: To the Boys and Girls of the British Empire*, Sir James Yoxall, Member of Parliament and a prominent member of the National Union of Teachers, wrote:

The Kaiser has been a bully in the European playground, and every boy (sic) knows well that there is no peace for others until a bully is tackled and knocked out.

In a later edition, Sir James added, in language which would have struck a chord with all good sports and people of integrity:

In all this war there is nothing for us to be ashamed of: We fight for honour. You know what honour is among schoolboys – straight dealing, truth speaking. And 'playing the game'. Well, we are standing up for honour among nations, while Germany is playing the sneak and bully in the big European school. Germany must be taught to 'play cricket', to play fair, to honour 'a scrap of paper'. A boy who behaved as Germany has done would be 'sent to Coventry' by all the School.[31]

The school classroom thus continued to be one of the key sites of conditioning and indoctrination. Patriotic messages and imperatives were conveyed by institutional changes to both the breadth and the content of the formal school curriculum. Central directives were designed to mobilise school communities. As in the example above by James Yoxall, the messages to Britain's children were simple, direct and unequivocal; this was not the time, the authorities argued, for a philosophical or moral debate concerning the validity of the present conflict. The language employed was familiar in both style and content, and was designed to resonate with an audience well versed in nationalistic literature and patriotic sentiment. For children, the Great War was reduced to a simple struggle in the formerly peaceful playground of Europe; between truth and deceit; between 'our honour' and the enemy's 'bad form'. War had once more become an extension of sport by any other – but far more deadly – means. The various forms of the 'game', which had once graced the playing fields of Eton and numerous other schools, was now played in the trenches of Flanders.

But what of the real thing – school sport played according to the established rules back in Britain? The impact of war on this important aspect of school life was extremely variable. With so many schoolmasters on active service, some schools, for example Deacon's School in Peterborough,[32] abandoned sports fixtures altogether for the duration of the war. Colfe's Grammar School in London experienced similar difficulties and, in the absence of competent coaches, the Football XI played no games against external opposition between 1915 and 1919.[33] The traditional matches against the Old Boys, for many schools one of the highlights of the sporting calendar, were early casualties of a war which had taken such enormous numbers of men out of the country. Games were much-reduced in Caernarvon County School in Wales for a very different reason: 'there was a strong feeling throughout the school that anything remotely 'showy' was out of tune with the spirit of the times'.[34] In direct contrast to those who argued that, whatever the logistical difficulties, this was no time to be playing games,[35] pupils in some schools openly criticised the cessation of sporting activity. In 1917 the boys at Handsworth Grammar School in Birmingham used the pages of their school magazine to make their feelings on the matter very clear to the school authorities:

The summer term is generally the most interesting and most crowded portion of the school year. On this occasion, however, we have very little to chronicle, mainly owing to the curtailment of the Inter-School Cricket programme and the absence of the customary House ties competition. As there has been much feeling regarding the practical abandonment of the school Cricket fixtures, we should like to enquire why the exigencies of outside affairs should affect the cultivation of sport in the school.[36]

Inter-school matches were far more difficult to arrange in wartime. In addition to staffing shortages there were other limiting factors. For away matches, these included increased rail fares and transport restrictions, especially after the government requested that all non-essential journeys be kept to a minimum.[37] Nevertheless, some schools managed to provide pupils with a decent fixture list. Emanuel School in London played twenty-three cricket matches and twelve rugby fixtures against other public schools in 1915 alone, the year in which they became Public School Sports Champions.[38] Games flourished at Hampton School in London, winners in 1916 of the Bowles Cup in the Middlesex secondary schools' athletics championships.[39] Some schools, for example Kent College in Canterbury and Northampton Grammar School,[40] played against services teams stationed nearby, continuing a pre-war tradition which saw school teams, usually comprising masters as well as boys, playing fixtures against local village teams and other adult clubs. Geoffrey Barber reported in a letter from his boarding school in Cambridge to his parents stationed in India how the Leys School 1st XI Hockey team played a series of matches against university undergraduates at Caius College and a team from a nearby 'military training college'. The letter was dated 26 January 1919.[41] The Armistice had been signed ten weeks earlier, but with so many men awaiting demobilisation from the armed forces the situation was still far from returning to normal, whatever that might mean after four years of conflict. Hurstpierpoint College kept their school cricket alive during the war by playing fixtures against 16th Royal Fusiliers, the 3rd Battalion Sussex Regiment and the RAMC.[42] In the absence of most professional sports during the war, such games could be relatively well attended and greatly appreciated by spectators. Other schools responded by making do with inter-house matches, in some cases inviting convalescing soldiers from nearby military hospitals to add to the small groups of supporters from the school community.[43] Pupils in some elementary schools also resumed their sporting activity after earlier stoppages. Alfred Whitehouse at St Nicholas Boys' School in King's Lynn was clearly delighted to be able to record in his logbook entry for 5 April 1917 that 'We now hold all Sports shields, 2 football, 1 for swimming and 1 for cricket – a record!'[44]

In some secondary schools new sporting activities were adopted during the war years. In 1917 the boys at City of London School took up boxing, a sport particularly suited to the demands of the age.[45] For many girls, for example those attending Merchant Taylors' School for Girls in Crosby, gymnastics became the new and preferred choice of physical activity.[46] In the elementary school sector, however, there was a resurgence of military drill at the expense of organised games and gymnastic exercises. Under pressure from the War Office, there was to be greater emphasis placed on the health of future soldiers and the mothers who would bear them. Lily Hewitt's end-of-term Report for the Spring Term 1915 at Busbridge School in Godalming records her performance in Drill – scored 9/10 and listed alongside all the usual subjects of the elementary school curriculum - but there is no reference at all to other forms of sport or physical exercise.[47]

As in the years before 1914 the formal subject-based curriculum and traditional sporting activities were only part of the education experienced by children, both in and out of school. During the Great War the wider curriculum, too, reflected the concerns of a nation pre-occupied with all things military. Previous wars had been distant, far-away events. They had been depicted but rarely experienced. Admittedly, men in military uniform were a relatively common feature, especially in garrison towns and naval ports or where members of the Volunteers and local Militia were particularly active. In 1914, however, the war had come to Britain, and even to Britain's schools. What excitement there was – for many children and their teachers – just outside the classroom window, or in the local streets, parks and fields!

Many buildings, including those schools which had been requisitioned, were no longer the familiar places they had once been. They had become fascinating hives of military activity. 'Our school' was now housing 'Our Lads'. Other schools, particularly in urban areas, found themselves with new neighbours, as one group of teachers and pupils discovered when an Observation Balloon Station was sited next to the Latymer School on the Huxley Estate in North London.[48] In the first months of the war, the general enthusiasm, which was generated by the raising and training of the Pals Battalions and Kitchener's New Armies, was shared by many school communities. The boys at their desks at King Edward VII School in Sheffield, for example, could clearly hear the marching songs of the 12th (City of Sheffield) Battalion York and Lancaster Regiment as they travelled from their training camp into the city. Many of these 'Sheffield Pals' were Old Edwardians – former pupils of a school which had been founded only a decade earlier.[49] Some teachers welcomed the opportunities for learning which the mass mobilisation of men and other related military activities gave to the children in their classes. On the morning of 23 February 1915 the children of St Gregory's School in Chorley were dismissed early 'on account of the Chorley Pals Battalion leaving the town for Caernarvon'.[50] Troop movements of any kind, not simply those containing men with obvious ties to the locality, were considered by some teachers to be of sufficient interest and excitement to warrant taking the pupils out of the classroom. When the Reserve Battalion of the Suffolk Regiment struck camp near the village of Barnack in Northamptonshire on 4 March 1915, Charles Allerton released all of the children in the village school so that they could witness the troops' departure.[51]

Visits to the locality by members of the royal family,[52] reviews of troops by high-ranking military officials,[53] 'Tank Days',[54] and military funerals,[55] were all valid reasons for organised school outings.

The arrival of new weapons of war – authorised or otherwise – often resulted in an exodus from school. Some such absences were officially sanctioned and organised activities. The author Ronald Blythe describes how the children in Standards II and VII at the village school in Akenfield in Suffolk were marched out to inspect a Zeppelin bomb which had fallen in a neighbouring field 'as an object lesson in science and patriotism'.[56] Teachers were firmly in charge on such occasions but, in an age when 'risk assessments' were not mandatory, some encounters with the military could have unintended consequences. There was enormous excitement, for example, when, after a lunchtime visit by a pilot in the Royal Flying Corps (RFC), the 200 boys at King Edward VII Grammar School in Melton Mowbray were rewarded with an impromptu aerial display. The pilot showed his gratitude to the school for the lunch which had been laid on for him by doing a series of risky stunts – much to the delight of the pupils, but to the dismay of the headteacher.[57] Other absences were incidents of impromptu truancy by individuals and, occasionally, large groups of pupils. The real scale of deliberate absence from school to watch the soldiers marching by, or to see new-fangled aeroplanes unexpectedly stranded on the local common after forced landings,[58] will never be known, hidden as so much of it undoubtedly was by the proffering of 'legitimate' excuses on a child's return to school. Once again, however, some school logbooks do refer directly to this problem. Many boys absented themselves from Hornby School in Lancashire on the afternoon of 20 September 1914 after the 'West Yorkshire Artillery went through the village at noon'.[59] Similarly, when bombs from a Zeppelin raid on the east coast of England on 19 January 1915 fell on the port of King's Lynn, Alfred Whitehouse noted in the St Nicholas Boys' School logbook the high level of unauthorised absence the following day. Over forty boys were absent, a few kept at home by parents fearful of further bombings, but the majority were 'absent visiting the places where bombs had fallen'.[60] War, by its very nature, rarely produces positive outcomes, even for those who emerge victorious. Gains are often illusory, short-term or massively detrimental to the other parties involved. Despite the huge human and economic cost of the Great War, however, it was a conflict which generated not just terror and fear, but fascination and critical analysis in equal measure. For schoolchildren – and adults – the war brought many additional opportunities for learning, intellectual enquiry and personal development, even if some war-related activities were frowned upon and regarded by teachers and others as distractions from the 'real' business of schooling. The war itself was very real, and it inevitably prompted reflection and further discussion.

The men, women and children of 1914–18 were not universally blinded by jingoism, nor were they passive recipients of 'The Old Lie'. School magazines tapped into the desire to find out more about the war. This was certainly the case at George Dixon Schools in Birmingham, where the Winter 1914 edition of the school magazine provided a detailed analysis of recent events under the heading 'The Pan-Germanic Plan'.[61] School Debating Societies argued about the causes of the war and its subsequent conduct and development. The boys at Westminster public school debated the personal responsibility of Kaiser Wilhelm II for the events of 1914,[62] whilst those at Bancroft's School in Essex considered 'German Culture' more generally.[63] Such debates were obvious opportunities for the propagation of the 'official' line and, at worst, blatant prejudice and nationalism. Some of the motions debated, however, suggest a far more considered response by senior pupils; the very same young men who would themselves be making important and, in many cases, life-changing decisions in the not too distant future. The emotive – and generally divisive – issues of enlistment and conscription were especially relevant to this particular generation of schoolboys. Debates at the Crypt School, a private school in Gloucester, reflected the concerns of the day. On 2 November 1915 the boys debated whether 'Compulsory military service should be introduced with the least possible delay'. The motion was defeated, but by the narrowest of margins: twelve votes 'For', thirteen votes 'Against'. The motion a year later in November 1916 was related to the previous one, but on this occasion reflects the realities of a war in which men were now forced – by the introduction of conscription in the Military Service Act of the same year – into making momentous decisions. The Crypt boys voted by twenty-five to five against the motion that 'The genuine Conscientious Objector is non-existent'. There are no verbatim reports of this particular debate, but the outcome suggests that this group of schoolboys, and probably many others in schools elsewhere,[64] were well aware of the vagaries and nuances of individual circumstance and personal response in wartime.[65] The implications for the future were also considered, this time by the Debating Society at Hurstpierpoint College. The motion at the meeting in December 1916 that 'England will be ripe for revolution after the war' was won by thirteen votes to four.[66]

The technology of modern warfare fascinated many school pupils. The topics discussed by the Scientific Society at Harrow County School for Boys included 'Submarines', 'Torpedoes', 'Modern Field Artillery' and 'Explosives'. Emmanuel School in London had hoped to install wireless telegraph equipment in 1914, but wartime restrictions prevented private installations. Undeterred, in 1915 the school formed a Wireless Society 'on theoretical and experimental lines pending the return of peacetime conditions'.[67] Some of the boys 'with scientific leanings' at Barrow Grammar School, however, strayed beyond academic discussion and decided to act upon their burgeoning interests. They were particularly 'fascinated by reports of gas on the Western Front', so much so that they began their own experiments with bromine and chlorine – presumably unsupervised – 'in the darker recesses of the labs'. There is no reference to any consequent lists of casualties in the official school history.[68]

The popular press produced thousands of war-related articles during the war and many of them found their way into schools. Headmaster Ernest Young of Harrow County took out a school subscription to the *Illustrated London News*, and also encouraged the younger boys to keep a scrapbook of the war.[69] Some publications were purchased and read by teachers before being passed on to their pupils. Masters at Bancroft's School read and then circulated *Land and Water*, a weekly magazine covering wartime developments, which was edited by Hillaire Belloc. The school's boarders took copies of national daily newspapers such as *The Daily Telegraph* and *The Daily Mirror*.[70] Popular culture, particularly in print form, continued to socialise children as it had done before 1914. In wartime, however, it was also used as a device to mobilise young people. The Great War became 'the great *imaginative* event … a force of radical change in society and its consciousness'.[71] Children read their magazines at home and at school. They discussed the contents in the street, in the school playground and in their boarding-school dormitories. They imagined and considered the part that they too would be called upon to play in the greatest of all conflicts. Their view of the world – a world most definitely at war – was shaped and conditioned by the contents of such publications. Magazines for boys were overtly militaristic. Stories in wartime editions of *The Magnet* included:

'The Hun Hunters' (1915)
'The Greyfriars Flying Corps' (1917)
'A Gentleman Ranker!' (1917)
'A Soldier's Son!' (1918)
'The Man from the Somme!' (1918)

The Boy's Own paper contained numerous similar articles penned by the prolific author Frank Ellis, including:

'The Boys who are Going to Win' (1914)
'To the "Old Boys" at the War' (1915)
'The Old School's Roll of Honour' (1915)
'England's Boys' (1915)
'I Serve!' (1916)

The titles of these articles contain terms and attitudes which the schoolboys of Britain would recognise, be familiar with, and continue to internalise. Exclamation marks conveyed imperatives for action. Role models guided the way. Novels such as those by John Buchan 'made the war both a moral melodrama and a history lesson'. The exotic locations, German spies and dashing heroes depicted in *The Thirty-Nine Steps* (1915) and *Greenmantle* (1916) combined to portray an exciting, if somewhat sanitised, conflict of ideas and culture. Rarely did the real face of war make an appearance in these ripping yarns. This is in stark contrast to much of the literature aimed at children in France, where a whole genre developed around the notion of *l'enfant heroique*. The language used in comparable French publications was often ferocious, preaching hatred towards the Germans and, in some cases, even advocating the martyrdom of child warriors fighting for *La Patrie*.[72]

The Great War provided the children in British schools with a new set of heroes and role models. Before 1914, hierarchical systems and organised team games had produced a whole panoply of senior pupils, prefects and team captains to admire and to emulate. The new heroes were forged in the heat of battle or sacrificed themselves in the service of others. Many were from the institution itself – former pupils of the school. News of awards for bravery to Old Boys, recorded in the *London Gazette* and graphically detailed and illustrated in newspapers such as *The Sphere* and *The Illustrated War News*, enhanced the noble histories, chivalric reputations and public standing of the elite public schools. The award of a Victoria Cross (VC), Distinguished Service Order (DSO) or Military Cross (MC) was a badge of honour for both the recipient and his Alma Mater. The new school heroes exemplified the values which such schools propounded and held dear. Many were from strong schools with strong cultures which had been shaped by traditions of service and the ritualised recognition of achievement over generations.[73] Honours and awards to men – and women – who had held posts of responsibility in their schooldays were particularly worthy of note; they were the characteristic products of the school, and role models both past and present. They reinforced the decisions made by teachers whose job it was to recognise and nurture 'brilliance' in all its manifestations. Dead heroes, those who had made the ultimate sacrifice, were the most potent symbols of all, typifying their school's contribution to the greater glory of the nation. Before the war had ended – and even more so afterwards – their contributions were enshrined in a cult of remembrance.

Throughout Britain, schools on the lower rungs of the hierarchy of schooling also marked the heroism of former pupils. For those schools founded in the wake of the 1902 Education Act, the war helped to establish traditions. The number of military awards won by former pupils combined with the statistics relating to those gaining promotions and especially commissions to mark a new school's ascendancy on the educational and social ladder. Elementary schools, too, celebrated wartime honours and awards. These schools provided the great majority of the millions of men who served in the British forces during the Great War. Most of the products of this form of schooling became privates in the army, able seamen in the Royal Navy and mechanics in the Royal Flying Corps. Many subsequently gained promotion to NCO. Relatively few gained commissions. Their awards, most commonly the Military Medal (MM), Distinguished Conduct Medal (DSM) or Meritorious Service Medal (MSM), reflected their place in the military as well as social hierarchy. Their schools marked the occasion of an award to a former pupil by an entry in the school logbook, or by declaring a half day holiday for the pupils, as happened several times, for example, at St Mark's School in Lambeth.[74]

School magazines routinely carried details of honours awarded to alumni serving with the colours. It was the annual Prize Day, however, that had traditionally provided the most high-profile opportunity to demonstrate the school's credentials to a wider public. The Head Master's or Head Mistress's Report was usually the highlight of an event which was sufficiently important to warrant coverage by the local newspaper. On such occasions the whole school community came together to 'praise famous men': the institution's heroes, both male and female, old and new. Prize Days were often held towards the end of the autumn term and the Report traditionally reflected upon the previous academic year. By the start of the new school year in September 1914, memories of the scholastic and sporting achievements of the previous year had been overshadowed by a series of momentous events which had challenged past certainties and disrupted normal routines. Some important decisions had to be made by the school authorities. Whilst many headteachers and governors were keen to use the annual Prize Day to parade their Roll of Honour, others questioned the wisdom of holding a celebratory event. The country was at war. The casualty lists were far longer than anyone had expected. Inevitably, individual institutions came to different conclusions regarding the advisability and viability of continuing with the most important celebratory event in the school calendar. Newport High School for Boys abandoned their annual Prize Distribution for the duration of the war.[75] The Prize Giving in December 1914 at West Norfolk and King's Lynn High School for Girls was an uncharacteristically low-key affair.[76] In July 1915 prizes at Meeching Boys' School in Newhaven were distributed directly to individual prizewinners without due ceremony - on the order of the managers as there was a war on![77] The Herbert Strutt School in Belper introduced an alternative format, foregoing the usual public event and holding instead a smaller ceremony in the school hall. In common with many other schools throughout the country, they also changed the nature of the prize, awarding certificates rather than the more traditional – and more costly – prizes of books. The Prize Certificates at Herbert Strutt School bore the inscription:

The Governors of the School, on the suggestion of the pupils and staff, have decided to abandon the Presentation of Prizes for the year 1914–15, owing to the urgent need for public and private economy at this crisis in the history of our beloved country.

In the interests of economy, this particular school decided to dispense with even the humble Prize Certificate in 1916.[78] Many schools, however, continued to award certificates (Plate 25) instead of prizes. Doris Phippen, a pupil in Form Commercial at Highbury Fields School in London, received a certificate for the academic year 1917–18, stating that she had 'reached a standard which in ordinary years would have earned her a prize', but then confirmed that 'No prizes are being given this year owing to the war'.[79] Particularly enterprising and considerate were the schools which combined the imperatives of wartime economy and service to others. The pupils at Helston Grammar School in Cornwall donated the value of their book prizes to The Belgian Relief Fund.[80] St John's School in Lemsford bought Christmas Parcels in 1915 for 'our boys at the front' instead of spending on prizes,[81] whilst Appleby Grammar School in Cumbria used the money set aside for prizes to support Netley Hospital.[82] Service to school met service to the nation when War Savings Certificates were awarded instead of books at the Prize Day at City of London School.[83]

Where schools continued to hold Prize Days, the purpose of the ceremony often underwent a subtle change. 'Prize Day' became 'Speech Day'. Even where there was no change of name, the focus of the event shifted from past to present. The great day was still an opportunity to award the customary 'glittering prizes' and to recognise individual academic brilliance or sporting achievement amongst the current cohort of pupils. This tended to be overshadowed, however, by the need for the Headteacher's Report to chronicle the school's contribution to the war effort, assert its willingness to serve and make sacrifices if necessary, and to describe the impact the war was having on the institution. The highlight of the evening was the naming and praising of new heroes. Miss Sara Burstall, the Head Mistress of Manchester High School for Girls referred in her 1917 Report to the war honours awarded to Winifred Bedson and Nora Rogers.[84] Other schools for girls proclaimed the wartime affiliations of former pupils to the Red Cross, the First Aid Nursing Yeomanry, Women's Army Auxiliary Corps and Voluntary Aid Detachments.

Institutional heroes were important, but there were many other local and national heroes for school communities to admire; men and women, boys and girls. Their wartime service, valour or ultimate sacrifice established them as powerful role models. Schools were often very keen to adopt them and to be associated with the ideals and values they represented, even if they were not direct alumni. Winners of the Victoria Cross (VC) – the highest award 'For Valour' – were often paraded and feted by local communities. Visits to schools from these now-famous uniformed servicemen, proudly displaying their medals, were always well received by pupils and teachers alike. Some, like Sergeant Major Daniels of the 2nd Battalion the Rifle Brigade, were from the same town or county but often had no direct links with the schools they visited. These local, as well as national heroes, were honoured nevertheless. Harry Daniels, who was born in Wymondham in Norfolk, was awarded the Victoria Cross for his actions at Neuve Chapelle in

March 1915. His celebratory and triumphant tour of Norwich, wearing his medal and carrying a framed copy of the award citation, included visits to schools. Upholland Village School in Wigan received a similar visit from Lance Corporal Edward Stanley Lee of 2nd Battalion Manchester Regiment, shortly after he was awarded the Distinguished Conduct Medal (DCM) for 'Conspicuous gallantry and devotion to duty' in September 1917. Here, in their very own classroom, the children of Upholland heard of daring deeds by a young man who had been one of their neighbours prior to his enlistment in January 1915. The soldier may well have told them how he and his Lewis Gun team were buried by an exploding shell; how he helped to dig out and attend to the wounded and, later, extinguished a heap of burning ammunition. For a brief moment, the children in this school and many others, came face to face with a real war hero, the closest that many of them would get to the realities of the war in the trenches.[85]

A few wartime heroes were shared with the nation. After the execution of Nurse Edith Cavell, shot by the Germans in October 1915 for harbouring Belgian refugees, one of the houses at George Green's School in Poplar was renamed in her honour.[86] Similarly, the boys of Bristol Grammar School organised a collection to fund a hospital cot in her memory.[87] When Lord Kitchener was lost at sea by enemy action in 1916, there was a national outpouring of grief for the hero who had raised Britain's New Armies. Lincoln Grammar School proudly reported in the *Lincolnian* that a former pupil, Able Seaman Cecil George, had gone down with Kitchener and HMS *Hampshire* in the waters off Orkney.[88] The major naval engagement of the war, the Battle of Jutland fought in the North Sea, also provided schools with other men – and boys - worthy of recognition and praise. Within days of the battle, which took place on 31 May and 1 June 1916, Peterborough Practising School 'had a service in memory of Lord Kitchener, and of the heroes of the Naval Fight off Jutland'.[89]

It was the death of John Travers Cornwell during the Battle of Jutland, however, that was to have the most impact on schoolchildren. 'Boy Cornwell' set the ultimate example to others by being awarded the Victoria Cross for his heroic actions on board the newly commissioned light cruiser HMS *Chester*. 'Jack', as he was generally known, had been educated at Walton Road School in Manor Park, Essex. He had also been a member of the St Mary's Little Ilford Boy Scout troop (Plate 26). After leaving school he was employed as a delivery van boy for tea merchants Brooke Bond & Co. With Britain at war, Jack joined the Royal Navy as a boy sailor at Devonport in July 1915. His father had withheld his permission for the boy's early military service, but Jack's application was supported by a reference from his headteacher and employer. On 31 May 1916, HMS *Chester* encountered four German cruisers and a firefight ensued. Despite being mortally wounded, Boy (First Class) Cornwell stayed by his gun when all around had fallen, steadfastly awaiting further orders. He died from his wounds in Grimsby Hospital two days later, aged sixteen. After Jack was mentioned in dispatches by Admiral Sir David Beatty, his story was quickly picked up by the press. On 15 July *The Spectator* suggested that a photograph of the now universally proclaimed young hero should hang in every elementary classroom in the country 'so that that the lustre of his deed may shine where boys and girls are quick to catch the reflection of lofty and honourable conduct'.[90] In the House of Lords on the following day Lord Beresford declared that 'An honour paid to Cornwell's memory would be an example to the boys of the Empire at their most susceptible age' and proposed the posthumous award of the Victoria Cross.[91] Thousands of people, including local dignitaries, former school friends, Scouts and other Royal Navy boys, attended the funeral in Manor Park Cemetery of this ordinary boy who had done extraordinary things in time of war. His epitaph read: 'It is not wealth or ancestry but honourable conduct and a noble disposition that makes men great'. British elementary schools observed Jack Cornwell Day on 30 September 1916 and millions of children throughout the Empire contributed to the Boy Cornwell Memorial Fund. John Travers Cornwell became 'the perfect symbolic hero'.[92]

Other children who made particularly impressive, albeit far less dramatic, contributions to the war effort were also held up as role models. Jennie Jackson from Burnley was celebrated for her fund-raising campaigns. 'Young Kitchener', as she was known, raised a remarkable £4,000 from street collections and the sale of promotional postcards and items made by women in the town. This money was used to purchase comforts for the troops and a motor ambulance for military service, which she duly presented, dressed in a made-to-measure uniform of a cavalry officer, to Queen Alexandra. Dressing up in mock uniforms was popular amongst children from all social classes, and usually conformed to gender stereotypes – boys as little soldiers, girls as little nurses. For those who could afford them, Gammages, the London toy shop, sold facsimile uniforms.[93] Most miniature uniforms, however, were homemade or, in the case of many of the images of uniformed children, were provided as patriotic props by enterprising local photographers.

Lessons in war were not confined to the schoolroom. The war manifested itself in many other ways in out of school activities. There was a ready market amongst children – and adults – for games and pastimes, which contained military themes. New board games appeared, with names such as 'Trencho' and 'From the Ranks to Field Marshal'.[94] Cigarette and other trade cards, which had first made their appearance in collectable sets in Britain in the 1890s, began to feature army regiments, the latest weapons and wartime heroes. A whole series of cards issued by Gallaher Ltd featured recipients of the Victoria Cross, Sergeant Major Harry Daniels VC of Norfolk included (Plate 27). It would be wrong, however, to suggest that the war changed everything. Traditional games and pastimes did not simply disappear with the onset of war, especially those enjoyed by many girls and younger children. Norah Hillman, who attended the village school in Steyning in West Sussex during the war, later recalled that many playground, field and street games were still enjoyed: games such as 'Tag', 'Hop-Scotch', 'Hide-and-Seek', 'Rounders' and a whole variety of skipping-rope games and action rhymes. On some occasions the teachers at her school even abandoned formal drill lessons in favour of popular 'round games' such as 'Here We Go Round the Mulberry Bush' and 'Poor Sally Sits-a-Weeping'.[95]

Uniformed youth movements also taught lessons in war. In the heady days of August 1914, their members had been mobilised to assist with the war effort. As the war continued into 1915 and beyond Boy Scouts and Girl Guides continued to serve their country on the home front. The Scouts of Hampton School in Middlesex worked in hospitals, cultivated allotments and helped their local police force.[96] A Scots battalion of Seaforth Highlanders, confined to camp on the outskirts of London, were eternally grateful to the Scouts from nearby Harrow County School for Boys who ran errands for them. Headmaster Ernest Young's troop also helped to deliver mail, handbills for Lord Derby's Recruitment Scheme and furniture, paper and clothing for the local War Help Committee.[97] Girl Guides also played their part in the war effort. Before the outbreak of war in 1914 many girls' schools, following the example set by the establishment of Scout troops in boys' schools, founded their own Guide groups or affiliated to local units. During the war the Guides were, according to a report in *The War Pictorial*, highly organised, disciplined and 'of the greatest value'. They were 'engaged in innumerable forms of war service'.[98] Girl Guides at Caernarvon County School in Wales collected sphagnum moss for use in wound dressings.[99] Elsewhere, Guides made swabs for the Red Cross, raised funds for charities, looked after the children of soldiers on active service, taught English to refugees,[100] and engaged in signaling and telegraphy.[101] By the end of the war, membership of the Guide movement in Britain alone exceeded 40,000, with an additional 23,000 members overseas.[102]

According to *The Times History of the War*, the Great War 'was found to affect every degree of childhood'.[103] The schoolchildren of 1914–19 experienced the impact of war on many different levels. For some the war was relatively remote. Others fought the war by proxy, their schools and communities inextricably bound to the men and women on the front line. Wartime heroes challenged them to do better and to follow their example. Millions of children responded by engaging with a multitude of initiatives and good causes on the home front. These lessons in war were, inevitably, one-step removed from the real thing. Distance made the conflict purposeful, exciting, and heroic. For some children, however, the war came perilously close. The home front itself became the front line.

Chapter 5

On the Front Line

These dear little ones died as truly for their country as any of our gallant men.

Alfred Warren, Mayor of Poplar (1917)
Memorial appeal for the children of North Street School

In 1917 the Great War came very close to home for one school community near London. As the boarders of Chigwell School peered out of their dormitory windows they witnessed an event which might well have filled the pages of their fictional schoolboy magazines. Passing over the school were two huge airships – German Zeppelins! The boys were transfixed by this night-time spectacle of enemy war machines in such close proximity. Any fear that they might have been feeling was soon overcome by the excitement which followed. They continued to watch as, in true *Boys' Own* fashion, the Zeppelins were shot down and destroyed.[1] This war, the first total war, had quickly blurred the familiar distinctions between combatant and non-combatant, between soldier and civilian, between battle front and home front. Battlefields were no longer located solely in foreign fields. New weapons of war extended the killing fields beyond the trenches. The development of bomber aircraft brought death and destruction to civilians in their own homes and places of work. Submarines were soon employed in the ancient practice of siege warfare on a scale hitherto unknown, denying the necessities for survival to whole countries, not just isolated cities as in previous conflicts. In the industrialised warfare of 1914 to 1918 those who made war did so technically and commercially as well as purely militarily. Women and children fought campaigns which supported the millions of men engaged in the more traditional forms of warfare. They produced the *matériel* of war in workshops and factories, and helped alleviate the worst effects of the German U-boat campaign by helping to feed the nation in its hour of need. In this war, the front line assumed different forms and shifted its terror and destruction to other locations. Soldiers were no longer the only ones manning that line or the only legitimate targets.

For centuries most of the people of Britain had been comforted by the belief that, unlike many of their counterparts on the continent of Europe, they were safe from invasion and the scourge of marauding foreign armies. The occasional attempts by foreign powers to land alien troops on these shores had been small scale and quickly dealt with.[2] Such abortive raids simply confirmed the island nation's belief in its own security and invincibility. The Royal Navy was Britain's shield and protector. Britannia increasingly ruled the waves in both home waters and far more distant seas. Britain's small Regular Army, it was also argued, was all that was necessary for colonial disturbances and, since the reforms of the late-nineteenth century, could always be reinforced if necessary by various forms of citizens' militia manned by part-time and part-trained volunteers.

When Britain's island fortress was assailed successfully by both sea and air in the first year of the war it came as both a shock to the general populace and a timely reminder to the military authorities of the new realities of modern warfare. The threat posed by Germany's growing naval force had been recognised for some time, especially after the introduction in 1906 of the Royal Navy's HMS *Dreadnought* led to a rapid and menacing naval arms race between the two countries. It was the Imperial German Navy, however, which took the initiative in the early stages of the war. In December 1914 a German battlecruiser squadron led by Rear Admiral Franz Hipper crossed the North Sea with seeming impunity and began a naval bombardment of towns on the east coast of England. The targets were Scarborough, the Hartlepools, and Whitby. In less than two hours the German ships fired over a thousand shells, hitting railways, factories, houses, churches and schools. In total, 137 British soldiers and civilians were killed and a further 592 were wounded.

The attack on Scarborough was recorded in the logbook of Gladstone Road School. The date was Wednesday, 16 December. The school buildings were rocked by the impact of huge explosive shells which had been fired from the warships stationed offshore. The school clock stopped. The time was 08.25, the time when many pupils customarily arrived for the morning session. Fortunately, only two pupils were on site when the bombardment began and these were quickly shepherded, uninjured, into the school cellar for protection by the caretaker, Mr Crawford. The School Hall and one classroom were badly damaged, so Gladstone Road School closed early for the Christmas holidays.[3] At nearby Orleton School, a preparatory institution, pupil Claude Elstone was eating breakfast in the dining hall:

I remember I was fooling about with two or three plates of porridge when the first big metallic crash came from the battle ships of the German fleet which had crept into the bay and were opening fire on the town. Mr Venables (Headmaster) came in and ordered the whole school to the west end of the buildings to await further orders.

Mr Venables then made his way to the South Cliff post office to send a telegram to all the parents:

Bombarded this morning. No damage to School. Boys all safe. Sending home tonight and tomorrow morning.

Over the Christmas period Orleton School was evacuated to Ilkley, where Mr Venables rented houses and hired a sports field from the local sports club.[4] When the new school term began in January 1915 at Gladstone Road School, the number of pupils at the school was much reduced. Many parents had already left the Scarborough district in fear of further enemy naval raids.

As the boys at Chigwell School had discovered, a similar threat appeared in the skies above Britain. The use of air power for military purposes had been anticipated, and not simply by the professionals in the armed forces. Manned flight was one of the marvels of the age, and many adults and schoolchildren followed the development of this new technology with great interest. In January 1914, some seven months before the Great War began, the relative merits and potential of different forms of aircraft were discussed by the Debating Society at Harrow County School for Boys. With Mr Wheeler in the Chair, the senior boys debated the motion that 'Aeroplanes would be more serviceable in warfare than dirigibles'. The motion was carried by fourteen votes to two.[5] The subsequent development of air warfare validated the theoretical arguments and verdict of Bob Hart and his fellow pupils at Harrow County. In the first months of the war and in the first enemy air raids of the war, however, it was actually the mighty Zeppelin airship which presented the gravest threat to Britain. These huge dirigibles were used quite deliberately to target civilian populations, a strategic development which the Harrow County boys may not have considered. Armies might legitimately be attacked from the air, but, surely, no one in their right mind would even contemplate the indiscriminate bombing of domestic targets full of innocent people.

The 'First Blitz' on Britain by German aircraft took place during the Great War. The scale, intensity and cost in economic and human terms may have been less than that of the better-documented and more familiar Blitz of the Second World War, but its impact was nonetheless traumatic. Air raids by German Zeppelin airships initially in the war, and by huge Gotha and other fixed-wing bomber aircraft later, destroyed lives and property. As early as September 1914 children began leaving London, the most obvious target for the German raiders, just as they were to do in much greater numbers in 1939. The logbook of Highgate Primary School in the city had made no mention of the outbreak of the war or, indeed, of any war-related events during the first six weeks of the conflict. On 15 September 1914, however, the first real impact of the war was noted: 'large numbers of children have been sent into the country on account of recent air raids'.[6] Children from Highgate and other schools found their way to the suburbs, accompanied or sent by their parents rather than being part of an organised precautionary dispersal as in the Second World War. Some of these early evacuees and their families took refuge in Epsom, where they were they joined the roll of Pound Lane School. The school logbook entry for 28 September 1914 demonstrates just how seriously the threat from the air was being taken:

Several children have been admitted to the school from London, they are leaving town for a time on account of the air raids. Some of the children were given drill for Zeppelin raids and were told to shelter under their desks.[7]

A Zeppelin raid on the coast of East Anglia on the night of 19 January 1915 resulted in the destruction of property, civilian casualties and widespread alarm. Zeppelin L4, commanded by Kapitanleutnant Count Magnus von Platen-Hallermund, followed the Norfolk coastline westwards from the town of Sheringham. It flew over Gresham's School in north Norfolk, where housemaster Wynne Williams noted in his journal:

At about eight o'clock they came over us at Holt and we put out all lights. The little boys in my boarding house were on the whole more excited than alarmed. Luckily for the inhabitants of the boarding house, the bombs all fell round a farmhouse, killing one or two sheep and a turkey, and dislodging some tiles. Next day the school repaired thither en masse to inspect the damage and the boys searched the small craters for bits of bombs.[8]

More bombs were dropped on small settlements such as Heacham and Snettisham before the airship reached the port of King's Lynn. Several of the eight bombs dropped by L4 hit the docks. One hit houses in Bentinck Road, killing Percy Goate and Alice Gazely, aged fourteen and twenty-six respectively.

Raids from Zeppelins and other German aircraft became increasingly frequent during 1915 and the years of war that followed. For people living in or near London, especially those situated under the favoured flight paths of enemy bombers, air raids – or the threat of them – became an almost nightly occurrence. Schools, and other civilian institutions and buildings, now found themselves in the target zone. Some, including Emanuel School in Westminster, continued with 'business as usual'.[9] As late as 1917, when attacks on the city became even more persistent, the sounding of air-raid alarms did not prevent the girls of George Green's School in Poplar from performing their Drill Display.[10] The first raids on London were a cause of excitement for some. The boys of Colfe's Grammar School in Lewisham welcomed the opportunity to visit bomb sites and collect souvenirs.[11] Their counterparts at Bancroft's School in suburban Essex similarly collected pieces of shrapnel – fired by anti-aircraft guns guarding the eastern approaches to the city – which had landed on the school roof.[12]

The grim reality of war, however, soon began to take its toll. For many people, what had at first been a novelty soon became nerve-racking. At a simple level, air raids led to sleepless nights, absences from school and disruption to normal routines. Excuses for non-completion of homework, or 'Prep' in boarding schools, such as those recorded in the wartime histories of George Green's School and Dulwich

College,[13] were far more likely to be genuine – and considered sympathetically – than was usually the case. A genuine fear of night-time raids led to the cancellation of evening productions in some schools.[14] Some things simply had to change, as Emanuel School eventually discovered when they were obliged to suspend their customary religious services on Sunday evenings due to the school's inability to comply with blackout regulations in the chapel. By 1917 the war had come so much closer to home than anyone had ever envisaged. Air raids presented a real threat to property and life. There were already some instances, albeit infrequent, of damage to school sites. During a night-time Zeppelin raid on Hull on 5 March 1916, for instance, a bomb had fallen on the running track at Hymer's College, leaving a crater 14 feet wide and 6 feet deep.[15] Fortunately, there were no casualties. Buildings and grounds, of course, could always be repaired or rebuilt, and some schools even took out insurance policies to cover the costs incurred as a result of bomb damage. Harrow School purchased such a policy and also invested in fire-fighting equipment,[16] whilst Cheadle Hulme School prepared for any potential conflagration by keeping the swimming pool half filled with water.

The most serious risk to schools posed by enemy air raids, however, was to the safety of their pupils. Schools in the most vulnerable areas simply could not afford to ignore the possibility of a direct hit on their site whilst school was in session. A whole range of air-raid precautions were gradually introduced to safeguard, as far as was possible, the civilian populations in towns and cities deemed to be at risk from the Zeppelin menace. Sirens, drills and shelters for the general public gave some reassurance, but many schools, especially those in the most vulnerable areas, adopted additional air-raid procedures. In response to 'inquiries which have been made by the Head Mistresses of the Bath, Liverpool Belvedere and Portsmouth High Schools',[17] the Board of Education issued a Memorandum in February 1915:

4. If the children were at School, it would probably be best to keep them inside the building and so far as possible engaged in their ordinary work or otherwise occupied. They should be kept as far as possible away from the windows, should not be assembled in a Hall which has no floor above it, and should not be disposed as to hamper their speedy escape in case of fire. They should not be dismissed until it has been ascertained that all danger has passed.

Some schools had designated 'shelters', but these were not the underground reinforced bunkers that the term often denotes. At Cheltenham County High School, the girls were ordered to move away from external walls and windows. Girls in classrooms on the ground floor then took shelter under their desk; pupils from the upper floors congregated in the ground floor corridor; those in the school hall had to file out and lie flat by the hedge outside.[18] The girls at Putney High

School in London did at least have sandbagged cloakrooms to shelter in, but the protection afforded by such measures in the case of a direct hit from high-explosive bombs is questionable.[19] Many school communities became well versed in the necessary procedures (Plate 28), even if some of their attempts to comply with other official requirements were not always successful initially. When Zeppelin raids on York began in 1916, for example, schools blacked out their windows so that night-time raiders would be unable to identify targets on the ground. At the Mount School, however, a chink of light visible from the exterior of the building led to the imposition by local magistrates of a five shillings fine on the school. When, during subsequent raids, the school's electricity supply was cut off in order to prevent future transgressions, the girls and their teachers assembled without any lights on. Nerves were steadied by Miss Graham who read aloud extracts from John Buchan's *The Thirty-Nine Steps* whilst waiting for the all-clear to sound.[20] At Ayton School, Herbert Dennis and his wife regularly patrolled the school grounds until after midnight on the nights of possible Zeppelin activity. The headmaster and the local sergeant of police conducted a joint tour of the school buildings to ascertain how the school might be blacked out in the event of Zeppelin raids. Within a month, all the lights in the school were screened. The same screens saw similar service twenty-five years later.

Air-raid precautions were necessary, but not always effective. During the Great War some schools were severely damaged and schoolchildren were amongst those killed and seriously injured by enemy bombing. The German raid on London on the morning of Wednesday, 13 June 1917 had particularly devastating consequences. Having crossed the English Channel, a force of seventeen hostile aircraft designated the England Squadron, and led by Hauptmann Ernst Brandenburg, reached the River Thames and headed for the capital.[21] The aeroplanes were Gothas; three-seater machines carrying shrapnel bombs for this particular raid. Air-raid sirens and other warnings alerted Londoners to the approaching danger. Many parents decided to keep their children at home; pupil attendance at Edmonton's Silver Street Senior Boys' School, for example, was reduced by fifty.[22] As the trajectory of the raiders became clearer, schools in the projected flight path, such as VC winner Jack Cornwell's former school – Farmer Road School in Leyton – thought it wise to close for the day.[23]

One group of aeroplanes deliberately targeted the East End of London. They began dropping their bombs at around 11.30 a.m. On hearing the first explosions, many schools in the vicinity which were still in session quickly implemented their practised air-raid drills. The *Daily Sketch* edition for the following day reported that:

A feature of the raid was the splendid way in which the schoolchildren responded to fire drill. At one school, as soon as the first bomb was heard, the children were marshalled into the covered playground by the teachers within one minute, and departed singing.

Another school had a narrow escape:

> In a second case the children were out of the school in less than a minute. They were just out in the playground when a bomb fell through the roof of the school, but did not explode. A second bomb fell in the playground without exploding.[24]

The newspaper went on to extoll the virtues of children singing patriotic songs and teachers reading to pupils sheltering under desks whilst, in the skies above them, the German raiders were intent on wreaking havoc and destruction.[25]

One school, however, did not escape the bombers. North Street School, a LCC-maintained elementary school in Poplar, was situated close to the River Thames and the East India Dock Road. At 11.40 a.m. a single 50kg. bomb crashed through the roof of the school. It killed pupils Rose Martin and Edwin Powell outright before exploding in the Infant's classroom on the floor below. Miss Allum, Miss Middleton and Miss Watkins worked heroically to remove their injured and dying pupils from the wreckage and to evacuate the remaining children to places of safety. There was no panic, at least amongst the pupils and their teachers. Some children quietly sobbed as they were led away from the scene of devastation. On hearing news of the explosion, many parents did panic. Mothers with children at the school rushed to North Street to be met by scenes of carnage as the bodies of the dead and mutilated children were carried out by the teachers and the emergency services (Plate 29). The school caretaker, Mr Benjamin Batt, carried out the body of his own son, Alfie, who had been killed in the explosion. In all, eighteen schoolchildren were killed and some thirty fellow pupils were seriously injured. When Mr Deller, the headmaster, called the register the following morning, he read the names of all who were on the school roll, casualties and survivors alike, and wept openly.[26]

One week later, on 20 June 1917, a funeral service was held for the children of North Street School. Thousands of East Enders lined the route of the funeral procession to pay their respects to the victims. Flags flew at half-mast and blinds were drawn as a mark of respect. There were sixteen coffins for the eighteen victims: fifteen contained named individuals, the last held the unidentified broken fragments of the remaining dead childern. In Poplar Parish Church the religious proceedings were led by the Rector of Poplar. The magnitude of the event was signified, however, by the presence and involvement of two other leaders of the Anglican Church: the Bishop of Stepney and the Bishop of London. Other dignitaries included Lord Crewe, Chairman of the LCC; Lieutenant-General Sir Francis Lloyd, Commanding the London District; and Mr Will Crooks, the local Member of Parliament. The school itself was represented by the teaching staff and twelve surviving pupils: six girls dressed in white, and six boys wearing their Boy Scout uniforms. As 'London's Massacred Innocents' were laid to rest in East London Cemetery, their graves were covered in hundreds of wreaths which had been sent by schools, hospitals, factories, military and official bodies and individuals from all parts of the country.[27]

In the months following the funeral a memorial appeal was launched by Alfred Warren, the Mayor of Poplar. Over £1,455 was raised by public subscription. At the subsequent unveiling of the memorial on 23 June 1919, General Ashmore paid tribute to the children by stating that 'They died for their country and had set an example which should never be forgotten'.[28] The memorial itself was erected in Poplar Recreation Ground and contained the names and ages of the North Street School pupils who had been killed on 13 June 1917:

LOUISE A. ACOMPORA	AGED FIVE YEARS
ALFRED E. BATT	AGED FIVE YEARS
LEONARD C. BAREFORD	AGED FIVE YEARS
JOHN P. BRENNAN	AGED FIVE YEARS
WILLIAM T.H. CHALLIEN	AGED FIVE YEARS
VERA M. CLAYSON	AGED FIVE YEARS
ALICE M. CROSS	AGED FIVE YEARS
WILLIAM HOLLIS	AGED FIVE YEARS
GEORGE A. HYDE	AGED FIVE YEARS
GRACE JONES	AGED FIVE YEARS
ROSE MARTIN	AGED TEN YEARS
GEORGE MORRIS	AGED SIX YEARS
EDWIN C.W. POWELL	AGED TWELVE YEARS
ROBERT STIMSON	AGED FIVE YEARS
ELIZABETH TAYLOR	AGED FIVE YEARS
ROSE TUFFIN	AGED FIVE YEARS
FRANK WINGFIELD	AGED FIVE YEARS
FLORENCE L. WOODS	AGED FIVE YEARS

The destruction of North Street School was, to use a term applied to such incidents in more recent conflicts, collateral damage. The raid appears to have been directed at London's dockland. Bombs dropped by the Gothas hit targets of economic – if not of overtly military – importance. Some were dropped on Liverpool Street Station and other railway lines;[29] one hit a passenger locomotive, killing seven people on board and injuring seventeen others.[30] Of less potential strategic importance, unless the comfort and morale of Tommy Atkins are taken into consideration, was the damage done to a warehouse and a factory, reported somewhat derisively by the

Daily Sketch as storing tea and making jam respectively.[31] Given the crude bomb-aiming devices employed in early military aircraft, it was always highly likely that some bombs would miss their intended targets and fall elsewhere.

For the people of the East End and beyond, however, the notion that the bomb which fell on North Street School was an unintended 'stray' was beyond belief or rational explanation. German aircraft had visited these shores before and had bombed civilian targets. On this occasion the 'Hun baby-killers' conducted their first daylight raid in brilliant sunshine and clear skies.[32] It was, to many who witnessed the raid, more evidence of German barbarity. Under a heading 'The East End Feels Ugly' the *Daily Sketch* reported on the immediate aftermath of the attack:

> The raid caused intense indignation, and during the remainder of the day there were many angry demonstrations outside the premises and houses of alien enemies. In several cases police assistance was necessary to disperse the women.

The atmosphere at the funeral procession a week later was far more dignified. Like the funeral of Jack Cornwell VC in the previous year, this was not a state funeral as such, but it served much the same purpose in channelling the nation's grief, national identity and solidarity. Unlike Boy Cornwell, however, the victims of war at North Street School were not regular servicemen or volunteers or conscripts. For many in Britain at the time, the tragic fate of the Poplar children said less about individual heroism and more about the cowardly nature of an alien race.

Much of the debate, both at the time and since, misses the point by asking the wrong question. The issue is not whether the attack on North Street School was deliberate; the key point to be considered is whether it was legitimate. This might be done in the context of explaining rather than excusing. The Great War was not simply bigger than any previous conflict – the metrics of involvement and expenditure quickly validate such a claim – but it was also patently different in the ways in which the belligerent nations made war. This may be the case with all wars, but the shock of the new between 1914 and 1918 was palpable. This was the first 'modern' war; a war in which earlier rules and conventions were forgotten or blatantly ignored in the race to develop new terror weapons which would bring about victory. Technological advances all too often sprinted ahead of ethical and moral considerations. New forms of weaponry targeted the mind as well as the body of the enemy. In this particular case General Erich Ludendorff had clearly recognised the value of psychological warfare, stating that the prime objective of the German air campaign was 'the moral intimidation of the British nation and the crippling of the will to fight, thus preparing the ground for peace'.[33]

Public opinion and individual sensibilities were undoubtedly appalled that such an outrage had occurred in a conflict between otherwise civilised nations. The raid of 13 June 1917 demonstrated that nowhere and no-one was safe. In total war they were all, the elderly and young alike, contributors to the war effort in some form or other. They were all now conscripts to the national cause, and the enemy would wage war against them accordingly, and with all the weapons of destruction at their disposal. This single raid on London claimed the lives of 104 Londoners in total and left a further 423 people injured. The explosions did not differentiate their victims: men, women and children of all ages were casualties of war on that day. British propaganda, however, ensured that it was the children who were remembered. The children of North Street School 'were recruited into the ranks of the honoured dead' as surely as if they had been listed as killed in action in the newspaper obituaries and lists of The Fallen.[34] In Germany, meanwhile, children in their school classrooms and morning assemblies recited '*Gotte Strafe England*' – 'God Punish England'.

In the weeks and months which followed the raid many local authorities and schools reviewed their safety procedures. The Managers of St Mark's Voluntary Aided Primary School in the London borough of Lambeth, for example, met in November 1917 to discuss the issue:

> A letter was read from the Council on air raid precautions and after careful discussion and consideration it was decided that the children should be mustered and immediately marched under the teacher's escort to the crypt of the Church when a warning of an impending raid was received.[35]

The letter in question may well have been the result of an earlier letter sent by the Board of Education to LEAs and governors of independent and voluntary schools in July 1917, just weeks after the Poplar tragedy. The Board's advice to schools was essentially that which had been issued previously in the Memorandum of February 1915. It did differ from the original in one important aspect: the letter was headed 'Strictly Confidential Information' and stated that 'it is desired that it should not be published in the press'. Point 4 of the revised advice, reflecting the concern of the authorities in the immediate aftermath of the bombing of North Street School, read:

> Every effort should be made to dissuade parents from attempting to enter the school premises and to remove their children.[36]

Many schools in vulnerable areas, however, were overtaken by events. Further raids by German aircraft throughout 1917 and 1918 provoked a response based on fear rather than pragmatism. There appears to have been little evidence of the 'Blitz spirit' which conditioned the British response to attacks from the air in the Second World War. Even rumours of air raids were sufficient to generate panic and hysteria in many towns and cities. Some of those affected directed their anger at public authorities. Others, including children, perpetrated acts of xenophobic rage against their 'alien' neighbours.[37] Many Londoners, in particular, fled the new front line; some to the city's parks for the night, others for temporary refuge in the suburbs, just as they had done in the wake of the earlier Zeppelin raids on the capital. School rolls reflected the transient nature of this diaspora. School attendance on days following night-time raids was often significantly lower; children were often too tired to attend, or their parents too fearful to send them to school. Many parents made informal arrangements for their children, sending them to friends in the country.[38] Schools outside London often saw an increase in numbers as they admitted children seeking temporary respite from the bombing raids. The consequences for some schools in London, however, was significant. Headmaster John Perkins of Sir John Cass School in the city noted in 1917 both the scale and the impact on the school and its pupils of the continuing air raids and the informal evacuations which followed:

> In consequence of air raids both day and night during the past term a large number of children have been sent into the country and 47 are attending school elsewhere ... long periods of absence on the part of some combined with serious nervous and mental disturbances on the part of many have seriously affected the character of the work and made normal progress quite impossible.[39]

1917 was, for the civilian population of Britain, the worst year of the war.[40] In addition to the attacks from the air, the island nation was by then besieged by an enemy which also used the sea, Britain's traditional first line of defence, to further its war aims. Mastery of the world's shipping lanes, especially those bringing vital supplies from the USA and Canada across the Atlantic Ocean, could no longer be guaranteed by surface ships alone. The Germans made full use of their U-boat fleet to blockade Britain. Enemy submarines wreaked havoc, sinking merchant ships carrying goods necessary for the British war effort. In April 1917 alone, 545,000 tonnes of supplies were lost through U-boat activity.[41] The most precious cargo for a people waging total war was food. Traditional sieges often ended not with the deployment of specialist weaponry, or with troops storming through a breach in the defensive walls of the citadel, but by the starvation of the populace within. The German U-boat campaign led to such serious food shortages that, by 1917, Britain's capacity for waging war was seriously compromised. Once again, the Great War expanded beyond the bloody battlefields of Flanders to new theatres and modes of conflict.

Food shortages became commonplace. When food was available it was generally of poor quality and increasingly expensive. The U-boat blockade prompted the government to appoint Lord Devonport as Food Controller in December 1916.

In a Royal Proclamation in May 1917, King George V appealed to his loyal people to consume less food. The slogan of the day became 'Eat Less Bread': a message that was broadcast through the media of posters and even school magazines.[42] The popular press, too, extolled the virtues of self-denial. The subsequent appointment of Lord Rhondda as Food Controller in June 1917 was a clear sign that compulsion – in the form of food rationing – rather than voluntary restraint would be necessary if Britain was to avoid losing the war through its inability to feed the people. By the end of the year the government produced lists of 'food requirements', differentiated according to age and gender. The monthly 'requirement' – or ration – for boys aged thirteen to eighteen, for example, was stipulated as 6lb. of bread, 2lb. meat, 10oz. of fat and 8oz. of sugar. The requirement for girls of the same age was 80 per cent of that for boys.[43]

The impact of food restrictions on schools of all kinds was substantial. Those which had traditionally provided food for pupils were forced to make economies. Boarders at the great public schools and those in smaller preparatory and private institutions suffered wartime deprivations along with the rest of the population. For many pupils from privileged backgrounds the absence of sufficient food was often the abiding memory of school life during the war. Evelyn Waugh later referred to 'my first experience of hunger' whilst a boarder at Lancing College.[44] Boys at Dulwich College were introduced to nut cutlets, tripe and a 'disgusting pie of swedes and potato'.[45] Pupils in less prestigious schools also noted a decline in culinary quality. A contributor to the July 1917 issue of *The Gaytonian* at Harrow County School for Boys was particularly concerned about the use of substitute foodstuffs. He referred to swedes looking and tasting like pieces of eucalyptus tree, and a bean 'which might be a coffee bean, a cocoa bean, or a might have bean. In my humble opinion it is the latter'. It was clear, he lamented, that the schoolboy had been 'made a martyr and the object of experiments in the food line'.[46]

Simple economic considerations led some schools, for example West Norfolk and King's Lynn High School for Girls, to tackle the escalating costs of running the school and feeding its pupils by raising boarding fees by £2 per term,[47] or by raising the unit costs of school meals as happened at Manchester High School for Girls.[48] In areas where wartime wages were beginning to rise faster than prices,[49] and the demand for secondary school places exceeded supply, this was a strategy which might just ensure financial viability for the school. A great number of schools, however, decided that a combination of imposed self-denial and self-help might help alleviate the situation. In May 1917 *The Felstedian Magazine* captured the mood of the times:

But this term everything is different. To begin with our food is rationed out to us; we do not eat in the old careless way; eating is now reduced to a science of calories, of pounds and ounces. Secondly, work on the land in term time is in full swing, and the purpose for which we are primarily sent here has for the moment taken second place.[50]

A new slogan appeared – 'Dig for Victory'. Both the Board of Agriculture and the Board of Education urged schools to do their bit by providing food for themselves and for others.[51] The latter circulated a letter in March 1917 stating:

The President of the Board desires to know what steps have been taken to add to the space cultivated by Schools with the object of increasing the food supply.

The headmistress of Newcastle High School for Girls responded by saying that a chicken run would be added to the school garden. Her counterpart at Sutton High School was less forthcoming, stating in her reply to the Board that:

Neither I nor any members of my Staff are experts on gardening; so we are afraid to undertake too much ground.

Harrow County needed no encouragement from the authorities; their playing field had been providing vegetables for the school dining hall for almost a year before *Circular 994*.[52] Other schools followed suit. The suggested appropriation of the hallowed turf of the playing fields for non-sporting purposes was met, not by incredulity, but by a recognition that 'business as usual' was no longer possible or appropriate. Evelyn Waugh at Lancing recalled that 'potato digging was added to our patriotic duties'.[53] In London, the boys of Dulwich College were engaged in the same activity,[54] whilst at Emanuel School pupils planted wheat and made their own bread.[55] Northampton Grammar School converted one acre of the school field to vegetable production and harvested four and a half tons of potatoes that same year.[56] Whilst many of the existing records appear to indicate that wartime school gardeners were predominantly male pupils, there are examples of girls cultivating plots (Plate 30).[57] When Mr Wright, the school gardener at Merchant Taylors' School for Girls in Crosby, joined the army in 1917 Miss Ryder, the Botany teacher, and a group of senior pupils started growing their own vegetables.[58] The Blue Coat School in Birmingham decided to help the campaign to grow more food indirectly, by leasing part of their site to the City Council for use as allotments.[59]

In the nation's elementary schools 'Digging for Victory' was encouraged and often expected. Collectively, the schools for the poorest sections of society gradually became mass producers of food.[60] For many of these schools, playing fields were a luxury rather than a necessity. Some, nevertheless, managed to acquire plots of land for cultivation. In King's Lynn, the staff and pupils St Nicholas Boys' School responded early to the national food crisis:

1917
9 March: 30 rods of land, on Curtis Field, have been taken from the Corporation by the LEA for use as a school garden. Mr Fisher took 10 of the older boys on Wed afternoon for an hour to roughly mark it out. The timetable is varied on five afternoons so as to set 10 to 20 boys free for instruction in gardening.

31 May: HMI A. Key Esq. visited the school garden this afternoon and congratulated us.

1918
9 March: Handicraft boys were erecting a tool shed on the school garden today.

Headteacher Alfred Whitehouse was clearly prepared, albeit with direction and approval from the Board of Education, to make this particular wartime activity a formal and valued part of the elementary school curriculum.[61] Teachers at St Mark's Voluntary Aided School in Lambeth combined theory with practice. The garden adjoining the girls' school was allocated to the 'first class' boys (sic), who then divided it into plots and sowed vegetable seeds. The same logbook entry noted that 'Instruction is given in Nature Study'.[62]

Much of the produce from school gardens was intended for consumption by the school community. At Kibble in Scotland, the reformatory school ground some of its own-grown oats for the first time.[63] Self-help was also the order of the day at Cowper Testimonial School in Hertford where in 1917 the 'Boys provided their own seed potatoes 7lb each ... (and the) ... Boys had all produce of plots'.[64] This was not always the case; many school gardens produced vegetables and other goods for the wider community. Several elementary schools in Hertfordshire, for example, donated surplus produce to soldiers and sailors on leave, and to military hospitals in Royston and Cambridge.[65] Schools in Trowbridge were regular supporters of the 'Vegetables for the Navy' campaign.[66] The needs of animals – and school funds – were also considered when the cricket field at The Herbert Strutt School in Belper was sacrificed and allowed to become a hay meadow. The crop was sold for animal fodder for the princely sum of 11 shillings.[67]

By the end of 1917 the campaign to waste less and grow more had succeeded in galvanising many school communities and keeping the real horrors of starvation at bay. British children generally did not have to endure the same degree and extent of hunger that their counterparts in Germany suffered during the 'Turnip Winter' of 1917–18, a period of severe famine greatly exacerbated by the British naval blockade of that country.[68] Nevertheless, the last full year of the war did not see a return to normality. Rationing continued, and getting sufficient food remained a priority for many. In December 1917, Mr Pullan at Peterborough Practising School noted that 'Attendance has been poor during the week, owing to the number of boys looking for food'.[69] In recognition of the difficulties facing many parents at the time, some school cookery rooms were used, as at Gowerton Intermediate School in Glamorgan in 1918, for demonstrations for the local community on food economy.[70]

The U-boat menace was eventually countered by Prime Minister Lloyd George's insistence on the convoy system across the Atlantic to protect Britain's vulnerable mercantile marine. The supply of food improved, but deficiencies in other areas brought further miseries to the nation's homes and schools. The shortage of paper hampered classroom activity – and the production of many still-running school magazines was suspended for the duration – but this was a relatively minor inconvenience. Keeping children warm and dry in the middle of winter was a far more serious concern for both parents and teachers. Coal was in short supply, especially for non-military usage. College Road Council School in Moseley was not the only school to send children home when, on several occasions, there was 'no coal for the boiler'.[71] At Rissington School in the Cotswolds the headteacher and the managers took the decision to shorten the school day and extend the Christmas holiday period in order to save coal.[72] Even after the Armistice in November 1918, the continuing shortage of fuel left many schools without heating. Some valiantly tried to remain open even on days when the weather conditions were particularly poor; the only alternative was to send the children back to possibly colder and unsupervised homes. When Meeching Boys' School in Newhaven opened its doors on 17 December 1918, for example, 'many children arrived in a wet condition'. Because of the coal shortage there were no fires lit in the classrooms so the pupils were sent to sit by the furnace in the nearby Church Institute in order to dry their clothes and boots.[73]

The old adage that an army marches on its stomach still rang true during the Great War. The 'army', however, no longer consisted purely of those who wore military uniforms and belonged to line regiments or other armed services. The whole nation, as well as its soldiers, sailors and airmen, was engaged in the war effort and needed to be fed. The allotments and school gardens, which were pressed into service in 1917 were, in reality, no more than a useful addition to a much more important theatre of activity – the fields and pastures in traditional agricultural areas. With so many men away at the battle fronts with Kitchener's New Armies, British agriculture was short of manpower. The introduction of Conscription in 1916 took more men away from the fields, despite many attempts by employers at Military Service Tribunals to retain experienced workers. Women and children were used to fill the gaps in the rural labour force. Schoolchildren became farmers, or more precisely farm labourers, in a variety of ways. The Cavendish Association, under the direction of the Ministry of National Service Agriculture Section, instituted an agricultural summer camp scheme in 1917. Once again, Ernest Young volunteered his boys at Harrow County. The headmaster was also the school's Scoutmaster and, accompanied by thirty-six boys and Miss Baldwin acting as 'Camp Mother', spent the summer holiday in Pershore in Worcestershire, helping to bring in the plum harvest. Other secondary schools joined the scheme. Over 4,000 school pupils contributed to harvest camps in both 1917 and 1918,[74] including the boys of Barrow Grammar School, who undertook the necessary but unenviable task of pulling up thistles.[75] Voluntary work of this nature was valuable, helping both the farmer and the school. For the latter it formed part of their contribution to the war effort, helped to develop institutional cultures and traditions, and did not detract from term-time study.

For many more children, however, working on the land was not always a matter of personal choice or holiday adventure. Child labour was certainly not new. It was, and still remains in some parts of the world, a key feature of pre-industrial economies. The 'family economy' meant that all but the most privileged children would be employed as soon as they could walk: fetching and carrying and, for girls especially, doing domestic chores. The Industrial Revolution in Britain shifted the locus of juvenile labour away from the home to the factory, but large numbers of children continued to work in agriculture. That was, of course, until the child 'was rescued by the school'.[76] Despite the Factory and Education Acts of the nineteenth century, however, entries in elementary school logbooks continued to reflect the tension between learning and earning. In rural areas, pupil absenteeism was particularly pronounced at harvest time. Throughout Britain many boys and girls also left school prematurely for full-time employment, irrespective of their academic ability, potential or personal ambition, in order to contribute to the family income. In wartime, the greater needs of the nation exacerbated the situation even further.

The outbreak of war in 1914 coincided with one of the key points in the farming calendar. Men who had enlisted early were no longer available to bring in the harvest. As many in Britain believed that this was a war that would be, according to the slogan at least, 'Over by Christmas', temporary measures were introduced to fill the gaps in the labour force. In August 1914 Prime Minister Asquith suggested that LEAs might use their discretion to permit the release from school of boys aged eleven to fourteen to help on the land in the autumn and winter months.[77] The Board of Education permitted local authorities to suspend school attendance by-laws. The Soke of Peterborough Education Committee, for one, acted quickly to allow school boys aged eleven years old and above to be employed in agricultural work up to the end of November 1914.[78] West Sussex LEA agreed to give 'all possible facilities for boys over twelve years of age to work on farms provided that adequate wages are given'. Between 1 September 1914 and 31 January 1915, 34 of the 62 LEAs in England and Wales granted exemptions, to a total of 1,388 boys and 25 girls. They were to be 'temporary labourers', for the duration of the harvest only. The Secretary of Gloucestershire LEA justified the use of child labour by asking rhetorically:

> What good would the three or six months schooling be to anyone if this country (were) to be starved and then beaten in the most tremendous war of all history?[79]

As the war dragged on, and nearly a quarter of a million men left agriculture for the armed forces, such arrangements were extended. Headmistress Florence Spurling recorded the consequent impact on Akenfield Mixed School in 1915:

> The farmers are taking boys from the school for the threshing and have all been told of the illegality of such a proceeding. Bertie Anderson (12) is allowed absence from school for Temporary Emergency Employment. Owing to the late harvest and the scarcity of labour through the War, many children are needed to keep on the farms.[80]

In the same year, Alfred Whitehouse in King's Lynn noted that for many parents the schooling of their children was not an immediate priority:

> 1915
> 4 June: 87.4% attendance. There is a large amount of illegal employment, especially fishing.
>
> 29 July: 82.6%. Many boys are fishing and samphiring.[81]
>
> 15 October: 88.4%. Many boys still absent employed by their parents as fisher boys.

There was little improvement in the following year:

> 1916
> 12 May: 86.1%. Many boys illegally employed, cockling etc.
>
> 6 October: Several boys have been absent for months, illegally employed, fishing, or as errand boys.
>
> 24 November: The parents of 6 boys were summoned for children's absence while employers were left alone.

The headteacher's final comment is a telling one. Some parents in the North End fishing community were evidently trying to make ends meet in an uncertain wartime economy. They may even have been hoping to profit from rising demand and prices for their catch. Others, in the first few decades of compulsory schooling, may not have accepted that school was the best place for their children to get an appropriate and useful education. Early employment in the family business was deemed to be essential in some cases; in Cumbria the son of a blacksmith left Levens School in Kendal early at the age of thirteen after his father's apprentice was conscripted.[82]

Many employers were equally unconvinced about the professed benefits of formal schooling. As *The Times History of the War* pointed out 'Neither mill-owners nor politicians wanted an educated proletariat in 1817; and some of them did not want it in 1917'.[83] For many farmers the extension of educational opportunity and provision for the lower classes simply increased their tax and rate bills, diminished the pool of cheap labour traditionally available to them, and ultimately threatened existing social hierarchies.[84] Agricultural employers were criticised for taking advantage of wartime conditions by employing children on low wages rather than adults. Many county education committees, with the power to exempt children from school, were dominated by farming interests. Despite the Board of Education's insistence that child release from school was 'an exceptional measure permitted to meet a special emergency', and opposition from many teachers and their professional organisations, the exemptions continued. From March 1917 any child aged twelve and above could be exempted on submission of a written statement from an employer and the agreement of the parents. Herbert Fisher, President of the Board of Education and later architect of the 1918 Education Act, claimed in August 1917 that as many as 600,000 children had been withdrawn from school prematurely in first three years of the war. There were regional variations. Huntingdonshire's exemption rate was particular high, both in numerical terms and in proportion to the eligible school population. In the farming region of Holland in Lincolnshire 900 children were exempted in the final school term of 1917. Over a third of the district's exemptions were for girls, including 118 cases where girls were excused attendance in order to look after the family home in the absence of working mothers and serving fathers. In the adjacent county of Norfolk, no girls were exempted at all. Some local authorities decided to allow less formal block exemptions. In July 1918 the Education Committee in Durham permitted twelve schools to end the school day at 1.40 p.m. so that the pupils could then work on local farms.[85] In Lancashire, the logbook entry for Hornby School on 30 August 1918 states: 'school closed for one week to enable children to help in the harvest field'.[86]

British industry also needed replacement labour. Much has been written about the opportunities – and evident dangers – for women who were employed in the workshops and factories which supplied the men doing the fighting at the battle fronts.[87] The munitionettes, however, were not alone in producing the weapons of war. Direct support for the military machine was provided by children too, but this is a story that has rarely escaped from the individual school histories and logbooks to be read by a wider audience. Some children worked on the industrial front line *as part of* their schooling; schools of all types actively contributed to the production of war *matériel* during the Great War. A great number of schools, as noted previously, took part in the horse chestnut collection campaign of 1917. A few went further in their war work by extending their range of collection items. When the Royal Naval Cordite Factory in Dorset appealed for quantities of acorns – yet another example of an ersatz product being used in the manufacture of munitions and, in this case, gas respirators – Longbridge Deverill School in Wiltshire supplied fifty bushels.[88] Cooking oil and scrap metal also found their way via schools to the munitions factories for recycling into armaments. Sandbags, respirators and other paraphernalia of trench warfare were produced by children in some of the nation's elementary schools.[89]

Much of this work was small scale and, essentially, a continuation and extension of the patriotic endeavours witnessed in school in the early days of the war. Comforts were supplemented by personal survival equipment; blackberry jam by cordite for artillery shells. War production was far more systematised in some of the public schools and grammar schools. Despite the general and traditional curriculum emphasis on the Classics, some public schools had workshop facilities which were turned over to small-scale weaponry production during the war years. Cartridge punches were made by the boys at Cheltenham College. Similar work was done at Oundle and Uppingham.[90] The Ministry of Munitions contracted Bedford School to make submarine valves and 13lb. shells, whilst Bradfield school made shell cases for Vickers in term time and during the school holidays.[91] Several schools in London had links with the Royal Arsenal at Woolwich. The Governors at Emanuel School provided a grant which enabled a working group of boys, masters and former pupils to make bullet punches for Woolwich.[92] Boys from Colfe's Grammar School worked in the Royal Arsenal during their holidays.[93]

Other children worked on the industrial front line *instead* of going to school. Indeed, the premature transition from classroom to factory floor was expected of children in some types of school. An industrialised war demanded a larger workforce. Many men were retained in reserved occupations to fight their particular war from the factory floor. The British government gradually improved processes of recruitment to the armed forces to ensure that skills needed were not wasted on the battle fronts. Where gaps in the workforce existed, women and children were employed, especially after the German Spring Offensive on the Western Front in March 1918 led to further reductions in the classes of men eligible for exemption from military service. The employment of women and children instead of men – the so-called 'dilution of labour' – was often resisted by trade unions and the

Labour movement, but the demands of total war were paramount. In 1915 Kibble School responded to a request from the Home Office that:

> The boys from the Reformatory and Industrial Schools of Scotland should come forward at the present juncture and help the country in active service and in the munition factories.

Four members of staff and 101 boys from Kibble began work at Beardsmore's Munitions factory on Clydeside, often on the night shift. In a letter to the school in 1916, the Paisley Trades and Labour Council objected to the boys' employment on the grounds of both 'dilution' and health and safety.[94]

Many other schoolchildren *chose* to work on the industrial front line. On reaching the age of fourteen they were fully entitled to leave school. The majority of those in the elementary schools did so as their schooling had officially ended. For the fee-paying pupils and scholarship winners in the secondary schools, however, there was the prospect of continuing in full-time education until the age of eighteen and beyond. That large numbers from the non-elite schools did not stay on has led some social commentators to refer to a national system of schooling characterised by educational and social 'waste'.[95] The notion of wasted talent and potential – within the context of a society, which systematised inequality of opportunity and, to an even greater extent, inequality of access to those opportunities – is supported by numerous case studies into social mobility in the early twentieth century.[96] This was not a problem caused by the war, but a reflection of the function of the British hierarchy of schooling more generally. But the choices made by individuals and their families were also an important factor. There are times in any given lifespan when, conditioned by external contexts and internal imperatives, considerations of 'what should be' and the prospect of 'what might be' are overtaken by 'what must be'. War, 'the locomotive of history', has the potential to change the nature of the opportunities available and to accelerate the decision-making process. During the Great War, boys from grammar schools and other state-maintained secondary schools were more likely to leave secondary education early for employment in engineering and related trades. Several boys left Deacon's School in Peterborough unexpectedly and without notice to work at Brotherhoods, a city engineering firm which had won wartime contracts to produce shells, sea mines and torpedoes for the Royal Navy. Another prospective pupil, the winner of a Soke of Peterborough scholarship to Deacon's, failed to materialise at all, having decided instead to take up an offer of paid employment at the same factory.[97] High wages at the nearby Vickers works also tempted many boys from Barrow Grammar School to forego the prospects of further education and careers in the professions.[98] In the heady and uncertain days of the Great War, opportunities for skilled work could not be dismissed lightly, especially when such openings often led on to supervisory and managerial positions.[99]

Wartime conditions also encouraged premature leaving amongst girls in schools which offered a secondary education. When, in 1914, Miss Shackleton stated in her Report that the Merchant Taylors' School for Girls was greatly interested in the war, and that staff and pupils would enlist if they could, she had probably not anticipated the response of some of her pupils. In her Report three years later the headmistress praised her girls' contribution to the war effort, but added a necessary caveat:

> It is most satisfactory to find the girls so anxious to help the nation at this crisis and so efficient in the work they undertake, but it should be remembered that if education is sacrificed at too early an age the country will suffer ultimately.

A minority of the pupils at this school left at fourteen to attend boarding schools. The majority of these middle-class girls, however, left at the same age, not for skilled trade apprenticeships, but to do work in the home. In wartime, with the world seemingly turned upside down, they were needed by parents to do the chores done previously by domestic servants who had left for more lucrative wartime employment.[100] Economic realities clashed with both personal ambition and institutional encouragement. In 1917, despite having gained Junior and Senior Certificates and Matriculation to University whilst at Greenhill School in Tenby, Doris Kingdom could not afford to continue her formal studies. Instead she left to do war work at the Cardiff Recruiting Office. When she later encountered in the street her former headteacher Mr Griffiths, a man renowned for his ambition for his pupils, she was given a thorough 'dressing down'.[101]

Much of the employment on the land and in factories was poorly paid and entailed long hours of arduous work. At times, in a country under attack from the air and sea and seriously short of food, producing the *matériel* of war was a hazardous business. Premature war-related employment, however, was not confined to working in agriculture or industry. For under-age schoolboy soldiers, choosing to leave school early was potentially far more perilous. The majority of boy soldiers, of course, had already left their schools and were in employment when they managed to 'convince' Recruiting Sergeants that they were ready to do their duty for King and Country. The author's paternal grandfather was fifteen when, in 1914, he left his job in a Kettering shoe factory to enlist in the 3rd/4th Battalion Northamptonshire Regiment. His initial army record lists his physical characteristics: height 5ft 5inches; build slight. The majority of boy soldiers made it as far as the training grounds and Home Service duties before a national and parliamentary campaign succeeded in having many of them discharged from the armed forces. Some did see overseas service. In 1916 *The Illustrated War News* included a photograph of an unnamed 15-year-old soldier:

> a lad so eager to do something for his country that he smuggled himself in. His zeal was appreciated, and some work was found for him as a helper in the buffet.[102]

Private Sidney Lewis was still of school age when he left the classroom for the trenches. Generally believed to be the youngest British soldier of the Great War,[103] Sidney enlisted in the East Surrey Regiment on 12 August 1915 at the age of twelve years and five months. In 1916 he fought for six weeks in the Battle of the Somme before his true age was discovered and his mother campaigned for his return home.[104] The understandable anxieties of parents were not shared by everyone. Boy soldier Private Horace Hanson was proclaimed a hero by his local newspaper the *Halifax Courier* with the headline 'BOY OF 14 IN THE FIRING LINE'. Horace joined the Royal Field Artillery (RFA) on 20 April 1915, seven weeks before his fourteenth birthday. The newspaper reported:

> We have seen both his birth certificate and his enlistment form. He has been at the front since January. He is a fine, well-built lad, and his youthful enthusiasm has set an example to many men of military age.

When Hampton School in Middlesex published their Roll of Honour in midsummer 1915, it contained the names of two underage boys: H.W.R. Maddox left Form 3A in March 1915 'at a little over fourteen' to join the army; C.F. Norman left before he was sixteen for the King's Royal Rifles.[105] A note in the Admissions Register at Greenhill School in Tenby stated that William Thomas Prydderch, the son of a Minister of the Gospel of Nant-y-Moel, Glamorgan, a pupil for only two terms, had left on the 16 March 1915 and 'Joined the Army'. This simple statement does not do justice to the dramatic scenes witnessed by one of the school's subsequent early leavers, Doris Kingdom:

> We arrived at school one morning in time to see the Head Master (the same Mr Griffiths) rushing off on the back of a motor bike to Carmarthen hoping to be in time to prevent one of his older boarders, a boy named Prydderch, from joining the army. He was about 16 and a half I suppose but a big fellow – and youths at that time rushed to join by putting their age on. The Head Master was too late. Prydderch had 'taken the shilling' and was in.[106]

Mr Griffith's example was not followed by all of his headteacher colleagues. Some openly colluded with the boys concerned and 'other responsible people' such as their parents and the military authorities.[107] One 15-year-old schoolboy became an officer on enlistment: Second Lieutenant Reginald Battersby of 11th Battalion East Lancashire Regiment had his application for a temporary commission signed by his grammar school headmaster.[108]

When boy soldier Richard Blades was discharged from the army in 1916 for 'lying on his attestation form', he returned home to his former employment until, on his eighteenth birthday, he promptly re-enlisted and served in France and Belgium for the last eleven months of the war. Others boy soldiers resumed their studies. One can only imagine the classroom discussions which followed the return to Gowerton Intermediate School in Glamorgan of two former pupils and boy soldiers discharged from the army in March 1918.[109] Such returns were temporary. At Helston Grammar School in Cornwall a County Scholar, named only as 'C.J.J.' in the records, ran away to enlist in October 1915. Following efforts to secure his return, the 16-year-old boy was discharged two months later. He went back to the school, passed the Oxford Local Senior Examination, then left again to take up employment as a clerk in the Direct Spanish Telegraph Company. In 1917, C.J.J. re-enlisted and served two years in the army.[110] Following massive losses of territory and manpower in the wake of the German Spring Offensive of March 1918, and real and general fears that the war might be lost on the battlefield, the British government decided that it might need to ready boy soldiers for war after all. The National Registration Amendment Act that same month required all boys aged fifteen and above to come forward and register.

The vast majority of children who left school prematurely – with official blessing and direction or otherwise – to fight the war in the fields and factories of the home front or become boy soldiers were drawn from the state-maintained schools. The nation's elementary schools, in particular, made a massive contribution to the war effort through their school collection, gardening and savings campaigns and their work as substitute farm labourers. The mass mobilisation of working-class children was not universally accepted, however, especially by those who pointed to perceived disparities of involvement based on social class. Emily Phipps, President of the National Federation of Women Teachers in 1915 (NFWT), made a particularly invidious comparison when she pointed out that, unlike the children in Britain's elementary schools, the pupils at Eton and Harrow were not expected to bring in the harvest.[111] The allotments which were tended by many pupils in the public schools and their involvement in many other wartime campaigns clearly did not count for some contemporary observers. The most important contribution of the public schools to the national war effort, of course, was determinedly elsewhere. Eton and Harrow, and indeed all those schools with OTC cadets, were busy preparing the next cohorts of officers for the armed forces. This was no soft option; boys were no longer playing at being soldiers, but were preparing themselves for a real war which would soon call upon their services. These boy soldiers were officer stock; replacements for the thousands of young men from similar backgrounds who had already perished in the trenches of Flanders and Gallipoli. As young army subalterns, their responsibilities were enormous and their life expectancy extremely short.[112] They were not yet on the front line, but they were already in the training camps.

On the outbreak of war in August 1914 cadets rushed back from their annual training camps to await orders. Colfe's Grammar School quickly discovered their place in the military hierarchy when their rifles were commandeered to be used in training sessions for the thousands of Londoners who had recently joined the colours.[113] Harrow School, too, drilled with dummy rifles after their real ones had been requisitioned.[114] Westminster School OTC, on the other hand, did their patriotic duty by making their rifles available to the Queen's Westminsters, the Royal Fusiliers and the London Scottish.[115] Some cadets were initially deployed in home defence duties in much the same way as Boy Scouts. Hymer's College in Hull received a telegram from the War Office on 7 August authorising deployment of the school's OTC to guard some nearby railway lines against possible espionage.[116] Morpeth Grammar School cadets acted as messengers,[117] whilst those from Northampton Grammar School served as orderlies at Duston War Hospital.[118] As the war gathered momentum, established cadet corps gained more recruits and diversified their activities. By November 1914 there were nearly as many cadets in the OTC at Hymer's College in Hull as there were Old Boys serving in the forces. Over 200 boys were drilling and there were specialist machine gun and signaling sections. The following year numbers exceeded 310 and a cycle dispatch rider section was established.[119] In some public schools the demands of the corps began to take precedence over traditional studies and sports activities. Dulwich College took the War Office requirement that senior boys did at least ten hours military training a week very seriously. Virtually all the boys over the age of fourteen were members of the OTC. Time for drill, signaling, operating field telephones, bayonet fighting, and lectures on chemistry and explosives was squeezed from timetabled lessons, games afternoons and leisure periods.[120]

Public schools with no previous history of providing military training soon felt under pressure to do so. The imperative to establish a school cadet corps was often internal. In 1915, at the very moment when rolls of honour were becoming benchmarks of contribution to the war effort and institutional status, the magazine at Bancroft's School in Essex, *The Bancroftian*, noted that only 5 per cent of serving former pupils had been commissioned. This, the magazine pointed out, compared badly with similar schools where 50 per cent and in some cases as many as 90 per cent of their alumni were officers. A Cadet Corps was quickly established. There was soon a distinct smell of metal polish around the school and the corps, as if to announce its presence to the world, 'marched around the district with the Woodford Bugles proudly blowing and the big drum banging'.[121] The cadet corps at Kent College, Canterbury, was similarly founded in 1915. The school's Head Master, Alfred Brownscombe, was its first Commanding Officer.[122]

Many grammar schools, for example those at Eastbourne, Ashby-de-la-Zouch, Hampton and Barrow, also established cadet corps during the war. Other secondary schools considered doing so but wartime staffing constraints dictated otherwise. In 1918 the Herbert Strutt School in Belper decided instead to pay 5 shillings per hour for boys to be drilled by an army Sergeant Instructor at the local Drill Hall.[123] In cases where schools took conscious decisions not to introduce cadet forces, such as at Harrow County School for Boys, this clearly did not preclude them from doing some soldiering; Ernest Young's pupils still did elementary drill and were taught the use of firearms.[124] By September 1915, however, fifty-eight Cadet Corps and ninety-one (Junior Division) OTC had been established in aided secondary schools recognised by the Board of Education.[125] The King Edward VII Grammar School in Melton Mowbray, founded just before the war, was one such school determined to provide the boys with military training on-site. In early 1915 a Cadet Force was introduced. An appeal fund raised £35 for the necessary equipment of belts and haversacks: two shillings and sixpence came from the school's own Sports Fund, the Governors donated £25, and the LEA forwarded five shillings for each cadet enrolled. The boys were asked to purchase their new uniforms, and most of the volunteers found at least half of the necessary 30 shillings. The fund for equipment ran out before dummy rifles could be purchased, so these were made by the school woodwork department instead. In December 1915 a fund-raising concert was held at which the Adjutant of the 1st (Grammar Schools) Cadet Battalion of the Leicestershire Regiment gave a patriotic recitation. The said Captain Brockington was also the LEA Director of Education. Four boys subsequently brought their own horses to school and formed a mounted detachment. The KES boys evidently took their training very seriously, parading on Wednesday afternoons instead of Games, drilling and counter marching after school, and undertaking field exercises and night marches whilst on their cadet camp at Burton Lazars racecourse in July 1916.[126]

Preparation for military service was clearly a priority for cadet forces, but it was not their only activity. They were involved in air raid precaution duties and, as at Bolton School after a Zeppelin raid in September 1916, various forms of 'street duty' in the days following German attacks.[127] In Glasgow, the Corps of Hutcheson's Grammar School worked as flag sellers, took part in processions and attended military funerals.[128] The wartime experience of the Cadet Corps at George Green's School in the London borough of Poplar, as recalled later by former pupil G.F. Fink, demonstrated the many ways in which cadets were connected to, and contributed to, their local communities on the home front. Buglers volunteered to sound the 'all clear' at police stations after air-raids. In June 1917, George Green's cadets represented their school at the funeral of the North Street School air-raid victims. They had earlier formed a guard of honour for the visit of Mrs Lloyd George when she had opened the Poplar Recreation Ground situated opposite George Green's School. Their military training involved drilling in the School Hall and on the roof of the school. The school's headteacher gave the cadets a direct association with real soldiers. Dr Burnett arranged for the corps to have a joint exercise at Upminster with some of his men from the Artists' Rifles. Unfortunately, the latter failed to turn up on the day, and the schoolboy cadets easily took their designated objective.[129]

Many schools thus became increasingly militarised during the war. Some, for example City of London School, made membership of the corps compulsory.[130] A few schools supplemented the work of the Corps by introducing Scout troops for boys not old enough to become cadets.[131] Hymer's College addressed the perceived needs of the other end of the school-age spectrum by introducing, in 1916, a more advanced military course for boys of eighteen; a programme which included fifteen hours of OTC work, practical mathematics, map making and surveying.[132]

Being a cadet during the Great War was not a universally popular experience for British schoolboys. The quantity and, for some OTC products, the quality of pre-service military training was questionable. One boy at Cheltenham College later recalled:

OTC parades became longer and more frequent, and we did too many field exercises, of which the point was quite obscure but which meant that we spent hours advancing in short rushes and falling down in cow pats and sheep-droppings.[133]

Dulwich College also instituted an additional programme for boys close to call-up age, but one Old Alleynian who experienced both the course and subsequent front-line active service remarked later that his school's War Special Section training would have been more useful for fighting the Boers than for fighting the Germans in the trenches in France.[134] The response to the tremendous amount of drill and military exercise at Charterhouse varied from house to house.[135] So much was dependent in all schools upon the commitment of senior boys and, especially, their teachers. When a Senior Monitor at Bolton School pointed out that membership of the Cadets was voluntary, Headmaster Lipscomb replied that so was the school.[136] Some parents – and there were those who did question the wartime escalation of nationalistic sentiment and militaristic provision in schools – were equally concerned about OTC membership. The historian A.J.P. Taylor attended Buxton College in the first years of the war. The college OTC had a drum and bugle band, drilled regularly, undertook long route marches and conducted manoevres with other school corps. Taylor noted later in his autobiography that Buxton College 'would have seemed a war-obsessed place' to parents, such as his, with distinct anti-war convictions:

One day in the summer of 1916 I came home with the news that Mr Gallagher had taken us out into the fields and shown us the trenches where the older boys trained in the OTC. My mother was horrified. In her mind's eye she already saw me in the trenches or the guardroom. The hateful war was closing in on me. She determined that I must move school at once.[137]

For many younger boys the war brought excitement and eager anticipation. The magazine at Felsted Preparatory School in Essex declared that nearly all the boys in the Junior House were 'trying hard to decide whether they ought to eventually adorn the Army, the Navy or the Royal Flying Corps'.[138] Older boys left their courses early to join the forces not simply out of a sense of duty. Stuart Cloete at Lancing College later recalled that:

> Something was going on that was too big to be missed – adventure on a heroic scale (and) the eagerness of a young man to test himself, to try out, as it were, his own guts.[139]

Former pupils, fondly remembered young men not much older than themselves, were already winning distinctions on the field of battle and heightening feelings of esprit de corps which transcended any erstwhile divide between home and battle fronts. Such excitement was tempered by varying degrees of realism. G.F. Fink summed up the mood of many when he wrote later that:

> Of course we were all playing at being soldiers but I think we were all aware that in a very short time we would all be involved in the real thing.[140]

For Cecil Lewis at Oundle School:

> (Life's) easy pattern (was) thrown out of symmetry. We very young men had no place, actual or prospective, in a peaceful world. We walked off the playing-fields into the lines.[141]

Chapter 6

Alma Mater

The picture taken that day is by me now: the vine winds over the white wall, a happy emblem of our occasion; and the five of us, all young and with an expression of subdued resoluteness and direct action, are looking on the world together.

Edmund Blunden (1928)
Undertones of War

The image recalled by Edmund Blunden in his autobiography was that of five young British infantry officers, posing together in one of the many group photographs captured for posterity during the Great War. It was taken in 1917, in the French town of St Omer. The soldiers were fellow subalterns in the 11th Battalion Royal Sussex Regiment. More remarkable, however, is that they had all been pupils and friends at the same school before the call-to-arms. Blunden, the wartime poet and front-line soldier, was joined in front of the camera by Vidler, Tice, Amon and Collyer, fellow Old Boys of Christ's Hospital School in Sussex. Old school ties connected them, even amongst the devastation of the Western Front on which they served. Vidler, in particular, had a penchant for school recollections and humorous mimicry, granting his old friends comforting memories and a brief release from present realities. These young men had far more in common than simply being brother officers who might, at any time, be attached to another battalion or regiment. They were more than just soldiers, more even than young gentlemen officers; they were part of a shared history, which both transcended the conflict and was reinforced by their collective participation in it. Old Boys, it seemed, never really left school.[1]

Blunden and his school friends were not alone in looking back to the golden days of their youth and to the institutions which shaped them. The Old Boys of Sherborne School continued to celebrate Founder's Day even if the war meant that, for those on the Western Front, their reunion was held a little too close to the front line.[2] On 31 July 1917, at the height of the Battle of Passchendaele, Old Bedford Moderns Edgar Mobbs and Norman Spencer reminisced about the old school and former schoolmates. Minutes later, Lieutenant Colonel Mobbs, renowned England rugby player and Commanding Officer of 7th Battalion Northamptonshire Regiment, was killed in action leading his men forward near the village of Zillebeke.

Whilst school communities looked out from Blighty and thought of their former pupils fighting on an increasing number of war fronts, their alumni looked back - to their Alma Mater. The notion of 'doing one's duty' was quite deliberately applied in many interconnected and indivisible ways: duty to King and Country, to family and community, and to school. The very notion of the 'Old Boy' was a relatively recent creation of the pre-war period and was, for the public schools especially, whose products were exported throughout the British Empire, inextricably tied to ideas of class, privilege and imperialism. In *The Old School Lie* Peter Parker has referred to the way in which the Old Boy, fanned by 'the incense fumes of nostalgia', was 'forever mourning his exile from the magic garden of his youth'. Reverence for the 'The School' assumed quasi-religious characteristics and significance.[3]

The Great War strengthened the ties between 'The School' and its 'Old Boys'. School magazines enabled both to take communion – to share thoughts and experiences in difficult times. Magazines were written in a language that was familiar and comforting, unlike the unintelligible 'foreign language' spoken by civilians and dismissed with such contempt by the battle-scarred poet Robert Graves on returning to Blighty.[4] For many former pupils serving in the trenches of the Western Front or other battle zones the school magazine – *their school* magazine – became an important medium of contact and information. Schools of all kinds produced special 'War Issues', containing the latest information gleaned from serving Old Boys and from the wider school community. Details of enlistments, commissions, promotions and, all too frequently, casualties were collated for publication. Men at the front saw their own names – and those of their friends – listed on the Roll of Honour, and knew that someone beyond their immediate family had recognised their contribution to the war effort. Old Boys waited eagerly in the trenches for receipt of the latest edition. After receiving his copy of the school magazine in 1916, Old Dixonian Geoffrey Smith wrote back to the George Dixon School in Birmingham:

8th Battalion Worcs. Regiment
B.E.F. France

Dear Sir,
    Many thanks for the copy of *The Crown* and also for promising to send it to me each term. One's school magazine is a link with home which no other paper can be. When I received your 'Crown' I was in the firing line and unable to acknowledge its receipt immediately. Under the circumstances I know you will accept my apologies.
    Wishing the school every success,
                    Yours Sincerely,
                    Geo. H. Smith
                    2nd Lieut.

The school printed the letter in the next copy of the magazine.[5]

Some Old Boys sent articles or diaries recording their war experience. The editor of *The Bridge* magazine at Handsworth Grammar School in Birmingham included one former pupil's progress report to one of his old teachers under the heading 'From a Minesweeper in the North Sea':

> Mr. Kay has recently received an extremely graphic and interesting letter from a well-known Old Boy, T.B. Howse, formerly Hon. Secretary of the B.T. Old Boys' Society. He entered the School of Wireless Telegraphy, and having passed his examinations which qualified him as an operator, was sent to sea on a trawler to get his 'sea legs' and the necessary practical experience of his work. He writes very cheerfully, as the following extract shows: 'I have the picture post card of the Old School fixed up in my silence cabin, and when on watch I often recall things that have happened which I thought I had quite forgotten'.[6]

Harrow County School for Boys made great efforts to keep in touch with Old Boys at the front and sent them copies of *The Gaytonian* free of charge. In return, former pupils of the school sent back simple and sincere narratives, occasionally containing examples of bravado and 'stiff-upper-lip' sentiments. The value of their scouting experience was recognised by one who wrote in 1915: 'My semaphore came in very handy this week. I was given 50 men to teach, as I knew it pretty well'. Another wrote from the trenches in 1917 'I shall never say the school football field is muddy after this'.[7]

John Clifford Walley wrote to De Aston School in Market Rasen, a school he attended from 1909 to 1914. After two short-term teaching appointments he enlisted in November 1915, aged nineteen, as an Officer Cadet in the Artists' Rifles before gaining a commission in 5th Leicestershire Regiment. His letter to the *De Astonian* in 1916 included many of the new army slang terms he had picked up, such as 'No bon' and 'Na pooh'. After mentioning contacts he had made with other old De Astonians on active service, he went on to say:

> (Trusting) that the staff and all the boys are 'A.1'. I suppose I still know most of the boys. Kind regards to all of them. I am looking forward to receiving the School Magazine about Christmas time.

Lieutenant Walley duly received the Christmas issue. Within its pages was the letter he had written. He then wrote back to promise that his magazine subscription would be forwarded as soon as he could obtain an English two shilling piece. Three months later, on 22 March 1917, he was killed in action near the village of Epehy in France.[8]

For pupils still at school, letters from young men they knew and admired added much to their knowledge of the war and all it entailed. School magazines did not have the immediacy of reporting, or contain the graphic imagery of conflict, characteristic of today's omnipresent media coverage, but they did introduce schoolchildren to other worlds. Pupils at Deacon's School in Peterborough experienced, albeit from a position of relative safety on this side of the English Channel, the early advances and subsequent setbacks of the BEF in Belgium in 1914.[9] In Wales, pupils in Gowerton Intermediate School followed fellow Gowertonians to Gallipoli and Passchendaele.[10] Some of the articles penned in *The Barrovian*, which from the early months of the war had urged the boys of Barrow Grammar School to serve in the forces, were clearly intended to be both informative and motivational. They included:

With the Canadians in France by G. Webster.
Trench Warfare in Gallipoli by W.T. Forshaw VC.
The Work of the Engineers by T.N. Riley.

The school's historian noted that 'much of this material was garnered carefully and presented dramatically so that the School could feel that it was, through its Old Boys, a real part of the fighting war'.[11]

Sutton High School's magazine contained a regular section entitled 'Old Girls' News in which it listed the contribution to the war effort of named former pupils. By 1915 nearly thirty were known to be working in Red Cross and other hospitals, and the magazine's editor appealed repeatedly for Old Girls to let the school know what they were doing in relation to the war especially. In the magazine's Spring 1918 issue, Elsa Chambers-Smith wrote of her wartime experience under the heading 'With the Y.M.C.A. somewhere in France', stating that:

I have been for the last ten months at the Y.M.C.A. Headquarters at the Advanced Base of the British Armies in France, this being the nearest place up the Line that any women (with the exception of a comparatively small number of nurses at the Field Dressing Stations), are allowed to go.[12]

Letters from Old Boys and Old Girls were generally informative and balanced accounts. Some 'tended to suggest that life at the Front was rather like school, tough but surprisingly enjoyable'.[13] Many contained rallying cries to those they fully expected to follow in their footsteps. In a world convulsed by change, many urged 'The School' to maintain traditions and old familiar ways; to provide a secure anchor back home. For Old Emanuels the school represented the England for which they fought and might be called upon to die.[14] Self-censorship, and editorial decisions taken by headteachers and others responsible for production of magazine issues,[15] meant that young readers were rarely exposed to operationally sensitive military detail or the worst excesses of brutality in front-line combat areas. Some correspondents did refer to what they had witnessed, but they were rarely truly descriptive. Nurses, too, alluded to the carnage on the battle fronts in general terms. Evelyn Cartridge, a member of a VAD Motor Ambulance Unit attached to No. 1 General Hospital BEF, wrote an article for the *White & Blue* magazine at The Alice Ottley School in Worcester informing her schoolgirl audience that:

> The awful suffering I have seen during the last fortnight has made the war seem very close indeed. One thing which always stirs my feelings is to arrive at the quay at Havre at about 6 a.m. and unload our battered and wrecked humanity on to the hospital ship, and then to see alongside a troop ship of bright and happy faces – just coming in from England.[16]

Increasingly, however, the need to record 'the final sacrifice' made by former pupils brought home 'the horror of war' in a way that letters from the front, and especially alternative and distorted representations 'of heroic deeds and daring exploits' in the popular press, never could.[17] The Names of the Fallen spoke for themselves.

Schools kept in touch with their former pupils in other ways. From 1916 Sherborne sent 'House Letters' to former pupils at the front.[18] Ex-pupils of Rugby School who served in the armed forces were each sent a postcard reminding them that 'Each day at noon work stops while the Chapel Bell rings and we think of you and wish you well'.[19] Barrow Grammar School sent a Christmas letter 'to all Old Boys in the King's Service on land and sea' and boys in the school were encouraged to stamp one envelope and to add their own individual message or question.[20] Letters and other forms of communication from home and school were so important. They formed a 'permanent and vital bond', building bridges between life and death, and between the past, the present and the future.[21]

There was one other important means of maintaining personal contact. Bessie Ashworth, a pupil at Bacup and Rawtenstall Grammar School in Lancashire during the war, remembered numerous occasions when men in uniform called in to see Mr Jackson, their old headmaster. They included:

> Some soldiers in khaki, other sailors in blue with bell-bottom trousers and round caps complete with the gilded names of their ships. I don't remember any boys wearing Air Force blue, though.[22]

During the Great War former pupils visited their Alma Mater before being sent abroad for the first time, just as others had done in the past before embarking for a new life in Canada, New Zealand or other British Dominions.[23] Such visits were important rites of passage for the visitors and tangible evidence of their transition to independent adulthood. Northop School noted the visit on 10 March 1915 of Private Fred Freeman of the RAMC, previously a pupil teacher at the school and now about to leave for France. On 18 January 1916 Private Freeman gave a lecture to the school's upper classes on his experiences of ten months in action, aided by a selection of suitable souvenirs from the battlefields. Northop School recorded numerous visits from Old Boys, many of whom had been forced to return home by wounds received in the Gallipoli campaign:

1915
15th October: Lieut Aynslie Astbury who was wounded in Gallipoli and now in hospital in England visited this his old school this morning and the scholars and staff gave him a rousing reception.

9th November: Pte Frank Price invalided from the Dardanelles wounded on Suvla Bay visited.

1916
3rd March: An old scholar Cpl Godfrey Jones wounded on the Dardanelles visited today.

27th October: Pte J Lovelock an old boy invalided at Gallipoli visited today.[24]

In November 1917, Sergeant W.S. Birse gave a talk to the pupils based upon his experiences with the Army Service Corps in the front line at Ypres. Mr Richardson, Northop School's headteacher, then set work based upon the talk to develop the pupils' writing skills. The essays which followed 'showed intelligence'. At Reading School, a somewhat more distinguished alumni, Captain C. St Q. Fullbrook-Leggatt DSO MC, inspected the OTC in 1916 and then proceeded to give a short address emphasising the importance of discipline and self-discipline.[25] Many schools invited former pupils to important school occasions. The 1916 Christmas Tea at Holt Schools saw the unveiling of yet another manifestation of a Roll of Honour, namely 'Framed photographs of 31 of our Old Boys serving with the forces'. One of the Old Boys in attendance then unveiled a Union Jack flag, which he had rescued from HMS *Triumph* after the battleship had been torpedoed and later sank in the Dardanelles. The proceedings finally came to an end when 'The scholars sang patriotic songs, and twelve girls gave a display of bandaging'.[26] Serving soldiers who were former pupils of Emanuel School in London frequently attended OTC church parades and Sunday Communion Service. The Old Emanuel 1915 Society, one of many school alumni organisations which were founded or were resurrected during the Great War, welcomed those OEs home on leave to their regular meetings.[27]

For many of the 126 boys of Kibble, going home on leave meant going home to the residential reformatory institution. Most had joined Scottish and Australian units. Many had kept up correspondence with the school, often expressing thanks for all it had done for them. Their visits over the Christmas period, often for several days at a time, allowed them the time to play football with the younger boys and afforded an opportunity to thank their headmaster James Love, a man who had regularly sent them small sums of money to help them make ends meet. The 'Old Boy' was thus not simply the product of the elite schools. Former pupils from schools across the social and education spectrum were proud of their place of schooling and, in return, their Alma Mater took great interest in their individual progress and achievements.[28]

The need for schools to communicate with their Old Boys, and vice versa, applied equally to former teachers. Schools and pupils wrote to 'Sir' too, keeping him up-to-date with the latest developments in the classroom and on the playing fields. Teachers and other staff on active service remembered in similar ways the schools in which they had recently worked. They too sent postcards and wrote letters back from the trenches, visited their schools when back in Blighty, donated souvenirs and gave talks about their wartime experiences.[29] When Mr F.W. Lamb left Auckland School in County Durham for his military training, the children in his class wrote a letter to him every month. His reply on one occasion was sincere and touching:

I miss you all very much and my greatest regret is that I shall probably not have the pleasure of again teaching some of you. By the time the war is over several of you will have left school.
Your sincere friend
F.W. Lamb.

He went on to remind the children of the importance of learning, diligence, duty, high purpose and honour. In keeping with traditional and gendered assumptions, he referred to how the girls would be able to teach him useful skills such as washing and scrubbing for his 'cookhouse fatigue', and informed the boys that they would need to learn how to sew buttons and darn socks.[30]

Visits from serving teachers were eagerly anticipated and a matter worthy of note in the school logbook. There was no reference to the war at all in the official record held at Busbridge School in Godalming until 25 January 1916, the day that Mr Seed reappeared in front of his pupils and staff, dressed in the uniform of a British Army NCO:

The school received a visit from Sgt Seed this morning, who is now an instructor in physical training and bayonet drill, having successfully passed a 21 days course at Aldershot gymnasia. Our Headmaster was only able to stay about an hour as he was on his way to Brentford Essex where he is to be attached to the 4th Gloucesters as drill instructor.[31]

The Old School was never far from such men and women's thoughts, even in the direst of circumstances. Teaching, for the vast majority of those employed across the educational spectrum – from the elite to the elementary schools, and the diverse range of institutions positioned between them – was more than a job; it was vocation. The Great War might cause individuals to question such sentiments, but it could not destroy them entirely. Whilst serving abroad, Malcolm White, formerly a master at Shrewsbury, still noted key dates in the school calendar and thought of major school events, such as the annual Sports Day. He visited the school regularly whilst on leave. In a letter to Evelyn Southwell, a close friend and former Shrewsbury colleague also serving in France, he compared the tension of waiting for the Somme Offensive to commence with waiting for a rowing match to begin. When the great battle finally got under way on 1 July 1916, Mr White, by then transformed by the exigencies of war into Lieutenant White of the Rifle Brigade, was killed instantly whilst leading his men forward.[32] His final letter to Southwell, who was killed just over two weeks later in the same battle, contained the following lines:

Our new house and Shrewsbury are immortal, which is a great comfort.[33]

Part III

Teachers at War

A man might rave against war: but war, from among its myriad faces, could always turn towards him one, which was his own.

Frederic E. Manning (1929)
The Middle Parts of Fortune

Chapter 7

Patriots

Won't you join up Comrades?
Erich Maria Remarque (1929)
All Quiet on the Western Front

Through the classroom window Paul Baumer and his fellow students watch as the news of war erupts on the streets of their small German town. Herr Kantorek, the schoolmaster, exhorts Paul and his classmates to do their patriotic duty and to enlist in the armies of the Fatherland. Later, during the ensuing conflict, Paul reflected with evident bitterness on the way in which the 'stern little man in a grey tail-coat, with a face like a shrew mouse' was prepared to sacrifice a generation of schoolboys on the altar of misguided patriotism:

> I can see him now, as he used to glare at us through his spectacles and say in a moving voice: 'Won't you join up Comrades?' These teachers always carry their feelings ready in their waistcoat pockets, and trot them out by the hour. But we didn't think of that then. There were thousands of Kantoreks, all of whom were convinced that they were acting for the best – in a way that cost them nothing. And that is why they let us down so badly.

Kantorek is one of the most memorable characters to emerge from the literature of the Great War. Erich Maria Remarque's celebrated book depicts this particular German schoolmaster as one of the 'blustering home-front patriots' who betrayed their young charges in the summer of 1914. The fictional Kantorek represents all those figures of authority, in all of the nations of Europe, who lunged headlong into war but should have known better.[1]

Herr Kantorek and other alleged purveyors of what the British poet Wilfred Owen dubbed the 'Old Lie' are not truly representative of the real teachers who responded to the call-to-arms in 1914. Just as there was no typical officer, private soldier or home-front civilian in the Great War, so too was there no typical teacher. The response by teachers, both masters and mistresses, to the exceptional circumstances of the years 1914 to 1919 varied enormously. The spectrum of their involvement in wartime activity ranges from immediate, but not necessarily unquestioning, commitment to the war effort to the opposite extreme of sustained anti-war campaigning.

There were some teachers who did appear to conform to the 'Kantorek' model. The new religion of jingoistic imperialism, imbued with the creed of duty, honour and self-sacrifice, found many converts within the pre-war teaching profession. C.H.P. Mayo, for example, a Mathematics Master at Harrow School who had supported Winston Churchill's quest for a place at Sandhurst Military Academy, was noted for his 'ecstasy in his proxy relationship with war'.[2] The Victorian Volunteer Movement, and its successor the Territorials, had also attracted teachers to the ranks of part-time soldiering. These included men from beyond the public schools, such as John Martin who introduced drill into St Augustine's School, a small parochial school in Peterborough, in the 1870s.[3] The growth of militarism within schools, however, was really made possible by the interests and activities of individual headteachers. Some, for example Mr Lipscomb at Bolton School, promoted and encouraged nationalistic values. He was 'a white-hot patriot (who) did everything he could to bring home to the boys the demands of the country'.[4] Others, supported by their governors, were keen to find a place for military training within the secondary school curriculum. The Cadet Corps founded at Morpeth Grammar School in 1910 was one of Headmaster Dakyn's 'favourite children'.[5] Some headteachers involved themselves directly in the Corp's organisation and activities. When the Newport High School for Boys Corps was founded in 1911, serving as a battery of the Newport Royal Artillery Cadets, Headmaster Battersby became an honorary major.[6] Even headteachers who were also ordained ministers saw no contradiction in promoting militarism within their schools. The Reverend Harold Buchanan Riley of Emanuel School in London and the Reverend William Parker of The King's School in Rochester both regularly wore military uniforms.[7]

The British declaration of war in August 1914 and the mass enlistment which followed gave such men an immediate opportunity to establish their schools' credentials. The production of a Roll of Honour, often at the instigation of the headteacher, was part of a process in which schools became active recruitment agents, encouraging their young men to join the colours. The realities of the Great War did not diminish enthusiasm and commitment to the war effort in some quarters; indeed, the mounting causality lists and home front deprivations may even have stiffened resolve. Chipping Camden School's wartime Speech Day in 1916, presided over by the khaki-clad Colonel the Honourable A.H. Bathurst, Chairman of Governors, included an unequivocal statement of martial intent. In his address to the school community Headteacher W. Matthew Cox stressed the 'the importance of drill and the use of the rifle'. In bellicose mood he went on to say that the school hoped to gain a rifle range in due course and that 'after a reasonable amount of time I am sure our boys will be able to shoot anybody or anything'.[8]

Like Kantorek, such men 'were convinced that they were acting for the best'. Unlike the fictional German schoolteacher, however, these real-life individuals existed within a complex network of institutional and local expectations and relationships. In the heady days of 1914, the headteachers of even the smallest schools worked with other pillars of the local community to awaken national sentiment and to help swell the ranks of volunteers. In the Parish of Northop in Wales, for example, Mr Richardson the headteacher joined with Mr Vaughan the Vicar, Mr Williams the Magistrate and Lord Justice Banks of Soughton Hall to wave the flag and rally the troops.[9]

The responsibility for sending so many young men to the trenches was thus a collective and communal one. It was also a weighty one. Playing the part – ascribed to them or assumed deliberately – came at a price. David Samuel at Aberystwyth County School was not alone in counting the cost of the war to his school community. In assemblies he would refer to former pupils killed in action and hope for the recovery of those wounded. He also kept a record book of press cuttings of those who 'brief years before walked the corridors of his School'.[10] Coming to terms with the death and maiming of Old Boys, and trying to make sense of the conflict as it unravelled to the remaining pupils, was part of each headteacher's war service.

Thousands of British schoolteachers, including headteachers, were not 'armchair warriors' of the type depicted in *All Quiet on the Western Front*. Many members of the teaching profession fell within the age range for military service. They joined with the rest of the adult population in having to decide upon their individual course of action in response to the general call-to-arms. They owed both a duty to King and Country and a responsibility for nurturing the children in their classrooms. War fever did not dupe these men and women, or force them unwillingly or unwittingly to rush headlong into uniform and combat or war-related activities. Like millions of their fellow Britons they experienced internal and external tensions over where their real duty lay. To argue otherwise is to deny this particular group of sensitive, intelligent and educated individuals of 1914 the same degree of respect for decision making that their counterparts a century later would routinely expect. Every individual actor is conditioned by the times and spaces in which they live, but personal agency differentiates them from the seemingly unthinking crowd.

When Britain declared war on Germany on 4 August 1914 teachers responded in myriad ways. Earlier chapters have shown how teachers who were also members of the Territorial forces attached to the BEF, for example John Paulson at Orme Road Boys School, responded to the order to mobilise and quickly re-joined their units to prepare for deployment overseas. Men from the public schools with OTC command experience, like George Tryon at Oundle, were swift to offer their skills and experience. In the weeks, months and years which followed, large numbers of their colleagues also enlisted in the armed forces. Many resigned from their teaching posts on hearing that war had been declared, informed their headteachers of their intention to enlist at the earliest opportunity or, as was the case with new appointment Arthur Schofield at Deacon's School, failed to appear at the start of the autumn term.

Amongst the thousands of Britons who made their way to the recruiting offices were male teachers from across the educational spectrum: the Oxbridge-educated master from the elite public school, the professionally-trained teacher in the maintained secondary school, and the certified elementary school assistant all took the King's shilling. The wartime history of the former is particularly well documented in the various institutional histories and, collectively, in Anthony Seldon and David Walsh's recent *Public Schools and the Great War*. Public school masters, like the boys they taught, were the products of a chivalric code cultivated in the boarding house and on the games field. It was to be expected that they too would serve their country when called upon to do so. Many – but not all – in this group of enlisted teachers had prior military experience gained whilst OTC cadets or as officers commanding school-based OTC. In 1914 Britain needed such leaders of men.

The story of Corrie Denew Chase exemplifies the social, educational and military background of many of the teachers from the public schools who enlisted at this time. Born in 1878, Corrie Chase came from a family with a long tradition of producing Anglican clergymen. He attended Blundell's School in Tiverton, where he played rugby and cricket and represented the school at the Public School Gym Competition at Aldershot in 1896 and 1897. After winning a Blundell's scholarship to Sidney Sussex College, Cambridge, he read Classics and, at some point in his undergraduate career, decided to enter the teaching profession. Two years as a teacher at Woodbridge School in Suffolk were followed by a period of further study of German at Heidelberg University and French at the Sorbonne in Paris. In 1905 he was appointed to teach Modern Languages at Campbell College, a relatively new public school which had been established in Belfast in 1894. When the school's OTC was founded in 1909, Mr Chase became Captain Chase. As Commanding Officer he led the Campbell College OTC contingent and accompanied them to the annual camps organised for British public schools at Tidworth (1911), Aldershot (1912) and Rugely (1913). The planned OTC Camp for 1914 was cancelled; the growing tensions on the Continent prompted one school, at least, to conduct a risk assessment. When war was eventually declared, Corrie Chase returned to Campbell College at the start of the new school year. By December, however, he had enlisted in the 16th (Pioneer) Battalion Royal Irish Rifles. At the age of thirty-six, and with his OTC credentials, he was commissioned with the rank of captain in the British Army. After training in Ireland and England he and his battalion, now part of the 36th (Ulster) Division, departed for France.[11]

Wilfrith Elstob's background was similarly conventional. Wilfrith was born in 1888, the son – like Corrie Chase - of an Anglican clergyman. After attending Ryleys Preparatory School in Cheshire, at the age of ten he became a boarder at

Christ's Hospital School. There he became a house monitor and a member of the 1st XV rugby team. In 1909 he gained his BA degree, and the following year a teaching diploma, at Manchester University. After studying in Paris, again at the Sorbonne, he joined the staff at the Preparatory School of Merchiston Castle School in Edinburgh as Senior French Master. On 11 September 1914 he enlisted as a private in the Public Schools Battalion, but just before joining them for training he accepted, instead, the offer of a commission in the Manchester Pals Battalion. Second Lieutenant Wilfrith Elstob joined 'A' Company of the 16th Battalion The Manchester Regiment and spent twelve months in training at Heaton Park in the city, at Grantham and at Larkhill Camp on Salisbury Plain. On 6 November 1915 the 16th Manchesters embarked for Boulogne.

Bernard William Vann also taught in a public school and, like Corrie Chase and Wilfrith Elstob, responded early to the call-to-arms of 1914. His social and educational background, however, demonstrates the importance of recognising individual nuances and avoiding any stereotyping of the men and women of 1914. On the outbreak of war, Bernard Vann was teaching at Wellingborough School. He was a graduate of Jesus College, Cambridge, where he had excelled on the sports field and in the debating chamber. He was a hockey 'Blue' and a sergeant in the OTC. Bernard Vann's early years, however, were not as conventionally privileged as those of Corrie Chase and Wilfrith Elstob. He did not attend a public school but instead was educated in the schools where his father Alfred Vann taught: South End Elementary School in Rushden followed by the nearby Chichelle Grammar School in Higham Ferrers where his father was appointed Head Master in 1899. On leaving school, and before going to university, Bernard taught for a while at Ashby De La Zouche Grammar School. During that period he also played association football for Northampton Town and Derby County, and hockey for Leicestershire. Teaching was not, however, his original vocation. After Cambridge he prepared for ordination to the priesthood. In January 1913 he was appointed Chaplain at Wellingborough School, where he also taught history and theology and coached football and cricket. When war was declared Bernard immediately applied to become an Army Chaplain. Frustrated by the lack of response from the War Office, on 31 August he enlisted instead in the 28th (County of London) Battalion – the Artists' Rifles. His Cambridge University degree, OTC experience, sporting pedigree and evident personal qualities outweighed any consideration of his relatively humble origins, and Private Vann was commissioned just two days later. Second Lieutenant Vann of the 1st/8th Battalion Sherwood Foresters departed for France in February 1915.

The new secondary schools also produced their share of teacher-soldiers. At Harrow County School for Boys, one of Bob Hart's teachers enlisted almost immediately war was declared. Russell Mervyn Wheeler (Plate 32), the school's Senior Master of English and History, was the son of Alfred Wheeler, schoolteacher in the village of Over in Cambridgeshire. Russell followed in his father's footsteps and joined the teaching profession. He trained first as a pupil teacher and then began teacher training at St Peter's College in Peterborough. In 1907, however, he enrolled at Fitzwilliam College, Cambridge, gaining a BA in History in 1910 and a subsequent MA in 1914. He joined the staff of Harrow County just after the school had opened in 1911 and, in addition to his teaching commitment, contributed to the development of the school Scout troop and chaired the Debating Society. On the outbreak of war, 31-year-old Mr Wheeler returned to Cambridge and trained for four months in the university's OTC, not as a student this time, but as an enlisted man in the Middlesex Territorials. On 27 January 1915 he gained his commission and soon saw action on the Western Front.[12]

Hundreds of teachers from the elementary school also enlisted early. To label such volunteers simply as 'teachers', however, fails to recognise how multi-dimensional many of them were. Evelyn Henry Lintott, for example, was better known as a sportsman than a teacher. Educated at the Royal Grammar School in Guildford, Evelyn then did his teacher training at St Luke's College Exeter in 1905 before taking a teaching post at Oldfield Road School in Willesden. Like Bernard Vann he was also an accomplished footballer and, as was the case for many amateur sportsmen at the time, combined full-time teaching with playing for what are now professional sides. His early clubs included Plymouth Argyle and Queen's Park Rangers. Evelyn played five times for the England Amateur team before turning professional and playing for Bradford City and winning a further seven England caps in the senior side. Despite his fame – sufficient to warrant his depiction on a cigarette card (Plate 33) – he continued to teach, this time at Dudley Hill School in Bradford. During the 1910–11 season Evelyn was also head of the Players Union.[13] Despite having the distinction of being the first professional teacher to be commissioned, his statement of attestation on enlistment in the 15th Battalion West Yorkshire Regiment recorded his occupation as 'Schoolteacher'.

The overwhelming majority of teachers – and men generally – who joined the British armed forces during the Great War served in the army. Archibald Walter Buckle, however, was a pre-war part-time member of the Royal Naval Volunteer Reserve (RNVR). Born in Brockley in south London in 1889, he became a schoolteacher at St Augustine's School in Paddington. In August 1914 he married his wife, Elsie, and was still on honeymoon when war broke out. He immediately reported for duty and joined the Drake Battalion of the 63rd (Royal Naval) Division (RND). This hybrid force, under the direct orders of the Admiralty but deployed as an infantry unit, was sent to Belgium in September 1914. Private Buckle was amongst the defenders of Antwerp.

In the absence of so many male teachers, schools throughout the country and across the educational spectrum were faced by an enormous logistical problem –

how on earth would they staff the curriculum? Many of the public schools replaced men such as Chase, Elstob and Vann with temporary staff. Often, these were former pupils or young men from similar backgrounds. All too often, however, this proved to be little more than a stop-gap rather than long-term solution. Harold Gostwyck May was, like so many teachers in the public school sector, both public school product and producer. Unlike many of his colleagues he was not a member of the OTC, nor was he a graduate of an ancient university. What he did possess, however, was an especially close association with the school in which he taught. In August 1914 he was a newly appointed Assistant Master at Sherborne School, having taught previously as a non-graduate for short periods at Clifton College, Llandovery College and Kelly College. He knew Sherborne well, having attended the school as a pupil from 1902 to 1907. Whilst there he became a Prefect and Head of House, captained the 1st XI cricket team, played in the 1st XV rugby team and represented the school in boxing competitions. This young man clearly had the personal qualities and many of the credentials needed by schools in this hour of crisis. His relative youth would bring a degree of dynamism to the school. The fact that he was of military service age, however, meant that his very temporary appointment created yet more instability. In November 1914 Harold May was commissioned into the 3rd Battalion Dorsetshire Regiment, along with temporary master Theodore Wood who had also joined the Sherborne teaching staff just three months earlier.[14]

Teacher training colleges might, in normal circumstances, have been expected to make good the shortfalls, especially in the non-elite schools. Their remit was to provide the growing number of elementary and secondary schools with well-qualified and thoroughly trained teachers. Their products, often former scholarship winners and educated to degree standard in specialist subjects, were intended to improve the quality of both instruction and leadership in the maintained schools. The events of August 1914, however, had shattered all notions of normality in these institutions too. The London Day Training College (LDTC), the original foundation of today's University College London Institute of Education (IOE), had opened its doors to both male and female trainee teachers shortly after the passing of the 1902 Education Act. When war began in 1914 many of its male students left without completing their courses or gaining their degrees and teaching qualifications. James Richard Garland (Plate 34) was one such trainee. Born in London in 1892, James gained a scholarship to Latymer School before becoming an undergraduate and trainee teacher at King's College London and the LDTC. When war was declared James was with the London University OTC on their summer camp. He enlisted immediately and was commissioned into 1st/2nd Battalion (London Regiment) Royal Fusiliers. James was one of seventeen of the fifty-six male trainees in the 1911 cohort at LDTC who enlisted in 1914. A further sixteen enlisted or were conscripted before the war ended. Their counterparts at

St John's Teacher Training College in nearby Battersea also mobilised early: their senior students made up 'A' Company in the 10th (Duke of Cambridge's Own) Battalion Middlesex Regiment.

Schools throughout the country could no longer rely upon the usual sources of supply for their teaching staff. Traditional notions of who might be qualified to teach the nation's children were about to be challenged. In the absence of direct action by central government, individual institutions were forced to find solutions to the staffing crisis themselves. For those in the maintained sector, providing schooling for the vast majority of British children, there were external expectations of what teachers might do in wartime. Schools did receive advice but direct orders were slow in coming. Government officials had clearly anticipated the dislocating effect that war might have on the nation's schools, especially if large numbers of teachers were to enlist. Joseph Pease at the Board of Education wrote to schools in 1914 stating that:

> If the schools could be kept open and effective, we would have done much. To reassure our countrymen serving with the colours we must maintain the balance and confidence of our life at home, by seeing that the children of this country are happy and occupied, living their normal life, well tended and undisturbed. As far as the education service is concerned, let us who remain in it make this our first duty.

Official advice, however, failed to keep pace with popular patriotism, the demands of an escalating conflict and the choices made by individuals in different occupations. Messrs Wheeler, Lintott, and Buckle were far from being isolated examples. The responsibility of keeping schools open weighed heavily on the shoulders of headteachers especially, yet even they were not immune from the call-to-arms, as Dr Burnett at George Green's School in London demonstrated when he left in 1915 to join the Artists' Rifles. Institutional pride could sometimes outweigh institutional needs, particularly when governors of schools, many of whom were active in local recruitment campaigns, encouraged members of the teaching staff to enlist.[15] In the early stages of the war, recruitment policy and practice was far too unsophisticated to differentiate between those who were keen and those who were vital for the war effort. There were some within the teaching profession who did have skills which were needed urgently. The expanded British army was in training, but there were insufficient trainers. In October 1914 a War Office Circular distributed via the Board of Education to school governors as *Circular 872* asked that teachers under the age of thirty-five with experience in Physical Exercises and Drill should be encouraged to enlist.[16] A year later, in October 1915, and with the need for manpower at the battle fronts even greater, the number rather than the skills of new recruits took priority. Arthur Henderson at the Board of Education consequently issued very different advice to that of his predecessor Joseph Pease, stating that in view of the increasing gravity of the international situation:

The balance of duty has now shifted and the claims of military service relative to those in the education service have now been increased. In their nature, education and war are as far apart as the poles. Education builds and war destroys. But there is time when the man who is building must leave his work to guard against a calamity which threatens the building itself.[17]

One of the great myths about the war fever of 1914 is that everyone in Britain was infected. The statistics for enlistment, however, do not support this argument. The figures for early enlistment – 300,000 volunteers in August 1914, plus a further 700,000 by the end of December that year – are truly impressive, yet they obscure the fact that this was but a small proportion of men of military age in England, Scotland and Wales who were eligible for military service and might have volunteered.[18] Also, the New Armies and other armed services were not truly representative of all geographical regions, social classes or occupations. There was a preponderance of volunteers from urban areas, the 'middling' classes and those formerly employed in white-collar jobs.[19] Many of the Pals battalions – and not just the Public Schools Battalions – attracted middle-class recruits. The proportion of self-employed and white collar professionals to manual workers was two enlistments to one. The principle of volunteerism soon came into conflict with notions of fairness.[20] Far more important, however, were the demands of national efficiency. The war of 1914 may have called for an army full of enthusiastic citizens, but the ongoing conflict demanded a far more considered and systematic deployment of skills across several fronts, including the home front. From 1916 conscription, rather than voluntary enlistment, would try to ensure that individual skills were matched with military needs, whether these were on the front lines of the battlefields or on the production lines in factories.

The way in which male schoolteachers in Swindon responded to the various demands for military manpower exemplifies the impact of individual decision making, the complexity of enlistment patterns and the subsequent insecurities for schools caused by staffing issues. By January 1916, thirty-seven teachers from Swindon were already serving with the armed forces, the great majority of them drawn from the elementary schools in the town. A further twenty-six had attested under the Derby Scheme,[21] continuing to teach in their schools but awaiting orders to report for duty. An additional fifty-five schoolmasters remained at their desks: thirty-six of them were over the age limit for military service and, remarkably, eighteen had been declared to be too unfit to serve. One teacher had chosen not to attest.[22] Increasing compulsion clearly did not negate the need for individuals to make decisions.

The Derby Scheme was followed by the introduction of conscription in The Military Service Acts of January 1916. A process of systematic exemption was introduced so that the 'necessary goods for civilian and military use' could be provided. Some occupations, such as coal mining, steel production, skilled agricultural, railways and munitions work, were 'certificated', 'reserved' or 'badged'.[23] Male members of the teaching profession, however, were conscripted in large numbers. Along with workers in commerce (trade and banking), the professions (especially clerks) and entertainment (hotel workers etc.), teachers generally were not considered to be vital to home-front production. Male workers in these groups were not indispensable; whilst they performed military duties there was, it was believed, a ready supply of cheap labour – usually women – ready to substitute for them.[24]

The Board of Education was clearly concerned about the impact this might have on secondary schools in particular. In November 1915 the Board had issued *Circular 926* stating that schoolmasters willing to serve should inform their headteachers, governing bodies and local authorities, and should also 'submit themselves for medical examination by an army doctor in order that they and the school authorities may know definitely whether they are fit or unfit'. The *Circular* also referred to:

> War Office advice that masters in Secondary Schools who are engaged in the work of training contingents of the OTC should not undertake military service, unless or until provision can be made for continuing that work efficiently.[25]

From 1916 even headteachers were at risk of being called up to fight. The departure of one headmaster, in particular, made quite an impact on his school. Ernest Basil Falkner MA MSc was on of the youngest headteachers in the country when in 1911, at the age of thirty, he was appointed to the headship of Haberdashers' Aske's Hatcham Boys' School in London. A graduate of Keble College, Oxford, he gained admission to the Head Masters' Conference as leader of a school which had only recently been recognised by the Board of Education. In 1916 Ernest Falkner was called up, awarded a commission in the Royal Naval Volunteer Reserve and subsequently attached to the Royal Naval Air Service. He made a brief return to the school shortly afterwards when he flew over the school one breaktime, much to the delight of the children of the school. In his absence the governors of the school, which had been founded by the Worshipful Company of Haberdashers, made a temporary appointment; Mr Lees, the Vice Master, was to be Acting Headmaster 'but with instructions to make no alterations of a permanent nature'.[26]

The introduction of conscription did not necessarily mean the automatic provision of more men for the armed forces. A system of Military Tribunals was established, in recognition of the varied ways in which one might serve in total war. Tribunals examined appeals for exemption from conscription lodged by those involved – both employees and employers – in non-reserved occupations.

Held locally, and consisting of community establishment figures and military representatives,[27] Tribunals operated within varied employment contexts and applied widely differing standards.[28] Tackling 'shirkers' was part of their role, but most were genuinely sensitive to local conditions and the need to balance the pressure for manpower from different quarters. Faced with severe staffing problems caused by early enlistments, many schools made full use of the appeal system to secure the exemption of teaching staff from military service. By 1916, the practical needs of most institutions were far more pressing and important than any kudos they might gain by having even greater representation at the front.

Headteachers did their best to retain their teaching staff, as did many governing bodies. They appealed to local Tribunals to be allowed to retain key staff who had been called up. Headmaster David Samuel at Aberystwyth County School appeared before his local panel to request total exemption for two of his science teachers, D.P. Ashton and E. Jones, and was successful.[29] At Nottingham High School, the governors made a firm stand on the call up of masters, declaring that those remaining were 'performing their full duty in a scheme of national service' and could not be spared from their important public service in school. Their efforts were not always successful, but they did manage to retain a nucleus of staff. [30] School governors also intervened in order to protect headteachers who had been notified of impending conscription. Few governing bodies were as accommodating as the one at Haberdashers'. At Deacon's School the governors appealed on behalf of Dr Davies and made it very clear, to their headteacher and to the panel, that the Head Master would not and could not be released from his duties. One LEA in Wales provided additional support for the governors in the schools which they maintained, passing a resolution in November 1915:

That the Governors of County Schools be notified that the Committee considers Head Masters to be indispensable to their respective schools and cannot be spared for military service, and that if any are called up in accordance with the new scheme of recruiting, the Committee will submit their objections to the local tribunal.[31]

Despite the best efforts of individual institutions to retain their staff, thousands of teachers were drafted into the armed forces. In October 1916 the Board of Education even wrote to members of the Girls' Public Day School Trust asking for details of male teachers still at their posts.[32] The Head Mistress of Nottingham High School for Girls responded:

There is one man teacher on this Staff – Mr Henniker, visiting teacher of Singing. He will be 42 on December 9 1916. He attested last summer. He is delicate and very small.

Her colleague at Sheffield High School for Girls replied that 'We are sorry we have no one of military age to offer'.[33]

A Board of Trade Report produced at the end of the war noted that 34 per cent of the 54,000 male teachers in the school labour force nationally were engaged in military service by July 1916. A year later the figure had risen to 39 per cent. In January and March 1918 further Military Service Acts were introduced. In April, and in the wake of the German Spring Offensive which had smashed through the British lines on the Western Front, a new Manpower Act was rushed through parliament. Men from previously exempt occupational classes, together with older conscripts – the age range had been extended to fifty-one – were hurriedly trained and transported across the English Channel to reinforce the battered British Fourth Army. By July 1918 some 23,000 British teachers, 42 per cent of the male workforce in schools, were serving in the armed forces.[34]

The vast majority of British servicemen who fought in the Great War of 1914 to 1918 had been educated in the nation's elementary schools. Similarly, most of the teachers who served during the war were elementary school teachers. Many of the latter were members of the National Union of Teachers (NUT). In 1920 this professional association published the:

National Union of Teachers
WAR RECORD
1914–1919
A SHORT ACCOUNT
OF DUTY AND WORK
ACCOMPLISHED
DURING THE WAR.

Over 15,000 NUT members – schoolmasters and schoolmistresses – are listed by name in this post-war Roll of Honour. A list of *Teachers Who Joined the Forces*, organised according to local branch membership, includes all those who contributed to the war effort in some way. A chapter entitled *Military Honours* records members who were decorated for bravery, whilst *The Gallant Dead* pays homage to 'The Fallen': those who were killed in action or died during the conflict. The overall roll of honour lacks sufficient detail to conduct a thorough analysis of patterns of service by teachers, unlike the smaller – but nevertheless substantial – data set contained in *Military Honours* and *The Gallant Dead*. The latter chapter contains the names of individual casualties followed by particulars of military rank, the service unit to which they were attached, and the name of the school where they were last employed. Most of the NUT members who served in the Great War were 'Tommies': over 98 per cent served in the British Army, very few served in the Royal Navy and even fewer joined the Royal Flying Corps. In rank, they ranged from humble private to lieutenant colonel in charge of a battalion. The great majority served in infantry regiments with city or county affiliations, or in the Royal Artillery (RFA, RGA) and Royal Army Medical Corps (RAMC). Very few were members of elite guards, lancers, hussars, or dragoon regiments. Whilst most had previously taught in council or parochial elementary schools, just over 4 per cent had last been employed in institutions described as 'colleges' or 'secondary', 'intermediate', 'higher grade' and 'upper standard' schools.

Direct military service was not the only way in which schoolteachers could serve their country. The conduct of war was no longer an exclusively male preserve, nor was it confined solely to front-line combat activity. The NUT *War Record* includes the names of 331 women who left their teaching posts and assumed new roles during the Great War. Some, like Miss Hettie Onions from Tredegar in the valleys of South Wales, joined the Women's Army Auxiliary Corps (WAAC). The logbook for the Georgetown Schools contains several references to her, and to her brother who had taught at the same school and had enlisted in the Monmouthshire Regiment:

1915
5 May: Miss Hettie Onions is absent, we regret the cause – her eldest brother Lieutenant Wilfred Onions died from wounds on the battlefront in Belgium.

1917
July: Miss Hettie Onions has been absent today being examined by a doctor in order to enlist in the Women's Auxiliary Corps.

3 September: Miss H Onions has left school during the holiday and enlisted in the WAAC.[35]

The WAAC was established in January 1917. Its members were volunteers, recruited to do administrative jobs for the British Army in this country and in France, thus releasing serving soldiers at a time of heavy losses on the battlefields. They wore uniform, did physical exercises every day, but were not granted full military status. This did not, however, prevent some of them from becoming casualties of war; nine WAACs were killed during a German air raid on the British Army Camp at Etaples in April 1918. Some 200 of the women listed by the NUT volunteered to become nurses, tending wounded troops in the many military hospitals which had been established behind the front lines and back in Britain. Miss G. Bytheway, a teacher from Palfrey Council School and a member of the Walsall District branch of the NUT, joined the Red Cross. Kate Elizabeth Ogg from Wingrove Council School in Newcastle worked as a nurse at the Northumberland VAD Hospital.

Not every teacher, of course, was a member of the NUT. Ishobel Ross (Plate 35) offered her services to the Scottish Women's Hospitals (SWH) in July 1916 after hearing Dr Elsie Inglis, the movement's founder, speak about their work and the desperate need for volunteers to go to Serbia. Ishobel was not a nurse, but she could cook. After attending Edinburgh Ladies College she qualified as a teacher of cookery at Atholl Crescent School of Domestic Science. On the outbreak of war she was teaching at a girls' school in the city. After joining the SWH, Ishobel kept a diary of her wartime experiences. On 3 August 1916 Ishobel and her fellow volunteers boarded the *Dunluce Castle*, 'a beautiful Hospital ship', and began the long and potentially hazardous ten-day journey to Salonika before joining the British and Serbian forces fighting the Bulgarian army in the Balkans. She spent nearly a year there, one of the women the Serbian soldiers dubbed 'the little grey partridges' on account of the colour of their uniforms.[36]

Male teachers who were not in the armed forces found other ways in which they could contribute to the war effort. Some, like A.F. Watts, Master in Charge of Junior School at the Crypt School in Gloucester, devoted their energies to auxiliary units. Working with the Red Cross from 1914, Mr Watts became Commander of Gloucester VAD 25 Hospital and then, as County Commissariat Officer, assumed responsibility for the food supply to twenty-three hospitals.[37] Two teachers from Colfe's Grammar School, Mr Creech and Mr Worthy, helped out on the home front by becoming Special Constables, a role which involved them manning London's air-raid shelters. Their colleague Mr FitzAucher served as a Volunteer Fireman in the city.[38] Cadet units continued to need leadership. School OTC – the production line supplying the stream of young subalterns to replace officers killed in action – were now crucial to the war effort. Robert Stuart Smith was Commanding Officer of 'D' Company in the OTC at King Edward VII Grammar School, Melton Mowbray. The headteacher held the rank of captain in the Corps:

> It was a role which suited him, and on parade he was every inch a soldier. His uniform was immaculate, each coil of his puttees precisely in place. His bearing was always confident, disciplined and athletic, and he took his duties with his usual seriousness.

Eager to enlist in 1914, Captain Stuart Smith was reminded by his school governors of Kitchener's pronouncement that nothing should be done which would impact adversely upon the training of cadets.[39] Male teachers who were over the age limit or deemed unfit for military service also helped out. When Headmaster Jacob at Felsted Preparatory School in Essex was rejected for military service he took a commission in the school's OTC instead.[40]

The British government also used teachers to perform administrative tasks at key points during the war. The provision of schooling throughout the country resulted in a ready-made network of institutions which could be called upon to disseminate information and associated materials to local communities. Teachers and their pupils were a workforce which might be deployed in special circumstances to assist with clerical or distributive tasks. In October 1915, the local Director of Education requested schools in Tredegar in South Wales to send one member of staff to the council offices at Bedwellty House so that they might support the Recruiting Officer with registration for the Derby Scheme. The Georgetown Schools sent three teachers to help out: Miss Ceinwen Evans from the Infant Department, Miss Adelaide Mills from the Senior Girls School and Mr Alexander Robson, Head of the Junior Mixed School. The impact of such work on individual schools could be substantial. Mr Robson continued to be involved in related duties until 1918, often attending meetings in Cardiff and Newport, which necessitated frequent absences from school.[41] The need to distribute ration books in response to the food crisis of 1917–18 also involved teachers. In what proved to be the final year of the war, Alfred Whitehouse at St Nicholas Boys' School in King's Lynn noted:

1918
18 March: Emergency holiday given tomorrow and Wednesday by LEA to enable teachers to assist in issuing Ration Cards at the Town Hall.[42]

The children, but not the teachers, at his school gained another enforced holiday some three months later. In early July 1918 many other schools also halted their normal activities. Schools throughout the Peterborough District, for example, closed for several days so that their teachers might be deployed in alternative war work.[43]

And what of those teachers who remained in their schools throughout the conflict, doing the best they could in the most difficult of circumstances, and trying to carry on with 'business as usual'? As previous chapters have illustrated, the usual patterns, routines and activities which had characterised the different types of schooling in the pre-war period were subject to the demands of a nation at war. The Great War did not stop the majority of teachers teaching and marking or exercising their pastoral duties. It did, however, make additional demands upon them, not all of which could simply be substituted for other customary activities. Teachers organised many more charitable activities, supervised collection campaigns, administered War Savings Schemes, helped their pupils to plant seeds and to harvest produce from Dig for Victory gardens, and spent their holidays in the harvest camps. They were expected to be propagandists, charged with the task of making sense of the war for their pupils. Many produced campaign maps and encouraged children to use marker flags to chart the latest great push. They sang the praises of Britain's wartime Allies, and learnt to play their national anthems. Teachers responded to questions prompted by the latest war news or lists of casualties in the local newspaper. Headteachers, in particular, became channels of communication for central government, disseminating to their staff suggestions on the teaching of patriotism and addressing their pupils on the dangers of inadvertent disclosure of information.[44] Staff in the boarding schools had additional responsibilities, which were vital to the wellbeing of pupils and colleagues alike. Mr Edward Balshaw, a Languages Master in his fifties who stayed at his post at Hurstpierpoint College throughout the war, was remembered more for his role as School Steward than for any teaching qualities he may have possessed. Even at the height of the food crisis and the rationing which followed, he made sure that the boys and remaining staff were well fed.[45]

Schools have always honoured their heroes. In the vast majority of cases the names on the honours boards belong to alumni; those former pupils who captained the school teams, were awarded the sacred duty of prefectship or gained scholarships to university. The exploits of such glittering stars, brilliant young men and women alike, were followed avidly by other pupils and their teachers, both during their time in school and in their subsequent careers. Even today, educational institutions of all kinds take pride in listing famous alumni on their websites. Exceptional teachers, too, are lauded by their schools, although far less frequently. For the majority, their academic qualifications and ability are generally taken as read and their classroom craft and personal qualities determine the nature of relationships they enjoy within the institution. For those who excel in other, often related, fields, however, the admiration of the school community will be manifest. Prowess on the sports field does wonders for their reputation, especially if it has been demonstrated at county or national level. Success on the battlefield had much the same effect.

The Great War afforded thousands of schoolteachers the opportunity to make a name for themselves, although very few would have genuinely stated this as the reason for them enlisting. The very act of joining the colours elicited the admiration, best wishes and sometimes farewell gifts from cheering pupils and colleagues. Who knew what glories lay ahead? They might be remembered for heroic deeds or, far more likely in the early military encounters, for being amongst the first to make the ultimate sacrifice. Two members of the teaching profession, albeit from different ends of the educational spectrum, hold the distinction of being celebrated nationally as 'firsts'. The first teacher to be killed on the battlefields of Europe was Lieutenant Alexander Williamson of Highgate School, a public school master who, as a member of the Special Reserve and 2nd Battalion Seaforth Highlanders, was with the BEF in France in the first weeks of the war. The young subaltern was killed in action on the River Aisne on 14 September 1914.[46] His story was reported in the *Times Educational Supplement* and, slightly later, in *The Captain*. In the latter publication, Lieutenant Williamson was portrayed as the epitome of the public schoolboy and schoolmaster.[47] The magazine proclaimed 'Everybody recognises the fact that the spirit of discipline and sportsmanship in our schools is bearing rich and glorious fruit on the stern fields of duty'.[48]

Plate 1. Bob Hart. From Harrow County School for Boys to the Honourable Artillery Company and the trenches of the Western Front. (*HCSB Archives*)

Bromley County Girls' School Form Room.

Plate 2. A secondary schooling for girls from the 'intermediate' classes. Bromley County Girls' School was founded in 1911, one of many institutions established in the wake of Balfour's 1902 Education Act to provide post–elementary education. (*Blades Collection*)

Plate 3. An education for gentlemen. Boys taking 'Bill' – or break – at Harrow School. England's elite 'public schools' catered for the sons of the privileged and wealthy upper classes. (*Blades Collection*)

Plate 4. Most public schools taught the 'Classics', but by 1914 some had introduced 'modern' subjects into the curriculum. The Science Laboratory at Ayton School, a small fee-paying institution in North Yorkshire. (*Blades Collection*)

Kingston Grammar School.
R. E. Black, D. W. Stoneham, F. W. Mudford,
R. C. Sherriff, J. M. Whitecross.

Plate 5. *(Left)* The rowing crew from Kingston Grammar School in 1912. Seated centre right is Robert Sherriff, author of *Journey's End*. (*Blades Collection*)

Plate 6. *(Below)* The Corps at Harrow School. A training for future army subalterns in the trenches of the Western Front. (*Blades Collection*)

Photos Copyright.

THE SERGEANTS OF THE CORPS.

A. H. Fry.

Sergt. A. C. Gibson-Craig.   Sergt. T. R. Castle.   Sergt.-Maj. J. Horton.
Sergt. J. F. Gurney.   Col.-Sergt. W. S. Darlington.
Sergt. E. J. Wheen.   Sergt. T. Evans.   Sergt. D. R. Drummond.   Sergt. E. W. Mann.   Sergt. G. J. Brownlow.   Sergt. J. P. Fitzgerald.
Sergt. E. W. Swan.   Sergt. E. M. Strong.

Plate 7. Sport was an integral part of the curriculum in most secondary schools, including those which educated girls. (*Blades Collection*)

Plate 8. Elementary schooling for 'other ranks'. Boys from the working classes were taught rudimentary literacy and numeracy – the 'three Rs' – and practical subjects to prepare them for early employment in the local workforce. (*Blades Collection*)

Plate 9. Gendered schooling. Working–class girls received an elementary schooling which prepared them for their future roles as wives, mothers and domestic servants. (*Blades Collection*)

Plate 10. Empire Day. A schooling for patriots and the future citizens of an imperial race. (*Blades Collection*)

FIG. 1.
Attention.

FIG. 2.
Stand at Ease.

FIG. 3.
Hips Firm.

Plate 11. Concerns over the fitness of the nation and the importance of discipline and obedience amongst the poorest classes led to the introduction of military-style 'Drill' in maintained elementary schools. (*Blades Collection*)

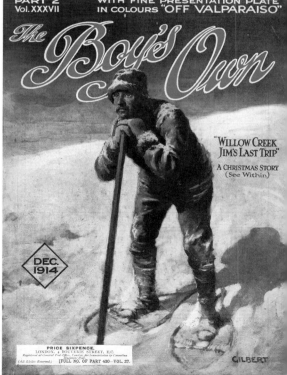

Plate 12. Daring deeds on the sports field and heroic actions in the far-flung posts of empire. *The Boy's Own* and other literature for schoolboys and schoolgirls conditioned young minds before and during the Great War. (*Blades Collection*)

Plate 13. Miss Susannah Knight, a teacher at St Gregory's School in Chorley who taught rudimentary French to men from Kitchener's New Army. (*Adam Cree*)

Plate 14. Future leaders of men. Cadets at an annual Public School OTC Camp. In 1914 their mock-military manoeuvres were disrupted by the real thing. (*Blades Collection*)

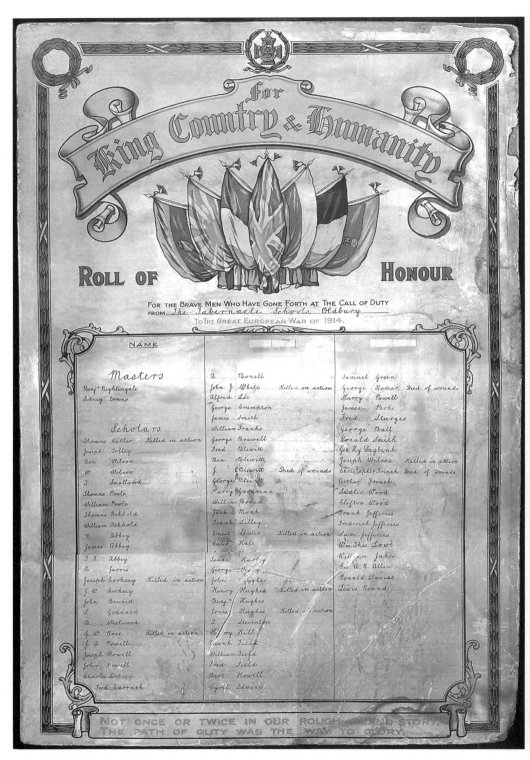

Plate 15. The Roll of Honour for the pupils and teachers of The Tabernacle Schools, Oldbury. (*www. genealogyforum.co.uk*)

Plate 16. Children as agents of the state. Pupils from Welsh elementary schools march through Cardiff in 1915 to encourage men to enlist in the armed forces. (*Blades Collection*)

Plate 17. From school to military hospital. In 1914 Lincoln Grammar School was requisitioned and became part of 4 Northern General Hospital. Over 45,000 British and Allied wounded servicemen were treated there during the war. (*The Garton Archive*)

Plate 18. British schools welcomed displaced Belgian refugees and children from other allied nations, and supported numerous charitable causes during the war. (*Blades Collection*)

BELGIAN RELIEF FUNDS
1915
OFFICIAL SOUVENIR

H.M. QUEEN MARY.
Specially chosen by Her Majesty.

Battersea school children have knitted large quantities of socks for our soldiers at the front. They gave a performance at the Grand Theatre, Clapham, to raise further funds. Photograph shows them rehearsing their part, " Knitting Socks for Soldiers."

Plate 19. 'Comforts' for the boys at the front. British schoolchildren took part in the national 'knitting frenzy', producing balaclavas, scarves, gloves and other items for the men in the trenches. (*Blades Collection*)

THE OVERSEAS CLUB
PATRON
HIS MAJESTY THE KING.
1915

CANADA AUSTRALIA S.AFRICA NEW ZEALAND NEWFOUNDLAND INDIA

Christmas Day Gifts
FROM THE SCHOOL CHILDREN OF THE EMPIRE
This is to Certify
that *Annie Harrison*
HAS HELPED TO BRING HAPPINESS ON CHRISTMAS DAY TO OUR BRAVE SAILORS AND SOLDIERS, WHO ARE FIGHTING FOR HONOUR, FREEDOM & JUSTICE.

Plate 20. Official recognition for helping with the war effort. (*Blades Collection*)

Plate 21. Girls from MHSG leaving their classrooms to deliver medical supplies to Red Cross military hospitals in the Manchester district. (*MHSG Archives*)

Plate 22. Children and teachers from the All Saints Schools in Wellingborough with their harvest of blackberries to be made into jam for the troops. (*J & M Palmer*)

Plate 23. Schools as war financiers. The War Savings Association at Newbattle School in Midlothian, Scotland. (*www.newbattleatwar.com*)

THE UNION JACK

" The red, white, & blue."

THE NATIONAL EMBLEM
OF THE BRITISH EMPIRE.

Life of St. George.

St. George—the patron saint of England—was a Roman military officer, born of a Christian family at Lydda, in Palestine. When the Emperor Diocletian began the persecution of the Christians, George remonstrated with him and resigned his commission. His famous adventure with the Dragon was as follows: Near the town of Berytus, in a lake, the Dragon had its home. It destroyed cattle and human beings, so that the people, believing their Gods had sent the Dragon for punishment, offered sacrifices chosen by lots. The King's daughter was one of these victims. St. George found the Princess by the lake and killed the Dragon when it came forth to destroy her. He refused to give up Christianity and was put to death after cruel torture on April 23rd, 303 A.D. Edward III made him patron saint of England.

St. George's Day,

APRIL 23rd, 1917.

R.S.P.C.A. School Souvenir
for Scholars' contribution
to the above Fund.

Plate 24. Flag Days. More opportunities for collective action and financial support for worthy causes. (*Blades Collection*)

Plate 25. Schools across the educational spectrum issued certificates of service instead of the customary prizes in their annual Speech Day presentation ceremonies. (*Blades Collection*)

Plate 26. 'Boy' Cornwell VC: elementary school pupil, Boy Scout and national hero at the Battle of Jutland in 1916. (*Blades Collection*)

Plate 27. Another hero to emulate and another cigarette card to add to the collection. (*Blades Collection*)

Der „Zeppelinunterricht" in einer Londoner Schule
(Nach englischer Darstellung)

Plate 28. The 'Home Front'. A British schoolteacher prepares his class for new forms of warfare – and new theatres of conflict. (*Blades Collection*)

THE SPHERE

AN ILLUSTRATED NEWSPAPER FOR THE HOME

With which is incorporated
"BLACK & WHITE"

Volume LXIX. No. 909. {REGISTERED AT THE GENERAL POST OFFICE AS A NEWSPAPER} London June 23, 1917. Price Sevenpence.

Copyrighted in the U.S.A.

DRAWN BY D. MACPHERSON AT L.C.C. SCHOOL

The AIR ATTACK on "THE FORTRESS" OF LONDON—CARRYING SOME of the VICTIMS to the HOSPITALS

The above drawing was made by the special artist of "The Sphere," who visited the L.C.C. school which was hit by German bombs on the morning of Wednesday, June 13. The firemen, policemen, and Red Cross men were ably assisted by men on leave from the front, both naval and military, who happened to be in the proximity of the school when the bombs began to fall. Our artist was also able to make a diagrammatic sectional view of the building showing how the bombs reached the infants' class-rooms after penetrating the girls' floor and then the boys' *(see p. 250)*

Plate 29. 'Total War'. On 13 June 1917, German Gotha bombers raided London. They dropped bombs on North Street School in Poplar, killing eighteen children in their classrooms. (*Blades Collection*)

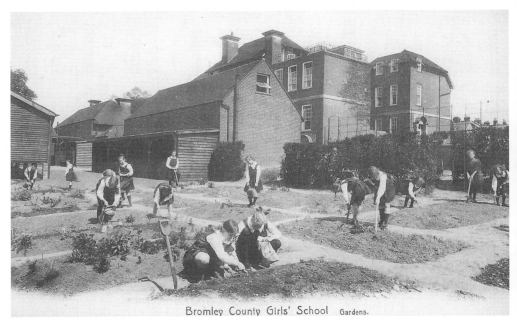

Bromley County Girls' School Gardens.

Plate 30. 'Digging For Victory.' The blockade of Britain by German U-boats in 1917 led to the introduction of vegetable gardens in many schools. (*Blades Collection*)

Plate 31. War work. Senior boys from Eton College waiting to unload war *matériel* from freight trains at Didcot Station. (*Blades Collection*)

Plate 32. Teacher as soldier. Lieutenant Russell Mervyn Wheeler, formerly schoolmaster at Harrow County School for Boys. (*HCSB Archives*)

GALLAHER'S CIGARETTES.

E. H. LINTOTT,
BRADFORD CITY, 1909–10.

Plate 33. Teacher and sporting hero. Evelyn Lintott combined his duties as an elementary school teacher with playing football for professional sides such as Plymouth Argyle, Queen's Park Rangers and Bradford City. (*Blades Collection*)

Plate 34. Lost to the teaching profession. In 1914 James Garland left the London Day Training College before gaining his teaching qualification. He was killed in action on the first day of the Battle of the Somme in 1916. (*King's College London Archives*)

Plate 35. The 'Little Grey Partridge'. In 1916 Ishobel Ross left her employment as a cookery teacher to join the Scottish Women's Hospital in Serbia. (*University of Aberdeen Press*)

CAPTAIN T. E. ADLAM, V.C.

SECOND-LIEUT. J. HARRISON, V.C., M.C.
Killed in action, May 3rd, 1917.

SECOND-LIEUT. D. S. BELL, V.C.
Killed in action, July 10th, 1916.

MEMBERS OF THE UNION.

Plate 36. Teacher as national hero. Three members of the National Union of Teachers were awarded Victoria Crosses 'For Valour' in the Great War. (*NUT Archives*)

Plate 37. Conscientious Objector. James Maxton – Scottish schoolteacher and later Member of Parliament – was dismissed from his teaching post and imprisoned for refusing to support the war or to undertake military service. (*Wikimedia Commons*)

Plate 38. Joseph Dines. Teacher, England footballer and 'Temporary Gentleman'. (*True's Yard Museum*)

Plate 39. 'Temporary Masters'. Members of the National Federation of Women Teachers marching in Lowestoft in 1917 for the right to vote – and for pay and conditions equal to those of their male counterparts. (*UCL Institute of Education Archives*)

Plate 40. Peace at last. Schoolchildren celebrating the end of the Great War in 1918. (*Blades Collection*)

Plate 41. A 'Lost Generation'. Headteacher Edward Adams unveils a simple wooden memorial to former pupils and staff who had joined the ranks of 'The Fallen'. (*Peterborough Library & Archives*)

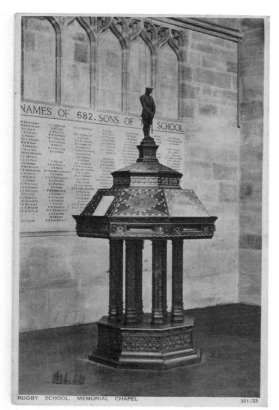

Plate 42. The memorialisation of war. The scale of the loss suffered by elite public schools such as Rugby was enormous, and has not been forgotten. (*Blades Collection*)

THE STAFF. 1924.

Mr. A. Bell. Mr. W. G. Hardwick. Mr. A. Winterbotham. Mr. R. S. Parr. Mr. H. W. Acomb. Mr. W. Thomas. Mr. W. H. Youngs. Mr. W. V. Davies. Miss G. A. Pringuer. Mr. W. D. Varney. Mr. A. Schofield. Dr. J. H. Davies. Mr. C. J. Robson. Mr. C. M. Spencer. Miss D. M. Whincop.

Plate 43. A collective experience of conflict. The staff of Deacon's School, Peterborough, in 1924. (*Peterborough Library & Archives*)

Plate 44. 'The Forgotten'. Lieutenant Commander Archibald Walter Buckle DSO. (© *Imperial War Museum*)

The distinction of being the first member of the British armed forces to be killed in action on British soil also belongs to a schoolteacher. Whilst manning the guns of the Heugh Battery guarding the town of Hartlepool, Private Theophilus Jones of the 18th Battalion Durham Light Infantry (RGA) was killed by an exploding shell. It was one of over a thousand shells which were fired by a detachment of three battlecruisers of the Imperial German Navy during their forty-two-minute bombardment of the east coast towns on 16 December 1914. Theo Jones was born in Darlington and taught in West Hartlepool before becoming headmaster of the village school at Thringstone in Leicestershire in 1913. Whilst there he became church choirmaster and also played for Coalville Rugby Club. Shortly after the declaration of war he enlisted in the Durham Pals. On leaving for training, Mr Jones' pupils had presented him with a prayer book.

Many schools still remember alumni who gained honours on the battlefield. The public schools quite rightly point to the number of military decorations won by their former students. Of the 627 recipients during the Great War of the highest award for bravery, the Victoria Cross, more than a quarter (163) were awarded to men educated in British and Dominion public schools. The disproportionate number of VCs and other military awards to men from Eton (thirteen VCs), Harrow (eight), Cheltenham (six), Haileybury (six), Wellington (five), Clifton (five), Dulwich (five) and other elite schools reflects the bravery and commitment of a whole generation of young men imbued with a code which expected – and celebrated – ideals such as service, duty and honour. That so many were also members of the 'Lost Generation' is testimony to their enormous contribution to Britain's war effort. Their stories are writ large in histories of the conflict. The trinity of military enlistments, decorations and casualties has become the defining experience of the Great War for many schools.

Teachers from the public schools were amongst the decorated war heroes. Five of them, including two mentioned earlier in this chapter, won Victoria Crosses. After leaving Merchiston and joining the 16th Manchester (Pals) Battalion in October 1914, Wifrith Elstob fought on the Somme and won a Military Cross for his leadership during the attack on Montauban on 1 July 1916. By the end of the greatest British offensive of the war, in which many of his fellow officers in the battalion were killed in action, he had been promoted to Acting Lieutenant Colonel. In April 1917 he commanded the battalion during the Battle of Arras and again in July in the Ypres Salient. For his bravery and leadership during fighting along the Menin Road on 31 July 1917 he was awarded the Distinguished Service Order (DSO). Wilfrith Elstob was subsequently awarded a VC for his actions near St Quentin in 1918. When the Germans launched their Spring Offensive on 21 March much of the British army was forced to abandon the front line and to retreat. Within hours of the initial attack, however, some units were unable or unwilling to fall back. The small number of 16th Manchesters left holding the redoubt on 'Manchester Hill' were completely surrounded and massively outnumbered. Despite being wounded three times, Lieutenant Colonel Elstob informed Brigade Headquarters that 'The Manchester Regiment will hold Manchester Hill to the last man'. According to one of the few survivors, when the position was finally overrun a German soldier demanded Wilfrith's surrender. He replied 'Never' and was shot dead.[49]

The former Master and Chaplain at Wellingborough School, Bernard Vann, served as an infantry officer throughout the war. Like Wilfith Elstob he fought in France – at the Battle of Loos in October 1915 – and progressed through the ranks. By October 1917 he was Acting Lieutenant Colonel commanding 1st/6th Battalion The Sherwood Foresters (The Nottinghamshire and Derbyshire Regiment). In the final months of the war Bernard Vann was in the thick of the fighting, part of the British forces attacking the Hindenburg Line during The Hundred Days campaign. His VC citation published by *The London Gazette* on 14 December 1918 read:

> For conspicuous bravery, devotion to duty and fine leadership during the attack at Bellenglise and Lehaucourt, on 29 September, 1918. He led his battalion with great skill across the Canal du Nord through a very thick fog and under heavy fire from field and machine guns. Col Vann rushed up to the firing line and with the greatest gallantry led the line forward. By his prompt action and absolute contempt for danger the whole situation was changed, the men were encouraged and the line swept forward. Lt Col Vann, who had on all occasions set the highest example of valour, was killed near Ramicourt on 3rd October, 1918, when leading his battalion in attack.

A letter to *The Times* from a fellow officer reminded readers of 'the magnificent example of this fine Christian Gentleman'. An obituary in *The Wellingburian* praised the ordained minister and school chaplain, and noted that during his time as a warrior on the battlefield:

> He never forgot that he was a priest of God, for it was his greatest joy to be able to do the double duty of commanding his battalion and giving Communion to the sick and wounded.[50]

The stories of Wilfrith Elstob, Bernard Vann and others like them have assumed an almost legendary status, representing as they do the ideal of the schoolmaster who combines service to others with steely determination, personal bravery and outstanding leadership qualities. The products of their social milieu and schooling, they too, like the young subalterns they taught and fought alongside, are justly celebrated.

Teachers from the non-elite schools were also decorated and honoured during the Great War. The frontispiece of the *War Record*, published by the NUT in 1920

(Plate 36), contains the photographs of three of the union's members who had also been awarded the Victoria Cross: Jack Harrison, Donald Simpson Bell and Tom Adlam. John ('Jack') Harrison's background was very different from that of Wilfrith Elstob and Bernard Vann. Born in 1890, Jack was the son of a shipyard plater and boilermaker in Hull. He taught at Lime Street Council School in Hull and played rugby, but not the Rugby Union code of the public schools. He played Rugby League, the version of the game popular in the industrial towns and cities of northern England. During the 1913–14 season, the last before the war, he scored a remarkable 52 tries for Hull FC. In November 1915, Jack joined the Inns of Court OTC and in August of the following year he became a (Temporary) Second Lieutenant in the 11th Battalion (Hull Tradesmen) East Yorkshire Regiment. He was awarded a Military Cross (MC) in March 1917 and just six weeks later was killed in action. On 3 May the Hull Brigade attacked the German lines at Oppy Wood near Arras in France. Jack's platoon was pinned down by heavy machine-gun fire. Armed only with a pistol and Mills bombs, Jack ran forward, dodging from one shell hole to another and weaving in and out of the barbed wire. His platoon watched as he fell whilst tossing the grenade in the direction of the machine-gun post. The enemy gun fell silent, but Jack was never seen again. His VC citation in *The London Gazette* of 14 June 1917 stated that 'His self-sacrifice and absolute disregard of danger was an inspiring example to all'.[51]

Second Lieutenant Donald Simpson Bell VC had also won fame as a sportsman before the war. He was a noted amateur footballer who played for Crystal Palace and Newcastle United. In 1912 he signed professional forms with Bradford Park Avenue in order to supplement his income from teaching. Born in 1890, Donald attended St Peter's School in Harrogate and then Knaresborough Grammar School. He trained to be a teacher at Westminster College, where he won his colours for soccer, rugby and cricket before returning to his home town to teach at Starbeck Council School. Donald enlisted in 1914 – arguably the first professional footballer to do so – and was quickly promoted to Lance Corporal before gaining a commission in the 9th Battalion (Alexandra, Princess of Wales's Own) The Yorkshire Regiment.[52] Second Lieutenant Donald Simpson Bell was awarded the Victoria Cross for his part in an attack on Horseshoe Trench on the Somme on 5 July 1916. In his last letter to his mother Donald stated:

When the battalion went over, I, with my team crawled up a communication trench and I hit the gun first shot from about 20 yards and knocked it over. We then bombed the dugouts and did in about 50 Bosches. The G.C.O. has been over to congratulate the battalion and he personally thanked me. I must confess it was the biggest fluke alive and I did nothing.[53]

Just five days later, during a similar attack on the German lines near the village of Contalmaison, Donald was killed in action.

The third member of the NUT to be awarded a VC, and the only teacher recipient to survive the war, was Captain Tom Adlam of 7th Battalion The Bedfordshire Regiment. He was a part-time soldier before the war, having joined the Territorials in 1912 whilst at teacher training college. In 1914 he left Brook Street School in Basingstoke to enlist as a private in the army. He won his VC on 27 September 1916 in an action at Thiepval during the Battle of the Somme. Tom died in 1975.

The stories of Jack Harrison, Donald Simpson Bell and Tom Adlam are as exceptional as any of those of the hundreds of British and Dominion servicemen who were awarded the highest decoration 'For Valour' during the Great War. They were, however, counted amongst hundreds of other British teachers who were awarded honours during the Great War and whose stories are generally forgotten today. The NUT *War Record* lists with evident pride the types and numbers of honours for war service won by its members, including many awarded by auxiliary forces and Allied governments:

Victoria Cross	VC	3
Distinguished Service Order	DSO	15
Distinguished Service Cross (Royal Navy)	DSC	1
Distinguished Flying Cross	DFC	2
Military Cross	MC	231
Military Medal	MM	188
Distinguished Conduct Medal	DCM	65
Distinguished Service Medal (Royal Navy)	DSM	1
Distinguished Flying Medal	DFM	1
Meritorious Service Medal	MSM	64
Royal Red Cross Medal	RCM	2
Croix de Guerre (France, Belgium)	C de G	24
Other foreign awards		22

'Military Honours' in National Union of Teachers *War Record* (1920) pp.79–92.[54]

France, Belgium, Egypt, Greece, Italy, Portugal, Roumania, Russia and Serbia all recognised the bravery and commitment of serving members of the NUT, both commissioned officers and other ranks. Major A.G. Church (RGA), formerly a teacher at Morpeth Central School in the East End of London, was awarded both the British DSO and MC and the Russian Order of St Vladimir With Crossed Swords and Bow. Corporal R.G. Chaytor (RAMC), who taught at Medomsley Council School in the Vale of Derwent before the war, was honoured by the Belgian government twice, receiving the Croix de Guerre and the Order of Leopold II in addition to his British Military Medal.

Honours were not earned exclusively for meritorious action in the front lines of battlefields. The French Government awarded the Reconnaissance Francaise to Miss E.M Ashton, a South Shields teacher turned cook at the Scottish Women's Hospital. Miss K. Bishop, formerly of Bedlington Colliery Council School in Northumberland, was awarded the Royal Red Cross Medal for her work as a Nursing Sister with the St John Ambulance. Mrs R. Woods, a VAD Hospital Superintendent who taught at Frant Church School in Heathfield in Sussex before the war, received the same medal. Similarly, not every decorated teacher was a member of the NUT. For their calmness and bravery in helping the children of North Street School in the aftermath of the German air raid on Poplar in June 1917, teachers Annie Allum, Gertrude Middleton and Wenceslia Watkins were awarded Order of the British Empire medals. A.F. Watts, teacher at the Crypt School in Gloucester and wartime VAD Commander was awarded the MBE and the Belgian Medaille Du Roi Albert in recognition of his support for military hospitals.[55]

According to the archive research company 'Ancestry', the most likely previous occupation of those decorated and honoured during the Great War, in proportionate terms, was that of teaching, followed closely by those employed previously as window cleaners, cotton mill workers, doctors, fishermen, servants, barbers, merchants, policemen and bankers.[56] Why this should be so is unclear, and it would be unwise to assert that teachers, a group which spanned the whole spectrum of society and diversity of personal experience, had particular qualities not evident in other occupational groups. Such comparative data is interesting, but does little to further understanding of why and how different groups or, more importantly, individuals behave in specific contexts. Military decorations rewarded individual commitment and bravery, but acts of heroism are born of many, often contradictory, factors. There is a fine line between courage and foolhardiness, between fear and cowardice, between self-sacrifice and self-preservation. As Donald Simpson Bell noted, it is the observations and judgements of others which label our actions and define our worth; an actor's sensitivities and motivations or impulses – the product of individual thought and reflection – are often unseen or unspoken. Only the decisions made and the actions taken are witnessed.

Historians of the Great War need 'to get closer to the difficult choices people made'.[57] Millions of British citizens chose to be 'active citizens'. The majority of the patriotic, adventurous, and brave – or just downright naive – enlisted in the first year of the war. Others followed their example later, sometimes, like Hettie Onions in Tredegar, in response to the loss of friends and family members in the early campaigns. The sincerity of their opinions was rarely, if ever, seriously challenged in the court of public opinion, unless, of course, one accepts the generally applied notion of 'war fever'. In Britain's hour of need they had heard the call-to-arms and responded accordingly. By 1916, however, the realities of this new war, prolonged and terribly bloody as it clearly and undoubtedly had become, had stemmed the flow of volunteers. The passing of the Military Service Act of 1916 was a deliberate and formal call-to-arms for those who had been passive in the first year of the war. Far from making matters clearer by stating the nation's expectations of its people, the introduction of conscription created a new set of parameters for personal decision making. Those individuals who feared the battlefield, had pressing domestic or business interests which kept them at home, or out of deep religious or political conviction opposed this or any war, were now called to account for their perceived passivity. External demands and expectations, bound up in concepts of duty, loyalty and community, clashed with internal impulses and beliefs such as self-interest and conscience.

How does or should one define bravery at such times? In *A War Imagined* Samuel Hynes argued that 'it is the nature of war to diminish every value except war itself and the values war requires: patriotism, discipline, obedience, endurance'. War, especially on the scale and intensity of the Great War, quickly polarises debate by instigating 'little wars' between 'national' and 'foreign', 'conforming' and 'non-conforming'.[58] This was an especially difficult time for those who opposed the war for idealistic reasons. Many who believed that the war was wrong on religious or humanitarian grounds chose non-conformity and, specifically, non-compliance with the terms of the Military Service Act. Choosing to say no to conscription, and the unpopularity, condemnation and even outright animosity that flowed from such a decision, demanded a different form of personal bravery.

From the first weeks of the war, the pressure on men to enlist had been intense. The visibility of patriotism was all important. Those not in uniform, for whatever reason, risked being given the white feather of cowardice. At a time when teachers were expected to be role models in thought and deed, public opinion could be particularly vehement towards those in the profession deemed to be 'shirkers' or 'slackers'. A fictional article which appeared in *The Magnet* in August 1915 entitled 'THE MASTER WHO STAYED AT HOME!' made it very clear how patriotic schoolboys should respond to teachers who did not play the game by serving King and Country in this hour of need. In real life too, the pupils and Old Boys of Uppingham School were dismayed that their Head Master Reginald Owen, newly appointed in November 1915 at just 28 years old, had chosen not to serve his country.[59] Governors, parents, and local and national communities shared equally high expectations of teachers. At Helston Grammar School in Cornwall teacher Mr Boxhall responded positively to Lord Derby's Scheme but his enlistment was deferred and he was still teaching in the school in 1917. One of the governors, however, Mr A.C. Cade, wrote to the *Western Daily Mercury* and made invidious comparisons between the privations suffered by his son serving in the army and Mr Boxhall who was 'at home and at ease'. Despite support from the majority of the governing body, Mr Boxhall later insisted on attending the necessary medical examination and left the school for military service in 1918.[60] Caernarvon County School in Wales, where several male teachers were not called up for military service, was dubbed 'Coward's Castle' by the local newspaper.[61] In this and many other schools teachers who stayed at home were left in an emotional no man's land, torn between duty to their school and duty to their country. Some high-profile school leaders found to their cost that this was also not a time to question the popular consensus. Dr Edward Lyttleton, the Headmaster of Eton, was forced to leave his post in 1916 after he had been denounced in the national press for making allegedly pro-German comments. This 'brave and rare voice' had given a sermon in March 1915 at St Margaret's Church in Westminster in which he did little more than propound the true Christian message.[62] Lyttleton 'did not think it right to surrender to the hysteria of jingoism',[63] urged compassion rather than condemnation, and suggested that the Great War be ended by a negotiated peace.

Until 1916 discretion may have been the better part of valour for those who questioned the righteousness of the war. The introduction of universal conscription, however, forced many individuals to state their beliefs and to declare their allegiances. Some of their friends and colleagues had earlier avoided this denouement by volunteering for non-combat service with humanitarian and medical units. Leslie Gilbert, a Quaker who taught A.J.P. Taylor history at Bootham School after the war, served indirectly by joining the Friends Ambulance Unit in 1915 as a nursing orderly on ambulance trains in France.[64] There were others, still working in schools, who, motivated by deep religious or pacifist conviction, chose now to appeal against their conscription. They were amongst the 16,500 Conscientious Objectors (CO) who appeared before British tribunals during the Great War.[65] Public declarations of non-conformity created additional difficulties for the teachers and schools involved. Those with confirmed pacifist beliefs were not universally condemned as is often believed to have been the case, but they certainly divided opinion. In November 1917 the Governing Body of Aberystwyth County School voted upon a series of resolutions to dismiss one of two teachers who had appeared before local tribunals on conscientious grounds. Dr D.J. Davies had been openly criticised by some of the governors for being 'a demoralising influence', whilst others countered this accusation by stating that he had never attempted to instil his views into others or even discuss his opinions in class. Parents and pupils also lent their support, the former by sending letters and the latter by mounting a demonstration. A large number of boys marched to the house of the Chair of Governors because, they asserted, 'One of the Masters ... is being unjustly persecuted because of his convictions'. The decision to dismiss Dr Davies was subsequently rescinded.[66] There were difficulties, too, at the King's School in Ottery St Mary in Devon, where staff shortages led to the appointment of a male teacher who was subsequently discovered to be a Conscientious Objector.

One mistress consequently resigned in protest, and after pressure from parents, the new teacher was dismissed by the governors.[67] Despite the serious issue of teacher supply during the war, Conscientious Objectors faced real difficulties in securing employment. The Governors of Hutcheson's Grammar School in Glasgow were not alone in resolving not to entertain applications for teaching posts from Conscientious Objectors.[68] Their counterparts at Aberystwyth County School similarly insisted that male candidates of military age gave reasons in their applications for vacant posts why they were not engaged in military service.[69] Such overt prejudice and discrimination continued even after the war had ended. Harold Bing, an 18-year-old when the Military Service Act came into operation, joined the No-Conscription Fellowship and, as an 'absolutist' who refused to engage in any activity which might support the war even indirectly, subsequently spent nearly three years in prison. On his release he was determined to become a teacher but encountered numerous advertisements for posts in schools stating 'No COs should apply'.[70]

One of the most famous Conscientious Objectors of the Great War was Bert Brocklesby. He was one of the 6,000 men who served prison sentences for their refusal to serve, one of 1,300 who refused to cooperate with the military authorities in any way, and a member of the Richmond Sixteen who were treated particularly harshly as a clear warning to others who might follow their example. Other members of the Brocklesby family did contribute to the war effort in different ways. In the South Yorkshire mining village of Conisbrough near Doncaster, Father John was chairman of the local War Fund Committee, mother Hannah was on the Ladies' Committee for Soldiers' Relief, and eldest son, George, worked in the Recruiting Office. Another son, Philip, enlisted in the York and Lancaster Regiment, and the youngest son, Harold, was in the OTC at Sheffield University before also serving in France. Bert, the second of the four Brocklesby boys, was twenty-five when war was declared. Unlike the other members of his family, his Methodist upbringing and unwavering belief in the literal word of the Bible led him to condemn the war. He had joined in the Mission Band and taught in the local Sunday school. In 1907 he trained to be a teacher at the Methodist College in London where he captained the rugby team and became College Precentor in charge of the college music programme. Bert then returned to Conisbrough to take up a teaching post. In January 1915 he preached a sermon at the Conisbrough Methodist Chapel in which he spoke out against the war. At his tribunal in Doncaster in 1916 his appeal against conscription was based squarely upon the Sixth Commandment: 'Thou shalt not kill'. He was directed to join the army's newly-formed Non-Combatant Corps, and when he refused to comply was arrested and sent to Pontefract Barracks followed by imprisonment in the cells of Richmond Castle. Bert and the other fifteen inmates were then sent to France on 'active service'. Now subject to the martial code, the penalties for disobedience were severe. Bert continued to refuse to submit to military direction, was court-martialled and, with over thirty others, sentenced to death by shooting. This sentence was then commuted to ten years penal servitude. Bert Brocklesby spent the rest of the war in English prisons until, in April 1919, he and other Conscientious Objectors were released by the British Government. Bert returned to teaching briefly, but then travelled to Vienna with the Friends War Victim Relief organisation to help feed children still suffering from the effects of war. Later work as a missionary in East Africa was followed by another spell of teaching back in England. Bert Brocklesby died in 1963. At the time of his arrest in 1916, his father had said: 'I would rather Bert be shot for his beliefs than abandon them'.[71]

Those in the teaching profession who openly opposed the war on political grounds also put themselves in an extremely precarious position. A handful of teachers went beyond conscientious objection to the war and became militant anti-war and anti-capitalist campaigners. One Old Boy of Hutcheson's Grammar School gained national infamy as a Conscientious Objector. Born in 1885, James Maxton (Plate 37) attended Grahamstown School, a Scottish public elementary school in Barhead near Glasgow where his father, also called James, was the headteacher. At the age of twelve the young James won a Renfrew County 'Free Place' scholarship to Hutcheson's. Later he became a pupil teacher at Martyrs' Public School before proceeding to the Training College for Teachers at Glasgow University. Whilst there he joined, briefly, the 1st Lanarkshire Rifle Volunteers. His growing radical views, however, soon led him to request a transfer to the unit's non-combatant ambulance section. On leaving college he taught at Sir John Maxwell School in Eastwood in the outer suburbs of Glasgow before transferring in 1908 to St James School in Bridgeton in the East End of the city, an area known for its acute social deprivation. His experience there reinforced his political radicalism – in 1904 Maxton had joined the Independent Labour Party (ILP) – and he rapidly gained a reputation as the 'children's advocate', the teacher 'who had been converted to socialism by the plight of his poorest pupils'.[72] In 1914 Maxton and other ILP members opposed the war. By then he had moved to Dennistoun School. After his arrest in December 1915 following a freedom of speech and anti-conscription demonstration in Glasgow his employer, the Glasgow School Board, dismissed him but then transferred him to Finniestown School. He was also given a final warning about his conduct.

The Military Service Act of 1916 led to Maxton's call up for the armed forces. In March of that year he appealed against his conscription and the tribunal, recognising his genuine and steadfast convictions, offered him the option of serving in the RAMC. His refusal branded him a Conscientious Objector. In the same month his arrest after supporting the Clydeside munitions workers and encouraging them to strike – an act considered by many to be tantamount to an act of treason in wartime – led to a trial at the High Court in Edinburgh.

Found guilty as charged and sentenced to one year in prison, he was released from Edinburgh's Calton Jail in February 1917. Undeterred, James Maxton continued to be politically active. By the time the peace treaty was finally signed at Versailles in June 1919 he was a full-time employee of the ILP and its Scottish Divisional Chair. He had met the Russian revolutionary Kerensky during the latter's visit to Britain and, ironically, had even been elected to the Glasgow Education Authority. After the Great War he was MP for Bridgeton from 1922 until his death in 1946 and became Chair of the ILP. Winston Churchill described him as the greatest parliamentarian of his age. Another future Prime Minister, Gordon Brown, wrote the definitive biography of this man of relatively humble origins and occupation who became an icon of the socialist movement in Britain.[73]

James Maxton was not the only radical teacher in Scotland. His friend and colleague John Maclean, who taught at Lorne Street Primary School in Govan, were both leading figures in the Socialist Teachers' Society which had been formed in 1905 and was particularly strong in Scotland.[74] Maclean was also directly and heavily involved in the Red Clydeside agitation. Like Maxton, he too was dismissed from his teaching post by the Glasgow School Board and imprisoned for his overt anti-war activities. Maclean was an influential member of the Co-operative movement and a declared Marxist and revolutionary socialist. In recognition of his support for the workers' revolution in Russia, the Soviet leadership appointed him Bolshevik Consul for Scotland. His further imprisonment, impassioned speeches and early death in 1923 combined to create a legendary figure for both the British Left and the movement for Scottish Independence.

War elicits myriad responses. The Great War is still remembered for the contribution and hardships of millions of individuals throughout the world. In Britain and all the other belligerent nations, narratives of glory combined with sacrifice continue to be told and valued. The stories of the tens of thousands who questioned the war of 1914–19 are also important and worth recalling: 'their strength of conviction remains one of the glories of a dark time'.[75]

Chapter 8

Temporary Gentlemen

To be a good officer, it is also necessary to be a gentleman.
Admiralty minute Adm.116/1734, 16 January 1918

March 1918, just hours before the German Spring Offensive smashes through the British lines. A small group of soldiers sit in a British dugout on the Western Front. Stanhope, Osborne, Raleigh and Trotter are all commissioned officers. Captain Stanhope is the archetypal brilliant young man of his generation; well-educated and the hero on the games field at his public school. The war has transformed him into a battle-blooded, hard-drinking company commander and leader of men. Lieutenant Osborne, senior in age but not in rank to Stanhope, is the avuncular former schoolmaster who played rugby for Harlequins and, on one occasion, for England. He converses in a form and style that many of his brother officers are familiar with, making references to school sport and 'colours' and the importance of hero worship. To Osborne, the German front line is 'about the breadth of a rugger field' away. The youngest officer, more boy than man, is Second Lieutenant Raleigh; the naïve and idealistic subaltern who has made the journey to the trenches from the same school as Stanhope. Raleigh has used his family connections to get him placed in the same company as his schoolboy hero.

If these three men conform to the classic representations of the British officer class at war, then the fourth officer in the scene certainly does not. Second Lieutenant Trotter is, instead, a grotesque caricature; a parvenu, an upstart, the new man who has somehow gained admittance to a once-exclusive club. His face is 'red, fat and round', and he has 'podgy fingers'. He is unable to button his tunic because 'he has put on weight during his war service', having, it is implied, taken full advantage of the previously unobtainable benefits of the officers' mess. Unlike Raleigh, Trotter is unable to share literary allusions with Osborne and is ungrammatical and colloquial in his speech. He drops his 'h's just like the mess servants, one of whom he believes is 'getting familiar'. Unlike the other three men in the dug out, Trotter was promoted from the ranks – and his fellow officers and other ranks know it. The war has made 'Temporary Officers' of them all, but in an age which held that an officer was a gentleman and gentlemen was an officer, Trotter was the only 'Temporary Gentleman' amongst them.

The dramatis personae in *Journey's End* are, of course, fictional characters.[1] They were created by Robert Sherriff, the young man from Kingston Grammar

School who, despite his school's ancient foundation and sporting links with the public schools, failed to gain a commission in 1914.[2] Much to his surprise and genuine disappointment, Sherriff discovered that one's Alma Mater, and its place in the educational hierarchy, really did matter. Army Regulations stipulated that new officers would need to have had a public school education or its equivalent. Evidence of active involvement in the Territorials, OTC or school Cadet Corps was an additional qualification. Sherriff's schooling did not qualify him for the award of the King's Commission. He was not accepted for officer training, whilst thousands of 'Raleighs' were.

The public-school educated subaltern, and the part he played in the Great War, has become the stuff of legend – and myth. Such young men have been described as 'waiting in the wings of history',[3] or, more prosaically, as members of a group who 'assumed the rights of a ruling elite, but also the obligations that went with them; not least the responsibility for leadership in war'.[4] They were undoubtedly young men from 'the right background', a 'gilded youth' imbued with visions of service to 'Empire', 'Nation', 'School' and the social class which defined such terms and from which they were drawn. War had become, in the popular imagination at least, a theatrical event; the sacrificial schoolboy its juvenile lead.[5] The teenage second lieutenant was 'the perfection of an iconography',[6] an idealised model of leadership which was thrown headlong into an all-consuming conflict. Early selection procedures did mean that the vast majority of commissions awarded in the first year of the war went to the products of the elite schools. Connections, whether through family or schooling, were everything, and of greater weight even than demonstrable ability, aptitude or potential. Proxy measures – such as evidence of academic or sporting prowess – reinforced other assumed and less precise indicators of an individual's suitability to lead companies of men on the battlefield.

Rolls of Honour produced by different schools challenge some of the enduring myths about officers during the Great War. As an earlier chapter has shown, the products of the elite public schools did not universally gain commissions. Admittedly, the vast majority from such schools who applied to become officers did become subalterns, but there were those, such as Charles Laidlaw from Perse School in Cambridge,[7] who chose not to apply for commissions and served in the ranks instead. Others were deemed to be unfit or unsuitable for leadership roles. John Kipling, son of the author Rudyard Kipling, was rejected initially on the basis of defective eyesight. Family connections eventually secured him a commission in the 2nd Battalion Irish Guards.[8] The second claim that all – or even most – of the officers in the Great War were the products of the elite public school system is also incorrect but persists, nevertheless, as a major constituent of Great War mythology. Whilst the most senior posts were generally held by former public school men – Eton College alone provided seven British Army Corps Commanders during the war[9] – the social background and previous schooling of junior officers became increasingly diverse as the war dragged on. Large numbers of BEF casualties in the first campaigns in Flanders were compounded by high rates of attrition amongst New Army company commanders during the major offensives on the Somme and at Passchendaele in 1916 and 1917 respectively. The German Spring Offensive of March 1918 stretched British manpower to the limit and created a crisis of both confidence and supply. The army, for so long dependent upon traditional sources of recruitment for its officers, was forced to be pragmatic and to recruit new men from beyond the usual gene pool.

During the Great War 229,316 commissions were granted.[10] Some 100,000 of these went to men with OTC experience gained in the public schools and universities. From Febuary 1916 young men leaving schools, universities or the Inns of Court with OTC Certificates continued to be commissioned, but they were joined as junior officers by the products of the new Officer Cadet Battalions (OCB). These provided a four-month course for men from the ranks; men who had front-line experience and had been recommended by their commanding officers for their proven ability and leadership qualities as NCOs. On successful completion of the course they were promoted to second lieutenant and became Temporary Officers – 'for the duration of the war only'. Nearly half of all wartime commissions were awarded to OCB graduates.[11] Most of the new officers were middle class, but many – some 40 per cent – were drawn from the intermediate and working classes of society. A War Office report in 1920 noted that hundreds of former miners, fishermen, carters, leather tanners, warehousemen and porters had held temporary commissions. These men had mostly been educated in Britain's maintained secondary and elementary schools, a fact clearly recognised by the focus and content of their officer training.

OCB courses were based on two related premises. The first was that good military leadership was not purely a matter of ability in the field. Gentlemen, it was argued in the early twentieth century, had an innate ability to lead, a way of doing things which the naturally deferential men in the ranks expected and appreciated. Effective junior officers had a certain style and qualities, which, if not inherent, might be learned and adopted by others. Would-be officers were therefore taught etiquette and manners for much of their time. They were taught 'conduct befitting officers and gentlemen' as well as drill, musketry and tactics.[12] This process of 'gentlemanlification', deemed to be unnecessary for those who had been to public school, often took place in the refined settings of Cambridge and Oxford colleges. Dining at High Table in Trinity or Balliol prepared them for the rigours of the officers' mess. The development of personal qualities was far more important than the honing of leadership strategies; 'good form' triumphed over technical capability.

The second premise, inextricable from the first and convenient to those in authority, was that working-class Tommy Atkins – representative of the great majority of other ranks – responded best to upper-class officers, or at least to those 'young swells' who were better mannered and more cultured than they were.[13] OCB training taught the importance of social status, presence and distance. The Temporary Gentlemen were thus forged out of necessity. In this particular respect, and as Sherriff's depiction of Trotter indicates, class barriers were not broken down by the Great War. If anything, they were maintained and reinforced by this temporary and, at times, uneasy device for officer supply.

Many schoolteachers became Temporary Officers during the Great War. Those with impeccable credentials – public school and Oxbridge educated, members of the corps, pre-war part-timers in the Special Reserve or Territorials, currently teaching in an elite school, for example – were generally awarded a commission in 1914. Public school men like Corrie Chase and Wilfrith Elstob taught in institutions which had traditionally schooled young men for leadership positions in all walks of life and, especially, in the armed forces. Schoolmasters such as these prepared boys for careers in the Regular Army, and helped them to gain access to the military academies at Sandhurst and Woolwich. They also joined with the majority of their pupils in combining professional careers with part-time soldiering. Such pre-war experience and affiliation enabled them to obtain commissions from the outset, although getting into the 'right' battalion or regiment might require additional useful connections. Whilst Regular Army career officers might sometimes refer to them disparagingly as 'the Temporary Gentlemen', they were patently gentlemen nevertheless; it was only their full-time in wartime officer status which was temporary.

George Arthur Tryon exemplifies the many public school masters who served in the Great War. He had close links with the clerical and military establishment through his father, Reverend A.W. Tryon and his grandfather, General Tryon, who had served in the Regular Army. After first attending De Aston School in Market Rasen, where his father was the incumbent of the parish church, George joined Uppingham School. There he became a member of the OTC. He continued his part-time military training during his undergraduate years at Cambridge University. Appointed to teach at Oundle School, he subsequently became a housemaster and captain of the school's OTC. When war was declared in August 1914 George Tryon had all the right credentials for a commission in His Majesty's armed forces. He was, by dint of breeding, schooling and profession, a gentleman and potential officer; his OTC training and leadership experience were additional qualifications which cemented his place in the military hierarchy. On volunteering for service he was immediately commissioned into the 6th Battalion King's Royal Rifle Corps (KRRC), posted to France in 1914, and eventually commanded the 4th Battalion KRRC. George Tryon was one of the young men from the right background depicted so well in John Lewis-Stempel's *Six Weeks: the Short and Gallant Life of the British Officer in the First World War*. Admittedly, he is not the stereotypical 18-year-old schoolboy subaltern with character but little worldly experience like Sherriff's fictional Raleigh, but he nevertheless epitomises the gentlemanly product of the public schools of England. Many, George Tryon included, were clearly men of great ability, combining the qualities and attributes of Stanhope and Osborne. They were an example to their fellow soldiers and eminently qualified for their leadership role; a role developed through their experience as teachers as well as their early conditioning in elite schools and their pre-war part-time military training.

Ernest Woodward's social and educational background was similar to George Tryon's, but his response to the call-to-arms was very different. He was educated at Christ's Hospital School where his father had been Senior Classical Master, won a scholarship to Hertford College Oxford, and then entered the teaching profession. He taught classics and coached rugby at Oundle before moving to the Perse School in Cambridge. On the outbreak of war he volunteered immediately but, unlike Tryon, refused to accept a commission, preferring instead to serve as a private with men from similar backgrounds in the 18th Battalion (Public Schools) Royal Fusiliers. On disbandment of the Public Schools Battalion in 1916 he became a second lieutenant in the 10th Royal West Surrey Regiment.[14] The wartime experience of another public school master, W.A. Tomlinson, was remembered by H.E. Walker, one of the pupils in his classics class at Felsted Preparatory School:

> During World War I he joined the army and remained a private until the Armistice, although I am sure that he could have obtained a commission. His experience of the food dished out to the men in the trenches probably accounts for the fact that he could always eat whatever was put in front of him in the Prep dining room.[15]

Mr A.C. Axe, a Music Master at Hurstpierpoint College, was turned down for a commission and served as a private in the Yorkshire Regiment.[16] Previous experience as a schoolmaster at a public school, no matter how prestigious, did not automatically guarantee officer status.

Beyond the public schools, some teachers who taught – and had been taught – in the aided grammar or grant-supported secondary schools were commissioned on enlistment. Military training in the OTC and Territorial battalions had not been restricted to those in or from the public schools. Schoolteacher Russell Wheeler and trainee teacher James Garland, for example, had both joined Senior Division OTC at university, whilst John Paulson had been awarded a part-time commission in the pre-war Special Reserve. Those employed as schoolteachers in elementary schools were far less likely, however, to be awarded a commission on enlistment, especially if their own schooling had taken place in such institutions. The military rank held by former schoolteachers who served in the Great War generally reflected the hierarchical nature of schooling in Britain; masters from the elite schools were far more likely to be commissioned, whilst the majority of Assistant Teachers from the elementary schools became other ranks.

Once again, The National Union of Teachers *War Record* provides data which, despite some obvious limitations, allow more detailed scrutiny of the above generalisations. As noted previously, although the *War Record* lists the names of nearly 20,000 NUT members who served, only those who were awarded military honours or who died in the conflict also have their rank recorded. The ranks of The Fallen are those held at the time of death, and it is therefore impossible to ascertain from this data set alone whether any given individual was commissioned on enlistment, subsequently during training, or on the basis of battlefield experience later in the war. Nevertheless, the statistics for those members of the NUT who are ranked amongst The Fallen show that this group of schoolteachers comprised commissioned officers, non-commissioned officers and private soldiers in roughly equal proportions.[17] Of the 1,413 male NUT members who served – and died – in the British Army:

449 (32 per cent) were commissioned officers
474 (33 per cent) were non-commissioned officers
490 (35 per cent) were privates or equivalent ranks.[18]

The statistics disguise the real lives of real individuals. For some of these men, however, it is possible to uncover personal histories which challenge the customary stereotypes. Second Lieutenant Joseph Dines (Plate 38) was one of the 449 commissioned teacher-soldier-officers referred to above. Born in 1886 in King's Lynn in Norfolk, Joseph attended All Saints National School in the town where, according to the 1901 Census, he became a monitor. He then became a pupil teacher in nearby Hunstanton before moving in 1909 to Peterborough for more formal teacher training at St Peter's College. In 1910 he returned to King's Lynn to teach at St Margaret's Church of England School, then moved to Highlands School in Ilford where he remained until the war. So far, Joseph's story is relatively unremarkable; he is one of the thousands of bright working-class children who were channelled into the teaching profession at this time. What set Joseph apart from many of his contemporaries, however, was his undoubted talent for playing football. Like Evelyn Lintott he combined a full-time teaching career with part-time and high-level sporting activity. He played for his local team King's Lynn FC, starring in their 1906 FA Cup match against Aston Villa. He captained the St Peter's College team. He played the occasional game for Milwall, Queen's Park Rangers and Liverpool, in a bygone age when professional teams would call upon amateur players to fill gaps caused by injuries. Known as 'the smiling footballer', Joseph was a determined amateur player, resisting all inducements to agree professional terms. He was called up for the England amateur squad in the 1909–10 season, eventually winning twenty-four international caps. At the Stockholm Olympic Games in 1912 Joseph Dines was in the gold medal winning England Association Football side.

In November 1915 Joseph Dines enlisted, at the age of twenty-six, as a private in the Army Ordnance Corps and was deployed as a storeman. He applied for a commission in December 1916 but was rejected. Sixth months later he was transferred to the 6th Battalion Middlesex Regiment stationed at Chatham, but shortly afterwards was posted to the Machine Gun School in Grantham to train on one of the other new weapons of the Great War – the tank. He applied for a commission in the Tank Corps, but once again was considered to be lacking in sufficient experience. In June 1918, however, Joseph – by this time Sergeant – Dines was commissioned into the 13th Battalion The King's Liverpool Regiment and was posted to France the following September. [19]

Why had it taken so long for this ambitious and talented man to become an officer? Perhaps his humble origins and lack of secondary education are all the explanation that is necessary. In the absence of records which might give clues to his personal qualities or potential for leadership, it is also difficult to find out about the man himself: his intelligence, communication skills, presence, manner and manners. What is indisputable is that he could teach, was college-trained and played sport at the highest level. Second Lieutenant Dines became an officer only in the last months of the war, one of the Temporary Officers and Temporary Gentlemen to whom the military authorities turned almost as a last resort. By then the German Spring Offensive had been halted, but at great cost to the British Officer Corps. Men like Dines were needed as replacements now, to be thrown into the fray as the final March to Victory in late 1918 unfolded. Perhaps the military authorities were far more sophisticated than many historians give them credit for, deploying Dines and others like him in roles which optimised their skills and experience. It has been claimed that in the history and traditions of the British Army, men from the two social extremes – young subalterns from the elite schools and foot soldiers from the ranks of the lower orders – were considered to be dispensable. Mature men like Joseph Dines, one of thousands of serving former elementary schoolteachers with experience of managing and disciplining young adults from the working classes, were arguably much more valuable as NCOs, leading young men from humble backgrounds in the trenches.

The reaction, from both fellow officers and the men they commanded, to those who had been elevated to officer status was mixed, an inevitable consequence of a British Army that was already deeply divided along caste lines.[20] Different regiments, and even different battalions within the same regiment, dismissed the perceived pretensions of others. Those holding commissions were a diverse group, ranging from men with impeccable backgrounds to those who were socially suspect. Robert Graves was the product of a genteel background, a public school education, the Charterhouse OTC and the Special Reserve. Graves congratulated himself on having chosen a regiment with battle honours – the Royal Welch Fusiliers – rather than facing the 'shame' attached to joining a county regiment. The author of *Goodbye To All That* was nevertheless dismayed by the less-than-warm reactions of Regular officers to his own attachment to their battalion.[21] Of the 200,000 commissions in the war only 16,000, including Graves's, were permanent,[22] but many Regulars, especially in the highest ranks, distrusted citizen soldiers.[23] The author Dennis Wheatley similarly recalled his own experiences as a Temporary Gentleman and took great delight in describing the characteristics of his fellow officers. Unlike Graves, he found the Regulars charming, the pre-war Territorials rude and city battalion men overzealous and keen to curry favour with their superiors.[24] There was clearly a pecking order no matter what social or educational background an officer came from, but for ex-rankers this situation was exacerbated by criticism of their origins, manners, badly-cut uniforms and other such superficialities.[25] The term 'Temporary Gentlemen' shifted in its application during the Great War. At first it was applied to any civilian who was commissioned 'for the duration only'. It gradually became a more derisive term for those of inferior origin.[26] Many officers from the upper social groups noted with alarm the 'marked influx of men into the general officer corps whose social occupations were not "pukka", and (who) would not have had a sniff of a Territorial, let alone a Regular, commission in 1914'.[27] The poet Wilfrid Owen referred to the Temporary Gentlemen in his letters as 'glorified NCOs' and 'privates and sergeants in masquerade'.

Ultimately, it was ability that counted. Good leadership manifested itself in many ways. Wheatley noted that 'whatever their limitations in brains', the 'hearty huntin', shootin' and fishin' type' officers in the county regiments 'were popular with their men and made admirable leaders'. Such men conformed to the dash and daring model of leadership that had been exemplified in *The Captain* and other schoolboy magazines. The gallant subaltern who loved his men and gave them cigarettes and smiles,[28] and the loyal Tommy who dutifully responded to such 'companionate paternalism', have became enduring legends of the war.[29] Their symbiotic relationship – underpinned by notions of devotion and deference – was the basis of trench harmony, at least according to officers such as Owen and Graves. Leading men to their deaths in no man's land demanded nothing less, and perhaps nothing more.

In an age when social standing and style was often mistaken for ability, the British Army persisted with a model of leadership which became less effective as the war became more technical. In modern texts on leadership, soft skills – the ability to form positive relationships with individuals and within teams – are still highly valued, but only when deployed as part of a wider strategic and technically effective mode of operation. In 1914 courage, leadership and example were still vitally important leadership attributes, and 'were not of course the prerogatives solely of the officer class, still less of public schoolboys'.[30] The new warfare, however, demanded far more of its officers and other ranks. Private David Lindsay observed the deficiencies of the officer class from a somewhat privileged position. Before the war he had been a Member of Parliament, played a major role in the founding of the National Portrait Gallery and the Victoria and Albert Museum in London, and had reputedly declined an invitation to become Viceroy of India. As the Earl of Crawford and Balcarres, Lindsay was of obvious officer stock, but in 1915, and at the age of forty-three, he enlisted as a private in the RAMC. Lord Crawford noted in his diary:

> I have come across hundreds (of officers) who are utterly incompetent to lead men, to inspire confidence or respect, to enforce discipline, to behave even as gentlemen. This war is going to be won by the NCOs and men, not the commissioned ranks.[31]

Dennis Wheatley similarly noted that men of real ability were rare. Robert Graves recognised, albeit with the familiar caveats, that commissioned ex-rankers often brought something new to the military equation:

> Though the quality of officers had deteriorated from the regimental point of view, their greater efficiency in action amply compensated for their deficiency in manners.[32]

Some recent historians have argued that the junior officers were one of the critical factors in Britain's victory on the Western Front.[33] The notion that these young men were drawn almost exclusively from the public schools of Britain is, however, inaccurate; part of a mythology of the Great War, which 'abolishes the complexity of human acts and gives them the simplicity of essences'.[34] Temporary Officers were a far less homogenous group than hitherto depicted, containing both real gentlemen who assumed leadership as a birthright, and others who were elevated to positions of authority by dint of experience and ability. The demands of war led to the temporary transformation of a small and exclusive officer class into an enlarged, diverse and non-traditional officer corps.

Many of the Temporary Officers gained further promotion. Former teachers from public schools, such as George Tryon, Bernard Vann and Wilfith Elstob, for example, became celebrated senior officers who commanded battalions. Some of the Temporary Gentlemen who had previously taught in maintained schools also moved up the military hierarchy during the course of the war. Amongst the members of the NUT listed under 'Military Honours' in the *War Record* were ninety-five British Army captains and eighteen majors. J.M. Wightman became a colonel in the Munster Regiment and Lieutenant Colonel E.T. Rees commanded a battalion of the South Wales Borderers. Some who later became senior officers had been promoted from the ranks. Archibald Walter Buckle, a teacher at St Augustine's Church School in London, was exceptional. As a pre-war member of the Royal Naval Volunteer Reserve (RNVR) he responded immediately to the call-to-arms in 1914. He joined the Drake Battalion of the Royal Naval Division (RND) and served at Antwerp during the attempt by British and Belgian forces to stop the advancing German Army. He was commissioned shortly afterwards in recognition of his actions during the division's campaign in Flanders. Archibald later fought with distinction in the battles of Arras, Passchendaele, the German Spring Offensive, and the victorious Hundred Days campaign of 1918. He was awarded the Distinguished Service Order (DSO) on an unprecedented four separate occasions for acts of personal bravery. By the end of the war (Temporary) Commander Buckle led the Anson Battalion RND, the unit in which the poet Rupert Brooke had also served. The fact that a classically educated poet is remembered far more today than the ex-elementary school teacher who led a battalion of the RND to victory in 1918 is indicative of the way in which traditional notions of brilliance continue to be celebrated.

The Great War disturbed the status quo in ways which would have been unthinkable before 1914. Joseph Dines, Archibald Buckle and the thousands of other Temporary Gentlemen were but a symptom of a world turned upside down, for the time being at least. The exigencies of war fostered temporariness of all kinds. Censorship, conscription, food rationing and new licensing hours for public houses were all part of a new reality. At the very heart of government, patrician rule gave way to the new men. By 1917 the British war effort was being directed by two men who had been educated in elementary schools: the Alma Mater of Prime Minister David Lloyd George and Chief of the Imperial General Staff Sir William Robertson were Llanystumdwy National School and Welbourn Village School respectively. Robertson was the only British field marshal to have risen from the ranks. 'Wully', as he was affectionately known, even dropped his 'h's like Second Lieutenant Trotter.[35]

Whilst the Temporary Gentlemen and their former colleagues in the teaching profession fought on the battlefields of Europe and beyond, they were replaced in their schools by 'Temporary Masters'. The enlistment of thousands of male teachers created immediate and enormous staffing problems in schools. The Military Service Acts of 1916 and 1918 made matters even worse, as men who had originally been able to continue their teaching were conscripted. The Board of Education's *Report* for 1913–14, published just a few months after the war started, noted that nearly 4,000 male teachers from the public elementary schools in England and Wales 'were occupied on naval or military duties'.[36] Initially, staff lost to the war were replaced. Where this was not possible, schools made other contingency arrangements. Secondary schools were particularly hard hit by teacher shortages. Harrow County School for Boys was one of many which experienced a massive turnover of teaching staff during the war; forty new teachers were appointed, seventeen of them staying for less than a year. In February 1915 *The Gaytonian* stated 'We must ask parents to suffer patiently the numerous changes in the staff. They are unavoidable and constitute part of the price we are paying for the war'. [37] By September 1916 only two of the original seven male teachers on the staff of Cowper Testimonial School in Hertford were still teaching there, namely the headteacher and a teacher declared unfit for military service.[38] Public schools suffered too. Hurstpierpoint College made twenty-eight wartime appointments; of the fourteen masters teaching there in 1914, only five remained by the end of the war.[39]

Teacher replacements included elderly retired men who were encouraged back into schools in much the same way that the War Office had used retired officers to fill the gaps in the British Army in the early stages of the war. These 'dug-outs' were not always the 'pathetically doddering' individuals described elsewhere,[40] but despite their experience few compared favourably with the energetic young male teachers who were now with the colours. At the other end of the age scale were the trainee teachers who, until the call-to-arms, had been preparing to enter the profession. As James Garland's story has demonstrated,[41] however, the expected cohorts of young blood were also in increasingly short supply. In the first weeks of the war some trainee teachers found that their school-based teaching experience placements were simply extended at the expense of their college-based training in education theory. This was no more than a temporary expedient. In the next few months large numbers of male trainees at the London Day Training College (LDTC), for example, left to join the armed forces without completing their courses. Some opted for war-related work rather than teaching. LDTC trainee teacher Samuel Atkinson, a prospective Chemistry and Physics teacher, left in the last year of his course for munitions work, as did fellow student Edward Hall who became an Analytical Chemist at Woolwich Arsenal. The situation in the colleges preparing young men for elementary teaching was no better. By the end of 1914, the Board of Education reported, 45 per cent of those in their final years of training had left for the forces.[42] In its *Report* the following year the Board noted that some 3,000 former trainees were serving with the colours.[43] Training colleges did their utmost to attract new trainees, but the numbers remained small and the majority of the new male recruits to the profession were drawn from the ranks of those deemed to be unfit for military service. Numbers in training dwindled and some colleges, including the LDTC and King's College London in 1915, were directed by the Board of Education to amalgamate for the duration of the war. Others, including Armstrong College in Newcastle, St Mark's in Chelsea, St Gabriel's in

Kennington, and the Municipal Training Colleges in Brighton, Leeds, Manchester and Sheffield, were requisitioned as military hospitals.[44] Teacher training, for men at least, virtually ceased during the Great War.[45]

Some of the substitute teachers were even younger than the trainees. Prefects and older pupils, many of them waiting for their own opportunity to enlist, were also deployed by schools. H.W. Skinner later recalled the responsibility that he and other senior boys were given at Kent College in Canterbury, supervising 'prep' and teaching some of the younger boys. In the absence of the masters, whose replacements were generally 'inferior material, particularly as regards discipline', Skinner noted that 'it seemed to make us feel that we were helping'.[46] The Herbert Strutt School in Belper and King Edward VI Grammar School in Retford also used prefects to maintain discipline and to teach junior classes.[47] The latter school also employed Old Boys who had returned wounded to Blighty.[48] These were boys and men they knew and trusted. Staffing shortages were so severe in some schools, however, that headteachers and governors often had no alternative but to appoint substitutes who were unfit, unsuitable or unwilling. One former pupil of Harrow County School for Boys recalled that many of the male teachers 'would never have been considered for appointment in normal times; (they were) poor teachers, wretched disciplinarians'.[49] George Diamond, a pupil at Cardiff High School during the war, remembered:

> There was only a curtain separated two classes; and it was great agony for boys on one side of it to suffer the stern rule of Mr Bissell, while from the other side came sounds of revelry as Form I enjoyed periods of rapturous indiscipline under one of those transient and embarrassed phantoms that now began to flit across the scene.

George also endured 'outbreaks of frenzied nihilism' from one temporary teacher and the pacifist views of another, 'the odd mathematician who devoted the whole period to denouncing the War and Britain's part in it'.[50]

In March 1917 the Board of Education issued *Circular 986* in an attempt to bring other suitable, if untrained, adults into the classroom. Headteachers were advised that those 'in Holy Orders or Ministers of a congregation' might be employed as assistants to teach in elementary schools. The Board of Education made two provisos, however: these 'emergency teachers' could not be employed in schools where they were also managers, and their term was for the duration of the war only.[51] Clergymen also contributed to the wider curriculum of some of the public schools. At Hurspierpoint College, for example, the Reverend H.S. Barber helped run the cricket, football, fives and cross-country teams throughout the war years.[52]

Headteachers inevitably bore the brunt of the difficulties faced by schools. As leaders in wartime they were accountable for problems which were often beyond their personal control. The authorities, local communities and parents expected their schools to stay open despite limitations on teaching space, shortages of equipment and, for schools within range of enemy aircraft, frequent air-raid drills and occasional bombings. Some headteachers addressed the shortage of staff by doubling up classes or by making enforced changes to the school curriculum. At the Herbert Strutt School in Belper, Manual Instruction for the boys ceased in 1917. Shortages of wood were compounded by the conscription of the subject teacher in March of that year. Mr Jolley, originally in a 'low medical category', had been sent on a Summer Course at Lancaster which, it was hoped, would enable him to teach the boys Physical Training (PT). Unfortunately for the school, Mr Jolley appears to have made such an improvement to his own physique that he subsequently received his call-up papers. Headmaster Tunnicliffe had little alternative but to end the teaching of PT as well.[53]

Another alternative for headteachers was to add to their own workload, teaching subjects other than their specialism,[54] or, in some cases, teaching timetabled lessons for the first time since their appointment. The disappearance of ancillary staff also created additional work. When Mr Clayton the electrician at Ayton School was drafted into the army, Headmaster Dennis and his Senior Assistant Mr Baker took it upon themselves to run the turbine and dynamo which provided the lighting at their private boarding school.[55] Similarly, at Humphrey Perkins School in Leicestershire, Headmaster F.R.E. Fernsby's salary was increased by his governors after he assumed direct personal responsibility for maintaining the school site. He had previously, and unsuccessfully, tried to prevent caretaker Harry Longton from enlisting. Mrs Longton had taken over her husband's duties, but by 1917 it was clear to all that she was unable to look after the grounds.[56]

Wartime staffing shortages were not, of course, unique to schools. The absence of so many men at the front led to the wholesale employment in industry, agriculture and commerce of temporary workers, including thousands of children who had left school prematurely and were pressed into employment. The largest group of substitute workers, however, was women. Increasing numbers of adult female workers contributed to the war effort in factories and munitions works. They kept public transport running and laboured in the fields to save the nation from starvation. In British schools, by far the largest group of substitute teachers were trained women teachers. In early 1915 the Board of Education reported, in the borrowed military language of the period, that:

In the Elementary Schools the gaps have been filled to a large extent by calling up what might be called the reserves of the profession. Many qualified women who left the service for marriage have offered their services in the emergency and with very satisfactory results.[57]

The major influx of women into the teaching profession had taken place before, rather than during, the war.[58] In July 1914, 73 per cent of the workforce in local authority schools were women; by November 1918 that figure had risen to 82 per cent.[59] Many women now returned to the classroom in the country's hour of need. The marriage bar, which was based upon the notion that women could not possibly look after the home and do a full-time teaching job, was temporarily suspended. In elementary schools, it was a comparatively straightforward task to appoint women teachers on an *ad hoc* basis. The logbook for Amberley Parochial School in Gloucestershire contains a series of entries which illustrate how one small village school overcame a wartime staffing problem:

1916
12 May: I shall not be at school on Monday 15 May as I am under orders to proceed to Bristol to attend Harfield barracks for a Medical Inspection. Walter Jones.

20 June: I am leaving tomorrow to join H.M. Forces. Walter Jones.

21 June: I entered upon my duties as Head Teacher pro tem. Fanny R. Jones.[60]

Mrs Higgins similarly took over as headteacher of Rissington School in the Cotswolds after her husband joined the forces in 1917.[61] The logbooks of many other elementary schools record the departure of male assistants and the arrival of their female replacements. Alfred Whitehouse at St Nicholas Boys' School in King's Lynn, for example, noted:

1916
18 September: Mr Anderson left at noon, having been called to the Army.
Mrs Susan Close from Bonner Hill Road Boys' School, Kingston on Thames, commenced duties here.[62]

Whilst women teachers were an established feature of girls' schools and mixed infant and junior elementary schools, they were only occasionally part of the workforce in secondary schools for boys before 1914. This was particularly the case in boys' public schools. Despite serious staff shortages during the war the employment of women was considered by many to be 'neither practical nor viable'.[63] Where women were appointed, they were often relatives of masters absent on active service. At Kent College in Canterbury, Mrs Jackson, wife of the French master who had enlisted, and Miss Hargreaves, sister of the Second Master, were appointed. They were joined on the staff by women new to the school: Miss Phare, who founded the school Scout Troop, Miss Fowler, Miss Lewis, and Miss Harris. G.W.R. Brownscombe, son of headmaster Alfred Brownscombe, remembered how the school 'carried on normally during those war years – carried on mostly by women'.[64] The arrival of a new schoolmistress, seen by many at the time as a somewhat alien and exotic species in the masculine bastions of the British public schools for boys, clearly had an impact at Bancroft's School in Essex:

> For the first and only time, a woman was appointed to the teaching staff, dark little Miss Clarke, with the pence-nez, and the flowing gown, too feminine to be impressive, but lively and much at her ease, soon known to everyone as 'Laura'. She was a very successful teacher. There was competition for her tea-parties.[65]

In the traditional grammar and the new secondary schools the recruitment of women teachers during the war was far more commonplace. King Edward VI Grammar School in Totnes operated with an emergency staff of two masters and four mistresses, one of whom was Mrs Hanks, the wife of headteacher Frederick Hanks.[66] At Morpeth Grammar School Miss E.M. Sheldon, a teacher of science, was the first of four women appointed after 1916.[67] Northampton Grammar School formally welcomed its first mistress in the pages of the December issue of *The Northamptonian* that same year.[68] In Birmingham, the George Dixon Schools appointed five women to the boys' school.[69] The massive turnover of staff at Harrow County School for Boys included four women teachers appointed as early as October 1914. A further eighteen women had arrived in the staffroom by the time the war ended.

The demands of the war had thus changed customary practice in many schools, but the battle to overcome the traditional prejudice against women teaching secondary-age boys was hard won. Women teachers in boys' schools faced additional criticisms and gender stereotyping. A letter to the *Times Educational Supplement* in 1916, the point at which increasing numbers of schools were looking for replacement staff, stated that 'the best and most brilliant women cannot teach boys to be men - it would be unnatural if they could'. Barrow Grammar School for Boys anticipated clashes between newly appointed schoolmistresses and adolescent male exuberance, but through the pages of the school magazine the authorities trusted that 'the boys will be chivalrous'. Several boys were subsequently punished for 'neglect and overt idleness in connection with lady members of Staff' but, the magazine later reported, the discipline of the five women teachers appointed during the war was 'as good as that of any man'.[70] At Eastbourne Grammar School, which appointed nineteen temporary staff, it was similarly noted that 'Miss Varnier carried out her duties as well as any of our former masters'.[71] Temporary masters, whatever their gender, were expected to conform to a masculine construct of teaching, dispensing firm discipline and holding the fort until the real masters returned. Some schools even had difficulty with terminology. At Bolton School women teachers were to be known as 'Masters' but addressed as 'Madam'. Other schools would rather not have had to employ women teachers. Mr William Thomas informed those who gathered for the Speech Day in April 1919 at Hackney Downs School in London that 'we cannot profess ... to have altogether enjoyed the innovation'.[72]

For many school communities, however, the arrival of mistresses was a breath of fresh air. The four who started at Harrow County School for Boys in 1914 were highly qualified – which was especially important in a school that was just three years old and eager to establish its credentials – and were welcomed by all. They quickly integrated and they and the colleagues who followed them made their mark. One Old Gaytonian, who had been so dismissive of other male temporary masters, recalled:

> In my later years most of the teachers were women, to whom I have always been deeply grateful. Some were fresh from college, but if they had apprehensions about tackling a class of teenage boys it rarely showed: and they proved far better than their temporary predecessors at maintaining both order and interest. Even our physical training instructor was for a time replaced by a women, whose physique was the subject of inevitable, but on the whole respectable comment.[73]

Whatever individual schools thought about women teachers, the shortage of teachers generally meant that few could afford to harbour such prejudices. Good teachers were in short supply, and those teachers who were available were generally women. Those training colleges which had managed to remain open continued to prepare young women for the profession. The usual economic rules pertaining to supply and demand operated uneasily during wartime, however. The need to keep teaching posts open to men serving with the forces – and who knew exactly how long that might be? – inevitably meant that their replacements could only be offered temporary contracts. Of the 256 female trainees who gained their teaching qualifications at the LDTC from 1910, 66 were later recorded under the heading 'Subsequent Career' as being employed in wartime temporary or 'supply' posts.[74] For some fifty other trainees there was no entry under this particular heading.

Elsa Tutin was one such trainee. She entered the LDTC in 1913 at the age of nineteen, having been previously educated at Chelsea County Secondary School and then spending a year as a Student Teacher at Broadwater Road School in London. Her course consisted of two parts. She studied Latin (graded 'weak to fair'), English ('good to very good') and History ('satisfactory') to University of London degree level at Bedford College. At the LDTC building in Southampton Place she studied educational theory and practice, interspersed with one-term teaching practices in associated schools. Her final report was written with prospective employers in mind. Miss Tutin had made good progress during the course, and her ability and force of character augered well for her future as a teacher. Her tutors at LDTC believed that she would be a valuable member of the school staff and, with more experience, develop into a very good teacher.[75]

In 1917 Elsa left London with a Second Class Honours Degree in English, a University Teacher's Diploma, and a Board of Education Certificate. Her first teaching post, during the academic year 1917–18, was at the County Secondary School in Newport on the Isle of White. On 10 June 1918 she was offered another 'Temporary War Appointment': for the next seven months Miss Tutin became a temporary master, teaching English to secondary-age boys at Deacon's School in Peterborough.[76]

For some schools, the dire shortage of teachers was compounded by their inability to pay decent salaries to replacements. Elsa Tutin's salary at Deacon's School was unusual at £130 per anum, the amount earned on average by a headmistress of an elementary school in 1914, and some £20 higher than the average salary paid to a female graduate working in a secondary school during the war.[77] Salaries at The Herbert Strutt School, however, were insufficient to retain temporary teachers. One female teacher stayed at the school for a week before transferring to one making a better offer, whilst another left after the school governors refused to match the salary offered by her old training college.[78] Educational institutions competing for limited staffing resources also found that they had other rivals enticing teachers, or would-be teachers, away from the classroom. A logbook entry for Pound Lane Elementary School in Epsom, which had already doubled-up its classes after three teachers had enlisted, records:

1917
2 October: Miss Wetherall away all the morning for an interview under the Ministry of Munitions. Her salary is so poor she is unable to live on it and therefore is obliged to leave the profession.

The LDTC register also lists the names of several female students who left the course early for more lucrative remuneration in munition works. Rose Moss entered the LDTC at the same time as Elsa Tutin but, in the autumn of 1916, took up munitions work. So too did Kathleen Wadsworth, who was working in a munitions factory within a year of starting her teacher training course. The LDTC had decided to grant permission for such interruptions; trainees were given the option of completing their course when the war ended or, for those holding scholarships who chose not to resume their studies, refunding the cost of their tuition. Kathleen Wadsworth withdrew completely in September 1917. Edith Viney, a new trainee in 1915 who subsequently did clerical work for the Ministry of Munitions, refunded just over £27 to her education authority after the war. Other trainees left prematurely for other reasons. Isabel Hadfield contributed to the war effort at the National Physical Laboratory in Teddington from 1915, leaving just months before the end of her course. Catherine Tolson, an entrant in January 1918, interrupted her course at Easter of the same year, at the height of Britain's manpower (sic) crisis, to do statistical work for the Ministry of National Service. Personal ambition gave way to pragmatism for a number of trainees who were paying their own fees. Gwendoline Naylor was granted leave of absence in April 1917 'owing to financial difficulties caused by the war' – or more precisely the impact of the war on her father's business – and did not return to LDTC. Three fellow trainees left during the same academic year for similar financial reasons.[79]

The Great War demanded considered responses, not simply feverish or blind emotional gestures. Like their male counterparts who enlisted in the forces, these young women sacrificed qualifications and career prospects. A century later, it is impossible to see beyond the decisions made by them. The inner workings of an individual's mind – balancing the choices available to them in a given but unique context – are rarely accessible. Some trainees may well have felt that they could best serve the war effort elsewhere. Short-term improvements in earnings, at a time when salaries for teachers were falling behind wartime wages generally, and real increases in the cost of living,[80] appear to have been a key factor for many. Whatever their personal motivations and decisions, many talented women were lost to the profession, and not simply 'for the duration'.

The changing nature of work and status for women teachers was part of a wider phenomenon. Women had always been a key part of the national workforce. Before the war millions of working-class women had worked out of necessity,[81] their contributions to the economy and society in general barely recognised. During the Great War traditional notions of women were disturbed temporarily.[82] Total war demanded that they be mobilised. Recruitment posters urged them to enlist. Women were officially encouraged to work, to enrol in ancillary organisations, to sign on in the war factories, and to undertake tasks which were the traditional preserve of male workers. They became active participants in a common enterprise. For many women, greater involvement meant more charity work, more caring and more knitting, but for many others it meant new roles, new experiences and greater responsibility.[83] The war made women more visible, more assertive, and more vocal in support of their rights. The pressure to serve came not simply from the authorities, but from women themselves. In July 1915, and following the shells crisis of that year, a Women's Right to Serve March, organised by Emmeline Pankhurst, was held in London. One of the banners at the march read 'The situation is serious. Women must help to save it'.[84] Amongst those marching were women teachers.

As the industrial unrest on Red Clydeside demonstrated clearly, militant trade union activity did not cease on the outbreak of war in 1914. Professional associations such as the NUT generally supported the war effort, as their *War Record* testifies. Within the NUT, women members debated ways in which they might contribute more directly to the war effort. The West Ham Women Teachers' Association (WHWTA), for example, encouraged its members to join the Women's Police Patrols. Dissatisfaction *within* the ranks of teachers, however, was ever-present. Arguments within the NUT for greater gender equality led to the formation of the Equal Pay League in 1904, re-named the National Federation of Women Teachers (NFWT) two years later. The NFWT kept up its campaign for equal wages and conditions during the war. Despite the work women teachers were engaged in, there was often virulent criticism and opposition from male members of the NUT. Women union leaders, many of whom were also committed supporters of the Suffrage Movement, were determined to challenge conventional versions of femininity and to counter gender-based assumptions. Ethel Froud of the WHWTA resigned from her teaching post in West Ham to become full-time Secretary of the NFWT, a post she had held part-time since 1913. She was a member of the Women's Social and Political Union (WSPU) and played in their fife and drum band, and was also on the Committee of the Women Teachers' Franchise Union. The case for equal pay, equal conditions and equal political rights was argued by Ethel Froud and her colleagues at every opportunity (Plate 39).

Support was certainly forthcoming for women teachers who had become temporary masters. In November 1916 NFWT President Miss G.M. Herbert urged women not to submit to traditional expectations of what they might do, arguing instead that 'teachers working in Boys' Schools should insist upon doing the whole work of the class so that the question of unequal work could not be used'. Rose Lamartine Yates, a member of the London County Council and advocate for women teachers, stressed the importance of teaching expertise and impact rather than gender attributes. Women teachers, she argued, had:

> proved equal to the task in spite of the handicaps of a war period, of a different code of discipline, no previous training and the boys' prejudice against a teacher, branded as inferior. The experiment therefore has proved women's interchangeability.[85]

A later President of the NFWT, Agnes Dawson, stated that 'women proved over and over again their ability, willingness and adaptability'. The notion that women teachers were interchangeable with their male colleagues was the most convincing case for equal status.

Nevertheless, when the teacher soldiers returned from war service, the employment of most temporary masters came to an abrupt end. Elsa Tutin's temporary war appointment at Deacon's School was terminated on 25 January 1919. Her staff file states simply: 'Left on return of Asst. Master'. Equal pay did not materialise. In 1918 a Departmental Committee on Teachers' Salary Scales recommended that male teachers should continue to receive higher salaries in recognition of their 'greater family responsibilities'. The wartime President of the Board of Education, H.A.L. Fisher, upheld this principle in the Commons, and LEAs shied away from the expense that equal pay arrangements would inevitably entail. The Burnham Committee's 4:5 salary ratio for female and male teachers reinforced the pre-war gender bias within the profession. Following the report of the Geddes Committee on National Expenditure in 1922 the salaries of all teachers were reduced.[86]

During the Great War Temporary Gentlemen and temporary masters were both elevated beyond their customary station in life. The traditional inhabitants of the officers' mess and staff common room greeted them with varying degrees of acceptance or resignation. Women teachers diluted the teaching force in much the same way that the Temporary Gentlemen had infiltrated the traditional officer corps. Dilution is a deliberately pejorative term, and both misleading and inaccurate. Hundreds of male and female teachers, representative of thousands of men and women from non-elite groups generally, demonstrated their expertise and proved their interchangeability with others traditionally considered to be their superiors. When the war finally ended, their services were summarily dispensed with. Those who had been 'Gentlemen' or 'Masters' resumed their traditional places in the social and educational hierarchies, their contributions barely remembered, their talents and potential subsumed within the prejudices of the age.

Part IV

Aftermath

Land of our Birth, our faith, our pride,
For whose dear sake our fathers died;
Oh, Motherland, we pledge to thee
Head, heart and hand through the years to be!

Rudyard Kipling (1906)
The Children's Song

Chapter 9

Peace

The people have drunk the wine of peace
In the streets of town.
They smile as they drift with hearts at rest
Uphill and down.

The people have drunk the wine of peace,
They are mad with joy.
Never again need they lie and fear
Death for a boy.

Lesbia Harford (1918)
The People Have Dunk the Wine of Peace

A t 11 am on 11 November 1918 the guns stopped firing. After four years of fighting, the Great War was over. For the men in the battle zones the immediate response to the ceasefire was one of relief rather than jubilation.[1] This was a moment for quiet reflection, a time for remembrance of lost comrades and thankfulness for personal survival. Back in Britain the mood was very different, at least for those who were not grieving for family members lost in the conflict. News of the Armistice had reached local communities almost immediately. From within their classrooms children and teachers in many cities, towns and villages knew that something of great importance was happening. In London they could hear church bells ringing, guns firing salutes and air-raid sirens sounding in celebration rather than warning.[2] In the Rossendale Valley in Lancashire all the textile mill hooters were blaring out.[3] In the Welsh village of Gowerton near Swansea 'works hooters, engine whistles, church bells and railway detonators indicated that the joyous moment of peace had arrived'.[4]

Confirmation that the war was over came in different ways. In most schools it was the headteacher who made the public announcement before making arrangements for the school community to mark the occasion. George Cook, however, remembered how his school in Wolverton was overtaken by events:

Just after dinner, on an ordinary school day, all of a sudden the young chaps from the works burst into the school. They knocked the headmaster over and they beckoned all of the kids out of the classrooms, and believe me, we didn't need any encouragement. We all flew out and the staff were just left standing there. Then we marched behind the band all the way round the town.[5]

Most schools, however, were already responding to the good news. In London, the logbook entry for Silver Street Senior Boys' School in Edmonton is typical of many written by headteachers on 11 November 1918:

Glorious news received that the Germans had signed the terms of the Armistice at 5 a.m., and that hostilities would end at 11 a.m. The boys cheered and the flag was flown.[6]

In this moment of victory, Britain's allies were not forgotten. In some schools the children marked the occasion by posing for photographs whilst dressed in patriotic costumes and waving the flags of allied nations (Plate 40). Stibbington School's logbook noted that 'The National Anthems of the Allies were sung and cheers given for each (and) shillings were distributed to each child'.[7] At City of London School there was singing in the school hall in the afternoon. When the 700 assembled boys were asked who they wanted to cheer for, they responded quickly and unanimously: Foch, the commander of the French Army.[8] Some responses to news of the Armistice were far more restrained. Michael Dykes Bower, a day boy at Cheltenham College throughout the war, remembered how calmly the Principal announced the news of the Armistice to his class before continuing with the lesson. Later that day, boys and masters congregated in the chapel to thank God for the nation's deliverance from conflict.[9] Similar services of thanksgiving were held in many schools. The boys of George Dixon School in Birmingham, for example, were taken to their nearby church, whilst at Peterborough Practising School pupils and staff assembled in the main classroom.[10] Lichfield High School for Girls had said prayers at noon every day throughout the war. At 12 o'clock on 11 November their 'war prayers' became prayers of thanksgiving.[11] Piety and celebration conjoined at Lancing College where a Te Deum in Chapel was followed by a bonfire which got out of hand.[12]

After formally recognising the historic importance of the day, many schools granted a half-holiday and closed for the rest of the session. The people of Britain had waited four long years for this moment and, not unnaturally, many parents decided that they wanted their children to share in the general mafficking in the streets. In the past, schools had given a 'half' for important national occasions such as Coronation Day and – an important precedent well within recent memory – the termination of the Boer War in South Africa in 1902.[13] Mr H. Sprigge, the headteacher of St Mark's Voluntary Aided School in Lambeth, was informed by his LEA inspector that the school should close for the afternoon.[14] Later that same day Mr Pullan, headteacher of the Peterborough Practising School, noted in his logbook that 'The Education Committee decided tonight to close the schools for the rest of the week'.[15]

Many schools throughout the country, however, were already closed. Behind the euphoria and scenes of celebration lay another, far more serious, justification for closure. When Head Boy and Cadet Sergeant Major William Katz, accompanied by his headmaster, hurried to King Edward VII Grammar School in Melton Mowbray on 11 November to raise the school flag, it belied the fact that the school was closed and in the midst of crisis. Two of the school's pupils, Dick and Marjorie Hollingshead, had only recently died. They, like millions of others around the world, were victims of the Spanish Influenza pandemic of 1918 to 1920.[16] The H1N1 strain of the virus, which surfaced again as recently as 2009, infected some 500 million people worldwide. Estimates for direct fatalities range from 50 to 100 million, figures far in excess of those killed in combat. The disease was no respecter of social class or wealth, and schools across the educational spectrum were affected.

At St Nicholas Boys' School in King's Lynn, Headmaster Alfred Whitehouse recorded the first incidence of influenza affecting his school exactly one calendar month before the Armistice, on 11 October 1918. The virus spread rapidly amongst the school and its community. On 21 October two teachers and 84 of the 195 boys on roll were absent and the King's Lynn Education Committee ordered the school to close for a week. It closed again on 4 November. One week later Mr Whitehouse noted in his logbook:

School re-opened. 147 present in the morning but owing to an Armistice having been signed between the Allies and Germany only 120 came in the afternoon. Great excitement and flag waving in town, 'God Save the King' sung and cheers given by boys.[17]

This was a pattern which was repeated in many schools. As the impact of the virus became increasingly apparent, some local authorities were forced to direct the closure of all schools under their control on behalf of the wider community. Three weeks after the Armistice the City of Peterborough Education Committee, for example, issued a letter to all its headteachers and managers:

Owing to the prevalence of Influenza throughout the City and to prevent the spread of infection, the Education Committee have with the approval of the School Medical Officer, resolved that the City Public Elementary Schools shall be closed until Friday, 13th December and re-opened on Monday, 16th December 1918. On Assembling on Monday, 2nd December, Head Teachers will please impress upon the children the object of the closure, and urge the absolute necessity for keeping away from crowds and crowded places in the interval.

Henry Wilson.
Clerk.[18]

Public schools were also badly affected by the virus. At one point Dulwich College had 400 absentees and all school work stopped for a week.[19] Unlike the day schools, however, boarding schools could not simply send pupils home. At Kent College in Canterbury the headmaster's wife, Mrs Brownscombe, became acting Matron and nursed eighty-seven boys, out of a total of ninety-two boarders, who had contracted the virus.[20] The boys of King's College in Taunton celebrated the Armistice 'with great gusto', only to find, according to the school's magazine, that 'on the following day the influenza fiend laid his chastening hand upon us'. As increasing numbers of pupils, masters and domestic staff were taken ill, the virus brought the school to a standstill. The Autumn Term ended early, but only sixteen boys were well enough to make the journey home for the vacation.[21] The fighting may have stopped in November 1918, but the influenza pandemic added new names – of boys, masters and domestic staff – to the lists of the dead at several public schools, including Malvern College, Harrow, and Ardingly in Sussex.[22]

The influenza epidemic reached one of its peaks just as the war ended. In the Allied nations, victory over Germany and the other Central Powers – countries in which the physical and psychological horrors of war were now exacerbated by defeat, shame, disease and revolution – was tainted. The return to normality which so many millions of people had been longing for did not happen immediately after the Armistice, if at all. Indeed, despite the celebrations on 11 November 1918, the all-pervasive sense of topsy-turveydom that had characterised the war years continued into 1919 and beyond. For the people of Britain victory had been achieved, but at enormous cost to individuals, families, institutions and wider communities. The nation would need to rebuild – 'reconstruction' was the term they used at the time – using an economic resource base which itself had been battered by four full years of total war.

For the rest of the 1918–19 academic year schools and their communities continued to adjust to the new post-war realities. The process of demobilisation brought home fathers, sons and brothers from the war fronts, and mothers, daughters and sisters from the war factories and hospital wards. Neighbours reappeared, most of them at least, as did many of the teachers who had responded to the call-to-arms at various points during the war. The structures which then and now govern the administration and daily routines of schools – the curriculum and timetable – were modified gradually, returning slowly to a state which might be recognisable as that which had existed before the war. But, of course, the war had not ended, not officially at least. The Armistice had halted the fighting but had not made the peace; that was a more lengthy process for the dignitaries and diplomats gathering in early 1919 at the Palace of Versailles just outside Paris. Consequently, the return to peacetime 'normality' in schools was frequently punctuated by activities which recalled the war, re-affirmed the nation's victory, or celebrated the peace anew.

The influenza virus, which had killed two pupils at King Edward VII School in Melton Mowbray and forced its closure on 11 November, also delayed the school's

Victory Party. Six weeks after the Armistice, surrounded by pictures of teachers who had served and fallen and a display of German war trophy weapons, the boys took part in games and dancing and watched a sketch performed by the staff.[23] The pupils at St Nicholas Boys' School, like thousands of schoolchildren throughout the country, were given the opportunity to see how their patriotic savings had been spent when, only two weeks after the Armistice, their LEA granted them a half-day holiday 'for the visit of the War Loan Gun' to King's Lynn. Impressive though this killing machine may have been to young minds inured to war, it paled in comparison with the war trophy which their headteacher took them to see at the start of the Spring Term. Mr Whitehouse noted in his logbook:

1919
9 January: The timetable was slightly varied this morning to enable the boys to visit 'U boat 28' in the Bentinck Dock by courtesy of the Officer in Charge.

Wartime habits, such as collecting for good causes, continued in peacetime, especially as evidence of the impact of modern weaponry upon human bodies was ever-present in the streets around them. The day after the school excursion to see the German submarine, Mr Whitehouse once more recorded:

1919
10 January: A collection among the boys realised 17s.6d. to supply 400 cigarettes to John Schread, an old scholar, blinded in the War.[24]

During the Summer Term 1919 there were further events designed to mark the achievement of both victory and peace. Individual schools joined with other community organizations in nationwide and officially sanctioned celebrations. On Friday, 23 May 1919 Empire Day was observed once more. Traditional modes of patriotic revelry were duly modified to suit a nation which had triumphed over adversity and near defeat. In London, the Lord Mayor, with a schoolgirl dressed as Britannia in attendance, welcomed over 1,000 children from the city's elementary schools to an entertainment at the Guildhall. Those assembled sent a telegram to the king 'conveying loyal greetings, with an expression of gratitude at the glorious conclusion of the war'. There were 'lusty cheers' as the Union Jack was unfurled. A Pageant of Peace followed for these sons and daughters of the Empire.[25] In Lichfield, the girls from Friary High joined with over a thousand other local schoolchildren for a service in Lichfield Cathedral. So inspirational was the mass rendition of Rudyard Kipling's *Children's Song* that the school adopted it as the school song.[26]

The Treaty of Versailles was signed on 28 June 1919, exactly five years to the day since the assassination at Sarajevo. The war on the Western Front had officially ended, but a whole series of smaller wars had erupted elsewhere on the fringes of an erstwhile peaceful continent of Europe. The boys at St Nicholas School were once again granted a holiday:

1919
4 July: Boys dismissed at 11.15 am to enable them to join a procession to welcome the Anglo–Russian Armoured cars in connection with the Victory Loan Campaign.

Two weeks later, schools throughout England took part in Peace Day, an event clearly designed to recognise the wartime experience and involvement of the nation's children. Alfred Whitehouse kept a particularly detailed record of that day's events in King's Lynn:

1919
19 July: All the children on the school registers assembled in the yard at 2 pm and proceeded in 4s (IGB) to the Tuesday Market Place and joined with the children from the other schools in the Peace Celebrations. *O God our Help*, *Land of Hope and Glory*, *Rule Britannia*, *God Save the King* were sung and cheers given for the King, Mayor and Mayoress. A procession was formed and tea took place at the Walks at 4 pm. Sports for prizes followed, then fireworks at 9.30 and a huge bonfire on the Walks banks at 11 pm with more fireworks. Rain somewhat marred the pleasure from 6.30 pm otherwise all was very much enjoyed.[27]

The city authorities in Lichfield organised similar festivities and gave a 'peace medal' stamped with the city arms to every child.[28] There was also great excitement for the children at the Georgetown Schools in Tredegar. They too were treated to a formal tea and were presented with commemorative medals struck especially for the occasion by the District Council.[29]

Commemorative pieces of china, customarily produced to mark events of national importance even in more recent times, were distributed by many local authorities to mark the coming of peace. The elementary schoolchildren of Cardiff, who in 1915 had marched in their thousands through the Welsh capital to encourage men to enlist (Plate 16), had already received a Peace Mug. Decorated with an image of the white dove of peace landing on a globe flanked by the flags of France, Italy, the USA and Great Britain, their mug was a memento to mark the signing of the Armistice. Thousands of other children received their china souvenir on Saturday, 19 July 1919, including pupils from schools in the Scottish Borders. Their Peace Mug also displayed doves and flags, but the centerpiece was an image of Britannia, the guardian of 'LIBERTY, JUSTICE, TRUTH, HONOUR'. It was inscribed:

PRESENTED BY
****
HERBERT J AYNSLEY.
*****
TO THE SCHOOL CHILDREN
OF BLYTH
BRIDGE
TO COMMEMORATE
PEACE DAY
****
19th DAY OF JULY 1919.

The boys and girls who attended Lamancha School and nearby Romanno School also celebrated the occasion. Their local newspaper, the *Peeblesshire Advertiser and County Newspaper*, reported how they assembled under the hoisted Union Jack to hear a speech on 'Patriotism and Empire' given by General Sir James Wolfe Murray of Cringletie and to receive their Peace Mugs from Lady Wolfe Murray. To the accompaniment of bagpipes, the children marched to Newlands Parish Church to praise the Lord for their recent victory and to solemnly remember 'Our Glorious Dead'. A programme of sports followed on the Riverside. At 7.30 p.m. the provision of milk and cakes and a hearty rendition of The National Anthem brought Peace Day to an end.[30] For the assembled children, this special day in the life of their school, community and nation was long and tiring but, thankfully, it had been interspersed with moments of great interest, excitement and refreshments. This truly was a day to remember. The adults who were members of the local Peace Celebrations Committee had ensured that it would be, not simply by the mode of that celebration, but by its content. Despite the horrors of the Great War, the old order had not simply survived, it had been vindicated.

When the school year finally ended in late July, the children at the St Nicholas Boys' School in King's Lynn belatedly received their souvenirs of peace. The kind gesture of their sovereign King George V, who had granted them some additional time off school, may well have impressed them more than the memento itself:

1919
31 July: Closed this afternoon for Midsummer holiday of five weeks, the extra week for Peace. Commemoration cards and Peace mugs (tin) given to each boy by the Mayor and Mayoress.[31]

The involvement of schools in the various celebrations of peace demonstrated just how important educational institutions were in the life of the nation at all times, and not simply in wartime. In an age when many take the existence of free and compulsory mass education for granted, it is worth remembering that this was not the case before 1914. One hundred years ago the provision, indeed the desirability, of schooling for all was a relatively recent and contested notion. Forster's Education Act of 1870 and Balfour's Act of 1902 had not met universal acclaim and their provisions were frequently attacked for being expensive and unnecessary. During the Great War, however, at least some of the country's new leaders recognised the vital importance of a system of education which prepared all the nation's people, including its youngest citizens, for the challenges faced by industrialised economies. They pointed not to the British system – if indeed the existing patchwork of provision for schooling warranted such a term – but to that operating in Germany. In September 1918, Prime Minister David Lloyd George argued the case for more and better schooling in this country:

> The most formidable institution we had to fight in Germany was not the arsenals of Krupp or the yards in which they turned out the submarines, but the schools of Germany. They were our most formidable competitors in business and our most terrible opponents in war. An educated man is a better worker, a more formidable warrior, and a better citizen.[32]

Education has been used throughout the ages and in many cultures to disseminate and reproduce dominant ideologies, to forge national identities and to fashion the roles and status of individuals within social and economic hierarchies. War, the locomotive of history, accelerates and amplifies these processes. In wartime, schooling may become, directly or indirectly, a casualty of war, but it is also 'implicated in the conduct, maintenance, and aftermath of wars'.[33] In the total war of 1914 to 1919 the nation looked, Janus-like, both outwards to the battlefields and inwards to its social and economic resources. Previously neglected or taken-for-granted areas of the body politic were subjected to renewed or reinvigorated inspection.[34] National survival demanded National Efficiency. The turmoil of armed conflict led those involved to question the pre-war status quo, to reshape educational and other provision in pragmatic fashion to meet each new demand of war, and then to embrace new forms of idealism upon which to base systemic change once the conflict had ended. In Britain, demands for a better society led to calls for National Reconstruction.

It is no coincidence that towards the end of both of the major military conflicts of the twentieth century significant education reforms in England and Wales were introduced by wartime governments. Whilst the provisions of the 1918 Act were less far reaching or long lasting than those of the 1944 Act, they were significant nevertheless. By 1918 something of a consensus had began to emerge amongst the disparate elements of Lloyd George's Coalition Government. The war had acted as a catalyst for the renewal of pre-war proposals for the continued expansion of formal schooling. The Liberal Party already had a track record of reform, but now they were supported – often uneasily, as is the nature of coalition arrangements – by a new political force at Westminster which had millions of adherents amongst the newly-literate and educated masses. During the war the Labour Party acquired a national platform for its views on schooling. Arthur Henderson took charge of the Board of Education and Keir Hardie became Minister of Education in May 1915. Labour set up its own Advisory Committee on Education in 1918,[35] having already advocated free and compulsory education for all to the age of sixteen the previous year.[36] Educational reform was firmly on the list of topics being considered for post-war Reconstruction.

They key architect of the 1918 Education Act was H.A.L. Fisher, the distinguished historian and Vice-Chancellor of Sheffield University referred to in earlier chapters. Following his election as a Liberal Member of Parliament in 1916 he was appointed President of the Board of Education. In late 1917 Fisher launched a national propaganda campaign, taking the case for educational reform to a variety of audiences throughout the country. Details of his proposals in the Education Bill before Parliament were greeted with widespread enthusiasm. He was heard by dockers in Bristol and elementary school headteachers in Gloucester.[37] His prospectus for educational reform was infused with 'war idealism',[38] and the need to convince the labouring classes, at a crucial point in the war, that their children would benefit from the huge sacrifices being made.[39] Fisher tapped into widespread concerns about access to secondary education, premature school leaving and the welfare of children generally. He promised greater opportunities for the sons and daughters of ordinary working men and women. The proposed reforms, he declared, were designed to repair the intellectual wastage which had resulted, especially in wartime, from a system of schooling which was based upon parental income rather than individual ability. Section 4.4 of the 1918 Act stated that:

> adequate provision shall be made in order to secure that children and young persons shall not be debarred from receiving the benefits of any form of education by which they are capable of profiting through inability to pay fees.[40]

Fisher's Act passed onto the statute books on 8 August 1918, the same day that the German lines were broken at the Battle of Amiens.[41] The Act was essentially a manifesto for the future, designed to promote greater opportunity by providing more scholarships, more maintenance grants, and more secondary schools.[42] The implications were clear: the narrow and precarious scholarship ladder was to be replaced, as one headteacher put it, by 'the widening of the high road to the University for those who deserve to go there'.[43] Other forms of post–elementary education were also considered. In recognition of the 'boy labour problem',[44] a contentious feature of many local economies which had been exacerbated by the war, the Act incorporated the recommendations of the 1914 Lewis Report: *Juvenile Education in Relationship to Employment after the War*. Elementary education became free and compulsory to the age of fourteen, at which point employment was to be combined with mandatory attendance at Day Continuation classes of eight hours per week until the age of eighteen. The 1918 Act was also intended to be a children's charter,[45] in recognition of general concerns about the health and behaviour of children and adolescents in wartime. Provisions for the reduction of child labour were accompanied by others promoting the establishment of nursery schools and the extension of school medical services.

Despite the high hopes generated by the promise of Reconstruction – creating 'schools fit for heroes' to paraphrase Lloyd George – the 1918 Education Act is rarely remembered today. Despite the verdict of later historians that Fisher's Act removed many of the perceived weaknesses of the pre-war education system,[46] it has been overshadowed by the 1944 Education Act. Butler's Act instituted a system based firmly upon the concept of 'Education for All', [47] albeit in the form of a 'Tripartite System' of secondary schooling which was, and still is, contested. Fisher's idealism was genuine, but it was hardly revolutionary. His provisions for the expansion of secondary schooling fell well short of the Labour movement's ambition for secondary education for all. Far from being an attempt at social engineering by the state,[48] Fisher's Act recognised the new realities of wartime Britain. Few working-class families before the war had been able to afford the fees for secondary education and only the very brightest of their children were awarded scholarships. During the war, however, changing employment opportunities, an increase in real wages and the narrowing of wage differentials between skilled and unskilled workers raised the standard of living for some families rapidly and dramatically.[49] In the last year of the war, as H.A.L. Fisher took his proposals to the people, the people themselves were already making decisions of their own. During the Great War they continued to balance opportunity with potential gain, choosing lucrative employment openings for their children when available to them, or accessing forms of schooling previously unobtainable.

Increasing affluence, combined with higher expectations and ambitions, had an impact which was patently felt in the schools themselves. By 1918 secondary schools in many towns and cities began admitting increasing numbers of both male and female fee-paying pupils. The expansion at Northampton Grammar School for Boys, for example, was so rapid that both the shooting range and the sports pavilion were converted for use as classrooms.[50] Essex County Council helped Chelmsford County High School for Girls to purchase a number of ex-army huts so that the school population, which had risen from 44 pupils in 1907 to 200 by 1917 and to 300 by 1919, could be fully accommodated.[51] At Manchester High School for Girls numbers on roll increased from 618 in 1916 to 725 in September 1918,

and nearby houses were rented to cope with the oversubscription.[52] The absence
of so many young men at the front had presented educated young women with new
employment prospects, and parents were increasingly willing to pay school fees to
secure such opportunities for their daughters. In many public schools the sudden
drop in pupil numbers in 1914, as senior boys enlisted,[53] was reversed.[54] Hymer's
College in Hull was bursting at the seams and temporary concrete huts had to be
built.[55] Demand for boarding places at Oakham School exceeded supply, but this
reflected not rising wages, but a parental clientele preoccupied with the war effort
and finding it increasingly difficult to find domestic help.[56]

During the first half of 1919 schools throughout the country adjusted from a
state of war to a state of peace. For most, the provisions of the new Education Act,
laudable though they might be, were not their main priority. Peace celebrations,
too, were important markers in the transition process, but getting back to some
degree of normality was far more important. For schools and the communities
which inhabited them, the Great War had taken many of their teachers and, in
some cases, their buildings. The content of their lessons had changed and greater
demands had been made upon extra-curricular activities. Patriotic spirit and
activity was everywhere, but it could not disguise the psychological wear and tear
that exposure to danger had produced. What all schools needed at this point was
what they had come to expect before 1914: classrooms full of children in good order
and being taught by their own well-qualified and experienced teachers. Cheadle
Hulme School in Cheshire was one of hundreds of schools whose premises had
been requisitioned by the military and medical authorities at the start of the war.
Returning to the school site and facilities after they were released by the Red Cross
in March 1919 was a major relief. Lincoln Grammar School returned to its pre-
war site in 1920. One by one the teachers returned to their schools. When the
Armistice was signed on 11 November 1918 thousands of men who had taught in
elementary schools before the war were still with the armed forces, the majority
of them overseas. The Board of Education began to make plans for their return to
the classrooms. The Board had calculated in late October 1918 that 16,442 male
teachers were serving with the military and a further 400 were engaged in munitions
work. In addition, there were 442 former elementary school mistresses engaged as
nurses or factory Welfare Supervisors and Canteen Superintendents. When the
military authorities signalled that teachers would be given a degree of priority in
the demobilisation process, the Board of Education issued *Circular 1073*. LEAs
were asked to submit the names of teachers still serving so that the Board might
forward them to the relevant officials.[57] Over the several months following the
ceasefire, teachers who had survived the conflict returned home and took up their
former careers. Those serving in distant theatres of war took longer to return but,
gradually, they too removed their uniforms, resumed their professional lives and
replaced the temporary appointments who had deputised for them.

Many teachers returned to their old jobs in their old schools. Some had been with the colours since the call-to-arms in 1914. Corrie Chase from Campbell College had spent the war commanding units which had dug support trenches and constructed roads, bridges and railways. He survived the carnage of the first week of the Somme Offensive in July 1916, kept the Menin Road clear at Hellfire Corner during the Battle of Passchendaele in late 1917, and was awarded the Military Cross in January 1918. On his demobilisation in February 1919 he returned immediately to his former employment. The school magazine welcomed him back and wished him 'a long stay amongst us'. Corrie Chase did not disappoint them; he remained at Campbell College until ill health forced him to relinquish his rooms there in 1960.[58] Tom Adlam VC, who had been awarded the highest military honour for his actions at Thiepval during the Battle of the Somme, did not return to Brook Street School in Basingstoke. After the Armistice he remained in the army and served in Ireland. He subsequently became headteacher of the village school in Blackmoor in Hampshire. During the Second World War he was recalled and served as Lieutenant Colonel Adlam in the Royal Engineers. Archibald Buckle, who had campaigned with distinction in the Royal Naval Division throughout four years of fighting, also resumed his teaching career. His meteoric rise from the ranks to lieutenant commander was reflected in his new appointment. On his return to London Mr Buckle became Headteacher of Rotherhithe Nautical School, an institution which had been transformed from a Higher Grade School in 1915 in response to an official report into the sinking of RMS *Titanic* three years earlier.[59]

Headteachers in the elementary schools recorded the return of their teacher-soldier colleagues, just as they had noted the date of their earlier departure for military service.[60] Many teachers had been absent for over four years, but a few had been called up only weeks before the war ended. Mr Allerton of Barnack School in Northamptonshire joined the RAF on 27 September 1918 and returned to school less than four months later on 13 January 1919.[61] Some teachers did not return to their posts. Mr Seed, the headteacher of Busbridge School in Godalming decided not to resume his headship and resigned in January 1919.[62] Maintained secondary schools also lost staff. Two teachers from Trowbridge and District High School for Boys, Mr Matthews and Mr Chandler, both decided to stay on in the armed services rather than resume their teaching careers.[63]

There were thousands of others, of course, who would not return from the killing fields and who were denied a welcome home and the opportunity to resume their lives and careers. They were amongst the ranks of The Fallen.

Chapter 10

The Fallen

To the Memory of the King's School Cadet Corps.
Beautiful in Life, More Beautiful in Death.
The King's School, Ottery St Mary, Devon.[1]

D espite the victory celebrations and the gradual return of schoolteachers
to their customary activities, previously cherished hopes of a return to
normality quickly proved to be illusory. Throughout Britain, and in all
the other belligerent nations, the real cost of the war was being counted in human
terms, and nothing would ever be the same again. The surviving combatants
returned home after demobilisation with tales to tell, but only if the narrator
had the strength to recall them, and then only to listeners receptive to stories
of wartime experience so very different from their own. An enormous number
of their comrades, however, remained where they had fallen: killed in action in
foreign fields or dead from their wounds despite the care and treatment given
in military hospitals. Institutions and communities, large and small, began to list
their dead and missing, and they began to pay homage to The Fallen.[2]

Since the end of the Great War, the institution of schooling has become one of
the chief means by which communities have attempted to come to terms with the
huge losses they suffered. Schools were key formative agencies at the time. Across
the educational hierarchy they prepared their children for conflict, mobilised
them for service in total war, celebrated their wartime heroics and memorialised
their deaths in battle. A century later, schools retain their role as guardians of the
past. The names of The Fallen continue to be honoured in many schools, their
individual and collective example used to reinforce corporate identity and to re-
assert cherished ideals and values. Remembrance does more than simply tell of the
past; it informs how we might be today.

For the great public schools, the process of remembrance has always been a
national as well as an institutional imperative. Membership of elite institutions
confers leadership responsibilities as well as the privileges of rank. Those who had
been educated in the elite schools assumed military command during the Great
War and paid a heavy price in doing so. Whilst the 'death of our best and brightest'
has become the stuff of legend,[3] the recent research findings presented by Anthony
Seldon and David Walsh in *Public Schools and the Great War. The Generation Lost*
demonstrate how important the elite schools were during the conflict. The casualty

figures for Britain's leading public schools speak for themselves. Of the 5,650 Old Etonians who served their country between 1914 and 1919, 1,175 were killed in action or died of wounds. A further 1,467 were severely wounded.[4] Marlborough College lost 733 former pupils, whilst the numbers of The Fallen at Wellington, Charterhouse, Rugby, Cheltenham and Harrow each exceeded 600. In these schools, and others like them, the death rate was disproportionately high: one in five of those who responded to the call-to-arms did not return after the war. Nearly 100 British public schools each recorded more than 100 war-related deaths.[5] Their stories of duty, bravery and sacrifice have been recorded for posterity by individual institutions, but they also hold a central position in the collective national memory of the Great War. Study the stories behind the names of The Fallen from any one of the public schools and they will resurrect the killing fields of Europe and beyond.

Sherborne School had 267 pupils on roll when war was declared. Between 1914 and 1919 over 1,100 Old Shirburnians served their country in some capacity. The school's archives contain the records of over 200 who died in the Great War. Their collective experience encapsulates the major contribution to the British war effort made by public schools of this kind. Over 90 per cent of the fatalities from Sherborne were officers. A few held commissions in the Royal Flying Corps and Royal Navy,[6] but the vast majority had enlisted in the British Army, including twenty-nine men who had held pre-war commissions in the Regular or Territorial forces. At the time of their deaths, twelve had reached the rank of army major, four were lieutenant colonels and one, a Sandhurst-trained Regular, was a full colonel. Of the nineteen NCOs and privates, eight were in the Royal Fusiliers and the King's Royal Rifle Corps, and a further five served with Canadian and New Zealand forces. Old Shirburnians served and fell in each year, and in every major land battle, of the Great War. The first casualty, missing presumed killed in France on 26 August 1914, was Second Lieutenant Ronald Campbell Ross of the 2nd Battalion The Royal Scots (Lothian Regiment), one of eight of the school's former pupils who died whilst serving with the BEF. At the Battle of Loos in 1915, five Old Shirburnian's perished. The Battle of the Somme claimed twenty-five more, including eight who died in various front-line regiments on 1 July 1916, the first day of the great offensive. In the Ypres Salient a further twent-five men were killed. The German and Allied offensives of 1918 claimed over twenty lives. Sherborne School alumni also perished in the so-called 'side-shows' of Gallipoli, Mesopotamia, Palestine, Salonika and German East Africa.

Similar narratives could be constructed for each of the many public schools in Britain. Smaller public schools may have fewer names on their memorials, and count a higher proportion of junior officers amongst their dead than schools which had traditionally supplied military leaders, but their contribution to the national war effort was considerable nevertheless. Death rates amongst their alumni, measured as a percentage of those who died from the number who served, are often comparable and in some cases higher. Scotland's oldest boarding school, Lorretto School near Edinburgh, had only 83 pupils on roll in 1914 but 592 of their Old Boys served during the war. The names of 148 former pupils are recorded on the school's Roll of Honour, a particularly high death rate of 25 per cent. Rydal School in North Wales was one of the smallest public schools, with only forty-five boys attending in 1914. Of the 243 former pupils who served, 63 (26 per cent) were killed.[7]

The public school alumni whose names are inscribed on memorials to The Fallen have been immortalised as Britain's 'Lost Generation'. Some 35,000 public-school educated service personnel were killed in the Great War. They were overwhelmingly male and drawn from the upper and middle echelons of society. They included the sons of prime ministers, peers of the realm and other leading figures in the British establishment. The elite fee-paying public schools had given them a preparation for life which was emulated but never quite replicated in lesser institutions. The importance of godliness and good learning, character and personal responsibility, honour and duty was drilled into them by teachers imbued with the same codes and traditions of schooling. For many pupils, their undoubted academic brilliance was subsequently validated by membership of prestigious colleges at the ancient universities of Oxford and Cambridge. Many, but not all, were as adept at understanding the Classics as they were at demonstrating their sporting prowess and leadership traits on the playing field. Their higher social status, and their own awareness of it, was reinforced by an almost total immersion in a form of schooling which, in also providing forms of military training explicitly denied to others, enabled them to assume command and leadership of others in times of war. In becoming front-line subalterns in 1914 and the years which followed, however, they increased their likelihood of becoming battlefield casualties.[8] The loss to the nation, and the country's future economic, social and cultural wellbeing, was inestimable. Their deaths ensured their individual and collective immortality. They were memorialised by their schools and enshrined in a wider cultural representation which depicted them as models of all that was righteous and worthy in British society. One hundred years after the conflict, and despite the huge social and economic changes which have taken place in Britain, the image of the sacrificial young second lieutenant leading his men over the top into no man's land remains as potent as ever.

The notion of a 'Lost Generation' is not without foundation. Britain and many other countries did lose a generation of men and women of great talent, energy and potential. There were many amongst the 35,000 who were, genuinely, paragons of the virtues which public schools held dear and sought to transmit to their charges. A master at Dulwich College in London said of one of his pupils, Paul Jones, that 'He was the very embodiment of all that is best in the public-school spirit, the very incarnation of self-sacrifice and devotion'. In *War Letters of a Public-School Boy*, published posthumously by Paul's father,[9] the schooling and accomplishments of one young man are set before the reader. The tone is unashamedly elegiac, for the letters are preceded by a memoir constructed by a grieving parent to honour 'the red sweet wine of youth' that had been poured onto the battlefield.[10] Paul Jones was a boy 'of high intellectual gifts and sensitive honour, who had shone with equal lustre as a scholar and an athlete'. He entered Dulwich College in September 1908 at the age of twelve and remained there for just over six years. He won Junior and Senior Scholarships, became a prefect, and edited the college magazine, *The Alleynian*. After a grounding in the Classics he transferred to the college's Modern side in order to pursue his real interests in English literature and history. Paul was, according to his father, a 'voracious and omnivorous' reader who, from an early age, made margin notes and discerning comments which demonstrated a maturity of thought beyond his years. He was a member of the college choir, played the piano, and was an aficionado of classical, especially Germanic, music. All things mechanical were of interest to Paul, and his parents provided him with model gas engines for experimentation. Politics also fascinated him, his interest manifested in both his musings on political theory and his frequent attendance as an observer at parliamentary debates in the House of Commons. A young man full of energy, he was one of Dulwich's best athletes and, in his final year there, was Captain of Football. As the war clouds in Europe gathered in 1914, Paul worked hard to secure a place at university, the natural next step for a young man of such obvious ability. In December 1914, with the war in Europe already in a state of stalemate, he was awarded a Brakenbury Scholarship to read History and Modern Languages at Balliol College, Oxford.

Thus far, Paul's story conforms to the stereotypical image – the very essence – of the brilliant public-school scholar and athlete. He was undoubtedly a product of his family background and his schooling at Dulwich College. Paul Jones was also, however, an individual and autonomous agent who navigated his way through the opportunities which opened up before him. He chose not to become a boarder at Dulwich and remained a day-boy throughout his school career. He read the great authors of ancient Greece and Rome but preferred the works of Shakespeare and Milton. His political idealism, carefully considered and rarely naïve, rejected feudal and capitalist doctrines which marginalised organised Labour and neglected the poorest in society. In April 1915 Paul decided to enlist. He was tall and muscular but extremely short-sighted and was thus refused a commission. Paul's story is a powerful reminder that behind the statistics of The Fallen, the customary representations of social class, and the pervasive and often mythologised narratives of the Great War, lies the human condition, with all its vagaries and inconsistencies.

Henry Paul Mainwaring Jones was eventually awarded a commission in the Army Service Corps. Frustrated by a role which denied him front-line action, he subsequently transferred to the Tank Corps, the point at which his short military career began to conform to the more familiar pattern experienced by so many of his contemporaries. He fought in the Battle of Arras, accompanied by subordinates who admired and loved him and judged him to be 'the best officer in our company'. On 31 July 1917 Paul Jones, still carrying photographs of Dulwich College and its playing fields as he advanced his tank into 'the zone of death' north east of Ypres, was killed by a German sniper's bullet.[11]

No society can afford to lose young men of such calibre and potential. The story of the Lost Generation, however, has assumed a mythological status which denies the contribution of others in the war effort. All too often the term has been used to validate notions of social hierarchy based upon birthright and wealth. It has been employed to emphasise the particular and greater contribution of an elite group, and by doing so sustain a project of social hegemony over other social classes. At its heart is a legend which deifies the 'Lost Legions of Youth', the 'strong, brave and beautiful' who, like Rupert Brooke, were all 'poets at heart' and steeped in classical notions of duty and heroism. They followed in the footsteps of familiar heroes, and laid down their lives for the common good. The death in battle of these young men was justified by their parents and teachers as 'a magnificent culmination of those splendid short lives'.[12] The stories of the privileged continue to be privileged over those of others who fought and died in the Great War.

This is not to deny the undoubted commitment, bravery and sacrifice of exceptional individuals such as Paul Jones, nor the disproportionate number of others like him from similar backgrounds who fell in the Great War, but it does call for a wider and less exclusive definition of the term 'Lost Generation'. No single social group has a monopoly of wisdom, talent or ability; to argue otherwise is to succumb to the stereotype and to deny the multiplicity of contributions and complexity of interactions in modern societies. The proposition that this 'cohort of supposedly extra-gifted young men who, had they lived, would somehow have averted the errors made by inter-war British governments is simplistic and reductive in the extreme.[13] The products of the public schools were not universally brilliant, brave and natural leaders, although many of them were. Nor were the men in the ranks routinely dull or lacking in initiative or other desirable qualities, even though some undoubtedly were. Lord Crawford's wartime diary is testimony to the diversity of aptitude and application amongst officers and men, or so-called 'quality' and 'other ranks'.[14]

The generation which fought during the Great War included millions of men and women whose social and economic circumstances had denied them access to a superior education. To return to the stark simplicity of statistics, the total number of British citizens killed in the Great War was in excess of 720,000.[15] The Lost Generation of the elite is but one part of a much larger and far more diverse 'Lost Citizenry'. Total war demanded enormous involvement and commitment from all sections of society. The new technology of warfare called for men and women with specific technical skills rather than traditional forms of knowledge. For Great Britain, the Great War was just that: a conflict which necessitated the greatest contribution from the greatest number of its people, the millions of citizens who collectively made up its body politic.

The great majority of Britain's citizen-soldiers, some 685,000 or 95 per cent of The Fallen, had not been educated in the elite public schools. Instead, they had populated the public-maintained elementary schools. For those with sufficient ability – and family circumstances which permitted it – a further period of education in the secondary schools or technical institutions had been possible. Before the war they had been employed across the occupational spectrum, from labouring in the fields and factories to undertaking the technical, commercial, supervisory and minor professional roles upon which the national economy and local communities depended. In wartime, the vast majority became plain Tommy Atkins, the other ranks slogging with rifle and pack across the mud of the Western Front and other theatres of war. Many made admirable NCOs. Some became officers by dint of battlefield experience and proven leadership expertise. These Temporary Officers, elevated despite their origins and schooling and disparaged by others as mere 'Temporary Gentlemen' for the duration of the war only, demonstrated what talent the nation possessed beyond the 'quality' classes. Unlike many in the public schools, most of the men from the elementary and secondary schools had not trained for war, but they died in their hundreds of thousands nevertheless. In sheer numerical terms this was indeed a generation lost.

In the aftermath of the Great War, schools of all types mourned their dead. The nation's grammar and secondary schools had, like the more prestigious public schools, lost many of their former pupils during the conflict. Ancient foundations, technically in the second rank of the educational hierarchy, suffered losses comparable to many of the smaller public schools. What differentiates the war record of The King's School in Peterborough and that of its namesake in Ely is the latter's designation as a public school and its higher proportion of officers to other ranks.[16] In Totnes, King Edward VI Grammar School lost 36 of the 129 Old Boys who served, a death rate higher than that of most public schools at 28 per cent. In this school too, the loss of so much talent and potential was a tragedy which had an impact beyond the confines of the institution itself:

> It is indeed sad, in reading through the old School Magazines of pre-war days, to trace the career of one promising boy after another, only to find, in the end, their names transcribed on the roll of the dead. The real meaning of that tragic war can nowhere be better seen.[17]

Such comparisons, invidious though they undoubtedly are when applied to the individual casualties of conflict, are intended to demonstrate that membership of the Lost Generation was not exclusively the preserve of those from the elite schools. There was often a fine line dividing schools with different designations. Northampton Grammar School, for example, which lost ninety-four Old Boys during the war, was not a public school in 1914 but received that designation in 1920 when it's headmaster became a member of the Head Masters' Conference.[18] Many grammar schools provided the traditional subjects and activities found in many of the smaller public schools, and admitted fee-paying clientele from similar backgrounds. They too lost their Old Boys in large numbers. Wallasey Grammar School lost 114 former pupils and teachers, Trinity School Carlisle lost 90, and Hull Grammar School lost 88.

In Scotland, many secondary high schools and academies each recorded over 100 dead. Allen Glen's School in Glasgow, which was founded in 1853 as an Endowed School for the sons of tradesmen and admitted many scholarship boys, lost 178 of its former pupils including 106 who had been awarded commissions. In the same city, Whitehill Secondary School recorded 198 deaths, Bellahouston Academy 149, and Kelvinside Academy 131. Elsewhere in Scotland, Boroughmuir High School in Edinburgh lost 179 former pupils. In the city of Dundee, The Fallen from Harris Academy, Morgan Academy and the High School numbered 169, 115 and 110 respectively.[19]

The new secondary schools in England and Wales, which had been established in the wake of the 1902 Education Act, also contributed to the numbers of The Fallen. Harrow County School for Boys lost some of the first boys to enter the school when it opened with such high hopes in 1911. The school roll that year numbered seventy-three, of whom sixty-three saw service during the war. Five of the school's original ten teachers also joined the colours. The school's Roll of Honour was tangible evidence of its contribution to the national war effort, but it came at a cost measured in human lives cut short by conflict. From that very first school cohort, sixteen Old Gaytonians and two teachers, including Bob Hart and Russell Wheeler respectively, did not live to see the Armistice of 1918. Throughout Britain the new schools recorded their losses. In Wales, Newport High School for Boys ended its first decade with eighty-three names on its war memorial.[20]

Thus the 'peers, public school boys and Oxbridge men',[21] notwithstanding the dysgenic impact of the war on the upper and professional classes,[22] were not the only casualties. Members of the elite groups were joined in death by the many from the less-prestigious and less well-known schools: the secondary school fee-payers and bright scholarship pupils who filled the varied rungs of the white-collar occupations in towns and cities. Though there were disproportionately fewer officers from such schools, our collective memory of many of those who did gain commissions and lay down their lives for their country has generally been marginalised by posterity. It is a similar story beyond the secondary schools, and especially beyond the officer corps. The assertion that 'it was the unskilled and uneducated who survived' may have some basis if one considers the numbers, for example, of agricultural labourers who spent the war in reserved occupations,[23] but it does a grave disservice to the memory of the millions of British citizens whose previous schooling took place in rural village schools and the elementary schools in towns and cities throughout the land. The young men from these schools filled the ranks of Kitchener's New Armies, advanced into no man's land when ordered to do so, and charged the machine guns of the enemy knowing the risks involved. Unlike their officers, they did not have servants to attend to their needs, nor were they granted the same amount of home leave or access to the same creature comforts behind the lines. Both officers and men were pounded by the new technology of warfare, yet the sensitive treatment of most officers displaying the new symptoms of conflict – shell-shock, or neurasthenia – was rarely extended to other ranks.[24] The sheer scale of casualties amongst this enormous group of men reduces individuals to statistics and overwhelms our collective memory.

Who now remembers humble Tommy Atkins? Who still honours his contribution, his sacrifice, his memory? A century after the conflict the simple memorial flame of an individual, unassuming life, is increasingly kept alight by family historians and institutional archivists. The Great War Centenary Commemorations have encouraged individuals and community groups to excavate the past, to re-discover material which was illuminated briefly in the immediate post-war years, packed away in cupboards and in attics in the years of austerity and further conflict which followed, to be forgotten by all but a few who cherished the memory of a lost grandfather or great uncle, or were fascinated by the names on a still-displayed war memorial. The customary service medals – 'Pip, Squeak and Wilfred' as they were known by many who received them – and the 'Dead Man's Penny' given to the family of each of the 722,785 British combatants who perished in the Great War, appear increasingly in local salesrooms and on internet auction sites. Their monetary value belies the cost to the individual's family, community and nation at the time.

In 1914 some seven million children of the lower classes in Great Britain were taught in public-maintained and voluntary elementary and primary schools, as the vast majority of their fathers and mothers had been. Collectively, these schools – over 20,000 of them – filled the ranks of the British Army, the Royal Navy and the Royal Flying Corps with their school leavers. The war of 1914–19 had an enormous impact on many of these schools, especially when one counts up their dead. St Luke's Parochial School in Finsbury in North London, for example lost fifty-four of its boys, all of them NCOs and privates. The names of The Fallen at West End Primary School in Elgin records the deaths of 115 former pupils, including 11 who gained commissions. One particular Scottish school contained what many at the time would have considered the dregs of society, boys and young men whose past histories did not entitle them, it was generally believed, to any form of respect. Yet the former pupils – more accurately 'inmates' - of Wellington Reformatory Farm School in Penicuik served their country with the rest of their generation. Founded in 1859 as a residential institution for the correction of young offenders, this school listed 404 Old Boys in its record of war service: 91 per cent of all who left the school between 1900 and 1918. Of these, 40 were killed and a further 184 were wounded. Despite their backgrounds, three became commissioned officers, fifteen were decorated and two were mentioned in dispatches.

The impact of the Great War, measured by the number of lives cut short by combat or disease, extended throughout the hierarchy of schooling. At the official unveiling of the Roll of Honour for St John's Boys' School in Peterborough (Plate 41), headteacher Edward Adams stood proudly by a painted wooden board containing a list of names of boys he had taught. The war was over, and the Roll of Honour contained the names of 130 former pupils and 2 teachers from the school who had 'made the supreme sacrifice during the Great War'. St John's was not an elite school. It was one of the larger elementary schools in the city of Peterborough which prepared working-class boys for relatively unskilled or semi-skilled employment in the local community. A few of those named had previously won scholarships to local secondary schools and appear on other memorials. Only one of the men from St John's, Second Lieutenant Charles Foote Snow of the Royal Field Artillery, was a commissioned officer. Many of them joined local county regiments. Over 40 per cent were members of the Northamptonshire Regiment, including seven career soldiers who died during the initial BEF campaigns in 1914. At least eight of the former pupils of the school died with the Northamptons in the fighting at Aubers Ridge and Loos in 1915. These men were not individually famous but their collective efforts were vital nevertheless. They were men of all ages, many in their late twenties and thirties, often with responsibilities at home for other family members, and whose loss was felt as keenly as that of the young and privileged. They, too, were lost to their families, to their friends, to their local community, and to the nation as a whole. St John's Boys' School – their school – no longer exists, having been subsumed within other institutions during the many re-organisations of schooling in the city of Peterborough over the past century. The individuals behind the names are rarely, if ever, lauded as heroic figures today, yet they were equally part of that Lost Citizenry of the early twentieth century.

The Fallen also counted teachers amongst its number. Many of the teachers who had left their schools for active service during the Great War were not demobilised. Instead, they too remained where they had been killed in action or had died from their wounds. Unlike Corrie Chase, Tom Adlam and Archibald Buckle they did not return to their homes, families and school communities. Teachers from the public schools were amongst the first casualties of the Great War. With their OTC experience and pre-war Territorial commissions they crossed the English Channel with the BEF and, like Lieutenant Alexander Williamson of Highgate School, died in the first skirmishes of the war. Fighting alongside them were other teacher Reservists from far less prestigious schools. Second Lieutenant John Paulson from Orme Road Boys School, a publically maintained secondary school in Newcastle-under-Lyme, was killed on 13 September at the village of Bucy-le-Long on the Aisne, attempting to stop the advance of the German Schlieffen Plan armies into France. In the months that followed, and as the initial war of movement ground to a halt, teachers from diverse backgrounds became casualties of the attempts to break through the lines of trenches which both sides had begun to construct. Private Albert Herbert from St Mark's Elementary School in Peterborough, an early volunteer to Kitchener's New Armies, was one of Edward Adams' former boys killed at Aubers Ridge in April 1915. Captain Sandy Morrison, a pupil, master and founder of the OTC at George Watson's School in Edinburgh, was killed at the Battle of Loos in September 1915.[25]

The campaigns of the following year resulted in enormous numbers of casualties. Private Arthur Axe, Music Master at Hurstpierpoint College, was killed on the first day of the Battle of the Somme.[26] He was joined on the casualty lists of 1 July 1916 by Private Matthew Higgins of 16 Battalion (McRae's) Royal Scottish Regiment, a graduate of Edinburgh University and teacher at Warrender Park School in the city, who died of his wounds six days later.[27] These men were victims of a simplistic military doctrine which asserted – on more than one occasion – that the massed guns of the artillery and charges across no man's land by wave after wave of infantry would break the stalemate. Despite such offensives – the term 'battle' no longer described the scale of the action and consequent slaughter – the armies of Europe remained stubbornly entrenched. Lieutenant Russell Wheeler of Harrow County School for Boys was killed defending the British front-line trenches near Dunkerque in November 1916, the year in which earlier hopes of dashing victories had given way to the grim realities of a war of attrition. His colleague at Harrow County, Captain Gordon Haswell of the 9th Battalion King's Own Yorkshire Light Infantry, had been killed on the first day of the Battle of the Somme. The German Spring Offensive of 1918 also took its toll. Lieutenant Colonel Wilfrith Elstob from Merchiston School was awarded his posthumous VC for refusing to surrender Manchester Hill to the enemy. Second Lieutenant Edgar Law from Whittlesey was killed on 5 April 1918 as he and fellow officers and men of the 6th Battalion Northamptonshire Regiment were pushed back by the Germans over territory taken by the British less than two years earlier.[28] Five days later Private William MacIlwraith, formerly Science Master at West End Primary School in Elgin, was killed whilst serving with the Royal Engineers Special (Gas) Company.[29] As the Allies counter attacked the casualties continued to mount. The March to Victory claimed the life of Second Lieutenant Joseph Dines from King's Lynn. The teacher and sometime England footballer was killed by machine-gun fire during the assault on the German Hindenburg Line near

Havrincourt in September 1918. He had been a commissioned officer for just three months and had been in France for less than two weeks. Just a few days short of the Armistice, Lieutenant Colonel George Tryon MC, former House Master at Oundle School, was killed in action at St Aubin, aged thirty-three. He had survived being wounded in France in 1915 and had endured the horrors of the Salonika campaign, only to fall on 7 November 1918 during the final assault on the German defences on the Western Front.

During the Great War over 2,000 British schoolteachers were killed in action or died subsequently of wounds received during military action. The exact number is difficult to ascertain as there is no single source of data. Instead, the reckoning of the dead was made by separate institutions and educational authorities, reflecting once again the fragmentation of educational provision in Great Britain. In its *Report* for 1917–18, published within weeks of the Armistice, the Board of Education stated that known fatalities amounted to 1,829 elementary and 329 secondary school teachers.[30] The Board's figures were clearly provisional and referred only to the publically maintained schools in England and Wales which the Board controlled. The National Union of Teachers (NUT) *War Record* lists 1,437 of its members who were amongst The Fallen. The overall numbers are but a small proportion of the total figure for British casualties, but the loss of so many members of a single profession is staggering nonetheless. When the number of losses from individual cities and districts is considered, however, some sense of the impact of such losses is gained. The Manchester District of the NUT lost fifty-seven members. Birmingham lost forty-five, Sheffield thirty-five and Liverpool twenty-eight. In London, twenty-seven members were lost from each of the NUT branches in Hackney, West Ham and West Lambeth. In Wales, the NUT branch in the Rhondda lost fourteen of its members. Some Local Education Authorities also kept records of The Fallen who had previously worked in the council schools. The Norfolk Teachers War Memorial housed in County Hall in Norwich lists fifteen teachers who were killed or died of wounds received at Gallipoli, in Flanders, the Pas de Calais or the Somme battlefields. The Scottish War Memorials Project lists the names of The Fallen, former pupils and teachers, from some 200 individual schools.[31] Mackie Academy in Stonehaven, for example, lost three former teachers, whilst Trinity Academy and Portree High School in Leith both list two former teachers on their war memorials.

The names of the The Fallen from teacher training colleges also make sombre reading. The London Day Training College lists thirty-nine of its alumni. Many, like James Garland in the 1911 cohort, were young trainees who, forsaking their studies in response to the call-to-arms, were forever lost to the teaching profession. Captain James Garland was killed, aged twenty-three, leading his men towards the German defences on 1 July 1916, the first day of the Battle of the Somme. St Peter's College in Peterborough lost forty-two former trainees and one college tutor, Mr

W.G. Chambers. The inscription on the college memorial lists their alumni by year of entry, and the majority of names are of men who left the college before 1914 to enter the teaching profession. They include Harrow County's Russell Wheeler, a trainee in 1904–5, and Joseph Dines from King's Lynn and Edgar Law from Whittlesey who were contemporaries in the 1909–10 group of trainees. Five of the men listed were more recent trainees, at St Peter's during the war but leavers before its closure in July 1915. The number of casualties amongst men who had trained at Jordanhill College in Glasgow was even greater. The college memorial lists 196 names, including twenty-nine who began their training in 1914 and 1915.

The statistics for teachers lost from British public schools support the more general assertion that this sector of schooling suffered disproportionate numbers of casualties during the Great War. The impact on some individual institutions was enormous. Arthur Axe was one of four masters from Hurstpierpoint College killed during the war.[32] Of the ten teachers from Shrewsbury School who served, five were killed, in addition to two former teachers and a member of the governing body. Merchant Taylors' School lost five of the thirteen teachers who served, Clifton College seven out of sixteen, and Dulwich College four out of ten. Eton, Harrow, Charterhouse, Lancing College and Christ's Hospital School are amongst the many great public schools which lost a member of their teaching staff.

The numbers of teachers amongst the dead of the Great War are, of course, small in comparison to the better known lists of former pupils who died in the conflict. Nevertheless, they are highlighted here because the impact of their loss on an individual school was arguably greater.[33] Unlike the many cohorts of former pupils who had left the school before 1914, serving teachers were still very much part of the institution when they enlisted. They were ever-present role models who, notwithstanding the vagaries and fortunes of war, were expected to return to their classrooms and to be there for their pupils in the future.[34] The death of a teacher, in whatever type of school, had an enormous impact on the children and remaining staff alike. At Dulwich College, for example, the loss of Mr Nightingale, Mr Beachcroft and Mr Kittermaster, three 'mild, unwarlike, dedicated and scholarly' masters, came as a 'great sense of shock'.[35]

The memorialisation of The Fallen began during the Great War. As news of individual casualties found its way back to schools and their communities, logbooks, magazines and governors' minutes recorded the names of former pupils and staff. The logbook for Northop School in Flintshire, for example, contains several such records:

1916
8 March: Official notice came today of the death of an old boy Walter Davey. Killed in the trenches.

1917
2nd July: Another old boy Walter Chambers has made the great sacrifice. Killed in Action in France RIP.[36]

At Harrow School, Head Master Lionel Ford had used the occasion of Sunday Evensong to read out the weekly list of Old Harrovians killed in action, and in special supplements the *Harrovian* had recorded details of how former pupils had met their fate on the battlefield.[37] In January 1916 Rugby School published Volume 1 – the first of seven - of *Memorials of Rugbeians Who Fell in the Great War,* which included biographies and photographs of each of the school's first 100 casualties.[38] After the Armistice in November 1918 there were further attempts by schools and many other public institutions to gather details of the dead, or to confirm the fate of those captured or missing from earlier engagements with the enemy. As late as March 1921, for example, The Harvey Grammar School in Folkestone placed an article in the *Folkestone Herald* appealing for details of Old Boys who had given their lives during the war so that a Roll of Honour might be produced.[39] By then, the process of transcribing names of The Fallen onto fitting memorials had begun throughout the land. For some communities there were difficult decisions to be made about which names should – or should not – be included. Should the names of the victims of the influenza pandemic sit alongside those who were killed in action on the battlefields? What of the man or women who subsequently died of wounds, many months or even years after the war ended? Commissioning authorities, generally parish councils or civic committees composed of local worthies,[40] and in schools, combinations of headteachers, governors, alumni and bereaved parents, also had to consider carefully the design of the memorial, striking a sensitive balance between the need to portray the dead as both heroes and victims of a necessary but bloody conflict.

The production of war memorials, some 54,000 of them across the country,[41] has been described by the Imperial War Museum as 'the largest public arts project in British history'.[42] Local initiative, rather than central direction, was responsible for the production of thousands of monuments to the dead. These 'sacred places in the landscape' can still be found in virtually every city, town and village,[43] decorating the walls of town halls, religious institutions and places of employment, or set as imposing sculptures in civic squares, churchyards and railway stations. From small plaques inscribed with the names of a few individuals to dedicated buildings containing the names of hundreds, the varied and ubiquitous memorials of the Great War bear witness to a nation's loss, and enable its people to come together 'in acts of communal mourning'.[44]

Schools throughout the country erected memorials to their dead. Many, such as that at St John's School in Peterborough (Plate 41), were simple but dignified affairs, with names and suitable inscriptions painted in white or gold on wooden boards. Where funds permitted, and often following appeals to the wider school community, more elaborate memorials were commissioned. At Harrow County School for Boys the scale of loss was less than that of many secondary schools, but the imperative to honour the alumni who had lost their lives was just as compelling. Ernest Young, who had led the school from its foundation and through the years of war but had relinquished his post as headmaster in 1919, returned on the evening of Tuesday, 22 February 1921 to unveil a memorial which was typical of many secondary school monuments to the dead. On a carved oak base were three brass panels containing the names of The Fallen: Bob Hart, Russell Wheeler and Gordon Haswell were joined by fifteen others, including Gerald Beet whose father had played a prominent part in organising the memorial appeal fund. Flanked on either side was the school Roll of Honour, an illuminated roll of names of all those from Harrow County who had fought during the war.[45]

Nowhere is the hierarchy of schooling more accurately represented than in the memorials produced after the Great War by the elite public schools. The long lists of their dead, and the monuments which perpetuate the memory of their fallen alumni, are on a very different scale. The War Memorial Chapel at Rugby School (Plate 42) pays homage to the '682 sons of the school' who:

> AT THE CALL OF KING AND COUNTRY LEFT ALL
> THAT WAS DEAR TO THEM, ENDURED HARDNESS,
> FACED DANGER, AND FINALLY PASSED OUT OF
> THE SIGHT OF MEN BY THE PATH OF DUTY
> AND SELF-SACRIFICE,
> GIVING UP THEIR OWN
> LIVES THAT OTHERS MIGHT LIVE IN FREEDOM.

The Memorial Chapel at Charterhouse was designed by Sir Giles Gilbert Scott who was also responsible for memorials at the catholic public schools of Ampleforth, Beaumont and Downside. The steps leading to the chapel at Durham School number ninety-eight, one for each of their dead.[46] At Haileybury, the war memorial is the dining hall, at Winchester and Sedburgh the Cloisters, and at both Berkhamstead School and Felsted School the new library was dedicated to The Fallen. Memorial halls were constructed at Marlborough College and at Bradford Grammar School. Glasgow Academy is itself a memorial to the 327 former pupils killed during the war, an endowed institution financed by the sale of shares and owned by the Glasgow Academicals' War Memorial Trust.[47] Elsewhere, sporting traditions influenced the nature of public school war memorials. Playing fields, often with accompanying cricket pavilions, were dedicated to fallen alumni at Christ College in Brecon, Loretto School in Edinburgh and Elizabeth College on Guernsey.[48] The new playing fields at Hurstpierpoint College were inaugurated in July 1921 with a 'School versus Ex-Servicemen Old Boys Cricket Match'.[49]

The names of the four masters killed in action adorn the pavilion clock.[50] At City of London School a memorial pavilion was opened in July 1925, its tearoom decorated with images of war and self-sacrifice. The inscription carved on the front of the building reads:

MCMXIV Libertatis Vindicibus Vitam Pro Patria Largitis Condiscipuli MCMXIX

(1914 To the memory of all champions of liberty who freely gave their lives for their country; fellow pupils raised this pavilion 1919).[51]

In other public schools the dead would be remembered with new classrooms, gateways and crosses.[52]

Whilst most memorials were retrospective some deliberately looked to the future, as at Wellington College where scholarships were established for sons of The Fallen.[53] Bereaved parents endowed schools with sports trophies and subject prizes so that future generations would gain some benefit whilst, at the same time, their sons' names would live for ever more. Some of The Fallen had made financial provision for their Alma Mater. Lieutenant E.H. Southcomb of the Manchester Regiment was killed in action on 31 July 1917. Before entering Shrewsbury School he had attended West Buckland public school in Devon, where he was remembered as a willing but not particularly successful athlete. On his death it was discovered that he had left a legacy of ten guineas to the School Sports Fund.[54] The dead would forever encourage their successors to 'Play up! Play up! And play the game'.

Throughout the land, school war memorials were unveiled with due ceremony and reverence. The forty-seven Old Lincolnians who had died in the Great War were formally honoured nearly a decade after the fighting stopped. The War Memorial at Lincoln Grammar School was designed by a member of the school community – Mr W.G. Watkins FRIBA, President of the Old Lincolnians Society – and consisted of a slab of Hopton Wood stone, framed by green Irish marble and divided into four panels by lines of gold mosaic. Above the names of The Fallen was the inscription: 'In memory of Old Boys of this School, who sacrificed their lives in the Great War, 1914–18'. The tablet was unveiled on Saturday, 26 February 1927 in the presence of school governors, staff, pupils, parents, and relatives of the dead. The guest of honour was Dr T.E. Page, an eminent classical scholar and Old Lincolnian. The school magazine, *The Lincolnian*, devoted three pages to the 'simple but impressive ceremony' in which the draped Union Jack covering the memorial was released and the dead were remembered as 'simple men' rather than 'paladins of romance' or 'proud knights'. The Old Boys were indeed men to remember, an example to others, who had endured squalor, sickness and suffering. The magazine article concluded with a line from Horace's Odes: 'Dulce et decorum est pro patria mori'.[55]

Many schools invited representatives of the wider community to officiate at their unveiling ceremonies. On 1 June 1920, the George Dixon War Memorial, commemorating forty-six fallen students, was dedicated by the Bishop of Birmingham.[57] The great public schools, of course, were able to invite Old Boys who were also leaders of the national community. When the war memorial at Harrow School was officially opened on 3 June 1926 those in attendance included Prime Minister Stanley Baldwin and Randall Davidson, the Archbishop of Canterbury.[58] The Memorial Arch at Clifton College was formally opened by none other than Field Marshal Douglas Haig, Commander of the BEF 1915–18 and a contemporary of Henry Newbolt at Clifton in the 1870s. In stark contrast, the unveiling of the war memorial at Hereford High School for Boys, a simple tablet containing the names of six former pupils who had lost their lives, was a private act with no public ceremony.[56]

School memorials were an attempt 'to build the war physically into post-war reality', thus providing tangible evidence that the war was finally over. They were pieces of art, combining brave and consolatory language with dignified images of innocence, duty and sacrifice. They were crafted not simply to remember the dead, but to console the living, those who needed to believe that the death of so many of their sons had been worthwhile and not in vain.[59] Chapels, playing fields and inscriptions replete with knightly epithets were appropriate tributes to the thousands of Christian gentlemen, sportsmen and warriors who had perished.[60] This was not the time, however, to point out, as Peter Parker did later in *The Old Lie*, 'the gulf between metaphor and actuality, between noble causes and battlefront realities'.[61] The true horrors of the Great War, portrayed so poignantly by Wilfred Owen and other war poets and artists,[62] signaled an end to romantic notions of warfare and dealt a 'death wound' to chivalry.[63]

In the years which followed the Great War a calendar of remembrance was established. The first anniversary of the Armistice was observed by many schools. On 11 November 1919 pupils and staff at Harrow County School for Boys stood to hear the names of those who died read out, and then sang a selection of suitable hymns. At Amberley Parochial School in Gloucestershire the logbook records the key ingredients of what would come to be known as a 'Remembrance Service':

1919
11 November: The first anniversary of Armistice Day was observed at 10.45 this morning when the Head Teacher addressed the schoolchildren (with the members of staff) and read the King's Letter. At eleven o'clock, silence was kept for 2 minutes.[64]

In 1920 schools observed the anniversary as part of a national programme of remembrance. On 10 November the body of the Unknown Warrior arrived at Dover Marine Railway Station, having travelled from Boulogne aboard HMS *Verdun*. Pupils from the Duke of York's Royal Military School formed part of the guard of honour and saluted the cortege before it resumed its journey to London. On 11 November the funeral procession of the Uknown Warrior moved slowly through the capital. Guns saluted, a formal ceremony was held at the newly constructed Cenotaph, or empty tomb, designed by Sir Edward Lutyens, and then the symbolic representative of all British service personnel who had died in the Great War was finally interned in Westminster Abbey. Schools throughout the country had re-arranged their timetables to mark the day. St Nicholas Boys' School in King's Lynn joined with thousands of other institutions in observing the 'Two minutes silence at 11 am with closed eyes'.[65]

By the following year many schools had their own war memorials in place. These physical manifestations gave greater focus to remembrance proceedings. They acted as secular altars, albeit with religious connotations, at the foot of which representatives from different parts of the school community – staff, prefects, cadets, governors, parents – might pay their respects to The Fallen by laying wreaths. No school is an island, however. The names of former pupils who died in the war often appeared elsewhere, on civic and other memorials erected to honour those in particular localities or organisations. St Nicholas Boys' School joined with other citizens of King's Lynn in a communal act of remembrance:

1921
26 January: Unveiling of (Town) War Memorial ... the boys met in the playground and marched in 4s to the Tower Gardens by 2.10 pm. After the unveiling by HRH Princess Mary, one of our orphan boys placed a laurel chaplet on the steps.[66]

Further afield, the battlefields of the Great War had witnessed the consecration of hundreds of cemeteries containing the physical remains of the dead, along with memorials listing the thousands of 'intolerably nameless names' of those whose bodies had not been recovered.[67] A recent account of the work of the Imperial (later Commonwealth) War Graves Commission has stated that post-war Britain 'achieved its most democratic expression in the celebration of its dead'.[68] The Commission's Director was Fabian Ware, formerly an Assistant Master at Bradford Grammar School and, from 1901, Inspector of Secondary Schools for the Board of Education. In the 'Empire of the Dead', manifested by row upon row of grave markers in foreign fields, the 'Brotherhood in Arms' was united in sacrifice. There was, in theory at least, to be no distinction in the form of memorial for rich and poor, for officers and men; all would lay beneath a simple white headstone, designed and made by the War Graves Commission.[69] Unlike the vast majority of school war memorials, however, carved on each stone was the rank – and in some cases, honorary title [70] – as well as the name and regiment of the victim of war buried there. This had been the customary practice of some schools which had lost former pupils in previous conflicts such as the Boer War and Victorian imperial expeditions. After 1918, however, most schools shared the belief at Rugby School that 'in their sacrifice, all were equal' and listed their fallen alphabetically or by date of death.[71]

During the 1920s members of several school communities travelled to the battlefields and cemeteries on the other side of the English Channel. Cranleigh School in Surrey may have been the first to do so as early as 1920.[72] In that same year Mr Franklin, headteacher of the Calton Schools in Gloucester, used his summer holidays to make a personal visit to the graves in Flanders of some of the boys he had taught before the deluge of war had overwhelmed them all. Unfortunately, he contracted typhoid during his pilgrimage and died early in the new school term on 16 September.[73] When pupils and staff from the Judd School in Tonbridge visited Ypres in 1922 the detritus of war still blighted the area, providing ample opportunity for the party to take souvenirs of helmets and bayonets from derelict tanks and other weapons.[74]

It was not unusual for schoolteachers to be involved in acts of remembrance which extended beyond their own individual institution, especially in smaller communities where a great many of the local casualties had lived in the same parish and attended the same village school. The men in one such village in Wales were commemorated in *A Record of the Services Rendered by Our Northop Men in The Great War 1914 -1919*. Compiled by Mr J.R. Richardson, this handwritten and leather-bound book was both a Roll of Honour of all who had served and a list of the men who had fallen:

> It has been compiled by one who throughout this war has taken great interest in the men themselves and in their doings, many of the men having been his pupils in Northop School. He deserves great credit for the care and accuracy with which the record has been compiled. The record will bear hopeful testimony to those who come after us, of the way in which the parishioners of Northop responded in those trying years, to their country's call upon her manhood to rise to her support in the hour of peril. It tells alas of how many were faithful even unto death.[75]

The Northop 'Record', completed in 1920, was duly placed with the Parish Registers.

One of the most remarkable acts of remembrance by any individual, however, was that of Susannah Knight (Plate 13), one of the teachers who were stranded in Europe when war was declared in 1914.[76] After arriving late for the start of the new school term, she combined her usual teaching role at St Gregory's School in Chorley with conducting classes in conversational French for the men of the Chorley Pals and other Territorial units who were then in training and awaiting deployment to the Western Front. She also organised a 'Smoking Concert', an opportunity for wounded Belgian soldiers to meet informally with men in the Pals. Susannah's school, a Roman Catholic elementary institution, welcomed the signing of the Armistice in November 1918 with mixed emotions. The war was over but the school re-opened on 11 November after being closed for four weeks and having had two children die as a direct result of the influenza virus.[77] In 1919 Susannah began a single-handed campaign to create a lasting memorial to the men of Chorley. She placed an advertisement in the *Chorley Guardian* of 5 April 1919 requesting biographical details from the families and friends of those who had served and died during the war. The advert recognised the different affiliations of The Fallen and the importance of every single individual:

All names to be in by the end of May. The names will be grouped with regard to the Churches they attended, and it is desired that no name, from the humblest to the greatest, may be omitted, so that our heroes may never be forgotten, and their names may be revered and honoured throughout the future generations.

The Memorial Album for 'Chorley's Glorious Sons, her Dead War Heroes' eventually contained entries for 775 men and included nearly 500 photographs. The great majority of the heroes were killed in action or died of wounds received on the battlefield between 1914 and 1918. Some, however, died of influenza and pneumonia or war-related and other medical conditions after the cessation of hostilities; Susannah's inclusive approach supported the belief of family members that their loved-ones' service should be recognised.

The production of the Memorial Album in three volumes, dedicated to the memories of The Fallen from just one town in the North of England and containing prayers for Catholics, Anglicans and Nonconformists alike, was a massive undertaking in itself. For Susannah Knight, however, the collation of casualty details was but a preliminary step. She intended to use the story of the men of Chorley to reinforce the bonds of friendship formed by Britain and her Allies during the war – the 'war to end all wars' – and to promote an enduring peace amongst nations. She began to add signatures to the Memorial Album. By the end of July 1921 Susannah had collected forty, including those of Field Marshal Haig, senior politicians Herbert Asquith, David Lloyd George, Winston Churchill and Stanley Baldwin, and even that of Prince Edward, the heir to the throne. H.A.L. Fisher, architect of the 1918 Education Act, also signed the album. The St

Gregory's School logbook records how Susannah then managed to secure leave of absence from her school in 1921. She travelled first to Europe, seeking audiences in Paris and Rome with royalty, military commanders and religious leaders. By the time she returned to her school in mid–August, suffering from exhaustion owing to the excessive heat in the Italian capital, the Chorley Memorial Album contained the signatures of Marshal Foch of France, King Victor Emmanuel of Italy and Pope Benedict XV. The album was blessed and its creator received the Apostolic Blessing.

The next overseas excursion was to be just as dramatic. The logbook for St Gregory's School noted:

1921
28 October: Miss Knight went to E(ducation) office on Thursday morning to make enquiries about her leave of absence to visit America. No definite answer could be given until after (the) meeting that night. She called at the Education office Friday morning. Leave of absence for one month with full salary granted. She came to school but left at 9.50 am to catch the train for Liverpool. Sailed Saturday by (the) *Scythia*.

Whilst in the USA, Susannah attended the Conference on the Limitation of Arms in Washington. The signatures of military and civilian delegates from Great Britain, France, Canada and the USA were added to the pages of the Memorial Album. They included General George Pershing, a large number of US Congressmen, the majority of Senators, members of the Cabinet, Vice President Calvin Coolidge and President Warren Harding.

Miss Susannah Knight retired from her teaching post at St Gregory's on 1 March 1933.[78] She returned to the USA in 1935, twenty years after the men from Chorley had embarked for France, and secured further signatures, including those of President Roosevelt and his wife, Eleanor. In all, the uncertificated assistant mistress from Chorley managed to add over 2,000 signatures of the great and the good to a simple memorial to 775 lost citizen soldiers. And then this act of remembrance was forgotten. The story of Chorley's fallen, overtaken by the passage of time and another world war, faded from popular memory. Just before Susannah's death in August 1950, however, the Memorial Album was re-discovered.[79] In November 1948 the re-bound album was displayed in public, before disappearing quietly once again, and until now, from our collective consciousness and national record.[80]

Chapter 11

The Forgotten

Shall they return to beatings of great bells
In wild train-loads?
A few, a few, too few for drums and yells,

May creep back, silent, to still village wells,
Up half-known roads.

Wilfred Owen (1918)
The Send-Off

Six years after the Great War ended, John Hughes Davies gathered together his colleagues at Deacon's School in Peterborough for a group photograph. In 'The Staff 1924' (Plate 43) Dr Davies is seated in the centre of the front row, a position traditionally reserved for school leaders on such occasions. Dr Davies had led the school since becoming its Head Master in 1913. In the decade which followed, both he and Deacon's School had known war and peace. The school community had responded to the call-to-arms in 1914, and by 1915 had published its own Roll of Honour in *The Deaconian* listing the names of Old Deaconians who had joined the colours. By the end of the war, over forty of these young men were listed amongst The Fallen. They had served with English, Irish, Scottish, Welsh, Australian, Canadian and Indian regiments. Most had been killed in action or died of wounds on the Western Front in Northern France and Belgium. Two died from sickness contracted in the trenches, and two died in POW camps in Germany. Their war graves and other memorials provide a simple narrative of the Great War, tracing the line of trenches from the Belgian coast to the point where the British and French defensive positions met, and bearing witness to the involvement of the boys from just one school in each year and every major battle of the war. Old Deaconians fell at Klein Zillebeke in 1914, Aubers Ridge and Loos in 1915, Vimy Ridge and Martinpuich in 1916, Ypres and Hill 70 in 1917, and Bapaumme and Canal du Nord in 1918. Further afield, they were laid to rest in the war cemeteries of Alexandria, Jerusalem and Mhow in India. Before the war these young men had been clerks, drapers, small-scale farmers and school teachers. Many had attended elementary schools before taking advantage of the new opportunities to access secondary education which Balfour's 1902 Education Act had created. Many had entered Deacon's School as fee-paying pupils, others as scholarship winners. The military ranks they held in wartime – there were twenty-three privates, eleven NCOs and seven commissioned officers – reflected their social and occupational backgrounds and the status of Deacon's School in the hierarchy of educational provision.

After the war a memorial to The Fallen from Deacon's School was commissioned. Designed by Mr Spencer, the school's art master, it consisted of a simple bronze tablet bearing thirty-six names.[1] After it had been cast, but before it was unveiled, a further six names were added to the list of the dead, and a small but matching supplementary tablet was cast. The War Memorial was officially unveiled on 13 April 1921 by the then Chairman of Governors, Mr John Henry Beeby. Three decades later more names were added to the list of former pupils killed in wartime. Dr Davies retired in 1948, having led Deacon's School through another world war. He returned four years later and stood in silence with former colleagues before unveiling a new War Memorial. To the forty-one names from the Great War were added the names of thirty-two Old Deaconians who had been killed in the Second World War of 1939 to 1945.[2] The Fallen from Deacon's School had not been forgotten, at least not by the school community. The Remembrance Day Service at 11 o'clock on 11 November became one of the most important events in the school calendar and, despite suggestions in the early 1990s that perhaps the ceremony was no longer relevant, continues to be so nearly a century later.

The Fallen of the Great War have remained with us, memorialised in wood and brass and stone, and enshrined in institutional and collective memory. They have quite rightly come to symbolise the suffering, the waste, and the idiocy of military conflict. Lawrence Binyon's poetic words remain as apt and poignant today as they did when he wrote them in 1914:

> They shall grow not old, as we that are left grow old:
> Age shall not weary them, nor the years condemn.
> At the going down of the sun and in the morning
> We will remember them.[3]

But what of those who did grow old, the cohorts of children who experienced the war and shared in its sufferings, and the adults who served on the home front in myriad ways, but survived to carry on their lives in the post-war world? And what of Dr Davies and the staff of his small secondary school, and the multitude of others like them, who did sit once more at the 'familiar tables of home',[4] and for whom the wars of the twentieth century were transient, but nevertheless momentous, interludes in lives and careers?

The impact of the Great War upon those who were counted amongst The Fallen has been well documented by historians and vividly portrayed by war poets and war artists. The hundreds of thousands of names listed on war memorials across the land and in foreign fields offer unequivocal evidence of the ultimate fate of many combatants. For the millions of British citizens who survived the four years of conflict, however, the impact of the war is far from self-evident. Beyond the relatively straightforward but, nevertheless, extensive task of making statistical tallies of the monetary or physical costs of the conflict it is all too easy to generalise but far more difficult to particularise.[5] The Great War was fought on such an enormous scale and with such intensity that it touched the lives of each and every institution and citizen. The magnitude of the conflict resulted in 'an enormous variety of different personal experiences for participants. Many different meanings were drawn from those experiences'.[6] Even within the same or similar social and occupational groups there were many disparate versions of wartime reality. For an individual school, and for the children and teachers who inhabited it, 'the intensity of its war experience' was determined by several factors.[7] Proximity to the theatre of war was a key determinant. Garrison towns and ports had long experience of the sights and sounds of military preparation, but in 1914 they were joined by hundreds of other communities, including schools, in providing billets or training facilities for a nation in arms. Huge numbers of highly visible military personnel,[8] complete with the trappings and paraphernalia of war, invaded formerly peaceful settlements. A home front emerged and Britain rapidly became an island garrison, a supply depot and a launchpad for military expeditions. Patterns of everyday life were disturbed by war collectivism and the production of increasing quantities of war material in an attempt to end the stalemate on the battle fronts.[9] Within months it became clear that the domestic front was itself a military target. The battlefields were not only overseas but, for those close to urban and industrial areas within range of enemy aircraft, they were also overhead. Despite the much-vaunted pre-war superiority of the Royal Navy, coastal towns in Eastern England were also open to direct assault. The vulnerability of many schools at the time was recorded in their official logbooks, governors' minutes and school magazines.

For many other schools, however, the war seemed far more remote. They were patently aware of the national emergency of 1914 and witnessed men and women from their families and communities responding to the call-to-arms, but otherwise little changed and they carried on with business as usual. In some parts of the country, for example in Wales or in some of the western counties of England, the initial impact of war was slight and deserving of merely a passing reference or, in some school logbooks, no mention at all until much later in the conflict. The real impact of war was felt for the first time at Kingswood School in Bristol, for example, when in 1916 its sanatorium was filled to overflowing with casualties from the Battle of the Somme.[10] As the demands of total war increased, however, and the soldier-citizens of Kitchener's New Armies began to fall in their thousands, proximity to war was not simply a matter of geography. The war began to make its mark throughout the land. Schoolchildren had increasingly close ties with the battle fronts. They provided comforts, adopted serving soldiers and prisoners of war, welcomed back former pupils home on leave and listened to their accounts of wartime experiences. In many schools the visitors were young men, not much older than the pupils themselves, who not too long ago had walked the same corridors and played on the same sports fields. A former pupil of Aberystwyth County School, J.R. Richards, recalled later that:

> The war came very close to us as one after another of the senior boys passed from the School into the Forces and the names of some we had known began to appear in the list of casualties.[11]

The experience of schooling during wartime may well have seemed, to the millions of British schoolchildren who lived through it, like something akin to a roller-coaster ride. The sudden and unexpected exhilaration of August 1914 soon gave way in most schools to sustained and productive war service schemes. Teachers came and went but they were often, especially in the boarding schools, the key voices which mediated the latest war news and tried to separate it from rumour. A lexicon of war charted the ups and downs of military campaigns and the national mood: advance, retreat, stalemate, offensive, gains, defeat – and then advance again.[12] By 1918 wartime restrictions, mounting casualties and gloomy prospects of victory began to have a serious effect. Many schools had become cold and grey places,[13] and some began to lose their initial enthusiasm for the war effort.[14] The celebration of victory in late 1918 and peace in 1919 was tempered by a growing recognition of the true cost of the conflict.

For many pupils, and especially those who were boarders, schools provided an important sheet anchor during a period of enormous turmoil and unpredictability. They were not, of course, the only or most important social institution inhabited by children who, like adults, had multiple affiliations. The closeness of war was felt even more keenly in many homes. The war destabilised families.[15] Fathers and older brothers enlisted, were conscripted, or served on the home front as, for example, policemen, anti-aircraft gunners or firefighters. Others transferred to war-related employment or served in the merchant marine. Many working-class mothers and older sisters worked in munitions plants, engineering and other factories, or on public transport. Pride in the family's contribution to the war effort was challenged by the emotional drain of goodbyes at railway stations and the vagaries and dislocations of home leave. Wartime service carried huge risks and exacerbated concerns for the welfare of loved ones, especially those far from home. A child whose father or brother had been killed in action or drowned at sea, or whose mother or sister had died in one of the many industrial accidents and explosions in munitions plants,[16] nevertheless went back to school at some point afterwards. The psychological and social effects of such a bereavement might well be imagined, but it would be difficult to assess properly the lasting impact upon a child's education and intellectual development. The number of British children and their families affected in this way ran into the hundreds of thousands. By 1921 War Pensions were being received by 192,000 British widows, with 344,000 dependent children.[17]

Financial provision was not accompanied by compassionate action, however. The bereaved children of the Great War form part of another lost – or forgotten – generation. The loss of so many fathers was a cause for official concern at the time, but that concern was for the wider impact upon society rather than upon the individual child, their family or their schooling. A perceived rise in juvenile delinquency during the war was generally explained, in the popular press especially, by the lack of disciplinarian father-figures.[18] During the war there was, as many school logbooks attest, a greater incidence of absence from school and unpunctuality, but much of this was a direct result of employment practices and opportunities and not simply incidents of wilful truancy. There were some instances of increased crime rates by juveniles, but this affected some areas more than others. Bath, for example, experienced an increase of 284 per cent in reported crimes by juveniles,[19] but in Hertfordshire the rate was no greater in 1916 than in previous years.[20]

The war did weaken family structures by diminishing children's access to, and close supervision by, important role models: fathers, mothers, elder siblings, other relatives, and their teachers in the schools. In families where wage earning took precedence over child rearing some children were undoubtedly neglected.[21] Schooling, too, was fragmentary and incomplete for many young people who were set to work prematurely. For those whose schools were on the front line during the German aerial bombing campaign, the dislocation and associated trauma were of even greater magnitude. Wider fears about a breakdown in society were unfounded, however. The moral panic over out-of-control juveniles was but one manifestation of wider concerns about the impact of the war on national life. Total war transformed Britain and other European nations by exposing their citizens to increasing bureaucracy and collectivisation and the erosion of individual freedoms. The economic framework was disrupted, and food shortages threatened personal wellbeing.[22] Everyday life and language was militarised, and huge reservoirs of aggression and violence were released deliberately by the state to further its war aims.[23] The great wonder is that the young people of Britain were not affected even more by such powerful forces of change.

The wartime records left by teachers generally concentrate upon the positive contributions they and their pupils made to the war effort. Only occasionally do they refer to the deleterious impact of war upon their classes. Miss Wise, a teacher at Norwich High School, a public school for girls, did notice that her pupils appeared to be 'suffering unconsciously from the strains of war conditions';

there was a general lack of excitement in the school, the pupils were more restless, inattentive and careless, and they seemed to have greater difficulty in getting down to serious study.[24] For Miss McDonald, a teacher of elementary schoolchildren at Badsey Council School in Evesham, the impact of wartime regulations on children's health was felt in June 1916:

> Several children being away under doctor's orders, suffering from general debility. Many children are very sleepy and tired owing to insufficient sleep. They are up much later at night-time than they should be, but have to get up early in the morning (Daylight Saving Bill).[25]

The wartime recollections of the schoolchildren themselves, many of them written by the products of the public and secondary schools, give but a fragmentary and not necessarily representative glimpse into young people trying to make sense of the world at war around them. It is difficult to assess the extent to which individual children recognised the 'deformations of civility' or the 'moral pollution' inherent in the *culture de guerre* which developed between 1914 and 1918.[26] The mental furniture upon which they drew was varied, differentiated by variables such as age, social origins, schooling, cultural perspective, geographical location and family circumstances. Bessie Ashworth, who attended Bacup and Rawtenstall Grammar School after winning a scholarship in 1914, states simply and economically that 'Four of the six years of my grammar school life were overshadowed by the horrors of that war'.[27] More detailed memoirs published after the war often, and perhaps not surprisingly, refer to a previous age, the ante-bellum. The 'before' stood in stark contrast to the 'then' of wartime and the 'after' of peacetime. Domestic details take pride of place in many wartime memories. Invidious comparisons were made on a whole range of topics relevant to the everyday experience of schooling: the staff, fixture lists, frequency of OTC drills and, of course, the quality of boarding school food. Evelyn Waugh later referred to his 'gross, innocent delight' when, as the war ended, Lancing College provided the boys there with more food.[28] There was, however, as in the country as a whole, a stoic acceptance of the demands and consequences of war,[29] and many schools did their utmost to introduce practical responses, such as school gardening projects, to the crises and challenges which arose.

Coping emotionally was another matter. When Evelyn Waugh wrote of the war years as 'the most dismal period in history for an English schoolboy', he was not simply referring to his personal experiences of cold and hunger. His mental furniture was that of a 'forgotten garrison', deserted by 'the masters who should have taught us' and forever subject to temporary and makeshift arrangements.[30] The awareness that no matter how bad conditions in the schools were, everyday life for the servicemen in the war zones was far worse, was some consolation. It could also be an overwhelming psychological burden, especially when employed as a motivational device by school authorities. Alec Waugh, Evelyn's brother, recalled how one of his schoolmates criticised his teachers for 'making our lives intolerable because we are too young' and then declared that:

> As soon as I am old enough I mean to go and fight; but I can't stick the way these masters croak away about the trenches all day long. If you play badly at rugger you are asked what use you will be in a regiment.[31]

At Campbell College, the Protestant public school in Belfast, Headmaster MacFarland used one particular phrase when reprimanding boys for poor behaviour or justifying wartime restrictions and hardships at the school: 'Remember the men in the trenches'.[32] A wartime schoolboy at Cheltenham College also recalled how:

> The war had a gloomy effect on the school. It was treated as a crusade to which everything, especially everything at all pleasant, must be sacrificed. We were expected to go without minor comforts 'because of the poor boys in the trenches'.[33]

Girls in some schools were subject to similar exhortations. Elizabeth Bowen, a pupil at Downe House, remembered later the psychological pressure which she and her fellow pupils were under during the war:

> The moral stress was appalling. We grew up under the intolerable obligation of being fought for, and could not fall short in character without recollecting that men were dying for us .... The war dwarfed us and made us morally uncomfortable.[34]

Temporary sacrifices were thus expected of those who had yet to make the ultimate sacrifice, but might well be called upon to do so before the war was over. In August 1917, when an end to the war seemed to many a distant prospect, Major Pilditch of the Royal Field Artillery observed that:

> Both sides are too strong for a finish yet. God knows how long it will be at this rate. None of us will ever see its end and children still at school will have to take it over.[35]

The great offensives of 1916, 1917 and 1918 redefined the nature of warfare. The Somme and Passchendaele were not battles in the previously understood sense,[36] but intensive and sustained acts of attrition. Thousands of casualties demanded thousands of replacements if the momentum of war was to be maintained. In 1918, many of those replacements, especially for the officer corps, were still at school, awaiting their turn to serve. Following in the footsteps of dead heroes was pressure enough, but it was something that senior boys in the public schools, especially, had prepared for and come to expect. For H.W. Skinner, a pupil and Sergeant in the Corps at Kent College in Canterbury until 1917,

> The main fear was that the War would be over before I was old enough to leave school and join up. In the event, I left school and volunteered for the R.F.C. where I eventually became a commissioned pilot.[37]

There were those who just missed the war, young men who were saved from its horrors but 'were forever divided from their elders'.[38] Their lives had been changed by the war, but their futures would be overshadowed by remembrance of The Fallen and their own stories all but forgotten.

The service personnel who survived the war returned home in 1919. A decade after the Great War had ended, Erich Maria Remarque stated in his introduction to *All Quiet on the Western Front* that his work would 'try simply to tell of a generation of men who, even though they may have escaped its shells, were destroyed by the war'.[39] The survivors have sometimes been included in a wider definition of the Lost Generation. Unlike those whose bodies were consigned to the military cemeteries but whose short lives have been memorialised, these were members of a generation which had lost its bearings and struggled to adjust to the demands of an unfamiliar post-war landscape. Many of those who had experienced combat saw themselves as a race apart, sharing 'the belief that in a sense none of them had ever really returned from France and Flanders'.[40] They were a damaged generation, scarred physically and mentally by the horrors of war;[41] a 'burnt-out generation',[42] injured further by the inability of Britain's government and its people to honour David Lloyd George's promise of a 'Land Fit For Heroes'. The return to civilian life was difficult. For those who did not consider their war adventures to be piteous, or had found comradeship and social purpose amidst the horrors of the battlefield,[43] peace was an anti-climax.[44] In 1914 thousands of patriotic citizens had willingly relinquished jobs and careers and fought for their country. In 1919 they came back to a post-war economy blighted by unemployment. The culture of remembrance paid attention to the dead, not the survivors. On 11 November 1921, the third anniversary of Armistice Day, many of those who had returned from the war demonstrated and held aloft placards stating 'The dead are remembered, but we are forgotten'.[45]

Some of the survivors appear in the photograph of 'The Staff 1924' (Plate 43). When Dr Davies took up the headship of Deacon's School in 1913 he inherited a teaching staff of six assistant masters. By 1924 there were fourteen assistant members of staff, and several of them had seen active service. Mr Schofield, the young trainee teacher who was appointed in 1914 but promptly enlisted when war was declared, returned in January 1919 to a 'Position kept open' after wartime service with the Northamptonshire Regiment and the RAF. Messrs Robson, Spencer, and Youngs had also served in Kitchener's New Armies. Reuben Scotney Parr attended Deacon's School before the war, later following the familiar route of many scholarship boys into a teaching career in the elementary school sector. In 1914 he enlisted in the locally recruited Huntingdonshire Cyclists Battalion and became a Sergeant Major Instructor (Physical Training). In 1919 he rejoined his old school as a PE master, a post he held for the next thirty-six years. Much to the delight of the Governing Body, which in 1924 included Councilor Isaac Whitsed as Chair and Edward Adams of St John's Boys' School,[46] Mr Parr introduced rugby – 'a game for gentlemen' – into the school curriculum. The war had also seen the appointment of several assistant mistresses. Miss Gladys Pringuer had, like Miss Elsa Tutin, been a 'Temporary War Appointment' for the duration of the war only. Unlike Miss Tutin and thousands of her fellow women teachers who were no longer required or wanted in the profession,[47] Miss Pringuer retained her post and spent a further decade at the school teaching mathematics. At Deacon's School, the masters had returned, but the school had expanded rapidly from nearly 150 pupils in 1914 to over 200 by 1924.

For many teachers resuming their careers after the war, the return to some degree of normality was welcome. At Lancing College Evelyn Waugh noted how the young masters 'came back to civil life with zest'.[48] For others, however, including the staff at Harrow County School for Boys, the transition from war to peace was far more difficult. In the early days of the war *The Gaytonian* had written breezily about the exploits of Mr Rayner and Mr Parry at the front, the latter an officer in the Royal Field Artillery 'sitting on a charger, easy and cool'. The magazine's editorial wondered 'How will these men ever settle down again to marking exercises?'[49] Of the ten masters who served, two, Russell Wheeler and Gordon Haswell, were killed in action. Frank Pettersson did not return to the school as expected, and James Paterson, who returned to Harrow County for only three months, was one of several who left teaching altogether, either on leaving the army or very shortly afterwards. Douglas Imrie returned to his post but left within a year, his health broken by the exertions of wartime service. Charles O'Sullivan, known to most boys as 'Sully', resumed his career after losing a leg in the war but left in 1919 to take Holy Orders. He died ten years later. During the 1920s he revisited the school some evenings and played the piano for hours at a stretch.[50]

The physical and psychological impact of the war on teachers was felt in many schools. The latent results of military service are difficult to measure,[51] but ex-combatants were generally more susceptible to other diseases and conditions and shortened lives.[52] The logbook at Meeching Boys' School in Newhaven noted on 19 October 1919 the absence that day of Mr Maguire, 'suffering from the effects of gas poisoning'.[53] Mr Amos returned to the headship of Badsey Council School in

Evesham in 1917 having been medically discharged from the army, but continued to be troubled by a shoulder wound.[54] The war was over, but for many ex-servicemen it 'was continuing to be fought within the psyche' after demobilisation.[55] The 'most profound impact of the human costs of the Great War ... was on the minds of the survivors'.[56] Charles Mitchell returned to Inverness Royal Academy as Principal Teacher in 1920, having been a captain in the Camerons and a recipient of the Military Cross. As was the case with so many of those who had served, he was reluctant to talk about his wartime experiences. The trauma of conflict, however, manifested itself dramatically on some occasions when 'he was moved to blazing indignation by any flippant reference to the war or to its casualties'.[57] Kenneth Cummins, a wartime pupil at Merchant Taylors' School in Liverpool, recalled how 'Masters left for the army too – and some came back again to teach – minus an arm or leg. Some were very fierce and would beat us'.[58] The wartime experience of those who, like Dr Davies, had remained in their teaching posts was very different from those who had fought on the battlefields. It was different in scale, intensity and potential outcome, but it could still be traumatic nevertheless. Those teachers who also were parents worked on, as did so many others throughout the country, but lived in fear of seeing the name of their son or daughter - or husband, wife, brother or sister – on the latest list of casualties. School leaders, in particular, shared these and other fears, and the responsibility of being *in loco parentis* to the children in their charge weighed heavily upon them. Head Master Sargant at Oakham School recalled the emotional tension of the war years:

> So the weary days dragged on. Each morning we opened the newspaper dreading to read of the death of some boy, who, but a few months before, had been a living member of the School.[59]

In a letter to his son, Robert Saunders, Headmaster of Fletching School in Uckfield, wrote of the losses of friends and neighbours, and of visions of dying and wounded boys upon whom he had urged 'the duty of patriotism'. He knew it had all taken its toll on him too:

> The war has pressed more heavily on us than is generally thought, even by ourselves, and I am afraid has aged us more than the four and a half years warrant as regards time.[60]

The deaths of family members or valued colleagues added enormously to the stress, and as institutional figureheads, their grief was public and shared by all. Hilda Adams, a pupil at Frenchay Church of England School in Bristol, remembered clearly the day in May 1917 when the son of her headteacher was killed in a training accident whilst serving with the RFC. Hilda noted that 'Mr Wardlow was in a terrible state when he got the news and he didn't open the school'.[61] In 1918, Frederick Sanderson, Head Master of Oundle School, received news in May that his son, Roy, had been killed, and in November the news that former housemaster and close friend George Tryon had suffered the same fate. Sanderson of Oundle died in post in 1922.[62]

The line between The Fallen and those who survived was sometimes a fine one. Many who died of wounds did so after the memorials had been unveiled. On Friday, 13 May 1927 mourners gathered at St John's Church in Lewisham. The congregation included school managers, schoolteachers, and schoolchildren. They stood alongside grieving friends and relatives, local councillors and a detachment of uniformed British servicemen. They were there to pay their last respects to one of the 'salamanders born in the furnace' of the Great War of 1914–19.[63] This was no ordinary funeral:

Full military honours were accorded the deceased hero, the coffin being conveyed from the house to the Church on a gun carriage drawn by six horses, with outriders. The coffin which was covered with the Union Jack, also bore the Commander's sword and five medals. A number of the deceased's comrades in the Anson Battalion walked beside the coffin and the boys of the Rotherhithe Nautical School formed a guard of honour in the church grounds.[64]

Inside the church, the service was conducted by Reverend Neill of St John's and by Chaplain Gouldie of the Anson Battalion. Finally, the hero's body was laid to rest in nearby Brockley Cemetery.

Archibald Buckle had died suddenly just days before, on 6 May 1927. His obituary in the *New Cross and Hatcham Review* stated that his widow, Mrs Elsie Buckle, had informed the Coroner's Inquest that her husband had been wounded on several occasions during the war. He had always made light of his injuries, had never complained, and refused steadfastly to apply for a disability pension. The newspaper continued:

Recently a boil appeared on his wrist and he was sent to Westminster Hospital. Medical evidence showed that death was due to bronchial pneumonia through osteomyelitis, probably accelerated by shrapnel wounds which had lowered the vitality. A verdict accordingly was recorded. The Coroner said death was accelerated by his war wounds.

Archibald Buckle (Plate 44) had returned to England after a distinguished military career in the Great War. By profession he was an elementary school teacher, in his spare time a member of the Royal Naval Volunteer Reserve. He had fought almost continuously from 1914 to 1918. He rose through the ranks to become a lieutenant commander and officer in charge of the Anson Battalion of the Royal Naval Division. On four separate occasions he was awarded the Distinguished Service Order for personal bravery and exemplary leadership. As to his personal qualities, a comrade-in-arms said that he:

> sometimes appeared staccato and abrupt, not over tactful to outside appearances. But it was a tactlessness born of a love of directness, hatred of pretence or of veneer. For to Buckle, sham of any sort was like a red rag to a bull, and second as a provocative only to injustice.

The teacher-turned-soldier returned to teaching in 1919 and became headteacher of Rotherhithe Nautical School in London, a post he held until his early and sudden death less than a decade later at the age of thirty-eight. Lieutenant Commander Archibald Walter Buckle DSO RNVR survived the war and was justifiably feted as a hero in his lifetime. And then he too was forgotten.

Despite frequent assertions between 1914 and 1918 that there would be business as usual,[65] schools experienced dislocation, hardship and loss, albeit in varying degrees. When peace finally arrived it was accompanied by a recognition that things would never be quite the same again. The certainties of the ante-bellum had been contested and, in some cases, destroyed by the deluge of total war. The culture of Remembrance stressed the pity of war rather than its supposed glory, and school leaders could no longer be sure of community support for blatantly militaristic elements within the curriculum.[66] The Great War forced individuals to take stock, to think about what really mattered to them, and to adjust accordingly to a different set of realities in the post-war world. It would be naïve, however, to suggest that this was always for the better. When the headmaster of Harrow County School for Boys waved goodbye to the party of visiting German Boy Scouts in August 1914, and almost immediately welcomed home Bob Hart and the school party from its aborted trip to Germany, he had expressed the genuine and sincere hope that none would fall victim to the horrors of a fast-approaching European war. After visiting the French Front in early 1918 the same man, Ernest Young, declared that it would be with 'a feeling of unmitigated disgust' that he would meet a German in the future.[67]

The Great War of 1914 to 1919 was considered by those who lived through it and by later historians to be the 'great divide';[68] a psychological chasm between the social world of 1914 and that which Dr Davies, his staff and his school inhabited in 1924. So much had happened during the war to test not just the millions of individuals who experienced it, but also the institutions within which they had lived, studied and worked and whose values they had espoused. The war changed everything, temporarily. Had the Education Act of 1918 been properly implemented and adequately financed, then the case for the Great War as a catalyst for fundamental and major change might well be justified. In reality, however, the war 'accelerated most of the major trends which were already in operation in pre-war England'.[69] Many schools, especially those offering forms of secondary education like Deacon's School, continued to expand in numbers. Whilst some placed greater emphasis than previously on scientific and technical education, the curriculum model which most secondary institutions offered after the war was still based firmly upon that of the socially superior elite public schools. The majority of British citizens continued to be educated in elementary schools. Access to secondary and higher education remained firmly linked to the ability to pay school fees, with a system of scholarships available to the deserving poor. Britain would experience another world war before 'Secondary Education for All' became a reality. So many of the changes which were introduced during the war were born of necessity, rather than idealism. They were pragmatic responses to pressing demands, rather than strategic changes of direction. Much of what was novel was intended to be for the duration of the war only, as the Temporary Gentlemen and the temporary masters discovered when the war finally ended. The Great War of 1914 to 1919 did not fundamentally disturb a more general structure of social differentiation which was, and still is, such a feature of educational provision in Great Britain.[70]

Epilogue

But their spirit lived on, their example was emulated, their names and memories were cherished, and here and there an Asquith or a Freyberg, a Hutchison, a Ramsay Fairfax, a Beak, or a Buckle, salamanders born in the furnace, survived to lead, to command, and to preserve the sacred continuity.

Winston Churchill (1923)

Lieutenant Commander Archibald Walter Buckle DSO is no longer part of the forgotten generation of the Great War. He was rescued from the enormous condescension of posterity when his grave was re-discovered nearly eight decades after his death and burial in 1927.[2] Members of the Royal British Legion in Brockley had been searching for the exact location of his final resting place in Brockley Cemetery for eighteen years. They eventually found his headstone hidden beneath overgrown shrubs and weeds, and covered by a dense thicket of brambles.

On Sunday, 30 October 2005 representatives from the Royal Navy, the Royal Marines and the British Army joined with hundreds of others who had assembled in Brockley Cemetery to pay their respects to one of the citizen-soldiers of the Great War. A small memorial slab of polished black stone – bearing an inscription telling simply of the dates of his birth and death, his age and details of his military rank, unit and honours – was placed by his grave, and remains there today.

Notes

A Note on Sources

1. Hastings, M. (2011) *All Hell Let Loose. The World at War 1939–1945*, London: Harper Press, p.xx.
2. Much of the information in, for example, King, P. (1997) *Hurstpierpoint College 1849–1995. The School by the Downs*, Chichester: Phillimore & Co Ltd is taken from the school magazine, *The Hurst Johnian*.
3. See, for example, Jones, A.E. (1975) *A Small School in the Great War. The Story of Sutton County School and its Old Boys in World War I* (published by the author).
4. See Hollis, C. (1960) *Eton: A History*, London: Hollis and Carter.
5. See Larrett, W.D. (1966) *A History of the King's School Peterborough*, Peterborough: Old Petriburgians Association.
6. See Pearson, R. (2010) *The Boys of Shakespeare's School in the First World War*, Stroud: The History Press.
7. May, T. (1975) *The History of the Harrow County School for Boys* (published by the school).
8. Marwick, A. (1965) *The Deluge: British Society and the First World War*, London: Macmillan.
9. See Dikotter, F. (2010; 2011 edn) *Mao's Great Famine*, London: Bloomsbury, p.xv.
10. Oral testimony from the home front is generally more elusive than that from Great War combat veterans. See Emden, R. van and Humphries, S. (2003) *All Quiet on the Home Front. An Oral History of Life in Britain During the First World War*, London: Headline Book Publishing, p.xiii.
11. This book contains many examples of schooling in England, Wales and Scotland, but far fewer from Ireland, an acknowledged deficiency which the author hopes to rectify in future volumes in the *Schooling and the Great War* trilogy.

Prologue

1. May (1975) p.65.

Introduction

1. Harrow County School for Boys later became part of the current Harrow High School.
2. My paternal grandfather, Richard Blades, enlisted in the army in 1914, witnessing 'things a boy should never have seen'. My great uncle Horace Groom enlisted at the same time and died on the Western Front in October 1918. For a good example of a family history of the Great War see Whithorn, D.P. (2003) *Bringing Uncle Albert Home. A Soldier's Tale*, Stroud: Sutton Publishing Ltd.
3. See, for example, Gilbert, M. (1994; 2004 edn) *The First World War. A Complete History*, New York: Holt Paperbacks.
4. See Cooper, S. (2012) *The Final Whistle. The Great War in Fifteen Players*, Stroud: The History Press.
5. See Carlyon, L. (2001; 2003 edn) *Gallipoli*, London: Bantam Books.
6. See Holborn, M. (Ed.) (2013) *The Great War*, London: Imperial War Museum and Jonathan Cape.
7. See Arthur, M. (2002; 2003 edn) *Forgotten Voices of the Great War*, London: Ebury Press.
8. See Walter, G. (Ed.) *The Penguin Book of First World War Poetry*, London: Penguin Books Ltd.
9. Blunden, E. (1928; 2010 edn)) *Undertones of War*, London: Penguin Classics; Brittain, V. (1933; 1998 edn) *Testament of Youth. An Autobiographical Study of the Years 1900–1925*, London: Virago; Graves, R. (1929; 2000 edn) *Goodbye to All That*, London: Penguin Classics.

10. Patch, H. and Emden, R. van (2007; 2009 edn) *The Last Fighting Tommy. The Life of Harry Patch, Last Veteran of the Trenches*, London: Bloomsbury.
11. See Joan Littlewood and Theatre Workshop (1963) *Oh What a Lovely War*.
12. See Faulks, S. (1993) *Birdsong*, London: Hutchinson.
13. BBC television programme *Blackadder* by Richard Curtis and Ben Elton, Series 4: *Blackadder Goes Forth*.
14. Barthes, R. (1957; 2009 edn) *Mythologies*, London: Vintage.
15. Winter, J.M. (1986; 1987 edn) *The Great War and the British People*, London: Macmillan Education Ltd, p.71.
16. Todman, D. (2005) *The Great War. Myth and Memory*, London: Hambledon and London, p.3.
17. Sheffield, G.D. (2000) *Forgotten Victory. The First World War. Myths and Realities*, London: Headline Book Publishing.
18. Winter (1986) p.1.
19. See, for example, Marlow, J. (1995; 2005 edn) *The Virago Book of Women and the Great War*, London: Virago; Grayzel, S.R. (2002) *Women and the First World War*, Harlow: Pearson Education Ltd.
20. Paxman, J. (2013) *Great Britain's Great War*, London: Viking.
21. Gregory, A. (2008) *The Last Great War. British Society and the First World War*, Cambridge: Cambridge University Press, p.292.
22. Colm Toibin article in *The Guardian* 10.08.2013.
23. Arthur (2002) p.1.
24. Parker, P. (1987; 2007 edn) *The Old Lie. The Great War and the Public School Ethos*, London: Hambledon Continuum.
25. Seldon, A. and Walsh, D. (2013) *Public Schools and the Great War. The Generation Lost*, Barnsley: Pen & Sword Military.
26. Seldon and Walsh (2013) p.6.
27. Pearson (2010); Oakes, J. (2009) *Kitchener's Lost Boys: From the Playing Fields to the Killing Fields*, Stroud: The History Press; Hilliam, D. (Ed) (2011) *Tig's Boys: Letters to Sir, From the Trenches*, Stroud: The History Press.
28. See Lowe, R. (Ed.) (1993) *Education and the Second World War. Studies in Schooling and Social Change*, London: The Falmer Press; Mayall, B. and Morrow, V. (2011) *You Can Help Your Country. English Children's Work During the Second World War*, London: Institute of Education.
29. Seldon and Walsh (2013) p.6.
30. Dikotter (2010) p.xvii.
31. Gregory (2008) p.8; Payton, P. (2012) *Regional Australia and the Great War. The Boys from Old Kio*, Exeter: Exeter University Press, p.xv.
32. See, for example, the Harrow County School for Boys and Harrow High School archive www.jeffreymaynard.com/harrow-county; the Garton Archive at Lincoln Christ's Hospital School www.christs-hospital.lincs.sch.uk; the Manchester High School for Girls Archive www.mhsgarchive.org
33. Dixon, C.J. (2006) *This Saddening List: The 1st World War Memorial, King Edward VII School King's Lynn*, Norwich: Gatehouse Press.

Chapter 1: Ante-bellum

1. May (1975) pp.19–34.
2. Maclure, J.S. (1979) *Educational Documents, England and Wales 1816–1968*, London: Methuen, pp.149–153.
3. Blades, B.A. (2003) 'Deacon's School, Peterborough, 1902–1920: a Study of the Social and Economic Function of Secondary Schooling', unpublished PhD thesis, University of London Institute of Education.
4. Aldrich, R. (1996) *Education for the Nation*, London: Cassell, p.87.
5. May (1975) p.43.
6. Smith, D. (1982) *Conflict and Compromise. Class Formation in English Society 1830–1914. A Comparative Study of Birmingham and Sheffield*, London: Routledge & Kegan Paul, p.105.

7. Blades (2003) p.158.
8. Wiener, M.J. (1981) *English Culture and the Decline of the Industrial Spirit, 1850–1980*, Cambridge: Cambridge University Press, p.132.
9. Mangan, J.A. (1983) 'Imitating Their Betters and Disassociating from Their Inferiors: Grammar Schools and the Games Ethic in the Late Nineteenth and Early Twentieth Centuries' in N. Parry and D. McNair (Eds) *The Fitness of the Nation*, Leicester: History of Education Society.
10. King, B. (1990) *P.G.S.G. A History 1905–1946. Cheltenham's Other Girls' School*, Cheltenham: Barbara King.
11. Wellingborough County High School advertisement. The school was founded in 1907 and administered by Northamptonshire County Council from 1911.
12. www.mhsgarchive.org
13. Foreword by Sir Michael Howard in Seldon and Walsh (2013) p.xii.
14. Seldon and Walsh (2013) p.11. HMC consisted of thirteen founder members in 1869, rising to 114 member schools in 1914.
15. See Seldon and Walsh (2013) pp.255–260.
16. Seldon and Walsh (2013) p.15. Of the 114 headteacher members of HMC in 1914, 92 were classicists.
17. Aldrich (1996) p.30.
18. Waugh, E. (1964; 1983 edn) *A Little Learning. The First Volume of an Autobiography*, London: Methuen, p.131.
19. Girouard, M. (1981) *The Return to Camelot: Chivalry and the English Gentleman*, London: Yale University Press, p.270.
20. Girouard (1981) p.176.
21. Girouard (1981) p.169.
22. Heward, C. (1988) *Making a Man of Him: Parents and Their Sons' Education at an English Public School 1929–50*, London: Routledge, pp.52–54.
23. Kipling, R. (1902) *The Islanders*, published in *The Times* 04.02.1902.
24. Treadwell, P. (1983) 'The Games Mania – The Cult of Athleticism in the Late Victorian Public School' in *History of Education Society Bulletin*, 32, 24–32.
25. Mangan (1983) p.1.
26. Sherington, G. (1983) *Shore: a History of Sydney Church of England Grammar School*, Sydney: Allen and Unwin, p.63.
27. Aldrich (1996) p.30; Treadwell (1983) p.26.
28. Arthur, M. (2005; 2006 edn) *Last Post. The Final Word from our First World War Soldiers*, London: Orion Books Ltd, p.60.
29. Hanson, N. (2005; 2007 edn) *The Unknown Soldier. The Story of the Missing of the Great War*, London: Corgi Books, p.285.
30. Huggins, M.J.W. (1982) *The Making of an English Public School*, Tedburn St Mary: Hiroona Publications, pp.68–71.
31. *Monmouthian* magazine April 1906 www.monmouthschool.org
32. Parker (1987) p.31.
33. Seldon and Walsh (2013) p.21.
34. Upland House 1908 *Annual Record* www.espmandewellhistoryexplorer.org.uk
35. Burton Grammar School www.burtongrammar.co.uk
36. Alderman, G. (1972) *The History of Hackney Downs School, Formerly the Grocers' Company's School*, London: The Clove Club, p.32.
37. Lees, T.C. (1947) *A Short History of Northampton Grammar School 1541–1941*, Northampton: The Swan Press, pp.75–76.
38. Dunlop, A.D. (1992) *Hutcheson's Grammar. The History of a Glasgow School*, Glasgow: Hutcheson's Educational Trust, pp.90–91.
39. Waugh, E. (1964, 1983 edn) *A Little Learning. The First Volume of an Autobiography*, London: Methuen, p.132.

40. Arthur (2005) p.28.
41. Emden, R. van (2005) *Boy Soldiers of the Great War*, London: Headline, p.14.
42. Graham, J.A. and Phythian, B.A. (1965) *The Manchester Grammar School 1515–1965*, Manchester: Manchester University Press, p.101.
43. *Nottingham High School for Girls*, GPDST publication, p.20.
44. Simon, B. (1977) 'The 1902 Education Act – a Wrong Turning', *History of Education Society Bulletin*, 19, 7–14, p.8.
45. Marwick (1965) p.23.
46. Waites, B. (1987) *A Class Society at War. England 1914–1918*, Leamington Spa: Berg Publishers Ltd, p.265.
47. Gregory (2008) p.278.
48. Aldrich, R. (2013) 'The British and Foreign School Society, Past and Present', *History of Education Researcher*, 91, 5–12, p.10; See also UCL Institute of Education blog articles by Green, A. (28.10.2013), et al.
49. Sanderson, M. (1987*) Educational Opportunity and Social Change in England*, London: Faber and Faber, p.18.
50. Armytage, W.H.G. (1970, 2nd edn) *Four Hundred Years of English Education*, Cambridge: Cambridge University Press, p.186.
51. Simon (1965) p.252 refers to the TUC resolution of 1905 condemning the 1902 Act and subsequent Regulations and demanding 'the formulation of an educational programme based upon the principles of equal opportunities for all'.
52. Blythe, R. (1969; 1978 edn) *Akenfield*, Harmondsworth: Penguin Books Ltd, pp.34–35.
53. Arthur (2005) pp.8, 14, 43.
54. Wright, S. (2012) 'Teachers, Family and Community in the Urban Elementary School: Evidence from English School Log Books c.1880–1918', *History of Education*, 41, 2, 155–173, p.155.
55. Thompson, F. (1945; 2008 edn) *Lark Rise to Candleford*, London: Penguin Books, p.254.
56. Arthur (2005) p.21.
57. Peterborough Practising School Logbook.
58. Simpson, L. (1984) 'Imperialism, National Efficiency and Education, 1900–1905', *Journal of Educational Administration and History*, 14, 1, 28–35, pp.33–34.
59. Marsden, W.E. (2000) 'Poisoned History: a Comparative Study of Nationalism, Propaganda and the Treatment of War and Peace in the Late Nineteenth and Early Twentieth Century School Curriculum', *History of Education*, 29, 1, 29–47, pp.29–32.
60. Ferguson, N. (1988) *The Pity of War, 1914–1918*, London: Penguin Books, p.201, refers to the 'relentless exposure' to nationalistic ideas and sentiment throughout the curriculum.
61. Peterborough Practising School Logbook.
62. Emden (2005) p.12.
63. Marsden, W.E. (1991) *Educating the Respectable: a Study of Fleet Road Board School, Hampstead, 1879–1903*, London: Woburn Press, p.151.
64. Dronfield Junior School Logbook.
65. Blythe (1969) p.39.
66. Lowe (1999) 'Education and National Identity', *History of Education*, 28, 3, 231–233, p.231.
67. Emden (2005) p.13.
68. Hornby School Logbook: 24 May 1907.
69. Dronfield Junior School Logbook.
70. Blythe (1969) p.169.
71. Emden (2005) p.13.
72. Stibbington School Logbook, in Cambridgeshire Environmental Education Service (2002) *Stibbington School Remembered, 1872–1982*, Peterborough: CEES.
73. St Nicholas Boys' School Logbook: 14 Febuary 1913.
74. Hornby School Logbook.

75. Corr, H. (2008) *Changes in Educational Policies in Britain, 1800–1920. How Gender Inequalities Reshaped the Teaching Profession*, New York: The Edwin Mellen Press, p.205.
76. Dyhouse, C. (2000) 'Good Wives and Little Mothers. Social Anxieties and the Schoolgirl's Curriculum' in R. Lowe (Ed.) (2000), *History of Education Major Themes*, London: Routledge Falmer, pp.437–438.
77. Marsden (1991) pp.xi, 216, 218, 234.
78. Simpson (1984) p.33.
79. Hurt, J.S. (1977) 'Drill, Discipline and the Elementary School Ethos', in P. McCann (Ed.) (1977) *Popular Education and Socialization in the Nineteenth Century*, London: Methuen, pp.170–176.
80. Jenkins, H.J.K. (1978) *A School in Woodston, 1728–1978*, Peterborough: St Augustine's School, p.28.
81. Penn, A. (1999) *Targeting Schools: Drill, Militarism and Imperialism*, London: Woburn Press, p.6.
82. Penn (1999) p.11.
83. Board of Education (1909) *The Syllabus of Physical Exercises for Public Elementary Schools*, London: HMSO.
84. www.workhouses.org.uk/trainingships
85. www.childrenshomes.org.uk/TSArethusa
86. *Night and Day* (1902) www.barnardos.org.uk
87. Storey, N.R. (2008) *Norfolk in the Great War. A Pictorial History*, Wellington: Halsgrove, p.10.
88. *The West Australian* 06.05.2011 p.4. Originally from the village of Wyre Piddle in Worcestershire, Claude travelled to Australia after the war and later served in the Royal Australian Naval Service.
89. www.workhouses.org.uk/trainingships
90. www.kibble.org/history
91. Betts, R. (1984) 'The Samuelson Commission of 1881–1884 and English Technical Education', *History of Education Society Bulletin*, 34, 40–52, pp.40, 46.
92. Daglish, N. (1998) 'Over By Christmas: The First World War, Education Reform and the Economy. The Case of Christopher Addison and the Origins of the DSIR', *History of Education*, 27, 3, 315–331, p.319.
93. Simpson (1984) p.28.
94. Simpson (1984) p.29.
95. Bernbaum, G. (1967) *Social Change and the Schools*, London: Routledge and Kegan Paul, pp.3–4.
96. Betts, R. (1984) p.30; Gordon, P. (1980) *Selection For Secondary Education*, London: Woburn Press, p.144.
97. Daglish (1998) p.319.
98. Blades (2003) p.251.
99. Sanderson, M. (1999) *Education and Economic Decline in Britain, 1870 to the 1890s*, Cambridge: Cambridge University Press, pp.28–29.
100. Sanderson, M. (1994) *The Missing Stratum: Technical School Education in England 1900–1990s*, London: Athlone Press, pp.21–24.
101. Jenkins, E.W. (1987) 'Junior Technical Schools, 1905–1945: the Case of Leeds', *History of Education*, 16, 2, 105–117, p.109.
102. McCulloch, G. (1989) *The Secondary Technical School. A Useable Past?*, Lewes: Falmer Press, p.31.
103. Soke of Peterborough Junior Technical School Admission Register, 1913–14.
104. Dent, H.C. (1970) *1870–1970. Century of Growth in English Education*, London: Longman, p.74.
105. Jenkins (1987) p.109.
106. Patch & Emden (2007) p.39.
107. Oakes (2009) p.48.
108. www.archive.spectator.co.uk/article/3rd-november-1906/9/the-girls-realm-annual

109. Parker (1987) p.18.
110. Hynes, S. (1990) *A War Imagined. The First World War and English Culture*, London: Pimlico, p.46.
111. Parker (1987) p.140.
112. Mangan (2000) pp.546–552.
113. Parker (1987) p.68.
114. Burk, K. (2000) *Troublemaker. The Life and History of A.J.P. Taylor*, Newhaven and London: Yale University Press, p.17.
115. Fifteen million toy soldiers were produced annually in Britain before 1914. Brown, K.D. www.museumofchildhood.org.uk/whats-on/exhibitions-and-displays/war-games/war-games-perspectives/toy-soldiers-and-the-first-world-war
116. Parker (1987) p.145.
117. Robb, G. (2002) *British Culture and the First World War*, Basingstoke: Palgrave, p.175.
118. Beckett, I.F.W. (1985) 'The Nation in Arms, 1914–1919', in I.F.W. Beckett and P. Simpson (Eds) (1985) *A Nation in Arms. A Social Study of the British Army in the First World War*, Manchester: Manchester University Press, pp. 4–5.
119. Ferguson (1998) p.4.

Chapter 2: Roll of Honour
1. May (1975) pp.65–66.
2. Hill, C.P. (1951) *The History of Bristol Grammar School*, London: Pitman, p.186.
3. St Gregory's School Chorley Logbook.
4. Marlow (1999) pp.25–26.
5. Dunlop (1992) p.92.
6. Lloyd, H.S. (1996) *The History of Aberystwyth County School (Ardwyn), 1896–1973*, Aberystwyth: The Ardwinian Association, p.83.
7. Emden, R. van (2013) *Meeting the Enemy. The Human Cost of the Great War*, London: Bloomsbury, pp.20–21.
8. Seldon and Walsh (2013) p.29.
9. Sargant, W.L. (1928) *The Book of Oakham School*, Cambridge: Cambridge University Press, p.51.
10. Bromwich, D. (1990) *King's College, Taunton. The First Hundred Years, 1880–1990*, p.21.
11. Arthur (2005) p.211.
12. Arthur (2005) p.151.
13. Seldon & Walsh (2013) p.30.
14. Members of the Shrewsbury School OTC subsequently paid a heavy price for their involvement in the Great War. See www.shropshirestar.com/news/great-war/2014/07/28/
15. Sir Michael Howard in his Foreword to Seldon and Walsh (2013) p.xii.
16. Wheatley, D. (1981) *The Time Has Come. An Autobiography*, London: Arrow Books Ltd, p.246.
17. Clark, C. (2012; 2013 edn) *The Sleepwalkers. How Europe Went to War in 1914*, London: Penguin Books, p.490.
18. Clark (2012).
19. Ferguson (1998) p.80.
20. Clark (2012) p.550.
21. Simkins, P. (1988; 2007 edn) *Kitchener's Army. The Raising of the New Armies 1914–1916*, Barnsley: Pen & Sword Military, p.75.
22. Terraine, J. (1965; 1997 edn) *The Great War*, Ware: Wordsworth Editions Ltd, p.60. By September 1915 the number of recruits had risen to 2,257,521.
23. Pennell, C. (2012) 'Rethinking British Volunteerism in 1914. A Rush to the Colours?', in *First World War: New Perspectives, Episode 2* www.podcasts.ox.ac/series/first-world-war
24. Ferguson (1998) p.201.
25. Pennell (2012).
26. Gregory (2008) p.2.

27. Gilbert (1994) p.63.
28. Gregory (2008) p.23.
29. Ferguson (1998) p.203.
30. Patch and Emden (2007) pp.55–58.
31. Ferguson (1998) pp.205–206.
32. Gregory (2008) p.13.
33. Ferguson (1998) p.199.
34. Gregory (2008) p.81.
35. Gregory (2008) pp.55, 58.
36. Ferguson (1998) pp.198–199.
37. Wright, C. (1985) *The Kent College Canterbury Book*, London: B.T. Batsford Ltd, p.40.
38. Brooke, R. (1914) *Peace*, line 1: 'Now, God be thanked Who has matched us with His hour'.
39. Beardwood, H.E. (1952) *The History of Colfe's Grammar School 1652–1952*, London: London University Press, p.130.
40. www.museumvictoria.co.au/ww1/stateschools
41. Gray, D.P. (2006) *The Uncommon Soldiers. Peterborough and District in 1914*, (published by the author), p.55.
42. Seldon and Walsh (2013) pp.31–32.
43. Douglas-Smith, A.E. (1965) *The City of London School*, Oxford: Basil Blackwell, p.336.
44. Seldon and Walsh (2013) p.31.
45. Cornwell, J. (2005) *King Ted's. A Biography of King Edward VII School Sheffield 1905–2005*, (published by the school), p.87.
46. www.pals.org.uk/sheffield
47. Seldon & Walsh ((2013) p.31.
48. Ives, A.G. (1970) *Kingswood School in Wesley's Day and Since*, London: Epworth Press, p.191.
49. Seldon and Walsh (2013) p.30.
50. Dunlop (1992) p.91.
51. Deacon's School Archive.
52. Gray (2006) p.121.
53. Gray (2006) p.130.
54. Gray (2006) pp.36–38.
55. Ferguson (1998) p.444.
56. www.birdbrook.net
57. Lloyd (1996) p.84.
58. Lloyd (1996) p.84.
59. www.monikie.org.uk
60. *The War Pictorial*, August 1918, p.34.
61. www.ww1.pgassociation.org.uk
62. Extract from McIlrath, H. *Larne Grammar School: the First Hundred Years* www.larne-in-ww1.irishgenealogy.net
63. Lloyd (1996) p.85.
64. May (1975) p.70.
65. Glover, E.P. (1957) *The First Sixty Years 1896–1956. The Newport High School for Boys*, Newport: R.H. Johns, p.30.
66. Ferguson (1998) pp.202–201.
67. Lewis-Stempel, J. (2010) *Six Weeks. The Short and Gallant Life of the British Officer in the First World War*: London: Weidenfeld and Nicholson, p.29.
68. Seldon & Walsh (2013) pp.254–261.
69. www.christcollegebrecon.com
70. www.winchester-house.org/History-of-the-School
71. www.roll-of-honour.com
72. Messenger, C. (2006) *Call-to-Arms. The British Army 1914–1918*, London: Cassell, p.293.
73. Seldon and Walsh (2013) p.13.

74. *The Captain* Volume XXVII 1912, p.76.
75. Sherriff, R.C. (1929; 2000 edn) *Journey's End*, London: Penguin Books.
76. Deacon's School Archive.
77. IWM *Searchlight* www.iwm.org.uk
78. Bannerman, C. (1999) *Further Up Stephen's Brae. The Midmill's Era at Inverness Royal Academy 1895–1979*, Inverness: St Michael's Publishing, p.19. *The Inverness Academical* 'War Service' issue June 1916.
79. Cornwell (2005) p.87.
80. Bolam, D.W. (1952) *Unbroken Community: The Story of the Friends' School Saffron Walden 1702–1952*, (published by the school), p.150.
81. Brooks, R. (1998) *King Alfred School and the Progressive Movement 1898–1998*, Cardiff: University of Wales Press, p.64.
82. Wake, R. and Denton, P. (1993) *Bedales School. The First Hundred Years*, London: The Haggerston Press, p.67.
83. Attributed to Trotsky, but possibly a mis-quotation.
84. A phrase used by Winston Churchill at the Guildhall in London on 9 November 1914.
85. Hornby School Logbook: 19 January 1906.
86. Wilks, H.C. (1979) *George Green's School, 1828–1978. A History*, London: Edward Arnold, p.60.
87. Gray (2006) pp.68, 17.
88. Board of Education letter to LEAs 8 January 1915.
89. Parker (2007) pp.240–241.
90. Board of Education (1915) *Report of the Board of Education for the year 1913–1914*, London: HMSO, pp.3–4.
91. Boville, M.K. (1986) *East Boldon School Centenary 1885–1995*, (published by the school), p.4.
92. Board of Education (1915)*Report of the Board of Education for the year 1913–1914*, London: HMSO, pp.3–4.
93. King, W. (1992) *Towards the Light. The Story of Cardiff High School for Boys 1898–1970*, Llanharan: Pallas Press, pp.62–63.
94. Kennedy, G. (1951) *The Story of Morpeth Grammar School*, Newcastle: The Old Boys' Association, p.90.
95. Lloyd (1996) p.88.
96. May (1975) p.93.
97. Davies, K. (1989) *The History of Fiddington Village School*, Fiddington History Circle, p.273.
98. Harrop, S. (1998) *The Merchant Taylors' School for Girls, Crosby. One Hundred Years of Achievement, 1888–1998*, Liverpool: Liverpool University Press, p.63.
99. Scott, F.W., Sutton, A. and King, N.J. (1992) *Hymers College. The First 100 Years*, Beverley: Highgate Publications Ltd, p.56.
100. Dickinson, P.G.M. and Jamieson, A. (1965) *The History of Huntingdon Grammar School*, (published by the school), p.23.
101. Deacon's School Archive.
102. Alderman (1972) p.32.
103. Board of Education (1915) *Report of the Board of Education for the year 1913–1914*, London: HMSO, pp.3–4.
104. Sheils, S. (2007) *Among Friends. The Story of the Mount School York*, London: James and James, p.67.
105. Later Lincoln School, now Lincoln Christ's Hospital School.
106. Lincoln GS returned to the original Wragby Road site in 1920.
107. www.rusholmearchive.org
108. www.mhsgarchive.org
109. Board of Education (1915) *Report of the Board of Education for the year 1913–1914*, London: HMSO, pp.3–4.
110. www.btinternet.com/james.fanning/newhaven
111. www.litherland-digital.co.uk

112. BBC *World War One at Home* www.bbc.co.uk/programmes/#p01qmh7f; www.nottinghamshire. gov.uk/rollofhonour
113. Newark School Peterborough Logbook: 17 November 1914, in Horswood, J. (1979) *A History of Newark School, Oxney Road, Peterborough*, Peterborough: The Teacher's Centre.
114. Brennan, P.J. (1997) *A History of the Cardinal Vaughan Memorial School 1914–1997*, Henley on Thames: Gresham Books Limited, p.13.
115. Sutton, R. (1959) *The Herbert Strutt School, Belper, 1909–1959*, (published by the school), pp.37–38.
116. St Nicholas Boys' School Logbook.
117. Sturges, G.W. (1958) *The Silver Link, Being a Short History of Huxley County Secondary School, formerly Silver Street Senior Boys' School, Edmonton, Middlesex 1901–1957*, (published by the school), p.11.
118. Peterborough Practising School Logbook.
119. www.winchester-house.org/History-of-the-School
120. Alston-Watson, G. (1941) *Ayton School Centenary History 1841–1941*, (published by the school), p.49.

Chapter 3: On Campaign

1. BBC *World War One at Home* www.bbc.co.uk/programmes/p01rjft9
2. Francombe, D.C.R. and Coult, D.E. (1937) *Bancroft's School, 1737–1937*, (published by the authors), p.94.
3. Gray (2006) p.43.
4. Emden (2005) pp.30–31.
5. *Cathedralian*, vol. 1, no. 4, Michaelmas 1914 in Collard, J., Ogden, D. and Burgess, R. (1992) *Where the Fat Black Canons Dined. A History of Bristol Cathedral School, 1140 to 1992*, (published by the school), p.59.
6. Myers, K. (2001) 'The Hidden History of Refugee Schoooling in Britain: the Case of the Belgians, 1914–1918', *History of Education*, 30, 2, 153–162.
7. Storr, K. (2003) 'Belgian Children's Education in Britain in the Great War: Language, Identity and Race Relations', *History of Education Researcher*, 72, 84–93, p.92.
8. Storr (2003) p.86.
9. Spinks, M. (2004) *Heads and tales. A History of Badsey Schools*, Badsey: The Badsey Society, p.72.
10. Palmer, B. (1999) *School in Barnack. A Short History*, (published by the school).
11. Waszack, P. (1984) *Roman Catholic Schools in Peterborough. A History*, Peterborough: Peterborough Arts Council, pp.12–14.
12. Alderman (1972) p.33.
13. Gilchrist, W.J.M. (1973) 'History of Gowerton Intermediate School, Glamorgan' in G. Bennett (Ed.) *Something Attempted, Something Done*, Llandybie: Christopher Davies (Publishers) Ltd, p.56.
14. Lloyd (1996) p.84.
15. Sutton (1959) p.39.
16. Seldon and Walsh (2013) pp.91–92.
17. Storr (2003) p.87.
18. Brennan (1997) p.13.
19. Myers (2001) pp.160–161.
20. Waszack (1984) p.14.
21. Storr (2003) p.90.
22. Barrès-Barker, M.C. (2007) *'Our Belgian Guests' – Refugees in Brent, 1914–1919*, Brent: Brent Archives 2010, pp.13–18 www.brent.gov.uk/museumarchive
23. BBC *World War One at Home* www.bbc.co.uk/programmes/p01qcrz
24. St Nicholas Boys' School Logbook.
25. Gray (2006) pp.59, 80.
26. Sheils (2007) p.68.

27. Reading, L. and Housley, D. (2006) *100 Years at City Road – A History of the George Dixon Secondary Schools, Birmingham*, (published by the school), p.23.
28. Storr (2003) p.84.
29. Moran (1994) p.273.
30. Waugh (1964) p.88.
31. The total number of public school pupils on roll in 1914, colated from figures in Seldon and Walsh (2013) pp.255–260, was 51,559.
32. Figures extrapolated from Board of Education (1915) *Report of the Board of Education for the year 1913–1914*, London: HMSO, pp.66, 76, 89, 99.
33. Gaskin, C., Vlaeminke, M. and Gaskin, K. (1998) *Moseley into the Millenium. The Story of Moseley School*, Studley: Brewin Books, p.44.
34. Francombe and Coult (1937) p.95.
35. Ysgol Sychdyn Logbook.
36. Lloyd (1996) p.88.
37. Bilton, D. (2003) *The Home Front in the Great War. Aspects of the Conflict 1914–1918*, Barnsley: Leo Cooper (Pen & Sword Books Ltd), p.158.
38. Davies, J.I. (1989) *The Caernavon County School. A History*, Caernavon: Gwynedd Archives and Museums Service, pp.257–258.
39. Spinks (2004) p.72.
40. Barnack School Logbook.
41. Boville (1986) p.5.
42. Payton (2012) p.73.
43. Hornby School Logbook.
44. Bannerman (1999) pp.27, 30.
45. Boville (1986) p.4.
46. St Nicholas Boys' School Logbook.
47. Wilks (1979) p.61.
48. Palmer (1999).
49. Wilks (1979) p.61.
50. Harrison, W. (1979) *Greenhill School, Tenby, 1896–1964*, Cardiff: University of Wales Press, p.222.
51. Dare, D. (1996) *The Unknown Founder. The Story of Helston Grammar School from 1550–1972*, Truro: Kelynen Publications, p.81.
52. St Nicholas Boys' School Logbook.
53. Chadderton, J.F. (1964) *Barrow Grammar School for Boys 1880–1960, an Informal Chronicle*, Barrow: James Milner Ltd, p.61.
54. Reading and Housley (2006) p.24.
55. Ferguson (1998) p.446.
56. Gray (2006) p.91.
57. St Nicholas Boys' School Logbook.
58. Clark, P.L. (1988) *Seventy Five Years. A History of Bacup and Rawtenstall Grammar School*, p.19 www.brgs.me/alumni/archives_history
59. Garside, B. (1957) *A Brief History of Hampton School, 1557–1957*, Richmond: Dimblebys, p.70.
60. Watson, N. (2000) *And Their Works Do Follow Them. The Story of North London Collegiate School*, London: James & James, p.61.
61. Norwich High School (1950) *Norwich High School, 1875–1950*, Norwich Goose Press, p.71.
62. Dunlop (1992) p.92.
63. Watson (2000) p.62.
64. Kirby, J.A. and Knight, P.M. (1985) 'Haberdashers' Aske's Hatcham Girls' School' in L.E. Ingerfield and M.B. Alexander 1985) *A Short History of Haberdashers' Aske's Hatcham Boys' School*, London: The Worshipful Company of Haberdashers, p.41.
65. Chadderton (1964) p.61.
66. Harrop (1988) p.65.

67. Kirby and Knight (1985) p.41.
68. Board of Education (1918) *Report of the Board of Education for the year 1916–1917*, London: HMSO, p.19.
69. www.wsch.eu/first-world-war
70. Norwich High School (1950), pp.69–70.
71. Gray (2006) p.73.
72. Merson, E. (1979) *Once There Was ... The Village School*, Southampton: Paul Cave Publications Ltd, p.76.
73. Ysgol Sychdyn Logbook: 21 October 1915; 10 January 1916.
74. Harrop (1988) p.65.
75. Parker (2007) p.77.
76. Beardwood (1952) p.134.
77. www.wsch.eu/first-world-war
78. www.wsch.eu/first-world-war
79. Norwich High School (1950).
80. Alderman (1972) p.32.
81. Watson (2000) p.61.
82. Waites (1987) p.273.
83. Fussell, P. (1975; 2000 edn) *The Great War and Modern Memory*, New York: Oxford University Press, p.66.
84. Nyazi, M. (1994) *The Best Days of Their Lives. A History of Busbridge School, Godalming, Founded 1 March 1868*, Godalming: Busbridge Books, p.60.
85. CEES (2002) p.12.
86. www.btinternet.com/~james.fanning/newhaven
87. Spinks (2004) p.72.
88. Parker (2007) pp.63, 71.
89. www.wsch.eu/first-world-war
90. Barnack School Logbook: 11 October 1917.
91. Board Of Education (1917) *Report of the Board of Education for the year 1915–1916*, London: HMSO, p.11.
92. St Nicholas Boys' School Logbook.
93. Board Of Education (1918) *Report of the Board of Education for the year 1916–1917*, London: HMSO, p.19.
94. Board Of Education (1919) *Report of the Board of Education for the year 1917–1918*, London: HMSO, p.3.
95. www.newbattleatwar.com
96. www.caldicott.com/magazinespring1918
97. Brown, C. (1989) *The Georgetown Schools (1877–1989)*, (published by the school), p.33.

Chapter 4: Lessons in War

1. Tropp, A. (1957) *The School Teachers. The Growth of the Teaching Profession in England and Wales from 1800 to the Present Day*, London: William Heinemann Ltd, p.208.
2. Lempriere, W. (1924) *A History of the Girls' School of Christ's Hospital, London, Hoddesdon and Hertford*, Cambridge: Cambridge University Press, p.77.
3. Brown, W.E. and Poskitt, F.R. (1976) *The History of Bolton School*, (published by the school), p.150.
4. Osmond, S.E. (1994) *A History of Calton Road Schools*, Parkend: Thornhill Press, p.36.
5. Broadway, C.M. and Buss, E.I. (1982) *The History of the School: 1882 B.G.M.S – D.A.H.S. 1982*, Luton: White Crescent Press Ltd, pp.42–43.
6. www.mhsgarchive.org; Lees (1947) p.90.
7. Douglas-Smith (1965) pp.389–392.
8. Sutton (1959) pp.40–41.
9. Beardwood (1952) p.133.
10. Lloyd (1996) p.85.

11. Parker (2007) p.81.
12. Martin, J. (1974) *A History of St John the Baptist Church of England Schools, Leicester 1881–1974*, (published by the school), p.97.
13. Corfe, T.H. (1960) *The School on the Hill. An Informal History of King Edward VII Grammar School Melton Mowbray 1910–1960*, (published by the school), p.53.
14. Wilks (1979) p.60.
15. Arthur (2002) p.171.
16. Arthur (2002) p.171.
17. Extracts from the Diary of Piete Kuhr, a 12-year-old schoolgirl from East Prussia, in Palmer, S. and Wallis, S. (2003) *A War in Words*, London: Simon and Schuster, p.4.
18. Beardwood (1952) p.131.
19. Spinks (2004) p.73.
20. Jobson, R. (1977) *The Story of a School*, London: Highgate Primary School, p.29.
21. Northop School Logbook.
22. Davies (1989) p.262.
23. *Amberley Parochial School. The History of a Village School. A Source Book* (1998), (published by the school), pp.86–87.
24. Davies (1989) p.269.
25. Parker (1987) p.273.
26. Pound Lane School Logbook.
27. Blythe (1969) p.171.
28. Parker (2007) p.75.
29. Brown (1989) p.31.
30. Davies (1989) p.273.
31. Martin (1974) p.97.
32. Deacon's School Archive.
33. Beardwood (1952) p.133.
34. Davies (1989) pp.269–270.
35. Chadderton (1964) p.63.
36. *The Bridge*, Midsummer 1917 www.handsworth.bham.sch.uk/history
37. Chadderton (1964) p.63; Cornwell (2005) p.90.
38. Scott-Giles, C.W. and Slater, B.V. (1966) *The History of Emanuel School 1594–1964*, London: Old Emanuel Society, p.128.
39. Garside (1957) p.72.
40. Wright (1985) p.45; Lees (1947) p.80.
41. Geoffrey Barber letters.
42. King (1997) p.159.
43. Cornwell (2005) p.90.
44. St Nicholas Boys' School Logbook.
45. Douglas-Smith (1965) pp.373–374.
46. Harrop (1988).
47. Nyazi (1994) p.58.
48. www.1900s.org.uk/1914-18-ww1-homefront
49. Cornwell (2005) p.87.
50. St Gregory's School Logbook.
51. Barnack School Logbook.
52. Brown (1989) p.33. The children of the Georgetown Schools watched as the Prince of Wales visited Tredegar on 21 February 1918.
53. Boville (1986) p.4. The children of East Boldon School witnessed a review of troops by General French in January 1916.
54. Sturges (1958) p.13.
55. Amberley Parochial School Logbook: 16 September 1915.
56. Blythe (1969) p.171.
57. Corfe (1960) p.48.
58. Amberley Parochial School Logbook: 16 November 1917.

59. Hornby School Logbook: 20 September 1914.
60. St Nicholas Boys' School Logbook.
61. Reading and Housley (2006) p.23.
62. Parker (1987) p.264.
63. Francombe and Coult (1937) p.94.
64. In a similar debate at Harrow County School for Boys the motion that conscientious objection was justifiable in some circumstances was passed by 23 to 18 votes. May (1975) p.69.
65. Lepper, C. (1989) *The Crypt School Gloucester 1539–1989*, Gloucester: Alan Smith Publishing Limited, pp.77–78.
66. King (1997) p.159.
67. Scott-Giles and Slater (1966) p.128.
68. Chadderton (1964) p.62.
69. May (1975) p.69.
70. Francombe and Coult (1937) pp.94, 97.
71. Hynes (1990) p.ix.
72. Smith, L.V., Audoin-Rouzeau, S. and Becker, E. (2003) *France and the Great War, 1914–1918*, Cambridge: Cambridge University Press, p.59.
73. Deal, T.E. and Kennedy, A.A. (1983) 'Culture and School Performance', *Educational Leadership*, 5, 14–15, 40.
74. Silver, P. and Silver, H. (1974) *The Education of the Poor. The History of a National School 1824–1974*, London: Routledge and Paul, p.150.
75. Glover (1957) p.30.
76. Walker, M. (2012) *West Norfolk and King's Lynn High School for Girls 1886 to 1979*, King's Lynn: K.E.S. Publications, p.29.
77. www.btinternet.com/~james.fanning/newhaven
78. Sutton (1959) p.45.
79. Mann, J. (1994) *Highbury Fields. The 'Most Interesting' School in London*, Winchester: Edgely Publications, p.79.
80. Dare (1996) p.81.
81. www.lemsfordhistory.co.uk
82. Hinchcliffe, E. (1974) *Appleby Grammar School – from Chantry to Comprehensive*, Appleby: J. Whitehead & Son Ltd, p.89.
83. Douglas-Smith (1965) p.371.
84. www.mhsgarchive.org
85. www.themanchesters.org/forum; www.wiganworld.co.uk
86. Wilks (1979) p.60.
87. Hill (1951) p.186.
88. WFA Occasional Paper 14 in the Garton Archive www.christs-hospital.linc.sch.uk
89. Peterborough Practising School Logbook: 13 June1916.
90. *The Spectator*, 16.06.1916, p.68.
91. *Hansard* 17.06.1916 5L, col. 921.
92. Gregory (2008) p.263.
93. Robb (2002) p.175.
94. Robb (2002) p.176.
95. From an article first published in the *West Sussex Gazette* 20 February 1997 www.pastimesproject.co.uk; See also Thompson (1945) p.325 on the delights and importance of playing in the countryside.
96. Garside (1957) p.70.
97. May (1975) p.74.
98. *The War Pictorial* (1918).
99. Davies (1989) p.273.
100. *The War Pictorial* (1918).
101. *The Times History of the War* (1918), Chapter CCXV, p265.
102. *The War Pictorial* (1918).
103. *The Times History of the War* (1918), Chapter CCXV, p.253.

Chapter 5: On the Front Line

1. Stott (1960) p.127.
2. The so-called Battle of Fishguard, when French Revolutionary forces landed in February 1797, is often referred to as 'the last invasion of Britain'.
3. BBC *World War One at Home* www.bbc.co.uk/programmes/#p01s4dhc
4. Crouch, D. (1991) *Orleton School. A Brief History*, (publisher unknown), p.6.
5. *The Gaytonian* 1914.
6. Jobson (1977) p.28.
7. Pound Lane School Logbook.
8. www.norfolkinworldwar1.org
9. Scott-Giles and Slater (1966) p.128.
10. Wilks (1979) p.61.
11. Beardwood (1952) p.132.
12. Francombe and Coult (1937) p.102.
13. Wilks (1979) p.65; Hodges, S. (1981) *God's Gift. A Living History of Dulwich College*, London: Heinemann, p.99.
14. Cornwell (2005) p.90.
15. Scott et al (1992) p.60.
16. Tyerman, C. (2000) *A History of Harrow School 1324–1991*, Oxford: Oxford University Press, p.443.
17. Board of Education letter to GPDST 2 February 1915.
18. www.messybeast.com
19. Pike, M. (1960) *The Oak Tree. The Story of Putney High School*, (published by the author), p.35.
20. Sheils (2007) p.70.
21. Estimates of the numbers of German aircraft involved range from fourteen to twenty.
22. Sturges (1958) pp.12–13.
23. www.leytonpast.info
24. This may have been the incident at Cowper Street Foundation School referred to by Hanson, N. (2008; 2009 edn) *First Blitz. The Secret German Plan to Raze London to the Ground in 1918*, London: Corgi Books, p.132.
25. *Daily Sketch* 14 June 1917, pp.1–3.
26. Reminiscences of Jack Brown, a 6-year-old survivor of the North Street School bombing www.bbc.co.uk/learningzone/clips/bombing-civilians-during-world-war-one/12738
27. *The Illustrated War News* 20 June 1917.
28. King, A. (1998) *Memorials of the Great War in Britain. The Symbolism and Politics of Remembrance*, Oxford: Berg, p.199.
29. Hanson (2008) p.126.
30. *The Illustrated War News* 20 June 1917.
31. *Daily Sketch* 14 June 1917, pp.1–3.
32. See Hanson (2008) p.149; Gilbert (1994) p.30.
33. Hanson (2008) p.69.
34. King (1998) p.199.
35. Silver and Silver (1974) p.150.
36. IOE Archives GDS/9/3/1.
37. Hanson (2008) pp.181, 304.
38. Parker (2007) p.56.
39. www.sirjohncasshistory.org
40. Taylor, A.J.P. (1965; 1988 edn) *English History 1914–1945, The Oxford History of England*, Oxford: The Clarendon Press, p.88.
41. Winter, J. (1988; 1995 edn) *The Experience of World War 1*, New York: Oxford University Press, p.102.
42. Gowerton Intermediate School Magazine, for example, in Gilchrist (1973) p.57.
43. Bilton (2003) p.161.

44. Waugh (1964) p.100.
45. Hodges (1981) p.98.
46. May (1975) p.195.
47. Walker (2012) p.30.
48. www.mhsgarchive.org
49. Taylor (1965) p.88.
50. Armour, D.J. (1995) *Felsted Preparatory School. The First 100 Years, 1885–1995*, London: The Athlone Press, p.16.
51. Board of Education *Circular 994*.
52. May (1975) p.73.
53. Waugh (1964) p.115.
54. Hodges (1981) p.98.
55. Scott-Giles and Slater (1966) p.127.
56. Lees (1947) p.80.
57. Parker (2007) p.90.
58. Harrop (1988) p.64.
59. Myhill, J.D. (1991) *Blue Coat. A History of the Bluecoat School, Birmingham, 1722–1990*, Warley: Meridian Books, p.89.
60. Parker (2007) pp.91, 64.
61. St Nicholas Boys' School Logbook. The entry for 24 May 1917 states that the school garden had received Board of Education approval.
62. Silver and Silver (1974) p.150.
63. www.kibble.org/history
64. Green, L. (1992) *A History of the Cowper Testimonial School Hertford*, Hertford: Hertford and Ware Local History Society, p.33.
65. Parker (2007) p.89.
66. www.wshc.eu/blog/item/the-first-world-war-home-front
67. Sutton (1959) p.40.
68. See the account by German schoolboy Heinrich Beutow in Arthur (2002) p.199.
69. Peterborough Practising School Logbook.
70. Gilchrist (1973) p.56.
71. Gaskin et al (1998) p.44.
72. Boyes, M. (1997) *A Cotswolds Village School from Victorian Times*, Cheltenham: The Rissingtons Local History Society, p.93.
73. www.btinternet.com/-james.fanning/newhaven
74. May (1975) p.75.
75. Chadderton (1964) p.63.
76. Thompson (1963) pp.367–368.
77. Horn, P. (1983) 'The Employment of Elementary Schoolchildren in Agriculture, 1914–1918', *History of Education*, 12, 3, 203–15, p.203.
78. Gray (2006) p.50.
79. Horn (1983) p.205.
80. Blythe (1969) p.170.
81. Samphire is an edible plant which grows naturally in some coastal areas.
82. www.levenshistory.co.uk/school
83. *The Times History of the War* (1918) p.256.
84. Parker (2007) p.97.
85. Horn (1983) pp.204–213.
86. Hornby School Logbook.
87. See, for example, Adey, K. (2013) *Fighting on the Home Front. The Legacy of Women in World War One*, London: Hodder & Stoughton Ltd.
88. www.wshc.eu/blog/item/the-first-world-war-home-front
89. Hornby School Logbook, 1915.

90. Pearce, T. (1991) *Then and Now. An Anniversary Celebration of Cheltenham College 1841–1991*, Cheltenham: Old Cheltonian Society, p.126.
91. Seldon and Walsh (2013) p.89.
92. Scott-Giles and Slater (1966) p.127.
93. Beardwood (1952) p.133.
94. www.kibble.org/history
95. Lindsay, K. (1926) *Educational Progress and Social Waste*, London: Routledge.
96. Sanderson (1987); Banks, O. (1955) *Parity and Prestige in English Secondary Education: a Study in Educational Sociology*, London: Routledge and Kegan Paul.
97. Blades (2003) pp.248, 251, 276, 282.
98. Chadderton (1962) p.64.
99. Waites (1987) p.267.
100. Harrop (1988) p.63.
101. Harrison (1979) p.230.
102. *The Illustrated War News* 14 June 1916, p.13.
103. *Sunday Times Online* 10 November 2013.
104. Messenger (2005) p.107.
105. Garside (1957) p.69.
106. Harrison (1979) p.229.
107. Emden (2005) p.49.
108. Emden (2005) p.106.
109. Gilchrist (1973) p.56.
110. Dare (1996) p.80.
111. Kean, H. (1990) *Deeds Not Words. The Lives of Suffragette Teachers*, London: Pluto Press, p.73.
112. Lewis-Stempel (2010).
113. Beardwood (1952) p.131.
114. Tyerman (2000) p.443.
115. Parker (1987) p.268.
116. Scott et al (1992) p.125.
117. Kennedy (1951) p.93.
118. Lees (1947) p.79.
119. Scott et al (1992) pp.125, 56.
120. Hodges (1981) p.99.
121. Francombe and Coult (1937) p.96.
122. Wright (1985) p.44.
123. Sutton (1959) pp.40, 47.
124. May (1975) p.67.
125. Board of Education (1916) *Report of the Board of Education for the year 1914–1915*, London: HMSO, p39.
126. Corfe (1960) pp.46–48.
127. Brown and Poskitt (1976) p.151.
128. Dunlop (1992) p.91.
129. Wilks (1979), pp.61–63.
130. Douglas-Smith (1965) pp.389.
131. Lees (1947) p.79.
132. Scott et al (1992) p.56.
133. Pearce (1991) p.130.
134. Hodges (1981) p.99.
135. Holden, W.H. (Ed) (1950) *The Charterhouse We Knew*, London: British Technical and General Press, p.70.
136. Brown and Poskitt (1976) p.152.
137. Taylor, A.J.P (1983) *A Personal History*, London: Hamish Hamilton, p.29, in Burk (2000) p.21.
138. Armour (1995) p.16.
139. Cloete, S. (1972) *A Victorian Son*, London: Collins, in Emden (2005) p.101.

140. Letter of 10 April 1978 by G.F. Fink in Wilks (1979), p64.
141. Emden (2005) p.308.

Chapter 6: Alma Mater
1. Blunden (1928) pp.144, 148.
2. Parker (1987) p.209.
3. Parker (1987) pp.19, 77.
4. Graves (1929) p.188.
5. *The Crown* Easter 1916 in Reading and Housley (2006) p.23.
6. www.handsworth.bham.sch.uk/history/midsummer-1917
7. May (1975) p.70.
8. www.roll-of-honour.com Lincolnshire: De Aston School.
9. *The Deaconian* Easter 1915. Deacon's School Archive.
10. Gilchrist (1973) pp.55–56.
11. Chadderton (1964) p.66.
12. *Sutton High School Magazine* www.ww1schoolarchives.org/sutton-school
13. Parker (1987) p.198.
14. Scott-Giles and Slater (1966) p.127.
15. Chadderton (1964) p.66; Ferguson (1998), p.221.
16. *White & Blue*, 79, 1916, p.698 at www.worldwar1schoolarchives.org
17. Reading and Housley (2006) p.23.
18. Parker (1987) p.207.
19. Lewis-Stempel (2010) p.18.
20. Chadderton (1964) p.66.
21. Audoin-Rouzeau, S. (1992) *Men At War 1914–1918. National Sentiment and Trench Journalism in France During the First World War*, Oxford: Berg Publishers Ltd, pp.140–142.
22. Clark (1998) p.18.
23. See, for example, Hornby School Logbook entries for 16 and 17 November 1909 referring to the 'Good-byes' of A.E. Thompson and the Kelsall brothers.
24. Northop School Logbook.
25. Oakes, J. and Parsons, M. (2005) *Reading School. The First 800 Years*, Peterborough: DSM, p.62.
26. Holt Schools Logbook in Bucknall, G.V.S. (1976) *Two Into One. Holt Schools 1834–1935*, Holt: Holt Magazine, p.34.
27. Scott-Giles and Slater (1966) pp.127–128.
28. www.kibble.org/history
29. See, for example, Peterborough Practising School Logbook, 14 and 18 November 1914; Northop School Logbook, 22 June 1917; Parker (2007) p.65.
30. Liddle, P.H. (1994) *The Worst Ordeal. Britons at Home and Abroad 1914–1918*, London: Leo Cooper, p.132.
31. Nyazi (1994) p.58.
32. Parker (1987) p.202.
33. Extract from 'Schoolmaster pals died on the Somme', *Shropshire Star*, 1 August 2014.

Chapter 7: Patriots
1. Remarque (1929) pp.15–17.
2. Tyerman (2000) p.43.
3. Jenkins (1978) p.28.
4. Brown and Poskitt (1966) p.150.
5. Kennedy (1951) p.93.
6. Glover (1957) p.30.
7. Scott-Giles and Slater (1966) p.38; Nolan, B. (1989) *The Picture History of King's School, Rochester*, (published by the school), p.24.

8. Cook, R. (1990) *Chipping Campden School 1440–1990*, Shipston on Stour: Peter I. Drinkwater, p.41.
9. www.northopwm.com/mr_richardson
10. Lloyd (1996) p.96.
11. Haines, K. (2005) *'Chevy' Chase ... a Real Mr Chips*, Belfast: Ballymaconaghy Publishing.
12. www.jeffrymaynard.com/Harrow_County
13. Later known as the PFA: The Professional Footballers' Association.
14. Sherborne School Archives.
15. Harrison (1979) p.222
16. Harrison (1979) p.222.
17. Lloyd (1996) p.88.
18. Winter (1986) pp.27–36.
19. Gregory (2008) p.81.
20. Gregory (2008) p.7.
21. The Derby Scheme was introduced in the autumn of 1915. It required eligible men between the ages of eighteen to forty-one who were not in a reserved occupation to declare – or attest – whether they would join the armed forces when called upon to do so. Those who made a positive response became members of the Army Reserve and wore a khaki-coloured armband emblazoned with a crown. Thirty-eight per cent of single men and 54 per cent of married men did not come forward. Conscription was introduced the following year.
22. Bavin, W.D. (1922) *Swindon's War Record*, p.63 in Gregory (2008) p.89.
23. Dewey, P.E. (1984) 'Military Recruiting and the British Labour Force During the First World War', *The Historical Journal*, 27, 1, 199–233, p.215.
24. Dewey (1984) p.220.
25. Board of Education *Circular 926*.
26. Ingerfield, L.E. and Alexander, M.B. (1985) *A Short History of Haberdashers' Aske's Hatcham Boys' School*, London: The Worshipful Company of Haberdashers, pp.20–21.
27. Becket (1985) p.17.
28. Becket, I.F.W. (2002) *The First World War: The Essential Guide to Sources in the UK National Archives*, Kew: Public Record Office, p.123.
29. Lloyd (1996) p.88.
30. Thomas, A.W. (1977) *A History of Nottingham High School 1513–1953*, Nottingham: J. and H. Bell.
31. Harrison (1979) p.224.
32. Board of Education *Circular 971a*.
33. IOE Archive GDS/9/3/1.
34. Board of Trade *Report on the State of Employment in the United Kingdom (1914–1918)* in Dewey (1984) p.205. Comparable figures for all male workers for the same years are 30, 40 and 46 per cent.
35. Brown (1989) p.32.
36. Ross, I. (1988) *Little Grey Partridge. First World War Diary of Ishobel Ross Who Served With the Scottish Women's Hospitals Unit in Serbia*, Aberdeen: The University Press.
37. Lepper (1989) p.76.
38. Beardwood (1952) p.133.
39. Corfe (1960) pp.46–49.
40. Armour (1995) p.82.
41. Brown (1989) pp.31–32.
42. St Nicholas Boys' School Logbook.
43. See also Newark School Logbook in Horswood (1979), and Peterborough Practising School Logbook.
44. Silver Street Senior Boys' School Logbook entry in January 1917, in Sturges (1958).
45. King (1997) p.156.

46. Parker (1987) p.261; Seldon and Walsh (2013) p.110; Kendall, P. (2012) *Aisne 1914: The Dawn of Trench Warfare*, The History Press.
47. A.J.N. Williamson returned to teach at his former school in 1912.
48. *The Captain* March 1915 in Parker (1987) p.261.
49. Bonner, R. (1998) *Wifrith Elstob VC DSO MC. The Manchester Regiment*, Knutsford: Fleur de Lys Publishing Ltd, p.17.
50. www.rushdenheritage.co.uk
51. www.hullwebs.co.uk
52. Peacock, A.J. (Ed) *Gunfire. A Journal of First World War History*, No. 31, pp.2–16, York: Smith & Son (Printers).
53. See Peacock (Ed) p.6.
54. The chart records the number of military awards, not the number of recipients.
55. Lepper (1989) p.76.
56. www.telegraph.co.uk/news/uknews/10649262
57. Dikotter (2010) p.xvii.
58. Hynes (1990) p.57.
59. Seldon and Walsh (2013) p.116.
60. Dare (1996) p.80.
61. Davies (1989) p.271.
62. Seldon and Walsh (2013) pp.117–118.
63. Hollis (1960) pp.296–296.
64. Burke (2000) p.36.
65. Beckett (2002), p.123.
66. Lloyd (1996) pp.94–95.
67. Holmes (1963) p.69.
68. Dunlop (1992) p.92.
69. Lloyd (1996) p.89.
70. www.ppu.org.uk
71. Ellsworth-Jones, W. (2008) *We Will Not Fight. The Untold Story of World War One's Conscientious Objectors*, London: Aurum Press, p.103.
72. Brown, G. (1986; 2002 edn) *Maxton*, Edinburgh: Mainstream Publishing, pp.38, 40.
73. Brown (1986).
74. Corr (2008) p.163.
75. Hochschild, A. (2011) *To End All Wars. How the First World War Divided Britain*, London: Macmillan, p.xvi.

Chapter 8: Temporary Gentlemen

1. Sherriff (1929).
2. See Plate 5 and pp.38-39 in this book.
3. Lewis-Stempel (2010) p.29.
4. Michael Howard in his Foreword to Seldon and Walsh (2013) p.xii.
5. Mangan (2000) pp.543–544.
6. Barthes (1957) p.9.
7. See p.38.
8. *My Boy Jack* (2007), Encosse Films Production, Director: Brian Kirk.
9. Seldon and Walsh (2013) p.40.
10. Messenger (2005) p.317. See also Simpson, P. (1985) 'The Officers' in I.F.W. Beckett and P. Simpson (Eds) *A Nation in Arms. A Social Study of the British Army in the First World War*, Manchester: Manchester University Press, p.64 and following.
11. Messenger (2005) p.333.
12. Graves (1929) p.202.
13. Lewis-Stempel (2010) p.62; Simpson (1985) p.65.
14. www.roll-of-honour.com

15. Armour (1995) p.25.
16. King (1997) p.156.
17. Figures for the Royal Navy and Royal Air Force are too small for meaningful comparisons.
18. Statistics in Winter (1998) p.83 indicate that these figures correlate with the proportion (38 per cent) of British students and teachers who became commissioned officers during the war.
19. www.thelinnets.co.uk/archive/joedines; www.liverpooldailypost.co.uk/liverpool-fc-news; www.lewishamwarmemorials.wikidot/person:dines-joseph; www.yourlocalpaper.co.uk 19 December 2014.
20. Gregory (2008) p.82.
21. Graves (1929) p.72.
22. Becket (1985) p.26.
23. Todman (2005) p.80.
24. Wheatley (1978) pp.291, 304.
25. Holmes, R. (2011) *Soldiers. Army Lives and Loyalties From Redcoats to Dusty Warriors*, London: Harper Press, p.196.
26. Petter, M. (1994) 'Temporary Gentlemen in the Aftermath of the Great War: Rank, Status and the Ex-Officer Problem', *The Historical Journal*, 37, 01, 127–152, p.139.
27. Lewis-Stempel (2010) pp.171, 59.
28. Lewis-Stempel in *Sunday Express* 09.02.2014.
29. Lewis-Stempel (2010) pp.52, 157.
30. Seldon and Walsh (2013) p.23.
31. Arnander, C. (Ed) (2013) *Private Lord Crawford's Great War Diaries. From Medical Orderly to Cabinet Minister*, Barnsley: Pen & Sword Military.
32. Graves (1929) p.203.
33. Lewis-Stempel. (2010).
34. Bartes (2009) p.170.
35. Taylor (1965) p.48.
36. Board of Education (1915) *Report of the Board of Education for the year 1913–1914*, London: HMSO, p.2.
37. May (1975) p.72.
38. Green (1992) p.32.
39. King (1997) p.156.
40. Parker (1987) p.73.
41. See p.129.
42. Board of Education (1915) *Report of the Board of Education for the year 1913–1914*, London: HMSO, p.2.
43. Board of Education (1916) *Report of the Board of Education for the year 1914–1915*, London: HMSO, p.3.
44. Board of Education (1915) *Report of the Board of Education for the year 1913–1914*, London: HMSO, p.155–156. At St Mark's College, 51 of the 70 Year 2 and Year 3 male students had already enlisted.
45. Tropp (1957) p.208.
46. Wright (1985) pp.49–50.
47. Sutton (1959) p.44.
48. Grounds, A.D. (1970) *A History of King Edward VI Grammar School Retford*, Worksop: R. Martin & Co. Ltd, p.227.
49. May (1975) p.72.
50. King (1992) p.63.
51. Board of Education (1918) *Report of the Board of Education for the year 1916–1917*, London: HMSO, p.10.
52. King (1997) p.156.
53. Sutton (1959) p.43.

54. For example, Mr Griffith at Greenhill School, Tenby, in Harrison (1979) p.234.
55. www.manannan.org.im/asox/history/Centenary
56. Elliott, B. (1965) *The History of Humphrey Perkins School*, (published by the school), p.155.
57. Board of Education (1915) *Report of the Board of Education for the year 1913–1914*, London: HMSO, p.2.
58. Bourke, J. (1996) *Dismembering the Male. Men's Bodies, Britain and the Great War*, London: Reaktion Books Ltd, p.195.
59. Thom, D. (1988) 'Women and Work in Wartime Britain' in R. Wall and J. Winter (Eds) (1988) *The Upheaval of War. Family, Work and Welfare in Europe, 1914–1918*, Cambridge: Cambridge University Press, p.318.
60. Amberley Parochial School (1988) pp.86–97.
61. Boyes (1997) p.77.
62. St Nicholas Boys' School Logbook.
63. Seldon and Walsh (2013) p.104.
64. Wright (1985) pp.43, 49.
65. Francombe & Coult (1937) pp.102–103.
66. Kelly, T. (1947) *The History of King Edward VI Grammar School Totnes and its Famous Old Boys*, (publisher not stated), p.74.
67. Kennedy (1951) p.90.
68. Lees (1947) p.79.
69. Reading and Housley (2006) p.23.
70. Chadderton (1964) p.60.
71. www.oldgramms.co.uk/history1899
72. Alderman (1972) p.33.
73. May (1975) p.72.
74. IOE Archive LDTC IE/STU/4/2.
75. IOE Archive LDTC IE/STU/4/2.
76. Deacon's School Archive.
77. Oram, A. (1996) *Women Teachers and Feminist Politics 1900–1939*, Manchester: Manchester University Press, P.124. See also Corr (2008).
78. Sutton (1959) p.39.
79. IOE Archive LDTC IE/STU/4/2–3.
80. Kean (1990) p.63.
81. Todman (2005) p.179.
82. Hynes (1990) p.91.
83. Copelman, D.M. (1996) *London's Women Teachers. Gender, Class and Feminism 1870–1930*, London: Routledge, p.228.
84. Gilbert (1994) p.345.
85. Copelman (1996) p.229.
86. Vaisey, J. (1958; 2012 edn) *The Costs of Education*, Abingdon: Routledge, p.204.

Chapter 9: Peace

1. Arthur, M. (2010) *The Road Home. The Aftermath of the Great War Told by the Men and Women Who Survived It*, London: Phoenix, p.21.
2. Arthur (2010) p.62.
3. Clark (1988) pp.19–20.
4. Gilchrist (1973) p.57.
5. Arthur (2010) p.62.
6. Sturges (1958) p.13.
7. Stibbington School Logbook: 11 November 1918.
8. Douglas-Smith (1965) p.388.
9. Pearce (1991) p.131.
10. Reading and Housley (2006) p.24; Peterborough Practising School Logbook: 11 November 1918.

11. Bird (1995) p.29.
12. Waugh (1964) p.124.
13. Hornby School Logbook: 11 March 1902.
14. Silver and Silver (1974) p.150. Logbook entry for 11 November 1918.
15. Peterborough Practising School Logbook: 11 November 1918.
16. Corfe (1960) p.54.
17. St Nicholas Boys' School Logbook.
18. Letter from the Soke of Peterborough Education Committee dated 29.11.1918, in Peterborough Practising School Logbook.
19. Hodges (1981) p.102.
20. Wright (1985) p.44.
21. *The Aluredian* vol. 4 no. 12 in Bromwich (1980) p.22.
22. Seldon and Walsh (2013) p.86.
23. Corfe (1960) p.54.
24. St Nicholas Boys' School Logbook.
25. *The Daily Graphic* Saturday, 24 May 1919, pp.1, 11.
26. Bird (1995) p.29.
27. St Nicholas Boys' School Logbook: 19 July 1919. The initials 'IGB' presumably refer to the marching order: the Infants' School, followed by the Girls' School, followed by the Boys' School.
28. Bird, J. (1995) *Hyacinths and Haricot Beans. Friary School Memories 1892–1992*, Lichfield: Lichfield Press, p.30.
29. Brown (1989) p.34.
30. www.newlands-kirkud.org
31. St Nicholas Boys' School Logbook.
32. *Manchester Guardian* 13 September 1918 in Daglish (1998) p.329.
33. Blair, E.E., Miller, R.B. and Tieken, M.C. (Eds) (2009) *Education and War*, Cambridge, Massachusetts: Harvard Educational Review, pp.1–2.
34. Wilson, T. (1986) *The Myriad Faces of War. Britain and the Great War, 1914–1918*, Cambridge: Polity Press, p.800.
35. Brooks, J.R. (1991) 'Labour and Educational Reconstruction, 1916–26: a Case Study in the Evolution of Policy', *History of Education*, 20, 3, 245–259, p.259.
36. Wilson (1986) p.815.
37. Osmond (1994) p.41.
38. Gordon (1980) p.181.
39. Dean, D. (1970) 'H.A.L. Fisher, Reconstruction and the Development of the 1918 Education Act', *British Journal of Educational Studies*, 18, 3, 259, p.259.
40. Gordon (1980) p.181.
41. The so-called 'Black Day of the German Army'.
42. Andrews, L. (1976) *The Education Act, 1918*, London: Routledge and Kegan Paul, p.18.
43. Headteacher Mr Griffiths' Report for 1917–1918, Greenhill School, Tenby, in Harrison (1979) p.227.
44. Hendrik, H. (1980) 'A Race of Intelligent Unskilled Labourers: the Adolescent Worker and the Debate on Compulsory Part-time Day Continuation in Schools, 1900–1922', *History of Education*, 9, 2, 159–173, p.160.
45. Perkin, H. (1989) *The Rise of Professional Society: England Since 1880*, London: Routledge, p.239.
46. Andrews (1976) p.89.
47. Tawney, R. H. (1922) *Secondary Education For All*, London: G. Allen & Unwin.
48. Perkin (1989) p.242.
49. Perkin (1989) pp.230–231.
50. Lees (1947) p.81.
51. www.messybeast.com

52. www.mhsgarchive.org
53. At Cheltenham College, Newick House was forced to close. Pearce (1991) p.126.
54. Seldon and Walsh (2013) p.107.
55. Scott et al. (1992) p.60.
56. Sargant (1928) p.51.
57. Board of Education (1920) *Report of the Board of Education for the year 1918*–1919, London: HMSO, p.17.
58. Haines (2005) pp.118, 122, 124. Corrie Chase died in 1965.
59. The school later moved to a new site in Blackfriars and is now the London Nautical School.
60. Peterborough Practising School Logbook. Mr Pullan noted the return of Mr Sibley on 3 February 1919.
61. Palmer (1999).
62. Nyazi (1994) p.60.
63. Berry (1994) p.45.

Chapter 10: The Fallen

1. Holmes, G.E.J. (1963) *The King's School. A History*, (published by the school), p.70.
2. Carlyon (2001), p.49, refers to the use of euphemisms: 'Soldiers weren't killed. They were *the fallen*'.
3. Lewis-Stempel, J. (2014) 'The Death of our Best and Brightest', *Sunday Express* 9 February 2014.
4. Hollis (1960) p.298.
5. From Seldon & Walsh (2013) pp.255–260.
6. Nine (including RAF) and one respectively.
7. From Seldon and Walsh (2013) pp.255–260.
8. Winter (1986) pp.64, 66.
9. Harry Jones was a political journalist and newspaper editor.
10. A phrase coined by Rupert Brooke in *The Dead* (1914).
11. Jones, P. (1918) *War Letters of a Public School Boy*, London: Cassell and Company Ltd.
12. Wohl, R. (1979) *The Generation of 1914*, Cambridge, Massachusetts: Harvard University Press, pp.209, 85–94.
13. Searle (2004) p.780.
14. Arnander (2013).
15. Todman (2005) p.44 argues that the most accurate figure for British deaths in the Great War is that calculated by Winter (1986), namely 722,785. There are great difficulties in accurately recording casualties when so many combatants changed service units, hence the evident imprecision and variations in the multitude of books on the conflict.
16. 59 per cent and 88 per cent respectively.
17. Kelly (1947) p.74.
18. Lees (1947) p.81.
19. Scottish War Memorials Project www.scottishmilitaryresearch.co.uk
20. Glover (1957) p.33.
21. Ferguson (1998) p.270.
22. Gregory (2008) p.162.
23. Ferguson (1998) p.270.
24. Bogacz, T. (1989) 'War Neurosis and Cultural Change in England, 1914–22. The Work of the War Office Committee of Enquiry into Shell-Shock', *Journal of Contemporary History*, 24, 2, 227–256, pp.23–232. It was argued that the development of 'character' in the elite schools made their products less likely to succumb to shell-shock.
25. Seldon and Walsh (2013) p.55.
26. King (1997) p.156.
27. www.scottishmilitaryresearch.co.uk
28. Deacon's School Archive.

29. www.scottishmilitaryresearch.co.uk
30. Board of Education (1919) *Report of the Board of Education for the year 1917–1918*, London: HMSO.
31. www.scottishmilitaryresearch.co.uk
32. King (1997) p.156.
33. Parker (1987) p.261.
34. Seldon and Walsh (2013) suggest that the death rate for public school teachers (26 per cent) was higher than that of public school pupils (20 per cent).
35. Hodges (1981) p.100.
36. Northop School Logbook.
37. Tyerman (2000) p.443.
38. Wearne, S. 'Sons of This Place' in *Attain Magazine* Summer 2010, accessed 14.10.2012 www.attainmagazine.co.uk/parents/sons-of-this place
39. Brown (1962) p.149.
40. King (1998) p.30.
41. Crane, D. (2013) *Empires of the Dead. How One Man's Vision Led to the Creation of WWI's War Graves*, London: William Collins, p.203.
42. Imperial War Museum *Searchlight* www.iwm.org.uk
43. Inglis, K.S. (1998; 2008 edn) *Sacred Places. War Memorials in the Australian Landscape*, Melbourne: Melbourne University Press.
44. Crane (2013) p.203.
45. www.jeffreymaynard.com
46. Wearne (2010).
47. McIntyre, C. (1990) *Monuments of War. How to read a War Memorial*, London: Robert Hale Ltd, pp.170–171.
48. McIntyre (1990) p.175.
49. McIntyre (1990) p.175.
50. King (1997) p.156.
51. www.lewishamwarmemorials.wikidot.com
52. McIntyre (1990) p.170
53. Seldon and Walsh (2013) p.196.
54. An extract from *West Buckland School 1858–1958. The First Hundred Years. A Review of a Century Recorded by Friends and Pupils* www.en.wikipedia.org/wiki/West_Buckland_School
55. WFA Occasional Paper Number 14.
56. Ruscoe, R.G. (1962) *Hereford High School for Boys: an Account of its First Fifty Years.1912–1962*, Herford: Hereford Times Ltd, p.15.
57. Reading & Housley (2006) p.25.
58. www.iwm.org.uk/memorials
59. Hynes (1990) pp.263–279.
60. Girouard (1981) pp.286–287.
61. Parker (1987) p.12.
62. Owen, W. *Dulce et Decorum Est* in Walter (2006) p.141.
63. Girouard (1981) p.290.
64. Amberley Parochial School Logbook.
65. St Nicholas Boys' School Logbook: 11 November 1920.
66. St Nicholas Boys' School Logbook: 26 January 1921.
67. Siegfried Sassoon's comment on the 58,000 names inscribed on the Menin Gate at Ypres.
68. Crane (2013) p.10.
69. Crane (2013) pp.17, 112, 118.
70. The inscription on one celebrated CWGC headstone in Lapugnoy Military Cemetery in France, for example, reads: 'CAPTAIN THE HON. T.C.R. AGAR-ROBARTES, MP. COLDSTREAM GUARDS 30TH SEPTEMBER 1915 AGED 35'. Tommy Agar-Robartes, son and heir of the 6th Viscount Clifden, was shot dead by a sniper on 30 September 1915.

He is also memorialised in Truro Cathedral, in the Church of St Andrew in Wimpole, Cambridgeshire, and in St Wilfred's Chapel in Church Norton, West Sussex.

71. Wearne (2010).
72. Seldon and Walsh (2013) p.203.
73. Osmond (1994) p.45.
74. Taylor (1988) p.49.
75. Introduction by John Banks, Churchwarden. Extracted from www.northopwm.com/sources_of_information
76. See p.26.
77. St Gregory's School Logbook: 11 November 1918.
78. St Gregory's School Logbook.
79. The Memorial Album had been retained by the daughter of the original printer.
80. Most of the information on Susannah Knight has been researched by Adam Cree.

Chapter 11: The Forgotten

1. Only thirty-five former pupils had actually died. L.J. Anker survived the war.
2. This summary of Deacon's School and the Great War has been adapted from documentary material gathered from the Deacon's School Archives, Commonwealth War Graves Commission records, and Memorial booklets researched and produced by Jane King in 2013–14.
3. Binyon, L. (1914) *For the Fallen*, in Walter (2006) p.235.
4. Binyon (1914).
5. Wohl (1979) p.221.
6. Todman (2005) p.3.
7. Becket (2002) p.172.
8. Becket (1985) p.18.
9. Waites (1987) p.273.
10. Ives (1970) p.191.
11. Lloyd (1996) p.85.
12. Holden (1950) pp.72–73 refers to rumours of defeat at the Battle of Jutland which percolated through to the pupils at Charterhouse on a 'black morning' in June 1916.
13. Seldon and Walsh (2013) p.94.
14. Brown, J.H. (1962) *A History of the Harvey Grammar School*, Folkestone: Old Harveians' Association, pp.148–149.
15. Wall, R. and Winter, J. (Eds) (1988) *The Upheaval of War. Family, Work and Welfare in Europe, 1914–1918*, Cambridge: Cambridge University Press, p.3.
16. The Silvertown explosion in London on 19 January 1917 killed 73 munitions workers and injured a further 400.
17. Beckett (2002) p.156.
18. See the article on fatherless children in Wales www.bbc.co.uk/news/uk-wales-26389055
19. Searle, G.E. (2004) *A New England. Peace and War 1886–1918*, Oxford: Clarendon Press, p.778.
20. Parker (2007) p.52.
21. Wilson (1986) p.158.
22. For details of the impact of war on children and schools in other belligerent nations see, for example, Chickering, R. (1998; 2004 edn) *Imperial Germany and the Great War, 1914–1918*, Cambridge: Cambridge University Press, p.120.
23. Wohl (1979) p.217.
24. Norwich High School (1950) p.75.
25. Spinks (2004) p.56.
26. Winter, J. and Prost, A. (2005) *The Great War in History. Debates and Controversies, 1914 to the Present*, Cambridge: Cambridge University Press, p.159.
27. Clark (1998) p.18.
28. Waugh (1964) p.125.
29. Liddle (1994) pp.10, 13.
30. Waugh (1964) pp.115–116.

31. Waugh, A. (1917) *The Loom of Youth*, London: Methuen.
32. Haines (2005) p.115.
33. Pearce (1991) p.130.
34. Greene (1934) p.42.
35. Fussell (1975) p.72.
36. Fussell (1975) p.9.
37. Wright (1985) p.50.
38. Parker (1987) p.273; Fussell (1975) p.110.
39. Remarque (1929) p.25.
40. Winter (1986) p.293.
41. Beckett (2002) p.156. Disability Pensions were initially granted to 1.1 million ex-servicemen, but this figure rose to 2.4 million by 1929, the result of the lingering effects of war-related medical conditions. See also Ferguson (1998) p.437 for details of neurasthenia victims and officer pensions. The latter continued to be distributed well into the 1930s.
42. Winter (1986) p.273.
43. Todman (2005) p.26.
44. Ferguson (1998) pp.361, 447.
45. Arthur (2010) p.193.
46. See p.34.
47. Grayzel (2002) pp.106–109.
48. Waugh (1964) p.124.
49. *The Gaytonian* June 1915, in May (1975) p.78.
50. May (1975) pp.78–79; www.jeffreymaynard.org
51. Winter (1986) p.277.
52. Winter (1986) p.274. Recent research by Professor Glyn Harper and colleagues at Massey University in New Zealand, published in the *British Medical Journal*, indicates a causal connection between war service and increased risk of premature death for survivors.
53. www.btinternet.com/-james.fanning/newhaven
54. Spinks (2004) p.73.
55. Fussell (1975) p.113.
56. Winter (1986) p.250.
57. Bannerman (1999) p.28.
58. Arthur (2005) p.211.
59. Sargant (1928) p.51.
60. Arthur (2010) pp.64–65.
61. *Waddelow Society Magazine* Autumn 2001 extracted from www.fwaterhouse.freeserve.co.uk/latestmagazine
62. Seldon and Walsh (2013) pp.122–123.
63. A description by Winston Churchill of RND commanders in his 'Introduction' to Jerrold, D. (1923) *The Royal Naval Division*, London: Hutchinson & Co.
64. New Cross and Hatcham Review 13.05.1927 www.homepages.paradise.net.nz/robbuck.1/pages/awbuckle
65. *The Gaytonian* October 1914 in May (1975) p.67.
66. See Cornwell (2005) p.105 concerning difficulties re-establishing the OTC at King Edward VII School in Sheffield.
67. May (1975) p.67.
68. Perkin (1989) p.224.
69. Perkin (1989) p.225.
70. Waites (1987) p.279.

Bibliography

Primary sources

Archive collections
Deacon's School Archive (Peterborough Library & Archives):
Admission Registers 1902–1926
Governing Body Minutes Books 1880–1926
Old Boys Minutes Book 1905–1932
Staff Register 1903–1956
Teacher Files 1914–1956
The Deaconian 1906–1980
Soke of Peterborough Junior Technical School Admission Register 1913–1914
Photographs 1903–1924

Girls' Public Day School Trust (GPDST) Archive (University College London Institute of Education):
Correspondence File 1914–1919

London Day Training College (LDTC) Archive (University College London Institute of Education):
Admissions Registers 1900–1920
Mark and Grade Books 1900–1920
Trainee Progress Reports 1900–1920

National Union of Teachers (NUT) Archive (Hamilton House, London):
War Record 1914–1919. A Short Account of Duty and Work Accomplished During the War (1920)

National Union of Women Teachers (NUWT) Archive (University College London Institute of Education):
NFWT Annual Reports 1917–1918
Central Council Meetings Minutes Book 1915–1919
West Ham Women Teachers' Association Minutes Books
The Woman Teacher 1919–1922
The Schoolmistress 1916–1918
Photograph collection

School Archive collections
Harrow County School for Boys: www.jeffreymaynard.com
Lincoln Christ's Hospital School (The Garton Archive): www.christs-hospital.lincs.sch.uk
Manchester High School for Girls: www.mhsgarchive.org
Sherborne School: www.flikr.com/photos/sherborneschoolarchives

School Logbooks
Amberley Parochial School, Gloucestershire: Amberley (1988)
Barnack School, Cambridgeshire: Palmer (1999)

Dronfield Junior School, Derbyshire: www.dronfield-jun.derbyshire.sch.uk
Holt Schools: Bucknall (1976)
Hornby School, Lancashire: www.hornbyprimary.lancsngfl.ac.uk
Newark School, Peterborough: Horswood (1979)
Northop School, Flintshire: www.northopwm.com/home-front-northop
Peterborough Practising School: Peterborough Library & Archives
Pound Lane School, Epsom: www.epsomandewellhistoryexplorer.org.uk/PoundLaneSchool/WW1
St Gregory's School, Chorley: www.mahara.saint-michaels.lancs.sch.uk
St Nicholas Boys' School, King's Lynn: True's Yard, King's Lynn
Silver Street Senior Boys' School, London: Sturges (1958)
Stibbington School, Cambridgeshire: CEES (2002)
Ysgol Sychdyn, Flintshire: www.northopwm.com/home_front_sychdyn

School magazines
Cathedralian
Monmouthian
Sutton High School Magazine
The Aluredian
The Bridge
The Crown
The Deaconian
The Gaytonian
The Inverness Academical
The Lincolnian
The Tauntonian
White & Blue

Periodicals and newspapers
Chorley Guardian
Daily Sketch
Manchester Guardian
New Cross and Hatcham Review
Peeblesshire Advertiser and County Newspaper
The Boys Own
The Captain
The Daily Graphic
The Illustrated War News
The London Gazette
The Magnet
The Navy and Army Illustrated
The Schoolmistress
The Spectator
The Sphere
The Times
The Times History of the War
The War Budget
The War Pictorial
The Woman Teacher

Private papers
Letters from Geoffrey Barber (Leys School, Cambridge) to his father 1918–1919

Official publications and correspondence
Board of Education (1914) *Circular 859* (Occupation of School Buildings for Military Hospitals and Other Military Purposes)
Board of Education (1915) *Circular 892* (Compensation for Military Occupation of School Buildings)
Board of Education (1915) *Circular 926* (The Release of Masters in Secondary Schools for Military Service)
Board of Education (1915) *Circular 930* (Appeals in Respect of Teachers Attested for Military Service)
Board of Education (1916) *Circular 949* (War Savings Associations)
Board of Education (1916) *Circular 968* (Teaching Staff Available in Secondary Schools)
Board of Education (1916) *Circular 971a* (Teaching Staff)
Board of Education (1917) *Circular 979* (School Gardens)
Board of Education (1917) *Circular 994* (Food Economy Campaign)
Board of Education (1917) *Circular 1009* (Propellant Supplies)
Board of Education (1918) *Circular 1073* (Teachers Serving in Armed Forces)
Board of Education (1919) *Circular 1122* (Extension to School Summer Holidays)
Board of Education letter 8 January 1915 to LEAs and Responsible Authorities *re* Requisitioning of School Buildings (IOE GDS/9/3/1)
Board of Education letter 2 February 1915 to Girls' Public Day School Trust and Memorandum *re* Air Raid Precautions (IOE GDS/9/3/1)
Board of Education letter 12 March 1917 to Schools *re* Increasing Food Supply (IOE GDS/9/3/1)
Board of Education letter 9 July 1917 to LEAs and Governing Bodies *re* Air Raid Precautions (IOE GDS/9/3/1)
Board of Education (1915) *Report of the Board of Education for the year 1913–1914*, London: HMSO
Board of Education (1916) *Report of the Board of Education for the year 1914–1915*, London: HMSO
Board of Education (1917) *Report of the Board of Education for the year 1915–1916*, London: HMSO
Board of Education (1918) *Report of the Board of Education for the year 1916–1917*, London: HMSO
Board of Education (1919) *Report of the Board of Education for the year 1917–1918*, London: HMSO
Board of Education (1920) *Report of the Board of Education for the year 1918–1919*, London: HMSO
Board of Education (1904; 1905 edn) (1909) *Syllabus of Physical Exercises for Use in Public Elementary Schools*, London: HMSO

Printed autobiographies, fiction and poetry
Binyon, L. (1914) *For the Fallen*
Blunden, E. (1928; 2010 edn) *Undertones of War*, London: Penguin Classics
Blythe, R. (1969; 1978 edn) *Akenfield*, Harmondsworth: Penguin Books Ltd
Bowen, E. (1934) 'The Mulberry Tree' in G. Greene (Ed.) (1934; 1985 edn) *The Old School. Essays by Divers Hands*, Oxford: Oxford University Press
Brittain, V. (1933; 1998 edn) *Testament of Youth. An Autobiographical Study of the Years 1900–1925*, London: Virago
Brooke, R. (1914) *Peace*
Brooke, R. (1914) *The Dead*
Buchan, J. (1916; 2008 edn) *Greenmantle*, London: Penguin Classics
Crane, S. (1899) *Do Not Weep, Maiden, For War is Kind*
Graves, R. (1929; 2000 edn) *Goodbye to All That*, London: Penguin Classics
Kipling, R. (1902) *The Islanders*
Jones, P. (1918) *War Letters of a Public School Boy*, London: Cassell and Company Ltd
Lloyd George, D. (1938) *War Memoirs of David Lloyd George*, London: Odhams Press Ltd
Manning, F.E. (1929; 1977 edn) *The Middle Parts of Fortune*, London: Peter Davies
Newbolt, H. (1892) *Vitaï Lampada*
Owen, W. (1917) *Dulce et Decorum Est*
Owen, W. (1918) *The Send-Off*

Pope, J. (1915) *The Call*
Remarque, E.M. (1929; 1986 edn) *All Quiet on the Western Front*, London: Heinemann Educational Books Ltd
Ross, I. (1988) *Little Grey Partridge. First World War Diary of Ishobel Ross Who Served With the Scottish Women's Hospitals Unit in Serbia*, Aberdeen: The University Press
Sherriff, R.C. (1929; 2000 edn) *Journey's End*, London: Penguin Books
Thompson, F. (1945; 2008 edn) *Lark Rise to Candleford*, London: Penguin Books
Waugh, A. (1917) *The Loom of Youth*, London: Methuen.
Waugh, E. (1964; 1983 edn) *A Little Learning. The First Volume of an Autobiography*, London: Methuen
Wheatley, D. (1981) *The Time has Come. An Autobiography*, London: Arrow Books Limited (1916)

Secondary sources (books)
Adey, K. (2013) *Fighting on the Home Front. The Legacy of Women in World War One*, London: Hodder & Stoughton Ltd
Alderman, G. (1972) *The History of Hackney Downs School, Formerly the Grocers' Company's School*, London: The Clove Club
Aldrich, R. (1996) *Education for the Nation*, London: Cassell
Alston Watson, G. (1941) *Ayton School Centenary History 1841–1941*, (published by the school)
Andrews, L. (1976) *The Education Act, 1918*, London: Routledge and Kegan Paul
Amberley P.S. (1988) *Amberley Parochial School. The History of a Village School. A Source Book*, (published by the school)
Armytage, W.H.G. (1970, 2nd edn) *Four Hundred Years of English Education*, Cambridge: Cambridge University Press
Armour, D.J. (1995) *Felsted Preparatory School: The First 100 Years, 1895–1995*, London: The Athlone Press Ltd
Arnander, C. (Ed) (2013) *Private Lord Crawford's Great War Diaries. From Medical Orderly to Cabinet Minister*, Barnsley: Pen & Sword Military
Arthur, M. (2002; 2003 edn) *Forgotten Voices of the Great War*, London: Ebury Press.
Arthur, M. (2005; 2006 edn) *Last Post. The Final Word from our First World War Soldiers*, London: Orion Books Ltd
Arthur, M. (2006) *Lost Voices of the Edwardians*, London: Harper Press
Arthur, M. (2010) *The Road Home. The Aftermath of the Great War Told by the Men and Women Who Survived It*, London: Phoenix
Audoin-Rouzeau, S. (1992) *Men At War 1914–1918. National Sentiment and Trench Journalism in France During the First World War*, Oxford: Berg Publishers Ltd
Banks, O. (1955) *Parity and Prestige in English Secondary Education: a Study in Educational Sociology*, London: Routledge and Kegan Paul
Bannerman, C. (1999) *Further Up Stephen's Brae. The Midmill's Era at Inverness Royal Academy 1895–1979*, Inverness: St Michael's Publishing
Barthes, R. (1957; 2009 edn) *Mythologies*, London: Vintage
Beardwood, H. (Ed.) (1952, 2nd edn) *The History of Colfe's Grammar School 1652–1952*, London: University of London Press Ltd
Beckett, I.F.W. (1985) 'The Nation in Arms, 1914–1918' in Becket, I.F.W and Simpson, P. (Eds) (1985) *A Nation in Arms. A Social Study of The British Army in the First World War*, Manchester: Manchester University Press
Beckett, I.F.W. (2002) *The First World War: The Essential Guide to Sources in the UK National Archives*, Kew: Public Record Office
Bernbaum, G. (1967) *Social Change and the Schools*, London: Routledge and Kegan Paul
Berry, K. (1994) *John of Gaunt School and the Trowbridge High Schools: the First One Hundred Years*, (published by the author)
Bilton, D. (2003) *The Home Front in the Great War. Aspects of the Conflict 1914–1918*, Barnsley: Leo Cooper (Pen & Sword Books Ltd)

Bird, J. (1995) *Hyacinths and Haricot Beans. Friary School Memories 1892–1992*, Lichfield: Lichfield Press

Blair, E.E., Miller, R.B. and Tieken, M.C. (Eds) (2009) *Education and War*, Cambridge, Massachusetts: Harvard Educational Review

Bolam, D.W. (1952) *Unbroken Community: The Story of the Friends' School Saffron Walden 1702–1952*, (published by the school)

Bonner, R. (1998) *Wifrith Elstob VC DSO MC. The Manchester Regiment*, Knutsford: Fleur de Lys Publishing Ltd

Bourke, J. (1996) *Dismembering the Male. Men's Bodies, Britain and the Great War*, London: Reaktion Books Ltd

Boville, M. K. (1986) *East Boldon School Centenary 1885–1995*, (published by the school)

Boyes, M. (1997) *A Cotswolds Village School from Victorian Times*, Cheltenham: The Rissingtons Local History Society

Brennan, P.J. (1997) *A History of the Cardinal Vaughan Memorial School 1914–1997*, Henley on Thames: Gresham Books Limited

Broadway, C.M. and Buss, E.I (1982) *The History of the School: 1882 B.G.M.S – D.A.H.S 1982*, Luton: White Crescent Press Ltd

Bromwich, D. (1990) *King's College, Taunton. The First Hundred Years, 1880–1990*, (publisher not stated)

Brooks, R. (1998) *King Alfred School and the Progressive Movement 1898–1998*, Cardiff: University of Wales Press

Brown, C. (1989) *The Georgetown Schools (1877–1989)*, Tredegar: Georgetown School

Brown, G. (1986; 2002 edn) *Maxton*, Edinburgh: Mainstream Publishing Company

Brown, J.H. (1962) *A History of the Harvey Grammar School*, Folkestone: Old Harveians' Association

Brown, W.E. and Poskitt, F.R. (1976) *The History of Bolton School*, (published by the school)

Bucknall, G.V.S. (1976) *Two Into One. Holt Schools 1834–1935*, Holt: Holt Magazine

Burk, K. (2000) *Troublemaker. The Life and History of A.J.P. Taylor*, Newhaven and London: Yale University Press

Cambridgeshire Environmental Education Service (2002) *Stibbington School Remembered, 1872–1982*, Peterborough: CEES

Carlyon, L. A. (2001; 2003 edn) *Gallipoli*, London: Bantam Books

Chadderton, J.F. (1964) *Barrow Grammar School for Boys 1880–1960, an Informal Chronicle*, Barrow: James Milner Ltd

Chickering, R. (1998; 2004 edn) *Imperial Germany and the Great War, 1914–1918*, Cambridge: Cambridge University Press

Clark, C. (2012; 2013 edn) *The Sleepwalkers. How Europe Went to War in 1914*, London: Penguin Books

Clark, P.L. (1988) *Seventy Five Years. A History of Bacup and Rawtenstall Grammar School* www.brgs.me/alumni/archive-history

Collard, J., Ogden, D. and Burgess, R. (1992) *Where the Fat Black Canons Dined. A History of Bristol Cathedral School, 1140 to 1992*, (published by the school)

Cook, R. (1990) *Chipping Campden School 1440–1990*, Shipston on Stour: Peter I. Drinkwater

Cooper, S. (2012) *The Final Whistle. The Great War in Fifteen Players*, Stroud: The History Press

Copelman, D.M. (1996) *London's Women Teachers. Gender, Class and Feminism 1870–1930*, London: Routledge

Corfe, T.H. (1960) *The School on the Hill. An informal History of King Edward VII Grammar School Melton Mowbray 1910–1960*, (published by the school)

Cornwell, J. (2005) *King Ted's. A Biography of King Edward VII School Sheffield 1905–2005*, (published by the school)

Corr, H. (2008) *Changes in Educational Policies in Britain, 1800–1920. How Gender Inequalities Reshaped the Teaching Profession*, New York: The Edwin Mellen Press

Crane, D. (2013) *Empires of the Dead. How One Man's Vision Led to the Creation of WWI's War Graves*, London: William Collins

Crouch, D. (1991) *Orleton School. A Brief History*, (publisher not stated)

Dare, D. (1996) *The Unknown Founder. The Story of Helston Grammar School from 1550–1972*, Truro: Kelynen Publications

Davies, J.I. (1989) *The Caernavon County School: A History*, Caernavon: Gwynedd Archives and Museums Service

Davies, K. (1989) *The History of Fiddington Village School*, Fiddington History Circle

Dent, H.C. (1970) *1870–1970. Century of Growth in English Education*, London: Longman

Dickinson, P.G.M. and Jamieson, A. (1965) *The History of Huntingdon Grammar School*, (published by the school)

Dikötter, F. (2010; 2011 edn*) Mao's Great Famine*, London: Bloomsbury

Dixon, C.J. (2006) *This Saddening List: The 1st World War Memorial, King Edward VII School King's Lynn*, Norwich: Gatehouse Press

Douglas-Smith, A.E., (1965) *The City of London School*, Oxford: Basil Blackwell

Dunlop, A.D. (1992) *Hutcheson's Grammar. The History of a Glasgow School*, Glasgow: Hutcheson's Educational Trust

Dyhouse, C. (2000) 'Good Wives and Little Mothers. Social Anxieties and the Schoolgirl's Curriculum' in R. Lowe (Ed.) (2000) *History of Education Major Themes*, London: Routledge Falmer

Elliott, B. (1965) *The History of Humphrey Perkins School*, (published by the school)

Ellsworth-Jones, W. (2008) *We Will Not Fight. The Untold Story of World War One's Conscientious Objectors*, London: Aurum Press

Emden, R. van (2005) *Boy Soldiers of the Great War*, London: Headline

Emden, R. van (2013) *Meeting the Enemy. The Human Face of the Great War*, London: Bloomsbury

Emden, R. van and Humphries, S. (2003) *All Quiet on the Home Front. An Oral History of Life in Britain During the First World War*, London: Headline Book Publishing

Faulks, S. (1993) *Birdsong*, London: Hutchinson

Ferguson, N. (1998) *The Pity of War, 1914–1918*, London: Penguin Books

Fussell, P. (1975; 2000 edn) *The Great War and Modern Memory*, New York: Oxford University Press

Francombe, D.C.R. and Coult, D.E. (1937) *Bancroft's School, 1737–1937*, (published by the authors)

Garside, B. (1957) *A Brief History of Hampton School, 1557–1957*, Richmond: Dimblebys

Gaskin, C., Vlaeminke, M. and Gaskin, K. (1998) *Moseley into the Millennium. The Story of Moseley School*, Studley: Brewin Books

Gilbert, M. (1994; 2004 edn) *The First World War. A Complete History*, New York: Holt Paperbacks

Gilchrist, W.J.M., (1973) 'History of Gowerton Intermediate School, Glamorgan', in G. Bennett (Ed.) *Something Attempted, Something Done*, Llandybie: Christopher Davies (Publishers) Ltd

Girouard, M. (1981) *The Return to Camelot: Chivalry and the English Gentleman*, London: Yale University Press

Glover, E.P. (1957) *The First Sixty Years 1896–1956. The Newport High School for Boys*, Newport: R.H. Johns

Gordon, P. (1980) *Selection For Secondary Education*, London: Woburn Press

GPDST *Nottingham High School for Girls*

Graham, J.A. and Phythian, B.A. (1965) *The Manchester Grammar School 1515–1965*, Manchester: Manchester University Press

Gray, D.P. (2006) *The Uncommon Soldiers. Peterborough and District in 1914*, (published by the author)

Grayzel, S.R. (2002) *Women and the First World War*, Harlow: Pearson Education Limited

Green, L. (1992) *A History of the Cowper Testimonial School Hertford*, Hertford: Hertford and Ware Local History Society

Gregory, A. (2008) *The Last Great War. British Society and the First World War*, Cambridge: Cambridge University Press

Grounds, A.D. (1970) *A History of King Edward VI Grammar School Retford*, Worksop: R. Martin & Co Ltd

Haines, K. (2005) *'Chevy' Chase ... a Real Mr Chips*, Belfast: Ballymaconaghy Publishing

Hanson, N. (2005; 2007 edn) *The Unknown Soldier. The Story of the Missing of the Great War*, London: Corgi Books

Hanson, N. (2008; 2009 edn) *First Blitz. The Secret German Plan to Raze London to the Ground in 1918*, London: Corgi Books

Harrison, W. (1979) *Greenhill School, Tenby, 1896–1964*, Cardiff: University of Wales Press

Harrop, S. (1988) *The Merchant Taylors' School for Girls, Crosby. One Hundred Years of Achievement, 1888–1988*, Liverpool: Liverpool University Press

Hastings, M. (2011) *All Hell Let Loose. The World at War 1939–1945*, London: Harper Press

Heward, C. (1988) *Making a Man of Him: Parents and Their Sons' Education at an English Public School 1929–50*, London: Routledge

Hill, C.P. (1951) *The History of Bristol Grammar School*, London: Pitman

Hilliam, D. (2011) *Tig's Boys: Letters to Sir from the Trenches*, Stroud: The History Press

Hinchcliffe, E. (1974) *Appleby Grammar School – from Chantry to Comprehensive*, Appleby: J. Whitehead & Son Ltd

Hochschild, A. (2011) *To End All Wars. How the First World War Divided Britain*, London: Macmillan

Hodges, S. (1981) *God's Gift. A Living History of Dulwich College*, London: Heinemann

Holborn, M. (Ed.) (2013) *The Great War*, London: Imperial War Museum and Jonathan Cape

Holden, W.H. (Ed.) (1950) *The Charterhouse We Knew*, London: British Technical and General Press

Hollis, C. (1960) *Eton: A History*, London: Hollis and Carter

Holmes, G.E.J. (1963) *The King's School. A History*, (published by the school)

Holmes, R. (2011) *Soldiers. Army Lives and Loyalties from Redcoats to Dusty Warriors*, London: Harper Press

Horswood, J. (1979) *A History of Newark School, Oxney Road, Peterborough*, Peterborough: The Teacher's Centre

Huggins, M.J.W. (1982) *The Making of an English Public School*, Tedburn St Mary: Hiroona Publications

Hurt, J.S. (1977) 'Drill, Discipline and the Elementary School Ethos', in P. McCann (Ed.) (1977) *Popular Education and Socialization in the Nineteenth Century*, London: Methuen

Hynes, S. (1990) *A War Imagined. The First World War and English Culture*, London: Pimlico

Ingarfield, L.E. and Alexander, M.B. (1985) *A Short History of Haberdashers' Aske's Hatcham Boys' School*, London: The Worshipful Company of Haberdashers

Inglis, K.S. (1998; 2008 edn) *Sacred Places. War Memorials in the Australian Landscape*, Melbourne, Australia: Melbourne University Press

Ives, A.G. (1970) *Kingswood School in Wesley's Day and Since*, London: Epworth Press

Jenkins, H.J.K. (1978) *A School in Woodston, 1728–1978*, Peterborough: St Augustine's School

Jerrold, D. (1923) *The Royal Naval Division*, London: Hutchinson & Co.

Jobson, R. (1977) *The Story of a School*, (published by Highgate Primary School)

Jones, A.E. (1975) *A Small School in the Great War. The Story of Sutton County School and its Old Boys in World War I*, (published by the author)

Kean, H. (1990) *Deeds Not Words. The Lives of Suffragette Teachers*, London: Pluto Press

Kelly, T. (1947) *The History of King Edward VI Grammar School Totnes and its Famous Old Boys*, (publisher not stated)

Kendall, P. (2012) *Aisne 1914: The Dawn of Trench Warfare*, Stroud: The History Press

Kennedy, G. (1951) *The Story of Morpeth Grammar School*, Newcastle: The Old Boys' Association

King, A. (1998) *Memorials of the Great War in Britain. The Symbolism and Politics of Remembrance*, Oxford: Berg

King, B. (1990) *P.G.S.G. A History 1905–1946: Cheltenham's Other Girls' School*, (published by the author)

King, P. (1997) *Hurstpierpoint College 1849–1995. The School by the Downs*, Chichester: Phillimore & Co Ltd

King, W. (1992) *Towards the Light. The Story of Cardiff High School for Boys 1898–1970*, Llanharan: Pallas Press

Kirby, J.A and Knight, P.M. (1985) 'Haberdashers' Aske's Hatcham Girls' School', an addendum in L.E. Ingarfield and M.B. Alexander (Eds) (1985) *A Short History of Haberdashers' Aske's Hatcham Boys' School*, London: The Worshipful Company of Haberdashers

Larrett, W.D. (1966) *A History of the King's School Peterborough*, Peterborough: Old Petriburgians Association

Lees, T.C. (1947) *A Short History of Northampton Grammar School 1541–1941*, Northampton: The Swan Press

Lempriere, W. (1924) *A History of the Girl's School of Christ's Hospital, London, Hoddesdon and Hertford*, Cambridge: Cambridge University Press

Lepper, C. (1989) *The Crypt School Gloucester 1539–1989*, Gloucester: Alan Smith Publishing Limited

Lewis-Stempel, J. (2010) *Six Weeks. The Short and Gallant Life of the British Officer in the First World War*, London: Weidenfeld & Nicolson

Liddle, P.H. (1994) *The Worst Ordeal. Britons at Home and Abroad 1914–1918*, London: Leo Cooper

Lindsay, K. (1926) *Educational Progress and Social Waste*, London: Routledge

Lloyd, H.S. (1996) *The History of Aberystwyth County School (Ardwyn), 1896–1973*, Aberystwyth: The Ardwynian Association

Lowe, R., (Ed.) (1992) *Education and the Second World War. Studies in Schooling and Social Change*, London: The Falmer Press

Lowe, R. (Ed.) (2000) *History of Education Major Themes*, London: Routledge Falmer

Maclure, J.S. (1979) *Educational Documents, England and Wales 1816–1968*, London: Methuen

Mangan, J.A. (1983) 'Imitating Their Betters and Disassociating From Their Inferiors: Grammar Schools and the Games Ethic in the Late Nineteenth and Early Twentieth Centuries', in N. Parry and D. McNair (Eds) (1983) *The Fitness of the Nation – Physical and Health Education in the Nineteenth and Twentieth Centuries: Proceedings of the 1982 Annual Conference of the History of Education Society of Great Britain*, Leicester: History of Education Society

Mangan, J.A. (2000) 'Duty Unto Death. English Masculinity and Militarism in the Age of the New Imperialism', in R. Lowe (Ed.) (2000) *History of Education Major Themes*, London: Routledge Falmer

Mann, J. (1994) *Highbury Fields. The 'Most Interesting' School in London*, Winchester: Edgeley Publications

Marlow, J. (Ed.) (1995; 2005 edn) *The Virago Book of Women and the Great War*, London: Virago

Marsden, W.E. (1991) *Educating the Respectable: a Study of Fleet Road Board School, Hampstead, 1879–1903*, London: Woburn Press

Martin, J. (1974) *A History of St John the Baptist Church of England Schools Leicester 1881–1974*, (published by the school)

Marwick, A. (1965) *The Deluge: British Society and the First World War*, London: Macmillan

May, T. (1975) *The History of the Harrow County School for Boys*, (published by the school)

Mayall, B. and Morrow, V. (2011) *You Can Help Your Country. English Children's Work During the Second World War*, London: Institute of Education

McCulloch, G. (1989) *The Secondary Technical School: a Usable Past?*, Lewes: Falmer Press

McIntyre, C. (1990) *Monuments of War. How to Read a War Memorial*, London: Robert Hale Limited

McIlrath, H. *Larne Grammar School: The First Hundred Years* www.larne-in-ww1.irishgenealogy.net

Merson, E. (1979) *Once There Was … The Village School*, Southampton: Paul Cave Publications Ltd

Messenger, C. (2006) *Call-to-Arms. The British Army 1914–1918*, London: Cassell

Myhill, J.D. (1991) *Blue Coat. A History of the Blue Coat School, Birmingham, 1722–1990*, Warley: Meridian Books

Nolan, B. (1989) *The Picture History of King's School, Rochester*, (published by the school)

Norwich High School (1950) *Norwich High School, 1875–1950*, Norwich: Goose Press

Nyazi, M. (1994) *The Best Days of Their Lives. A History of Busbridge School, Godalming, Founded 1 March 1868*, Godalming: Busbridge Books

Oakes, J. (2009) *Kitchener's Lost Boys. From the Playing Fields to the Killing Fields*, Stroud: The History Press

Oakes, J. and Parsons, M. (2005) *Reading School. The First 800 Years*, Peterborough: DSM

Oram, A. (1996) *Women Teachers and Feminist Politics 1900–39*, Manchester: Manchester University Press

Osmond, S.E. (1994) *A History of Calton Road Schools*, Parkend: Thornhill Press

Palmer, B. (1999) *School in Barnack. A Short History*, (published by the school)

Palmer, S. and Wallis, S. (2003) *A War in Words*, London: Simon and Schuster UK Ltd

Parker, D. (2007) *Hertfordshire Children in War and Peace, 1914–1939*, Hatfield: Hertfordshire Publications

Parker, P. (1987; 2007 edn) *The Old Lie: The Great War and the Public School Ethos*, London: Hambledon Continuum

Patch, H. and Emden, R. van (2007; 2009 edn) *The Last Fighting Tommy. The Life of Harry Patch, Last Veteran of the Trenches, 1898–2009*, London: Bloomsbury

Paxman, J. (2013) *Great Britain's Great War*, London: Viking

Payton, P. (2012) *Regional Australia and the Great War. The Boys from Old Kio*, Exeter: Exeter University Press

Peacock, A.J. (Ed) *Gunfire. A Journal of First World War History*, No. 31 pp.2–16, York: Smith & Son (Printers)

Pearce, T. (1991) *Then and Now. An Anniversary Celebration of Cheltenham College 1841–1991*, Cheltenham: Old Cheltonian Society

Pearson, R. (2010) *The Boys of Shakespeare's School in the First World War*, Stroud: The History Press

Penn, A. (1999) *Targeting Schools: Drill, Militarism and Imperialism*, London: Woburn Press

Perkin, H. (1989) *The Rise of Professional Society: England Since 1880*, London: Routledge

Pike, M. (1960) *The Oak Tree. The Story of Putney High School*, (published by the author)

Reading, L. and Housley, D. (2006) *100 Years at City Road – A History of the George Dixon Secondary Schools*, (published by the school)

Robb, G. (2002) *British Culture and the First World War*, Basingstoke: Palgrave

Ruscoe, R.G. (1962) *Hereford High School for Boys: an Account of its First Fifty Years. 1912–1962*, Hereford: Hereford Times Ltd

Sanderson, M. (1987) *Educational Opportunity and Social Change in England*, London: Faber and Faber

Sanderson, M. (1994) *The Missing Stratum: Technical School Education in England 1900–1990s*, London: Athlone Press

Sanderson, M. (1999) *Education and Economic Decline in Britain, 1870 to the 1990s*, Cambridge: Cambridge University Press

Sargant, W.L. (1928) *The Book of Oakham School*, Cambridge: Cambridge University Press

Scott, F.W., Sutton, A. and King, N.J. (1992) *Hymers College. The First 100 Years*, Beverley: Highgate Publications Ltd

Scott-Giles, C.W. and Slater, B.V. (1966) *The History of Emanuel School 1594–1964*, London: Old Emanuel Association

Searle, G.E. (2004) *A New England. Peace and War 1886–1918*, Oxford: Clarendon Press

Seldon, A. and Walsh, D. (2013) *Public Schools and the Great War. The Generation Lost*, Barnsley: Pen & Sword Military

Sheffield, G.D. (2001; 2002 edn) *Forgotten Victory. The First World War: Myths and Realities*, London: Headline Book Publishing

Sheils, S. (2007) *Among Friends. The Story of the Mount School York*, London: James & James

Sherington, G. (1983) *Shore: a History of Sydney Church of England Grammar School*, Sydney: Allen and Unwin

Silver, P. and Silver, H. (1974) *The Education of the Poor. The History of a National School 1824–1974*, London: Routledge & Kegan Paul

Simkins, P. (1988; 2007 edn) *Kitchener's Army. The Raising of the New Armies 1914–1916*, Barnsley: Pen & Sword Military

Simpson, P. (1985) 'The Officers', in I.F.W. Becket and P. Simpson, (Eds) (1985) *A Nation in Arms. A Social Study of the British Army in the First World War*, Manchester: Manchester University Press

Smith, D. (1982) *Conflict and Compromise. Class Formation in English Society 1830–1914. A Comparative Study of Birmingham and Sheffield*, London: Routledge & Kegan Paul

Smith, L.V., Audoin-Rouzeau, S. and Becker, E. (2003) *France and the Great War 1914–1918*, Cambridge: Cambridge University Press

Spinks, M. (2004) *Heads and Tales. A History of Badsey Schools*, Badsey: The Badsey Society

Storey, N.R. (2008) *Norfolk in the Great War. A Pictorial History*, Wellington: Halsgrove

Sturges, G.W. (1958) *The Silver Link, Being a Short History of Huxley County Secondary School, formerly Silver Street Senior Boys' School, Edmonton, Middlesex 1901–1957*, (published by the school)

Sutton, R. (1959) *The Herbert Strutt School, Belper, 1909–1959*, (published by the school)

Taylor, A.J.P. (1965; 1988 edn) *English History 1914–1945*, The Oxford History of England, Oxford: The Clarendon Press

Tawney, R. H. (1922) *Secondary Education For All*, London: G. Allen & Unwin

Terraine, J. (1965; 1997 edn) *The Great War*, Ware: Wordsworth Editions Ltd

Terraine, J. (1982) *White Heat. The New Warfare 1914–1918*, London: Sidgwick & Jackson

Thomas, A.W. (1977) *A History of Nottingham High School 1513–1953*, Nottingham: J. and H. Bell

Thom, D. (1988) 'Women and Work in Wartime Britain', in R. Wall and J. Winter (1988) (Eds) *The Upheaval of War. Family, Work and Welfare in Europe, 1914–1918*, Cambridge: Cambridge University Press

Thompson, E.P. (1963; 2013 edn) *The Making of the English Working Class*, London: Penguin Books

Todman, D. (2005) *The Great War. Myth and Memory*, London: Hambledon and London

Tropp, A. (1957) *The School Teachers. The Growth of the Teaching Profession in England and Wales from 1800 to the Present Day*, London: William Heinemann Ltd

Tyerman, C. (2000) *A History of Harrow School 1324–1991*, Oxford: Oxford University Press

Vaisey, J. (1958; 2012 edn) *The Costs of Education*, Abingdon: Routledge

Waites, B. (1987) *A Class Society at War. England 1914–1918*, Leamington Spa: Berg Publishers Ltd

Wake, R. and Denton, P. (1993) *Bedales School. The First Hundred Years*, London: The Haggerston Press

Walker, M. (2012) *West Norfolk and King's Lynn High School for Girls 1886 to 1979*, King's Lynn: K.E.S. Publications

Wall, R. and Winter, J. (Eds) (1988) *The Upheaval of War. Family, Work and Welfare in Europe, 1914–1918*, Cambridge: Cambridge University Press

Walter, G. (Ed.) (2006) *The Penguin Book of First World War Poetry*, London: Penguin Books Ltd

Waszak, P. (1984) *Roman Catholic Schools in Peterborough. A History*, Peterborough: Peterborough Arts Council

Watson, N. (2000) *And Their Works Do Follow Them. The Story of North London Collegiate School*, London: James & James

Whithorn, D.P. (2003) *Bringing Uncle Albert Home. A Soldier's Tale*, Stroud: Sutton Publishing Ltd

Wiener, M.J. (1981) *English Culture and the Decline of the Industrial Spirit, 1850–1980*, Cambridge: Cambridge University Press

Wilks, H.C. (1979) *George Green's School, 1828–1978. A History*, London: Edward Arnold

Wilson, T. (1986) *The Myriad Faces of War. Britain and the Great War, 1914–1918*, Cambridge: Polity Press

Winter, J.M. (1986; 1987 edn) *The Great War and the British People*, London: Macmillan Education Ltd

Winter, J.M. (1988; 1995 edn) *The Experience of World War I*, New York: Oxford University Press

Winter, J and Prost, A. (2005) *The Great War in History. Debates and Controversies, 1914 to the Present*, Cambridge: Cambridge University Press

Wohl, R. (1979) *The Generation of 1914*, Cambridge, Massachusetts: Harvard University Press

Wright, C. (1985) *The Kent College Canterbury Book*, London: B.T. Batsford Ltd

Articles

Aldrich, R. (2013) 'The British and Foreign School Society, Past and Present', *History of Education Researcher*, 91, 5–12

Barrès-Barker, M.C. (2007) *'Our Belgian Guests'* – *Refugees in Brent, 1914–1919*, Brent: Brent Archives www.brent.gov.uk/museumarchive

Betts, R. (1984) 'The Samuelson Commission of 1881–1884 and English Technical Education', *History of Education Society Bulletin*, 34, 40–52

Betts, R. (1991) 'The Issue of Technical Education, 1867–1868', *History of Education Society Bulletin*, 48, 30–37

Bogacz, T. (1989) 'War Neurosis and Cultural Change in England, 1914–22. The Work of the War Office Committee of Enquiry into 'Shell-Shock'', *Journal of Contemporary History*, 24, 2, 227–256

Brooks, J.R. (1991) 'Labour and Educational Reconstruction, 1916–26: a Case Study in the Evolution of Policy', *History of Education*, 20, 3, 245–259

Daglish, N. (1998) 'Over By Christmas: The First World War, Education Reform and the Economy. The Case of Christopher Addison and the Origins of the DSIR', *History of Education*, 27, 3, 315–331

Deal, T.E. and Kennedy, A.A. (1983) 'Culture and School Performance', *Educational Leadership*, 40, 5, 14–15

Dean, D.W. (1970) 'H.A.L. Fisher, Reconstruction and the Development of the 1918 Education Act', *British Journal of Educational Studies*, 18, 3, 259

Dewey, P.E. (1984) 'Military Recruiting and the British Labour Force During the First World War', *The Historical Journal*, 27, 1, 199–223

Hendrick, H. (1980) "A Race of Intelligent Unskilled Labourers': the Adolescent Worker and the Debate on Compulsory Part-time Day Continuation Schools, 1900–1922', *History of Education*, 9, 2, 159–173

Horn, P. (1983) 'The Employment of Elementary Schoolchildren in Agriculture, 1914–1918', *History of Education*, 12, 3, 203–15

Jenkins, E.W. (1987) 'Junior Technical Schools, 1905–1945: the Case of Leeds', *History of Education*, 16, 2, 105–117

Lewis-Stempel, J. (2014) 'Death of Our Best and Brightest', *Sunday Express* 9 February 2014

Lowe, R. (1999) 'Education and National Identity', *History of Education*, 28, 3, 231–233

Marsden, W.E. (2000) 'Poisoned History': a Comparative Study of Nationalism, Propaganda and the Treatment of War and Peace in the Late Nineteenth- and Early Twentieth-Century School Curriculum', *History of Education*, 29, 1, 29–47

Myers, K. (2001) 'The Hidden History of Refugee Schooling in Britain: the Case of the Belgians, 1914–1918', *History of Education*, 30, 2, 153–162

Petter, M. (1994) ' "Temporary Gentlemen" in the Aftermath of the Great War: Rank, Status and the Ex-Officer Problem', *The Historical Journal*, 37, 01, 127–152

Simon, B. (1977) 'The 1902 Education Act – a Wrong Turning', *History of Education Society Bulletin*, 19, 7–14

Simpson, L. (1984) 'Imperialism, National Efficiency and Education, 1900–1905', *Journal of Educational Administration and History*, 14, 1, 28–35

Storr, K. (2003) 'Belgian Children's Education in Britain in the Great War: Language, Identity and Race Relations', *History of Education Researcher*, 72, 84–93

Thom, D. 'Women, War & Society 1914–1918', in Imperial War Museum *Women at Work Collection* http://www.tlemea.com/Thom.asp

Toibin, C. (2013) 'History Students Will No Longer Tolerate or Believe Grand Narratives', *The Guardian* 10 August 2013

Treadwell, P. (1983) 'The Games Mania – The Cult of Athleticism in the Late Victorian Public School', *History of Education Society Bulletin*, 32, 24–31

Wearne, S. (2010) 'Sons of This Place', *Attain Magazine* Summer 2010

Wright, S. (2012) 'Teachers, Family and Community in the Urban Elementary School: Evidence from English School Log Books c.1880–1918', *History of Education*, 41, 2, 155–173

Dissertations and theses
Blades, B.A. (2003) 'Deacon's School, Peterborough, 1902–1920: a Study of the Social and Economic Function of Secondary Schooling', University of London Ph.D. thesis

Other Media
BBC *Learning Zone*: www.bbc.co.uk/learningzone/clips/bombing-civilians-during-world-war-one/12738
BBC Online: www.bbc.co.uk/news/uk-wales-26389055
BBC Television: Curtis, R. and Elton, B. *Blackadder* Series 4: *Blackadder Goes Forth*
BBC *World War One at Home*: www.bbc.co.uk/programmes/p01qcrz; www.bbc.co.uk/programmes/#p01qmh7f; www.bbc.co.uk/programmes/p01rjft9; www.bbc.co.uk/programmes/#p01s4dhc; www.litherland-digital.co.uk

Kirk, D. (2007) *My Boy Jack*, Encosse Films Production
Pennell, C. (2012) 'Rethinking British Volunteerism in 1914. A Rush to the Colours?' in *First World War: New Perspectives, Episode 2*, Oxford University www.podcasts.ox.ac.uk/series/first-world-war

Websites
www.1900s.org.uk/1914-18-ww1-homefront
www.archive.spectator.co.uk/article/3rd-november-1906/9/the-girls-realm-annual
www.barnardos.org.uk
www.birdbrook.net
www.brgs.org.uk/history
www.btinternet.com/-james.fanning/newhaven
www.burtongrammar.co.uk
www.caldicott.com/magazinespring1918
www.childrenshomes.org.uk/TSArethusa/
www.christcollegebrecon.com.
www.en.wikipedia.org/wiki/West_Buckland_School
www.epsomandewellhistoryexplorer.org.uk/PoundLaneSchool/WW1
www.fwaterhouse.freeserve.co.uk/latestmagazine
www.homepages.paradise.net.nz/robbuck.1/pages/awbuckle
www.hullwebs.co.uk
www.iwm.org.uk/memorials
www.kibble.org/history
www.lemsfordhistory.co.uk
www.levenshistory.co.uk/school
www.lewishamwarmemorials.wikidot/person:dines-joseph
www.leytonpast.info
www.liverpooldailypost.co.uk/liverpool-fc-news
www.manannan.org.im/asox/history/Centenary
www.messybeast.com
www.mhsgarchive.org
www.monikie.org.uk
www.monmouthschool.org
www.museumofchildhood.org.uk
www.museumvictoria.co.au/ww1/stateschools
www.newbattleatwar.com
www.newlands-kirkud.org
www.norfolkinworldwar1.org
www.nottinghamshire.gov.uk/rollofhonour
www.oldgramms.co.uk/history1899
www.pals.org.uk/sheffield

www.pastimesproject.co.uk
www.ppu.org.uk
www.roll-of-honour.com
www.rushdenheritage.co.uk
www.rusholmearchive.org
www.scottishmilitaryresearch.co.uk
www.shropshirestar.com/news/great-war/2014/07/28
www.sirjohncasshistory.org
www.telegraph.co.uk/news/uknews/10649262
www.thelinnets.co.uk/archive/joedines
www.themanchesters.org/forum
www.wiganworld.co.uk
www.winchester-house.org/History-of-the-School
www.workhouses.org.uk/trainingships
www.wsch.eu/first-world-war
www.ww1.pgassociation.org.uk
www.ww1schoolarchives.org/Sutton-School
www.yourlocalpaper.co.uk

Index

(Plate images in **bold**)

Adams, Edward vi, 41, 191, 211
Adams, W.B. 18
Adlam, Tom **36**, 141-2, 182
Agricultural work 100-02
air raids **28**, **29**, 86, 88-94, 96
Alderson, Irving 57-8
aliens 55, 69
Allerton, Charles 52, 58, 76, 182
All Quiet on the Western Front 123
Allum, Annie 92, 143
Amiens, Battle of (1918) 179
Amiens Dispatch 30
Amos, Frank 52, 212
Antwerp, Battle of (1914) 128, 158
ANZAC 58
Arethusa, TS 19
Armistice xxi, 171, 174, 176, 181
    celebrations **40**, 172-4, 201
Arras, Battle of (1917) 139
Ashton, E.M. 143
Asquith, Herbert 28-9, 64, 101, 201
Atkinson, Samuel 159
attendance (and absenteeism) 18, 77, 101
Aubers Ridge, Battle of (1915) 191, 192, 203
Axe, A.C. 153, 192, 194

Barnardo, Thomas 19
Brabazon, Reginald 16
Blythe, Ronald 14, 77
Baden-Powell, Robert 12
Baggley, Aubrey 11
Baldwin, Stanley 198, 201
Balfour, Arthur 4
Balliol College, Oxford 151, 186
Barber, Geoffrey 75
battlefield tourism xvi, 200
Baumer, Paul 123
Beale, Dorothea 13
Beet, Gerald 196
Belgian Refugee Fund **18**, 54, 82 (see also refugees)
Belgian schools 54
Bell, Donald Simpson **36**, 141, 142
Bing, Harold 146
Binyon, Lawrence 204

Bishop, K. 143
Blackadder Goes Forth xvii
blackberries **22**, 63
Blades, Richard 106, 108
Blue, Dugald 33
Blunden, Edmund xvii, 113
Board of Education 4, 18, 42, 90, 95, 98, 101, 130, 158
    Circulars xi, 43, 65, 66, 130, 132, 133, 160, 161, 179, 181, 193, 199
    Regulations 4, 5, 13
    Revised Code 14
Boy Scouts **26**, 12, 24, 26, 51, 83, 85, 111, 214
boy soldiers 106-8
Boys' Own Paper, The **12**, xiv
Brazil, Angela 23
British and Foreign Schools Society 14
British Army 29, 41, 64
    Boer War 18
    casualties 15
    commissions 10, 39, 150 (see also 'Temporary Gentlemen')
    New Army 29, 42
    recruitment 29, 155
    reform of 10
    Regulars 29, 87, 152, 156, 184
    senior officers 150
    soldiers' slang 115
    teacher soldiers 128, 154
    fitness trainers 130
    under-age enlistment 107-8
    Fourth Army 134
    36th (Ulster) Division 126
    Highland Mountain Brigade 44
    Royal Field Artillery 39, 107, 191, 209, 211
    cavalry regiments 135
    Tank Corps 155, 187
    Royal Engineers 142, 192
    Army Service Corps 118, 186
    RAMC 4, 5, 75, 147, 157
    Artists' Rifles 38, 111, 115, 127, 130
    Bedfordshire Rgt 142
    Cameron Highlanders 58
    Dorsetshire Rgt 129
    Durham Light Infantry 139

East Lancashire Rgt 108
East Surrey Rgt 39, 107
East Yorkshire Rgt 141
Highland Light Infantry 32
Honourable Artillery Company xv, 38
Huntingdonshire Cyclists 39, 42, 211
Irish Guards 150
King's Own Yorkshire Light Infantry 192
King's Royal Rifle Corps 33, 107, 152, 184
King's Liverpool Rgt 155
Lancashire Fusiliers 44
Leicestershire Regt 110, 115
Lincolnshire Rgt 32
London Scottish 38, 109
Manchester Rgt 39, 83, 127, 197
Middlesex Rgt 32, 128, 130, 155
Monmouthshire Rgt 135
Munster Rgt 158
Norfolk Rgt 58
Northamptonshire Rgt 11, 33, 34, 39, 57,
    106, 113, 191, 192, 211
Queen's Westminster Rifles 44, 109
Queen Victoria's Rifles 59
Royal Fusiliers 33, 69, 129, 153
Royal Irish Rifles 126
Royal Scots 184, 192
Royal Sussex Rgt 75, 113
Royal Welsh Fusiliers 37
Seaforth Highlanders 85, 135
Sherwood Foresters 127, 140
Scottish Rifles 12
South Wales Borderers 10, 37, 159
Suffolk Rgt 76
Welch Rgt 37
West Surrey Rgt 153
West Yorkshire Rgt 128
Worcestershire Rgt 57
York and Lancaster Rgt 32, 76, 146
Yorkshire Rgt 141, 153
Militia 10
Special Reserve 33, 138, 153, 156
Territorial Army 11, 28, 29, 33, 45, 51, 57,
    124, 125, 128, 142, 150, 152, 153, 156, 184,
    191, 201
Volunteer Movement 10, 18, 124, 147
British Expeditionary Force (BEF) xv, 10, 28,
    29, 151, 184
Brittain, Vera xvii
Brown, Gordon 148
Brownscombe, Alfred 110, 162
Buchan, John 73, 79-80
Buchanan Riley, H. 124
Buckle, Archibald Walter 44, 128, 158, 213-4
Burnett, Dr 111, 130
Burgess, George 11
Burnham Committee (1918) 168
Burstall, Sara 6, 82

Buss, Frances Mary 13
Bytheway, Miss G 135

cadets (see Officer Training Corps)
Captain, The xiv, 138, 156
Carlyon, A.K. 3
Cambridge, University of 75, 127, 151, 152
casualties, war related xvii, 34, 40, 44-6, 89, 95,
    135, 151, 191-4, 200, 205-6
Cavell, Edith 83
Chambers, W.G. 194
charities 18, 24, 54, 58, 82
Chase, Corrie Denew 126, 182
Chaytor, R.G. 142
children
    militarisation of 24, 207
    impact of war on xvii, 83, 85, 205-9
Choles, Claude 20
Chums 23
Church, A.G. 142
Churchill, Winston 124, 148, 201, 216
Church of England 4, 14
cigarette cards 27, 33, 84
Citizenship 15
coal shortages 100
'comforts' 19, 60
commissions 36-40, 151
Commonwealth War Graves Commission
    (CWGC) 199
Conscientious Objectors 37, 78, 145-8
conscription (see Military Service Acts)
Cornwell, Jack 26, 83
County (High) Schools for girls 2, 30, 3, 6
Crane, Stephen 26
Crawford, Lord 157, 187
cricket 9, 28, 45, 53, 74-5, 99, 126, 127, 129,
    141, 160, 196
curriculum, school
    before 1914 5-9, 13-22
    wartime 68-76, 99, 104, 161
    post-war 174, 214

Dardanelles 58, 118
Dawson, Agnes 167
Davies, D.J. 145
Daniels, Harry 27, 82-3, 84
Davies, J.H. 43, 133, 203-4, 210
Day Continuation Classes 180
debating societies 78, 88
demobilisation 174, 181, 182
Dennis, Herbert 48, 91, 161
Derby Scheme 131, 137
Dig for Victory campaign 30, 98-100
Dillon, Norman 9
Dines, Joseph 38, 154, 192-3, 194
Distinguished Service Order (DSO) 80, 139,
    158, 214

Disraeli, Benjamin 13
Donaldson, A.E. 37
Drill 11, 11, 13, 18-19, 75-6

Edinburgh, University of 192
Education Acts
    1870 4, 14, 178
    1902 xi, 4, 13-14, 129, 178, 203
    1918 178, 215
    1944 13, 178, 180
elementary schools xix, 13-14, 39, 98
    collection campaigns 22, 24, 63-65
    comforts 19, 56-7
    curriculum 8, 9, 14-16, 18, 99
    Drill 11, 13, 18-19, 75-6
    Empire Day 10, 16-17, 71, 175
    memorials 41, 191
    recruitment marches 16
    rolls of honour 15, 35, 39-40
    sport 18, 75, 176, 177
    teachers 13, 33, 38, 41, 6, 33-4, 35, 99, 126,
        128, 131, 134-5, 147, 151, 153-4, 155, 158,
        159, 160-1, 162, 165, 181, 182, 192, 193,
        201, 208, 211, 213 (see also headteachers)
    War Savings 23, 66, 68
Elisabethville 54
Elstob, Wilfrith 126-7, 139-40, 157, 192
Ely, Isle of 33
Empire Day 10, 16-17, 71, 175
Endowed Schools Commission 7
England Squadron 91
evacuees 88, 96
Evans, G.L. 11

Fallen, The xx, 40, 154, 183
Faulkner, Basil 132
Faulks, Sebastian xvii
Fernsby, F.R.E. 161
First Blitz 88
Fisher, H.A.L. 40, 103, 168, 179, 201
flag days 24, 72
Foch, Ferdinand 172, 202
food
    shortages 96-98, 100, 208
    rationing 97, 137, 138
Football (Association) 33, 9, 127-8, 141, 154
    Bradford City 33, 128
    Bradford Park Avenue 141
    Crystal Palace 141
    Derby County 127
    England Amateur Team 128
    King's Lynn FC 154
    Liverpool 154
    Milwall 154
    Northampton Town 127
    Newcastle United 141

Plymouth Argyle 128
    Queen's Park Rangers 128, 154
Ford, Lionel 53, 195
Forster, W.E. 4, 14
Franklin, Mr 200
Franz Ferdinand, Archduke 28
Friends Ambulance Unit 145
Froud, Ethel 167

Gallipoli, Battle of (1915) xvi, 58, 71, 116, 118,
    184, 193
Garland, James 34, 129, 153, 159, 193
Geddes Committee 168
German Army 158
George V, King 57, 97, 177
Gilbert, Leslie 145
Girl Guides 24, 85
Girls' High Schools 21, 6, 43, 45, 60, 69, 81,
    82, 90, 97, 98, 116, 172, 180
Girls' Public Day Schools Trust 13, 133
Girl's Realm 23
Glasgow School Board 147-8
Glasgow, University of 33, 147
Gotha bombers 191
governors, school ix, 3, 11, 34, 43, 53, 81, 95,
    104, 110, 124, 130, 132, 133, 136, 144, 145-6,
    195
grammar schools 5, 7, 110, 163
    requisitioning of buildings 17, 45, 181
    sport 5, 6, 45, 74-5, 150
Graves, Robert xvii, 156, 157
Great War, the
    causes xvi, 28-9
    impact on individuals xvii, 83, 85, 205-9,
        211-2
    legacy for education 215

Hadley, Henry 27
Haig, Sir Douglas 198, 201
Haldane Reforms 10
Hall, Edward 159
Hardie, Keir 179
Harford, Lesbia 171
Harrison, Jack 36, 141-2
Hart, Bob 1, xiv-xvi, 3, 12, 36, 189, 196
Hartlepool, bombardment of 31, 87, 139
Harvest Camps 101
Haswell, Gordon 192, 196, 211
Head Masters' Conference 7, 132, 189
headteachers 41, xix, 3, 8, 17, 124-5, 130, 132,
    134, 137, 160-161, 212
Heidelberg, University of 126
Henderson, Arthur 131, 179
Henty, G.A. xiv, 24
Herbert, Albert 33, 192
Herbert, G.M. 167

heroes **12**, **26**, **27**, **36**, 80-84
HMI 4, 5, 14, 70
Hodges, Charles 9
horse chestnuts 64-65
hospitals
    schools requisitioned 17, 44-6
    school contributions to **21**, 60-3, 82, 83, 99
    pupil volunteers 51, 61-2, 68, 75, 85, 109, 116
    teacher volunteers **35**, 135-6, 143
Hughes, Thomas 23
Hundred Days Offensive (1918) 140, 155, 158
Hynes, Samuel 144

Industrial Schools Act (1857) 20
Independent Labour Party 147
influenza pandemic 173-4, 195, 201
Inglis, Elsie 136
Ireland, political situation in 8, 29, 31

Jackson, Jennie 84
Jones, Edwin 34
Jones, Paul 185
Jones, Theophilus 139
Journey's End **5**, 39, 149-50
Junior Technical Schools 22
Jutland, Battle of (1916) **26**, 73, 83
juveniles
    delinquency 207
    employment of 101-3, 105, 180
    literature for **12**, xiv, 23, 24, 138, 144, 156

Kantorek, Herr 123
Kelsey, Beatrice 27
Kerensky, Alexander 148
Kingdom, Doris 106, 107
Kipling, Jack 150
Kipling, Rudyard 9, 24, 150, 169, 175
Kirk, Tom 28
Kitchener, Lord xxi, 29, 83
Knight, Susannah **13**, 26-7, 200-2
'knitting frenzy' **19**, 56-7

Labour Party 179
Laidlaw, Charles Glass Playfair 38, 150
Lamb, F.W. 119
Law, Edgar Felix 33, 39, 192, 194
Lee, Edward 83
Lewis Report 180
Lewis-Stempel, John 152
Lindsay, David 157, 187
Lintott, Evelyn **33**, 128
Llewellyn, Marjorie 70-71
Lloyd George, David 29, 49, 64, 158, 178, 201, 210
London County Council **25**, 11, 14, 52, 167

London Day Training College **34**, 129, 159, 164, 165-6, 193
Local Education Authorities 3, 5, 6, 42, 52, 73, 101-3, 133, 172, 173, 181, 193
London, University of vi, 33, 129, 164-5
Longbottom, Frederick 57
Loos, Battle of (1915) 140, 184, 191, 192, 203
Louvain, University of 30
'Lost Citizenry' 187, 191
'Lost Generation' xvi, 139, 185
Lusitania, RMS 31
Lyttleton, Edward 145

MacFarlane, J.R. 56
MacIlwraith, William 192
MacQuillan, James 36
magazines
    for boys **12**, xiv, 23, 138, 144, 156
    for girls 23
    produced by schools xx, 78, 114-7
Magnet, The 144
Manchester, University of 64, 127
Manning, Frederick 121
Marshall, Albert ('Smiler') 15
Martin, H.C. 19
Martin, John 19, 124
Maxton, James **37**, 147
May, Harold Gostwick 129
MacLean, John 148
memorials
    school war memorials 41, **42**, 193-8
    Unveiling ceremonies 197-8, 204
    parents 196, 197
    Chorley Memorial Album 201
Meritorious Service Medal (MSM) 81
Middleton, Gertrude 92, 143
militarisation
    of childhood 24-5, 84
    of language 47, 79, 80, 115, 124, 161, 207
Military Cross (MC) 80, 139, 141, 182
Military Medal (MM) 81
Military Service Acts 78, 132, 134, 144-7, 158
Militia 10
Ministry of Food 63
Ministry of Munitions 65, 104, 165
Mobbs, Edgar 113
Mons, Battle of (1914) and retreat from 30
Morrison, Sandy 192
Mitchell, Charles 212
Municipal Training Colleges 160
munitions workers
    children 104
    schools 104-5
    teachers 159, 165, 181
    women xviii, 161, 165-6, 206
Munro, Hector 27, 60

New Army, Kitchener's xxi, 29, 131, 151
Newbolt, Henry 3, 198
National Curriculum 5, 15
National Efficiency 18, 20, 64, 65, 131, 178
National Egg Collection 63
National Federation of Women Teachers 39, 167
National Schools 14
National Union of Teachers 167
    War Record (1920) 36, 134-5, 140-3, 154, 157, 193
Norfolk Teachers War memorial 193
North Street School, bombing of 29, 92-95, 110, 143

Officer Cadet Battalions (OCB) 151-2
Officer Training Corps (OTC) 6, 10-12, 19, 27-8, 68, 108-12, 118, 132, 136, 141, 151-153, 156, 208
    annual camps 14, 27-28, 129
    universities 33, 129, 146, 151
    teachers 33, 125-9, 132, 136, 152-3, 192
Ogg, Kate 135
Oh What a Lovely War xvii
O'Sullivan, Charles 211
Owen, Reginald 144
Owen, Wilfred xvii, 123, 198, 203
Onions, Hettie 135, 143
Overseas Club 20, 58
Oxford, University of 7, 151, 186

Pals battalions 32, 76, 131
    Chorley Pals 76, 201
    Durham Pals 139
    Grimsby Chums 32
    Manchester Pals 127, 139
    Sheffield Pals 32, 76
Parker, Peter xviii, 114, 198
Parr, Reuben 43, 211
Passchendaele, Battle of (1917) xxi, 113, 151, 158, 182
Patch, Harry xvii, 23, 31
Paton, John 33
patriotism 10, 30, 40, 70-71, 177
Paulson, John 33, 125, 153, 192
peace celebrations 40, 176-7, 181
Peace Day 176-7
peace medals 176
Peace Mugs 176, 177
Pearson, Ralph 46
Pease, Joseph 130-1
pensions, war 207
Pershing, General George 202
Peterborough 21-2, 52, 54
Pettersson, Frank xv, 211
Physical Education 19
Physical Deterioration, Report on (1904) 18

playing fields, school 9, 44, 98, 99, 196
Pope Benedict XV 202
Pope, Jesse 1
premature school leaving 105-6
preparatory schools xix, 11, 38, 66, 87, 97, 112, 127, 136, 153
Princess Mary 57, 199
Pringuer, Gladys 43, 211
prisoners of war 27, 60, 203
Prize Certificates 25, 81-2
Prize Days 36, 81-2
propaganda 72-73, 95, 179
Public Schools
    boarding 97
    Cadet Corps and OTC 6, 14, xiv, 10, 11-12, 27-8, 68, 109
    casualties 183, 191, 194
    character training 8-10
    clientele 3, 215
    commissions 32, 36-7, 150, 157 (see also subalterns)
    culture and ethos xviii, 8, 23, 80, 151, 209-10,
    curriculum 8, 68, 109
    debating societies 78
    enlistments 33, 37-8
    food shortages 97
    foundation of 7-8
    girls schools 7, 13, 133, 207 (see also GPDST)
    influenza pandemic 174
    'Lost Generation' xiii, 185-7
    memorials 42, 196, 198
    military honours 139, 80,
    'Old Boys' 114
    refugees admitted 53
    remembrance 183-5
    sport 7, 9-10, 39, 75, 149
    teachers 126-7, 129, 138, 152-3, 159-60, 162-3, 191-2, 194
    war work 31, 56, 104, 108
Pullan, L.C. 47, 172

Quaker schools 40, 145

rationing 97, 137, 138
recruitment 16, 29-32, 131
Red Clydeside 147, 148, 166
Red Cross 135, 136, 142, 143, 181
Refshauge, John 32
refugees
    Belgian 30, 51-4
    Serbian 53
    schools for 54
    fundraising for 18, 54
Remarque, Erich Maria 123, 210
remembrance

culture of 183, 198
  services 198, 204, 210, 214
  battlefield visits 200
requisitioning of school buildings 17, 42-6
Richardson, J.R. 71, 118, 125, 200
Robertson, Sir William 158
Robson, Alexander 137
Ross, Ishobel 35, 135-6
rowing 5, 9, 39, 120
Rowling, J.K. 23
Royal Air Force (RAF) 211
Royal Flying Corps (RFC) 77, 184
Royal Naval Division (RND) 128, 158, 214
  Anson Battalion 158, 213, 214
  Drake Battalion 158
Royal Naval Volunteer Reserve (RNVR) 72,
  128, 132, 158, 213
Royal Navy 19, 20, 72-3, 83, 87, 184
rugby football 9, 75, 113, 126, 127, 129, 139,
  141, 146, 149, 153, 211
Russell, John 41
Russia xiv, xv, 29, 69, 72, 142, 148, 176

salaries, teacher 165, 168
Salonika 136, 184, 193
Samuel, David 125, 133
Samuelson Commission (1881) 21
Sanderson, Frederick William 213
Sandhurst, Royal Military Academy 10, 39,
  124, 152, 184
Sarajevo, assassination at xiv, 28, 175
Sargant, Walter 212
Sassoon, Siegfried xvii
Saunders, Robert 212
Scarborough, bombardment of 31, 87-8
Schlieffen Plan xv, 30, 51, 192
Schofield, Arthur 43, 33, 126, 210
scholarships
  to secondary schools 5, 6, 13, 105, 129, 147,
    179, 180, 186, 189, 191, 203, 208, 211, 215
  to universities 38, 126, 138, 153, 165, 186
  as memorials 197
School Boards 5, 14, 17
Scottish War Memorials Project 193
Scottish Women's Hospitals 35, 61, 135-6, 143
'Secondary Education for All' 13, 180, 215
secondary schools xix, 3-7, 13, 21, 39, 105, 179
  (see also public schools, grammar schools,
    scholarships etc.)
  buildings 43-4
  casualties 188-9, 193
  establishment of 4-5
  clientele 5, 13, 55, 97, 189-90, 215
  culture and ethos 6
  curriculum 5, 6, 11, 18, 21, 72, 124
  fees 6, 14, 180
  for boys 3, 32, 36

  for girls 2, 21, 6, 18, 54-5
  premature leavers 105-6
  refugees 52, 54-5
  rising school rolls 151, 180, 211
  sport 75
  staffing in wartime 158, 162-5, 182
  teachers 43, 126, 127-8, 132, 135, 149-158,
    192-3, 203
  war work 60-1, 101
Second World War 204
Seldon, Anthony xix, 126, 183
Serbia 136
Shackleton, Miss 44, 106
Sheffield, University of 40, 146, 179
Sherriff, R.C. 38, 149
Skinner, H.W. 160, 210
Smith, William Alexander 24
social class 4, 5, 13-15, 33, 41, 149-152, 156,
  187, 215
Socialists Teachers' Society 148
social mobility 105
Somme, Battle of (1916) xxi, 120, 139, 141,
  142, 151, 182, 184, 192, 193, 205
Sorbonne, University of Paris 126
Southcombe, E.H. 197
Special Reserve 33, 138, 153, 156
sport 13, 18, 74-76
  importance in school curriculum 5, 6, 7, 9,
    13, 18, 53, 120, 138, 196-7
  in wartime 45, 74-6, 88, 98, 109, 180
  involvement of teachers in 33, 38, 9, 127,
    128, 138, 141, 149, 154
  rowing 5, 9, 39, 120
  rugby 9, 75, 113, 126, 127, 129, 139, 141,
    146, 149, 153, 211
  cricket 9, 28, 45, 53, 74-5, 99, 126, 127, 129,
    141, 160, 196
Spring Offensive, German (1918) xxi, 104, 108,
  134, 139, 149, 151, 155, 158
St David's Day 71-2
St Peter's College 15, 128, 154, 193-4
Stuart Smith, Robert 136
subalterns 8, 10, 109, 113, 136, 138, 140, 149,
  150, 153, 155, 156, 185
Swedish Gymnastics 19

Taylor, A.J.P. 24, 111-2, 145
teachers 13, 22, 23, 28, 32, 33, 34, 35, 36, 37,
  38, 39, 41, 43, 44 (see also headteachers,
  'Temporary Gentlemen', 'Temporary
  Masters' etc.)
  elementary school 13, 33, 38, 41, 6, 33-4, 35,
    99, 126, 128, 131, 134-5, 147, 151, 153-4,
    155, 158, 159, 160-1, 162, 165, 181, 182,
    192, 193, 201, 208, 211, 213
  members of OTC 33, 125-9, 132, 136,
    152-3, 192

munitions workers 159, 165, 181
public school 126-7, 129, 138, 152-3, 159-60,
    162-3, 191-2, 194
secondary school 43, 126, 127-8, 132, 135,
    149-158, 192-3, 203
Volunteers 10, 18, 124, 147
Teacher Training Colleges 15, 129-30, 146-7,
    159-60, 163-6, 193-4
  Armstrong, Newcastle 159
  Glasgow University 147
  Jordanhill, Glasgow 194
  King's, London 34, 159
  London Day Training College 34, 129, 159,
    164, 165-6, 193
  Methodist, London 146
  St Gabriel's, Kennington 159
  St John's, Battersea 130
  St Luke's, Exeter 128
  St Mark's, Chelsea 159
  St Peter's, Peterborough 15, 128, 154, 193-4
  Westminster, London 141
technical education 19-22, 43, 188, 215
technology of war 8, 25, 78, 88, 94, 156, 187-8,
    190
'Temporary Gentlemen' 149-158, 168, 188, 215
'Temporary Masters' 158, 162-168, 215
Temporary Officers 149-152, 155, 157, 188
Territorial Army 11, 28, 29, 33, 45, 51, 57, 124,
    125, 128, 142, 150, 152, 153, 156, 184, 191,
    201
Thomas, S.E. 36
Thomas, William Jenkyn 11, 164
Thompson, Leonard 14, 16
Tomlinson, W.A. 153
total war xii, xviii, 30, 55, 86, 95-6, 132, 166,
    178, 187, 207, 214
Trewby, Norman 35-6
Tribunals, Military 100, 132-3, 145, 146, 147
Trinity College, Cambridge 151
Tripartite System 22, 180
Tryon, George Arthur 33, 125, 152-3, 157, 193,
    213
Turner, Edith 14
'Two Nations', Disraeli's 13
Tutin, Elsa 164-5, 167, 211

U-boats xxi, 26, 48, 64, 65, 71, 72, 78, 86, 96,
    100, 104, 175
Unknown Warrior 199
universities 33, 179
  OTC contingents 10, 33, 128, 153
  recruits 33
  Cambridge 75, 127, 151, 152
  Edinburgh 192
  Glasgow 33, 147
  Heidelberg 126

London vi, 33, 129, 164-5
Louvain 30
Manchester 64, 127
Sorbonne (Paris) 126
Sheffield 40, 146, 179
University and Public Schools Brigade 33

Vann, Bernard William 127, 140, 157
Venables, Mr 87-8
Versailles, Peace Conference and Treaty of 174,
    175
Victoria Cross (VC) 26, 27, 36, 80, 82, 83, 84,
    139, 140-42
Voluntary Aid Detachments (VAD) 45, 117,
    135, 136, 143
Volunteer Movement 10, 18, 124, 147

wages, wartime 97, 101-2, 105, 166-7, 180
Walker, Louisa 16
Walley, Clifford 115
Walsh, David xix, 126, 183
War Pensions 207
War poets xvii, 1, 26, 113, 114, 123, 156, 158,
    171, 187, 198, 203, 204
Ware, Fabian 199
Warren, Alfred 86, 93
Watkins, Wenceslia 92, 143
Watts, A.F. 136, 143
Watts Naval Training School 19-20, 73
Waugh, Alec 209
Waugh, Evelyn 8, 12, 55, 97, 98, 208, 211
West Ham Women Teachers' Association 167
Wheatley, Dennis 28, 156, 157
Wheeler, Russell Mervyn 32, 88, 127, 153, 189,
    192, 194, 196, 211
Whitby, bombardment of 31, 87
White, George Baden 17
White, Malcolm 120
Whitehouse, Alfred 17, 47, 73, 75, 77, 99, 101,
    137, 162, 173, 175, 176
Wightman, J.M. 158
Wilkinson, John 12
Williamson, Alexander 138, 192
Women's Army Auxiliary Corps (WAAC) 135
Women's Right to Serve March 166
Women's Social and Political Union
    (WSPU) 167
women war workers xviii, 86, 101, 103-4, 132,
    161, 166
Woods, R. 143
Woodward, Ernest 153
Woolwich Royal Arsenal 104, 159
Woolwich, Royal Military Academy 10, 152

Yates, Rose Lamartine 167
YMCA 58

Young, Ernest 3, 12, 26, 79, 85, 101, 196, 214
youth organisations 12, 24-6, 51, 83, 85
  Boys' Brigade 24-5
  Boy Scouts **26**, 12, 26, 51, 84, 85, 109, 214
  Church Lads' Brigade 25
  Girl Guides 24, 68, 85
  Jewish Lads' Brigade 25
  Lads' Drill Association 25
Yoxhall, James 73-74
Ypres, Battles of (1914-17) 118, 139, 184, 187, 200, 203

Zeppelin raids **28**, 77, 86, 88-9, 90, 91, 110

Index Of Schools
(Plate images in **bold**)

Aberystwyth County School 27, 34, 36, 43, 53, 57, 69, 125, 133, 145, 146, 206
'Akenfield' Mixed School, Suffolk 17, 77, 102
Alconbury School, Huntingdonshire 61
Alice Ottley School, Worcester 117
All Saints National School, King's Lynn 154
All Saints Schools, Wellingborough **22**
Amberley Parochial School, Gloucestershire 72, 162, 198
Ampleforth, Gloucestershire 196
Appleby Grammar School 182
Armadale Public School, West Lothian 39-40
Ashby-de-la-Zouch Grammar School 110, 127
Atholl Crescent School of Domestic Science, Edinburgh 136
Auckland School, Durham 119
Ayton School, Yorkshire **3**, 48, 91, 161

Bacup and Rawtenstall Grammar School, Lancashire 60, 117, 208
Badsey Council Schools, Evesham 52, 57, 64, 71, 208, 212
Ballarat Agricultural High School, Australia 32
Bancroft's School, Essex 51, 78, 79, 89, 109, 163
Barnack School, Cambridgeshire 52, 57, 58, 65, 76, 182
Barrow Grammar School for Boys 60, 78, 101, 105, 110, 116, 117, 163
Bath High School 90
Beach Road Council Schools, Litherland 46
Beaumont College, Windsor 196
Bedales School, Hampshire 41
Bedford Girls' Modern School 69
Bedford Modern 113
Bedford School 104
Bedlington Colliery Council School, Northumberland 143

Belgian School, Peterborough 54
Belgian National School, Manchester 54
Bellahouston Academy, Glasgow 189
Belmont School, Brighton 11
Birdbrook School, Essex 34
Blue Coat School, Birmingham 98
Blundell's School, Tiverton 10, 126
Blyth Bridge School, Peeblesshire 177
Bolton School 68, 110, 111, 124, 163
Bootham School, York 145
Boroughmuir High School, Edinburgh 189
Bradfield School, Sheffield 104
Bradford Grammar School 196, 199
Bristol Cathedral School 51
Bristol Grammar School 26, 83,
Broad Street Boys' School, Whittlesey 33
Broadwater Road School, London 164
Bromley County Girls' School **2**, **30**
Brook Street School, Basingstoke 142, 182
Burton Grammar School 11
Busbridge School, Godalming 63, 76, 119, 182
Buxton College 111

Caernarvon County School 43, 57, 72, 74, 76, 85, 145
Caldicott School, Abingdon 66-7
Calton Road Schools, Gloucester 68, 200
Campbell College, Belfast vii, 8, 126, 182, 209
Cardiff High School for Boys 43, 160
Cardinal Vaughan Memorial School, London 47, 53
Charterhouse, Surrey 7, 9, 37, 111, 156, 184, 194, 196
Central High School for Boys, Manchester 45
Cheadle Hulme School, Cheshire 45-6, 90, 181
Chelmsford County High School 180
Chelsea County Secondary School, London 164
Cheltenham College 27, 104, 111, 172, 209
Cheltenham County High School 90
Cheltenham Ladies' College 6, 13, 37
Chichelle Grammar School, Higham Ferrars 127
Chigwell School, Essex 86, 88
Chipping Campden School 124
Christ College Brecon 37, 196
Christ's Hospital Girls' School, Hertford 68
Christ's Hospital School, Sussex 113, 127, 153, 194
City of London School 29, 32, 69, 75, 82, 111, 172, 197
Clifton College, Bristol 37, 129, 139, 194, 198
Colfe's Grammar School, London 31, 62, 69, 71, 74, 89, 104, 109, 136
College Road Council School, Moseley 56, 100
Clongowes Wood, Dublin 37

Cowper Testimonial School, Hertford 99, 159
Cranleigh School, Surrey 200
Crypt School, Gloucester 78, 136, 143

Dartford Grammar School 38
Deacon's School, Peterborough 43, vi, 5, 21,
   33, 34, 39, 44, 74, 105, 116, 126, 133, 165,
   167, 203-4, 210-11, 215
De Aston School, Market Rasen 115, 152
Dennistoun School, Glasgow 147
Downe House, Berkshire 209
Downside, Somerset 196
Dronfield School, Sheffield 16, 17
Ducie Avenue School, Manchester 39-40, 45
Dudley Hill School, Bradford 128
Duke of York's Royal Military School,
   Dover 43, 199
Dulwich College, London 7, 28, 97, 98, 109,
   111, 174, 185-7, 194
Dundee High School 189
Durham School 196

East Boldon School, South Tyneside 42, 57, 58
Eastbourne Grammar School 110, 163
Elizabeth College, Guernsey 196
Emanuel School, London 75, 89, 90, 98, 104,
   116, 118, 124
Eton College, Berkshire 31, 7, 64, 74, 108, 139,
   145, 150, 184, 194

Farmer Road School, London 91
Felsted Preparatory School, Essex 97, 112, 196,
   136, 153
Fletching School, Uckfield 212
Fleet Road School, London 16, 18
Frant Church School, Heathfield 143
Frenchay Church of England School,
   Bristol 212
Friends' School, Saffron Walden 41

George Dixon Secondary Schools,
   Birmingham 55, 59, 78, 114, 163, 172, 198
George Green's School, London 42, 58, 70, 83,
   89, 110-11, 130
George Heriot's School, Edinburgh 8, 37
Georgetown Schools, Tredegar 67, 73, 135,
   137, 176
George Watson's School, Edinburgh 37, 192
Gibbons School, London 66
Giggleswick School, Yorkshire 28
Girls' Council School, Thetford 63
Gladstone Road School, Scarborough 87-8
Glasgow Academy 32, 196
Glasgow High School 37
Godolphin School, Salisbury 61, 62

Gowerton Intermediate School, Glamorgan 53,
   100, 108, 116
Grahamstown School, Glasgow 147
Greenhill School, Tenby 106, 107
Gresham's School, Norfolk 89

Haberdashers' Aske's Hatcham Boys'
   School 132
Haberdashers' Aske's Hatcham Girls'
   School 60
Hackney Downs School, London 11, 44, 52,
   62, 164
Haileybury, Hertfordshire 9, 139, 196
Hampton School, Middlesex 60, 75, 85, 107
Handsworth Grammar School,
   Birmingham 74, 115
Harris Academy, Dundee 189
Harrow County School for Boys, Middlesex 1,
   32, vi, xiv-v, 3-6, 12, 26, 36, 43, 78, 79, 85,
   88, 97, 98, 101, 110, 115, 127-8, 159, 160,
   163, 164, 189, 192, 194, 196, 198, 211, 214
Harrow School, Middlesex 3, 6, xiv, 3, 7, 10,
   53, 90, 109, 124, 195, 198
Harvey Grammar School, Folkestone 195
Heald Place School, Manchester 45
Helston Grammar School 82, 108, 144
Herbert Strutt School, Belper 47, 53, 69, 81,
   99, 110, 160, 161, 165
Hereford High School for Boys 198
Highbury Fields School, London 82
Highgate Primary School, London 71, 88
Highgate School, London 138, 192
Highlands School, Ilford 154
Holy Trinity Girls' School, Trowbridge 62
Hornby School, Lancashire 15, 18, 42, 57-8,
   77, 103
Hull Grammar School 189
Humphrey Perkins School, Leicestershire 161
Huntingdon Grammar School 44
Hurstpierpoint College, Sussex 75, 78, 138,
   153, 159, 192, 194, 196
Hutcheson's Grammar School, Glasgow 11-12,
   27, 33, 60, 110, 146, 147
Hymer's College, Hull 90, 109, 111, 181

Inverness Royal Academy 58, 212

Jewish Free School, London 52
Judd School, Tonbridge 200

Kelvinside Academy, Glasgow 189
Kent College, Canterbury 31, 75, 110, 160, 162,
   174, 210
Kibble School, Paisley 20, 99, 105, 119
Kimbolton School, Huntingdonshire 21

King Albert School, London 54
King Alfred School, London 41
King's College, Taunton 27, 174
King Edward VI Grammar School,
   Sheffield 32, 40, 76
King Edward VI Grammar School, Melton
   Mowbray 70, 77, 110, 136, 173, 174
King Edward VII Grammar School, Retford 7,
   43, 160
King Edward VII Grammar School, Totnes 7,
   163, 188
King's School, Auckland 8
King's School, Canterbury 7
King's School, Ottery St Mary, Devon 145, 183
King's School, Peterborough 5, 21, 188
King's School, Rochester 124
Kingston Grammar School, London 5, 38-9,
   149-50
Kingswood School, Bristol 33, 205
Knaresborough Grammar School,
   Yorkshire 141

Lamancha School, Peeblesshire 177
Lancing College, Sussex 8, 12, 55, 97, 98, 112,
   172, 194, 208, 211
Larne Grammar School, County Antrim 36
Latymer Upper School, London 7, 76, 129
Leys School, Cambridge 75
Lichfield High School for Girls 172, 175, 176
Lincoln Grammar School 17, vi, 45, 83, 181, 197
Littlecote Council School, Grimsby 42
Liverpool Belvedere School 90
Llanystumdwy School, Gwynedd 158
Longbridge Deverill School, Wiltshire 104
Loretto School, Musselburgh 196
Lorne Street Primary School, Glasgow 148
Loxford School, Ilford 8

Mackie Academy, Stonehaven 193
Malvern College, Worcestershire 7, 174
Manchester Grammar School 7, 12, 33, 37
Manchester High School for Girls 21, vi, 6, 45,
   60-1, 69, 82, 97, 180
Market Street Schools, Ely 57
Marlborough College, Wiltshire 7, 27, 37, 184,
   196
Medomsley Council School, Durham 142
Meeching Boys' School, Newhaven 46, 63-4,
   81, 100, 211
Merchant Taylors' School, Crosby 27, 194, 212
Merchant Taylors' School for Girls, Crosby 43,
   60, 61, 75, 98, 106
Merchiston Castle, Edinburgh 8, 127, 139, 192
Monikie School, Dundee 35, 40
Monmouth School 10
Monson Road School, London 10

Morgan Academy, Dundee 189
Morpeth Central School, London 142
Morpeth Grammar School,
   Northumberland 43, 109, 124, 163
Moseley Road School, Manchester 45, 56, 100
Mount School, York 44, 54, 91

Newbattle School, Midlothian 23, 66
Newcastle High School for Girls 98
Newport High School for Boys 36, 81, 124,
   165, 189
Northampton Grammar School 11, 69, 75, 98,
   109, 163, 180, 189
North London Collegiate School 6, 13, 60, 62
North Street School, Poplar 29, 86, 92-5, 110,
   143
Norwich High School 60, 61, 62, 207
Nottingham High School for Girls 13, 133

Oakham School 27, 181, 212
Oldbury Tabernacle Schools, Sandwell 15
Old Fletton Council School,
   Huntingdonshire 42, 54
Orleton School, Scarborough 87-8
Oundle School 8, 21, 32, 33, 104, 112, 125, 152,
   153, 193, 213

Pate's Grammar School for Girls,
   Cheltenham 6
Perse School, Cambridge 153
Peterborough Junior Technical School 22
Peterborough Practising School vi, 15, 16, 47,
   83, 100, 172
Poland Street School, London 52
Portree High School, Leith 193
Portsmouth High School 90
Pound Lane School, Epsom 72, 88, 165
Preston Grammar School 35
Putney High School, London 90-1

Repton, Derbyshire 27
Rissington School, Oxfordshire 100, 162
Romanno School, Peeblesshire 177
Rotherhithe Nautical School, London 182,
   213, 214
Royal Belfast Academical Institution 37
Royal Grammar School, Guildford 128
Rugby School 42, 7, 8, 23, 37, 117, 184, 195,
   196, 200,
Rydal School, Colwyn Bay 185
Ryleys Preparatory School, Cheshire 126

Sheffield High School for Girls 134
Sherborne School, Dorset vi, 53, 113, 117, 129,
   184
Shrewsbury School 7, 27, 28, 120, 194, 197

Silver Street Senior Boys' School, London 47,
    91, 172
Sir John Cass School, London 96
Sir John Maxwell School, Glasgow 147
South End Elementary School, Rushden 127
St Augustine's School, London 128, 158
St Augustine's School, Peterborough 19, 124
St Columba's College, St Albans 8
St Edward's, Oxford 53
St Gregory's School, Chorley **13**, 26, 76, 201-2
St James' School, Glasgow 147
St John's, Johannesburg 8
St John's Boys' School, Peterborough **41**, 191,
    195, 211
St Luke's Parochial School, London 190
St Margaret's Church of England School,
    King's Lynn 154
St Mary's Boys' School, Hitchin 69
St Nicholas Boys' School, King's Lynn vi, 17,
    47, 54, 58, 60, 66, 72, 75, 77, 99, 137, 162,
    173, 175, 176, 177, 199
St Paul's School, London 7
St Peter's School, Harrowgate 141
Stanley Street Infant School, London **25**
Starbeck Council School, Harrowgate 141
Steyning Village School, Sussex 85
Stibbington School, Cambridgeshire 17, 63,
    172
Sutton High School 98, 116
Sychdyn School, Flintshire 56, 61
Sydney Church of England Grammar School,
    Australia 9
Sydney Grammar School, Australia 8

Thringstone School, Leicestershire 139
Trent Bridge Elementary School,
    Nottingham 46

Trinity Academy, Leith 193
Trinity School, Carlisle 189
Trowbridge and District High School 182

Upholland Village School, Wigan 83
Upper Canada College, Toronto 8
Uppingham School 7, 104, 144, 152
Upland House School, Epsom 11

Wallasey Grammar School 189
Walton Road School, Manor Park 83
Warrender Park School, Edinburgh 192
Watts Naval Training School, Norfolk 19-20,
    73
Welbourne Village School, Lincolnshire 158
Wellingborough County High School for
    Girls 6
Wellingborough School 127, 140
Wellington College, Berkshire xiii, 7, 10, 27,
    33, 37, 139, 184, 197
Wellington Reformatory Farm School,
    Lothians 191
West Buckland School, Devon 197
West End Primary School, Elgin 190, 192
Westminster School 7, 78, 109
West Norfolk and King's Lynn High School for
    Girls 81, 97
West Town Infants School, Peterborough 59
Whitehill Secondary School, Glasgow 189
Wingrove Council School, Newcastle 135
Winchester House School, Deal 38, 47-8
Winchester School 7, 196
Wintringham School, Grimsby 32
Woodbridge School, Suffolk 126
Worksop College 32